PowerPoint® for Windows® 95

The Visual Learning Guide

Other Prima Visual Learning Guides

Internet for Windows: America Online 2.5 Edition
Windows 95: The Visual Learning Guide
Word for Windows 95: The Visual Learning Guide
Excel for Windows 95: The Visual Learning Guide
WinComm PRO: The Visual Learning Guide
PROCOMM PLUS for Windows: The Visual Learning Guide
WordPerfect 6.1 for Windows: The Visual Learning Guide
Word 6 for the Mac: The Visual Learning Guide
Cruising America Online
Quicken for Windows: The Visual Learning Guide
1-2-3 for Windows: The Visual Learning Guide
ACT! 2.0 for Windows: The Visual Learning Guide
Excel for the Mac: The Visual Learning Guide
Windows 3.1: The Visual Learning Guide
Excel 5 for Windows: The Visual Learning Guide
PowerPoint: The Visual Learning Guide
Word for Windows 6: The Visual Learning Guide
WordPerfect 6 for Windows: The Visual Learning Guide
WinFax PRO: The Visual Learning Guide

Upcoming Books!

Cruising America Online 2.5
Access for Windows 95: The Visual Learning Guide
Internet for Windows, Microsoft Network Edition
Sidekick 95: The Visual Learning Guide
Quicken 5 for Windows: The Visual Learning Guide

How to Order:

Individual orders and quantity discounts are available from the publisher, Prima Publishing, P.O. Box 1260BK, Rocklin, CA 95677-1260; (916) 632-4400. For quantity orders, include information on your letterhead concerning the intended use of the books and the number of books you wish to purchase.

PowerPoint® for Windows® 95

The Visual Learning Guide

Grace Joely Beatty, Ph.D.

David C. Gardner, Ph.D.

PRIMA PUBLISHING

Project Editor: Susan Silva

If you have problems installing or running PowerPoint® for Windows® 95 (version 7) contact Microsoft at (206) 882-8080. Prima Publishing cannot provide software support.

ISBN: 0-7615-0210-6
Library of Congress Catalog Card Number: 95-69849
95 96 97 98 AA 10 9 8 7 6 5 4 3 2 1
Printed in the United States of America

Acknowledgements

We are deeply indebted to Tina Terhark who gave generously of her time to test every step in the manuscript.

Lisa Anderson did all the work necessary to convert this book into the Windows 95 edition. Thanks, Lisa. You're terrific! David Coburn did a great technical edit.

Suzanne Stone, copy editor; Prima Creative Services, interior layout; Emily Glossbrenner, indexer; and Paul Page, cover design, contributed immensely to the final product.

We are personally and professionally delighted to work with everyone at Prima Publishing.

Bill Gladstone and Matt Wagner of Waterside Productions created the idea for this series. Their faith in us has never wavered.

Joseph and Shirley Beatty made this series possible. We can never repay them.

Asher Schapiro has always been there when we needed him.

Paula Gardner Capaldo and David Capaldo have been terrific. Thanks, Joshua and Jessica, for being such wonderful kids!

We could not have met the deadlines without the technical support of Ray Holder, our electrical genius, Diana M. Balelo, Frank E. Straw, Daniel W. Terhark and Martin J. O'Keefe of Computer Service & Maintenance, our computer wizards.

Thanks to David Sieverding of Elegant Digital Imaging in Steamboat Springs, Colorado, for his help on how to send a file to a service bureau.

A very special thank you to Rosemary Abowd of Genigraphics who performed minor miracles to help us write Chapter 9, *Producing Slides through a Service Bureau*. Her professionalism and generosity were extraordinary.

Contents at a Glance

Customize Your Learning

Prima Visual Learning Guides are not like any other computer books you have ever seen. They are based on our years in the classroom, our corporate consulting, and our research at Boston University on the best ways to teach technical information to non-technical learners. Most important, this series is based on the feedback of a panel of reviewers from across the country who range in computer knowledge from "panicked at the thought" to sophisticated.

Each chapter is illustrated with color screens to guide you through every task. The combination of screens, step-by-step instructions, and pointers makes it impossible for you to get lost or confused as you follow along on your own computer.

LET US KNOW...

We truly hope you'll enjoy using the book and PowerPoint® for Windows® 95. Let us know how you feel about our book and whether there are any changes or improvements we can make. You can contact us through Prima Publishing at the address on the title page or send us an e-mail letter. Our Internet address is write.bks@aol.com. Thanks for buying the book. Have fun!

David and Joely

Part I: Creating a Basic Presentation

CHAPTER 1

Beginning a Basic Presentation

Gone are the endless hours of laying out and formatting presentation materials. PowerPoint 7.0 has 24 preformatted layout designs that automatically center text, create bulleted lists, and import clip art and charts. You can even use a Spelling Checker to help proofread. In this chapter you will do the following:

- ✔ Create a new presentation
- ✔ Choose predesigned layouts from AutoLayout
- ✔ Enter text
- ✔ Use the Spelling Checker

OPENING POWERPOINT FOR THE FIRST TIME

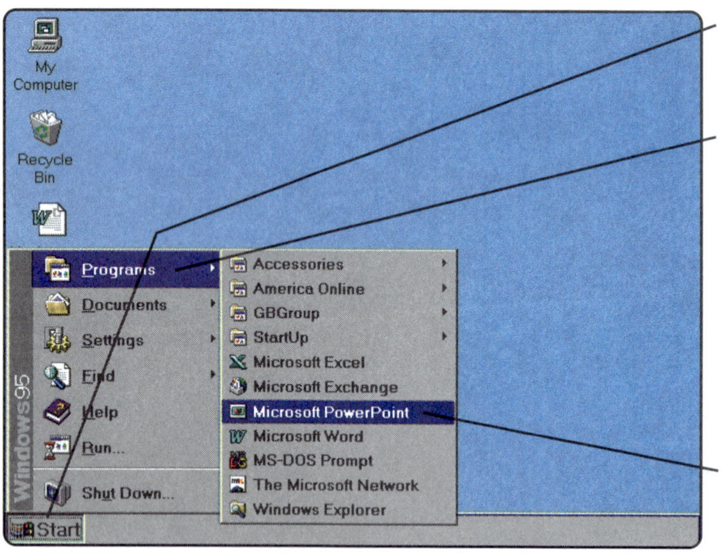

1. **Click** on **Start**. A menu will appear.
2. **Click** on **Programs**. Another menu will appear. Windows provides for tremendous customization, so your screen will probably look different than the one you see in this example.
3. **Click twice** on **Microsoft PowerPoint.** After a lengthy hourglass intermission, a Microsoft PowerPoint message box will appear.

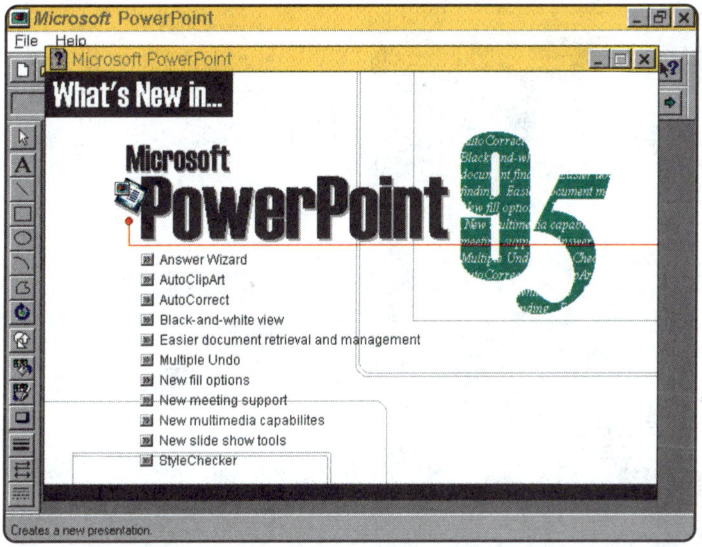

The first time you open PowerPoint, a screen will appear which will describe the new features of PowerPoint 95.

Then the opening PowerPoint screen will appear briefly.

Viewing Tip of the Day

Every time you boot up PowerPoint, you will see a Tip of the Day.

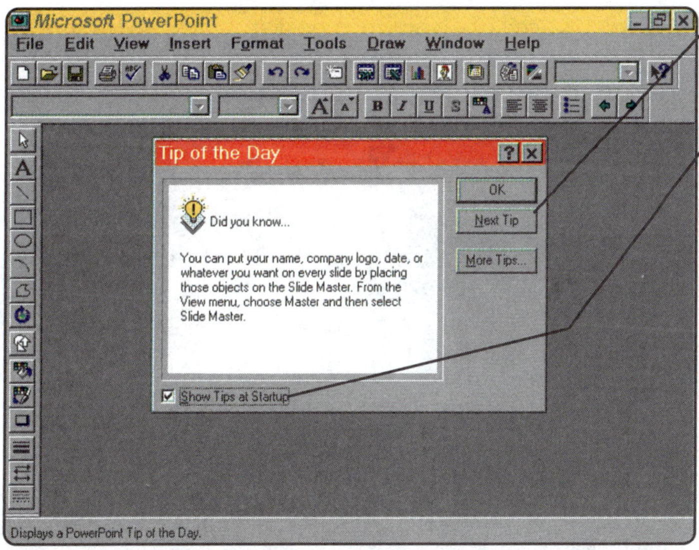

1. **Click** on **Next Tip** to see another tip.

If it drives you crazy to see a Tip of the Day every time you start PowerPoint, **click** on **Show Tips at Startup** to *remove* the ✓ from the box. This will prevent PowerPoint from automatically showing tips.

If you choose this option, you can still see tips by choosing the Tip of the Day command from the Help menu.

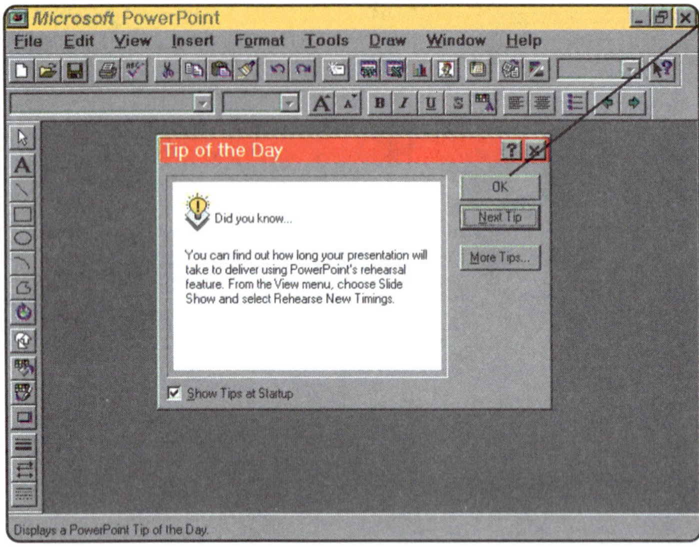

2. **Click** on **OK** to close the dialog box. A PowerPoint dialog box will appear on your screen.

CREATING A NEW PRESENTATION

You can use any one of the options in the New Presentation dialog box to begin a new presentation. In this section you will choose Blank Presentation. "Blank" refers to the fact that the presentation is not yet dressed up with a predesigned color scheme. (Most people who are planning to make overheads from their presentation will want to create them using the Blank Presentation format. Overheads show up best in black and white.)

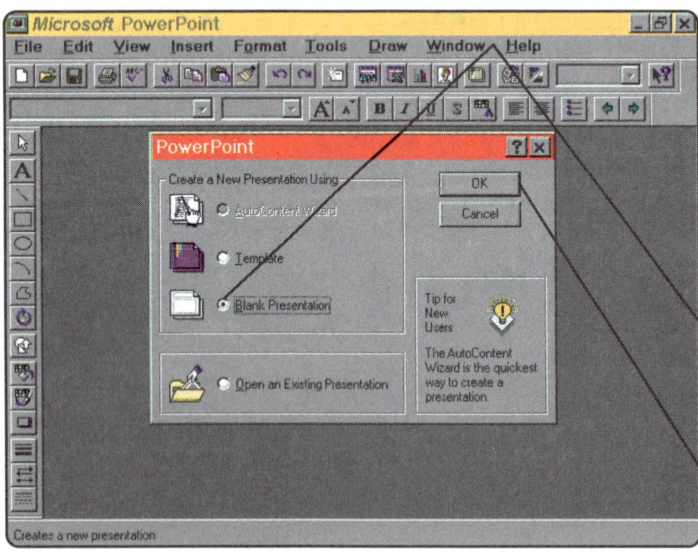

You will dress up your presentation in Chapter 3, "Choosing a PreDesigned Template." You will learn how to use all the options on this menu as you go through the chapters in this book.

1. **Click** on **Blank Presentation** to insert a dot in the circle.

2. **Click** on **OK**. The New Slide dialog box will appear.

USING AUTOLAYOUT

AutoLayout contains 24 preformatted layout designs that are set up to center text, make a bulleted list, and add clip art and charts. You can mix AutoLayout slides with individually designed slides. "Slides," by the way, is a generic term. You can create your presentation as slides, overheads, or an on-screen presentation. In this chapter you will create five slides.

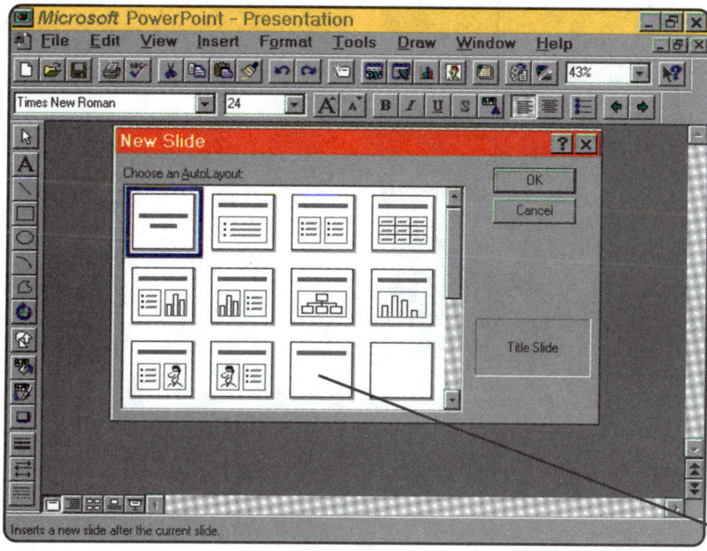

Creating a Title Slide

1. **Click** on the **Title Only** slide. A dark border will appear around the slide to show that it is selected.

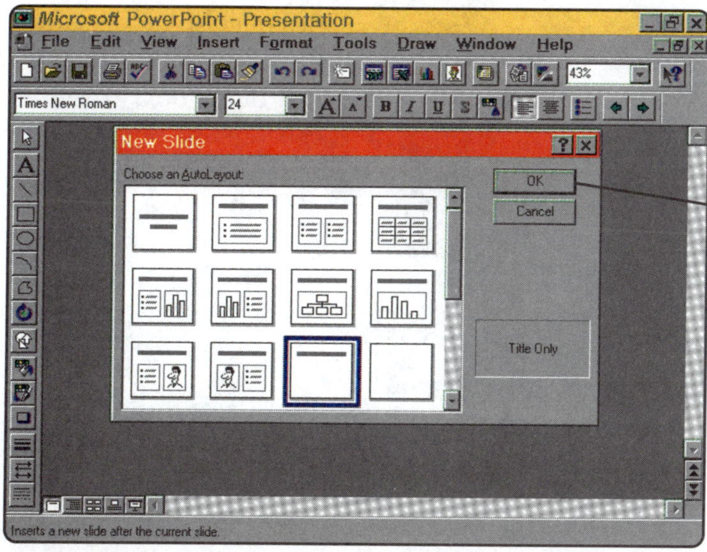

Notice that a description of the slide appears in the right corner of the dialog box.

2. **Click** on **OK**. After a pause, the Presentation screen will appear.

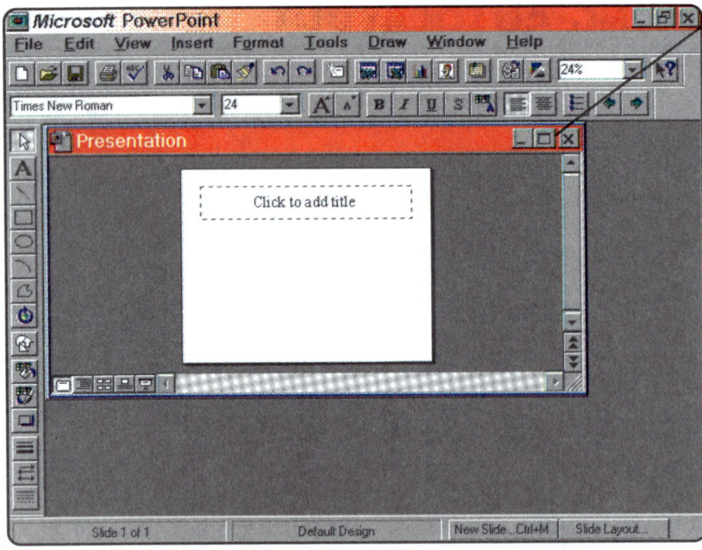

3. Click on the ☐ to maximize the Presentation dialog box if it's not already maximized.

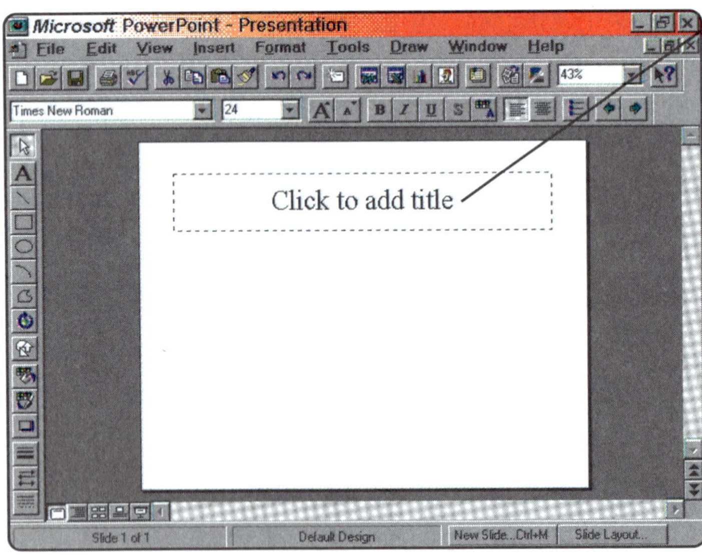

4. Click anywhere inside the dotted-line border. The instructions will disappear, the border will change to a series of slash marks, and the cursor will flash in the center of the box. This box is called a *text block*.

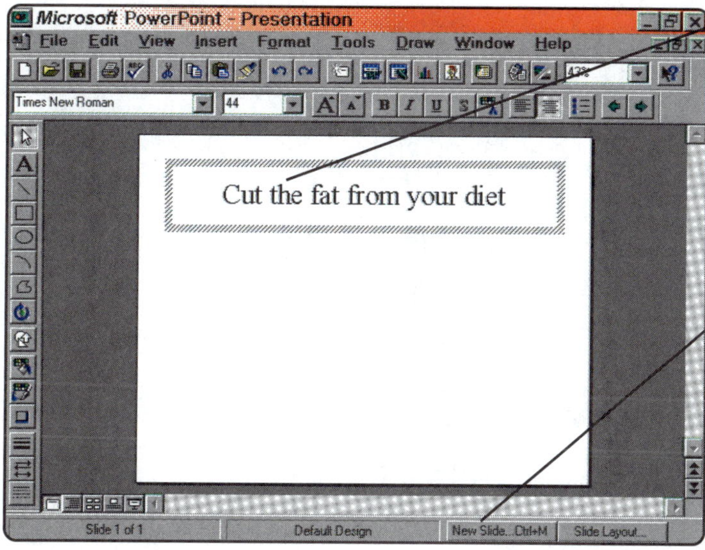

5. **Type Cut the fat from your diet.** (Don't include the period.)

Notice that the title automatically centers itself.

6. **Click** on **New Slide** so that you can create the next slide. The New Slide dialog box will appear.

Creating a Slide with a Title and Subtitle

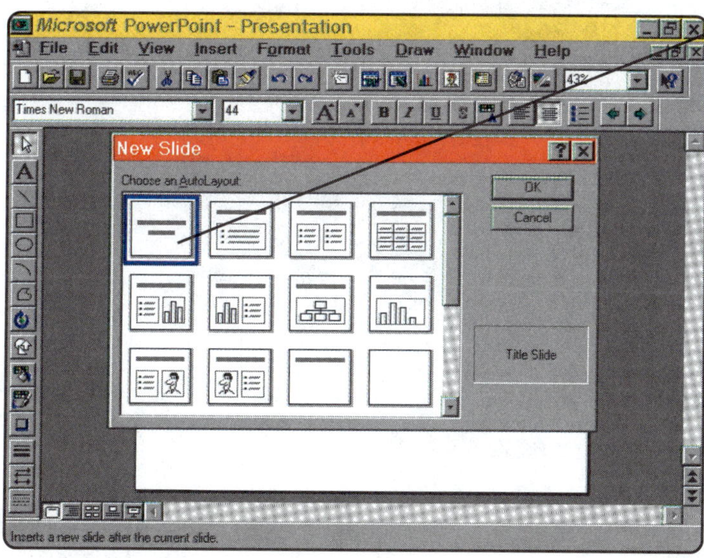

1. **Click** on the **Title Slide** which is the first slide.

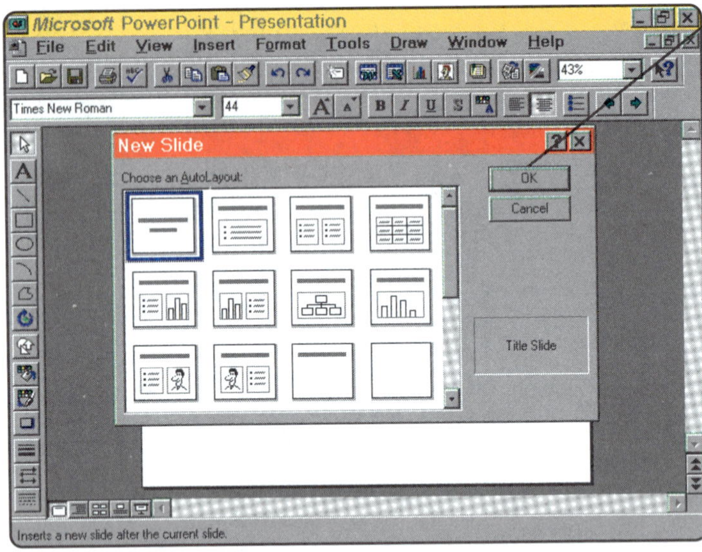

2. **Click** on **OK**. The Presentation screen will appear.

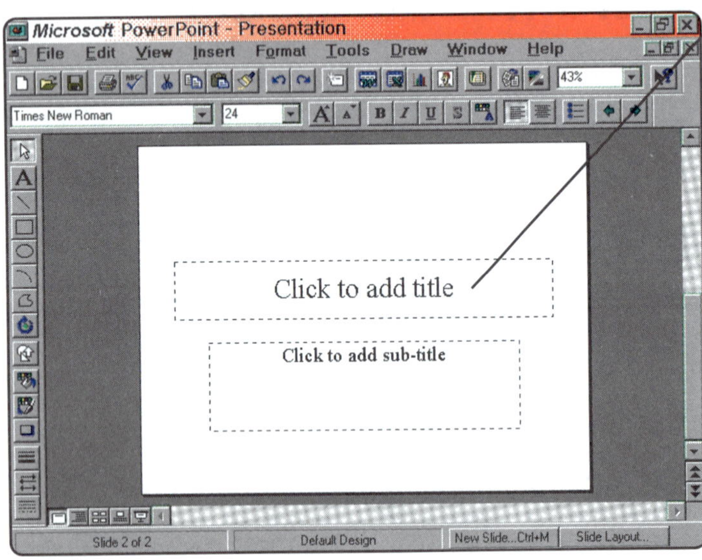

3. **Click anywhere** inside the title text block. The instructions will disappear, the border will change to a series of slash marks, and the cursor will flash in the center of the block.

4. **Type How much fat is in your food?**

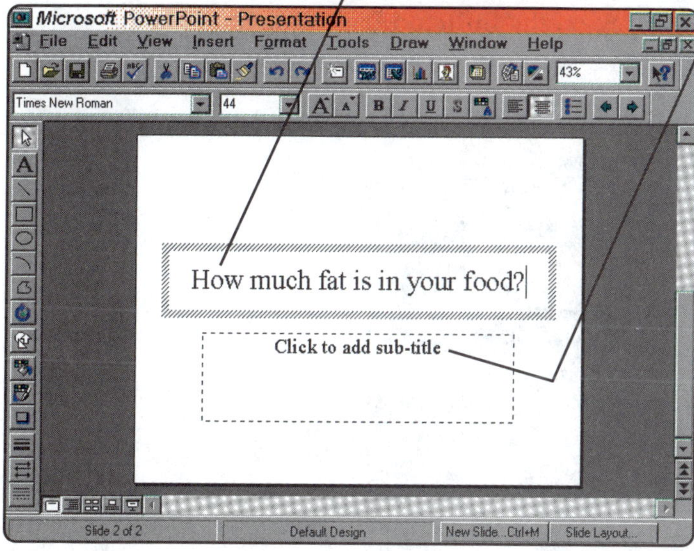

5. **Click** inside the **subtitle text block**. The cursor will flash in the center of the text block.

6. **Type Let's look at a milk carton label.** (Include the period.)

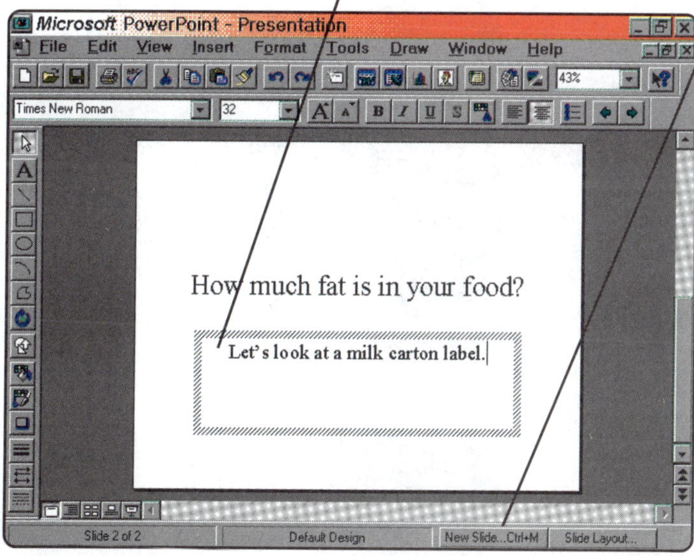

7. **Click** on the **New Slide button**. The New Slide dialog box will appear.

Creating a Bulleted List

1. **Click** on the **Bulleted List Slide** if it is not already selected. (It is the second slide in the top row.)

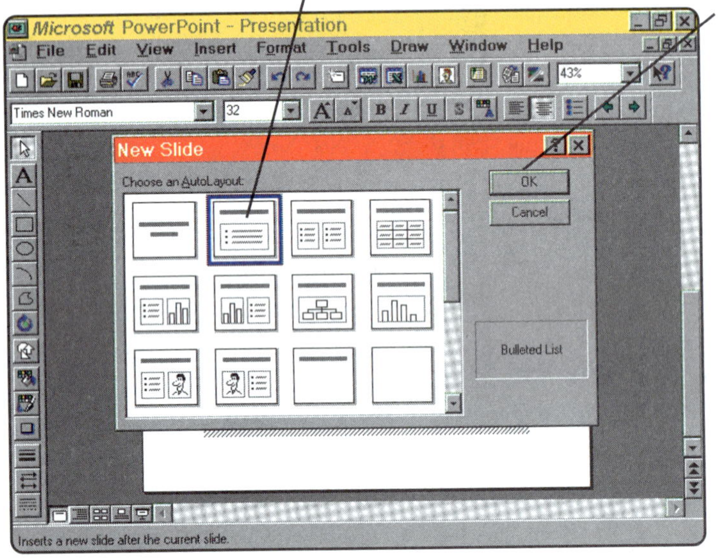

2. **Click** on **OK**. The Presentation screen will appear.

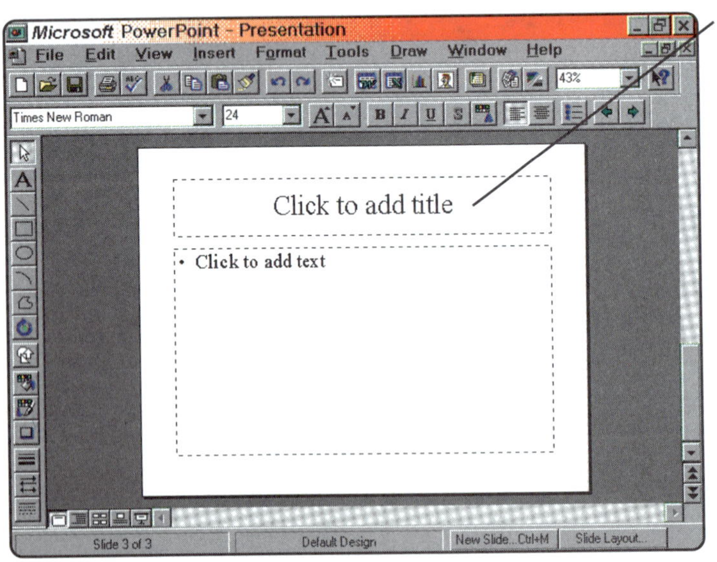

3. **Click** on the **title block**. The cursor will flash in the center of the text block.

4. Type Ways to Cut Fat. (Don't include the period.)

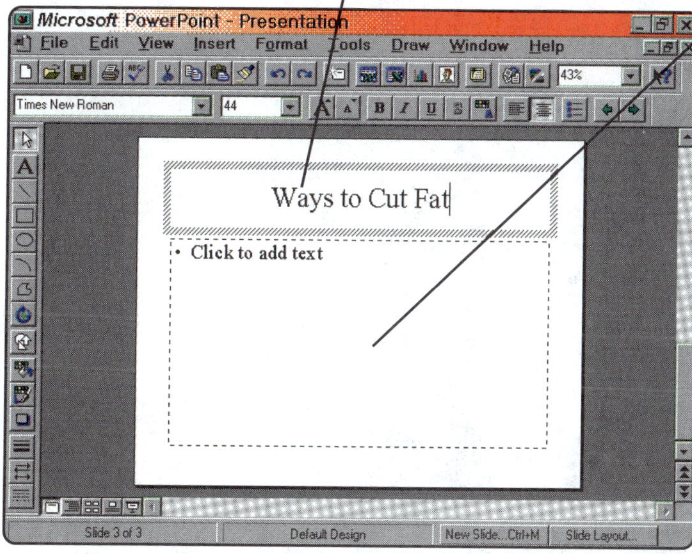

5. Click anywhere inside the bulleted text block.

Notice that after you click, the instructional text disappears but the bullet remains. The cursor will flash to the right of the bullet.

6. Type Reduce obvious fats like butter, oils, and cheese. (Don't include the period.)

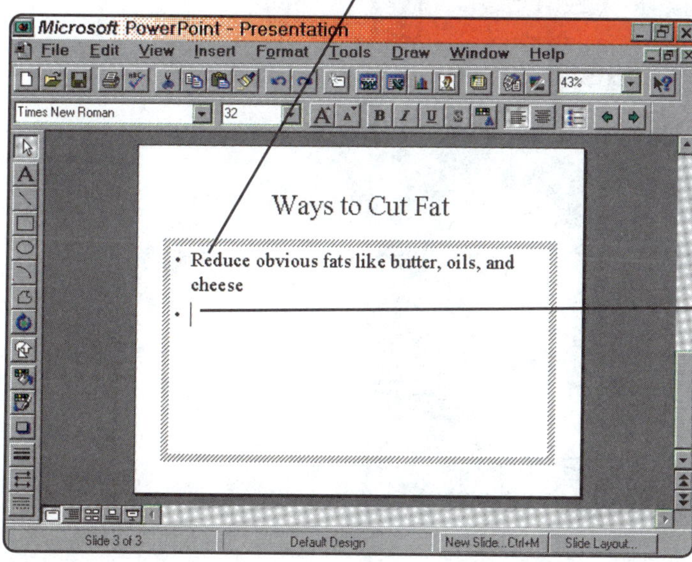

Notice that the word "cheese" automatically wraps to the second line and indents.

7. Press Enter. Another bullet will appear.

8. **Type Identify and reduce hidden fats**. (Don't include the period.)

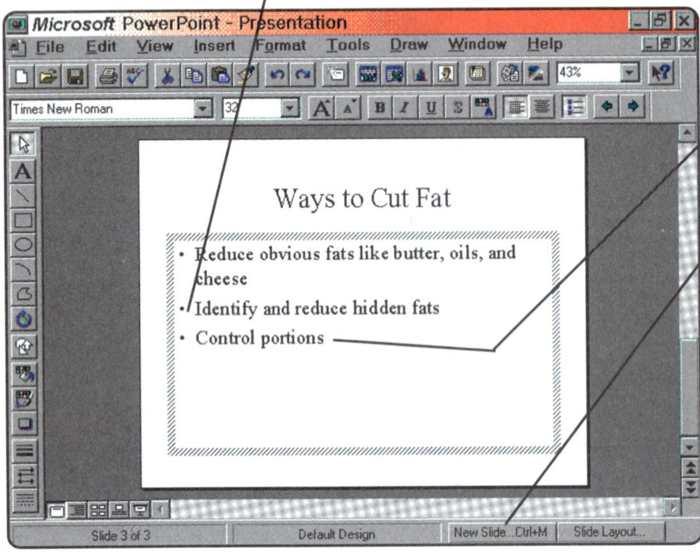

9. **Press Enter**. Another bullet will appear.

10. **Type Control portions**. (Don't include the period.)

11. **Click** on the **New Slide button**. The New Slide dialog box will appear.

Creating a Slide with Two Columns of Text

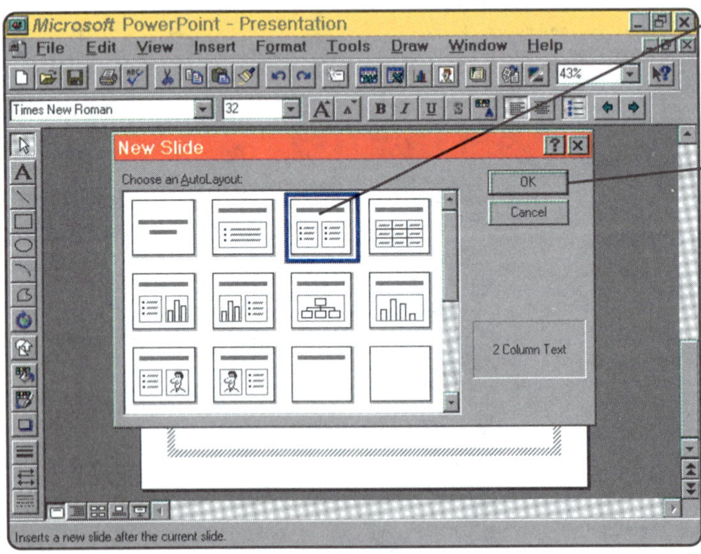

1. **Click** on the **2 Column Text** slide. (It is the third slide in the first row.)

2. **Click** on **OK**.

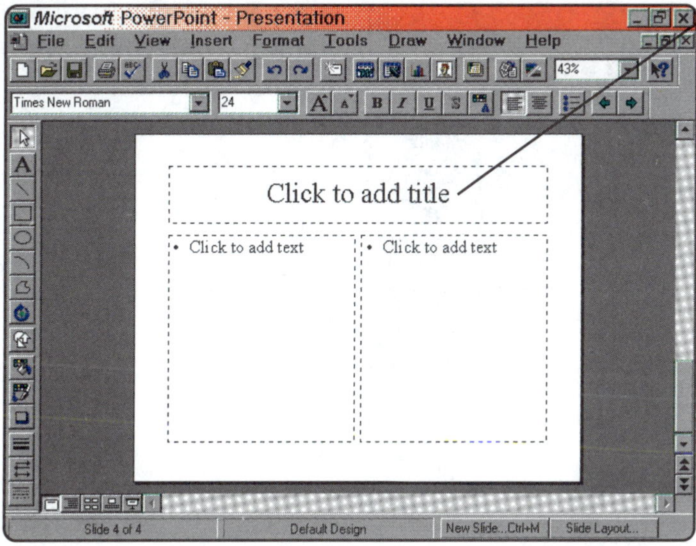

3. Click inside the **title block**. The cursor will flash in the center of the text block.

4. Type Lowfat Milk - 2% Milkfat and **press Enter** to add a line to the text block.

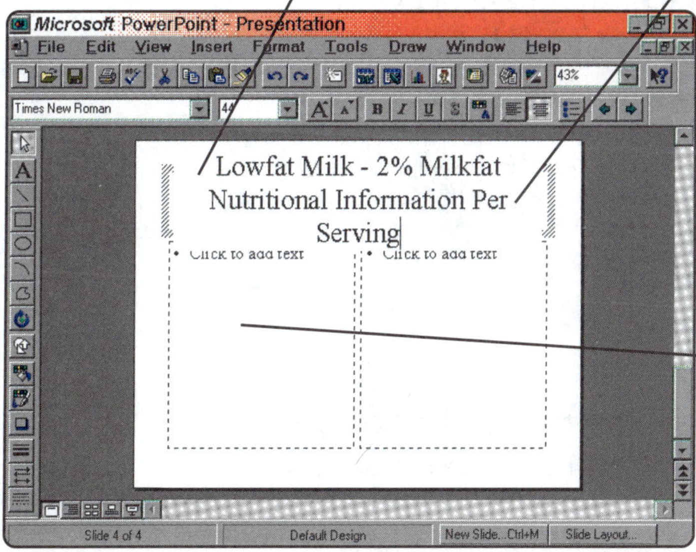

5. Type Nutritional Information Per Serving. (Don't include the period.) Notice that the text automatically wraps to a new line. In Chapter 5 you will change the font in the title block so that it will not obscure the text below it.

6. Click anywhere inside the left text block. The text will disappear but the bullet will remain. The cursor will flash to the right of the bullet.

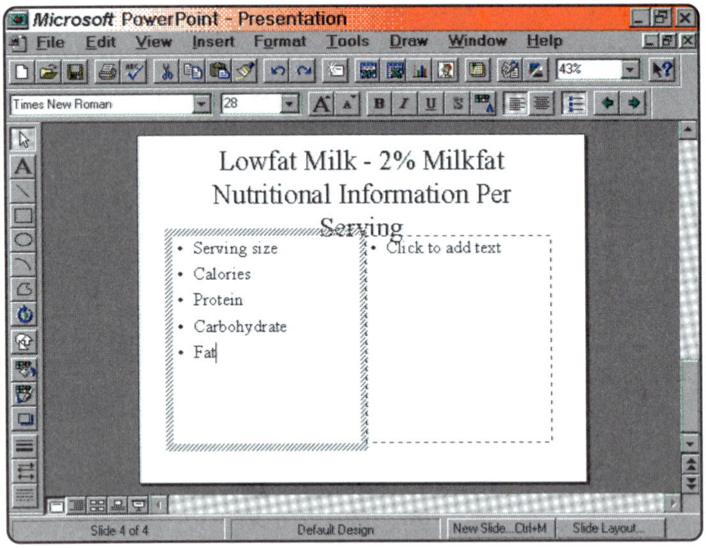

7. **Type** the following lines and **press** the **Enter key** between each item to create a new bullet:

Serving size
Calories
Protein
Carbohydrate
Fat

8. **Click** inside the **right text block**.

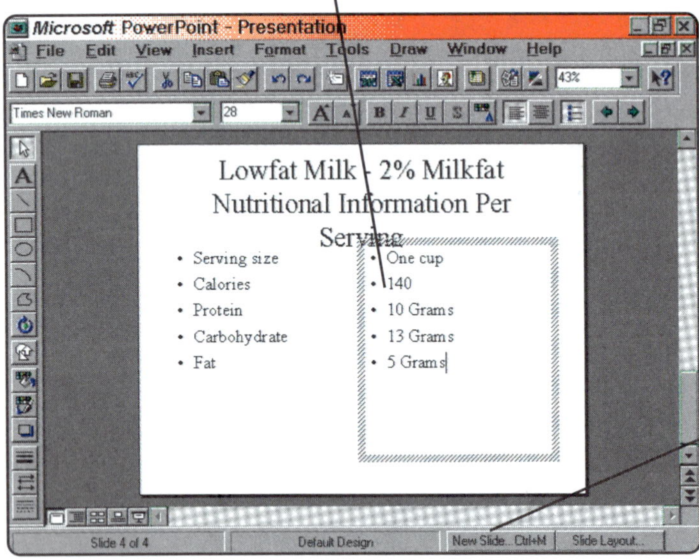

9. **Type** the following lines, and **press** the **Enter key** between each item to create a new bullet:

One cup
140
10 Grams
13 Grams
5 Grams

10. **Click** on the **New Slide button**. The New Slide dialog box will appear.

Creating a Slide With Two Text Areas

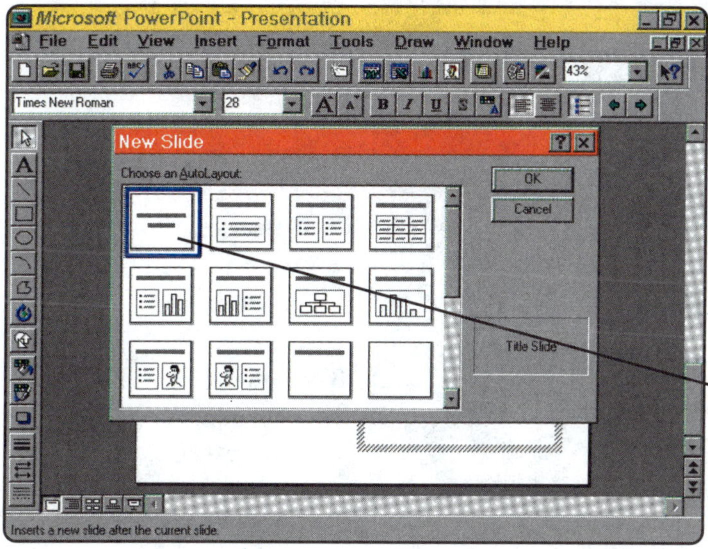

Don't feel limited by the label that AutoLayout gives to the predesigned slides. If the general layout of the slide is appropriate, use it. You can expand a text block to contain more lines of type than you see in the example.

1. **Click twice** on the **Title Slide screen**. The Presentation screen will appear. (Clicking twice is the same as clicking once plus clicking on OK.)

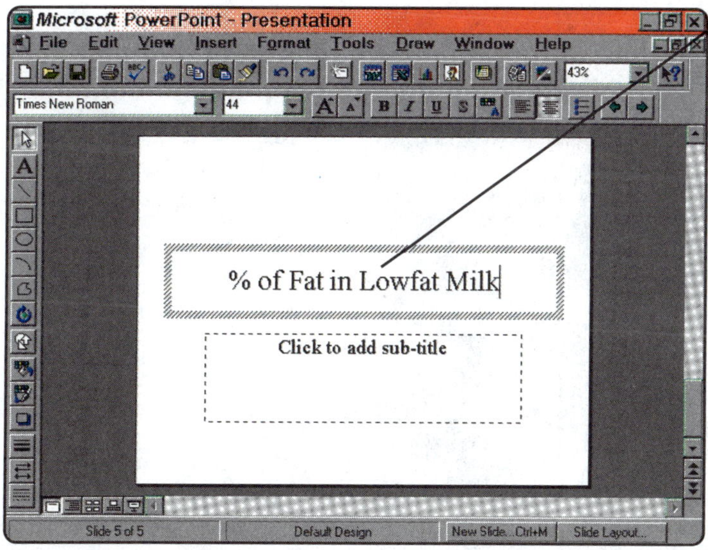

2. **Click** inside the **title block**. The cursor will flash in the center of the text block.

3. **Type % of Fat in Lowfat Milk**. (Don't include the period.)

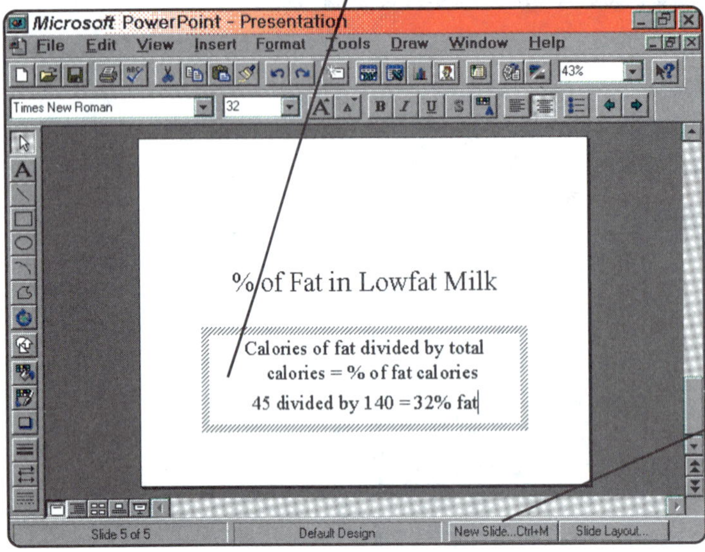

4. **Click** inside the **subtitle block.**

5. **Type Calories of fat divided by total calories = % of fat calories.** (Don't include the period.)

6. **Press Enter.**

7. **Type 45 divided by 140 = 32% fat.** (Don't include the period.)

8. **Click** on the **New Slide button.** The New Slide dialog box will appear.

Creating a Slide with One Text Line

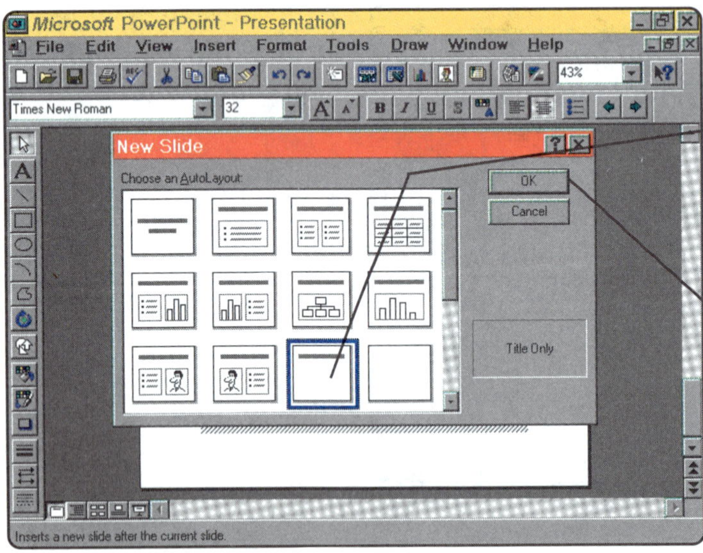

1. **Type** the number **11** on the keyboard.

2. **Confirm** that the **Title only screen** is selected. (This screen is the 11th slide from the beginning.)

3. **Click** on **OK.**

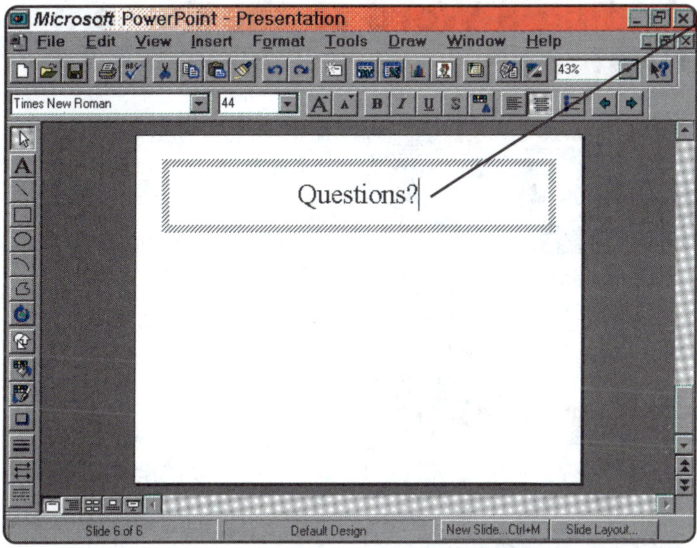

4. **Click** inside the **title block**. The cursor will flash in the center of the text block.

5. **Type Questions?**

USING THE SPELLING CHECKER

Be sure to check your spelling. There are few occasions more embarrassing than having your spelling errors seen larger than life by an entire audience. The Spelling Checker in PowerPoint works the same way it does in Word and other Windows-based word processing programs.

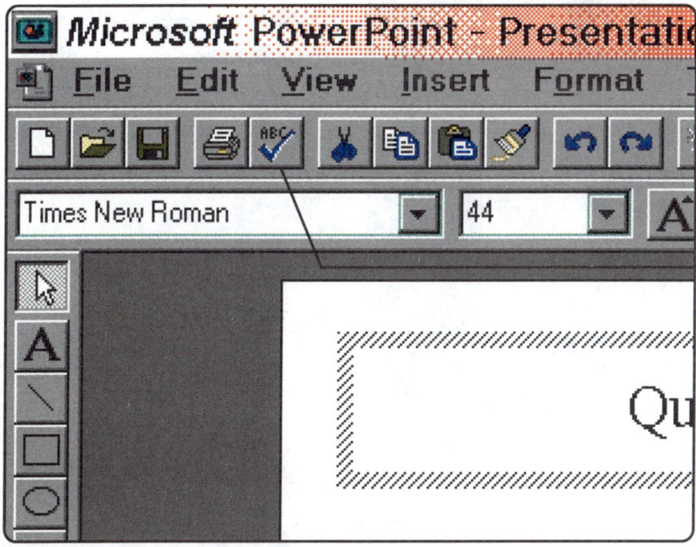

Starting the Spelling Checker

1. **Click** on the **Spelling Checker button** on the toolbar. The Spelling dialog box will appear.

Adding a Word to the Custom Dictionary

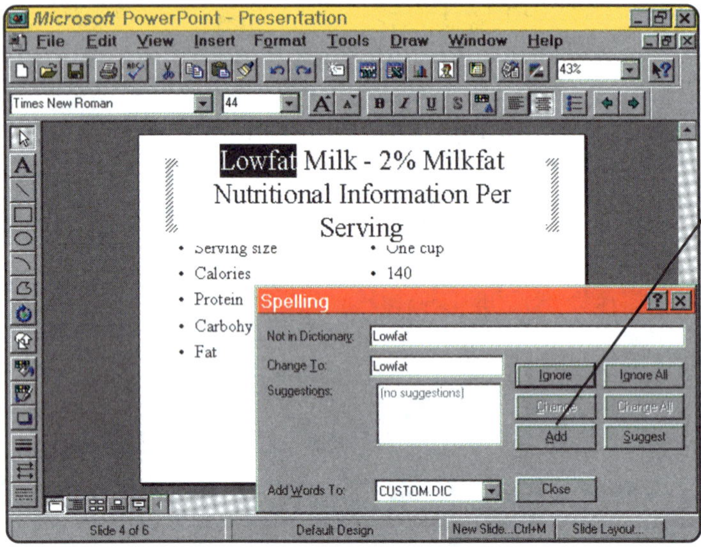

In the presentation you just typed, there are two words that can be added to the custom dictionary.

1. **Click** on **Add** to add Lowfat to the Custom dictionary.

2. When the Spelling Checker identifies Milkfat as an unknown word, **click** on **Add** to add it to the Custom Dictionary.

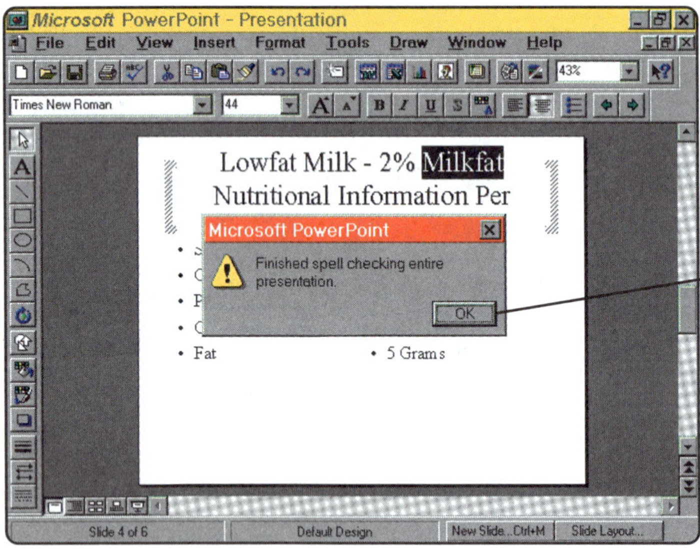

Because there are no other misspelled or unknown words, a PowerPoint message box will tell you it has finished checking the spelling.

3. **Click** on **OK** to close the Spelling Checker.

You'll name and save the presentation in the next chapter.

CHAPTER 2

Naming, Saving, Closing, and Opening a File

PowerPoint uses standard Windows-based commands to name, save, and close a file. In this chapter you will do the following:

✔ Name and save a file
✔ Close a file
✔ Close PowerPoint
✔ Open an existing presentation

NAMING AND SAVING A FILE

In this section you will name the presentation you created in Chapter 1.

1. **Click** on the **Save button** in the toolbar. Because you have not named the file, the File Save dialog box will appear.

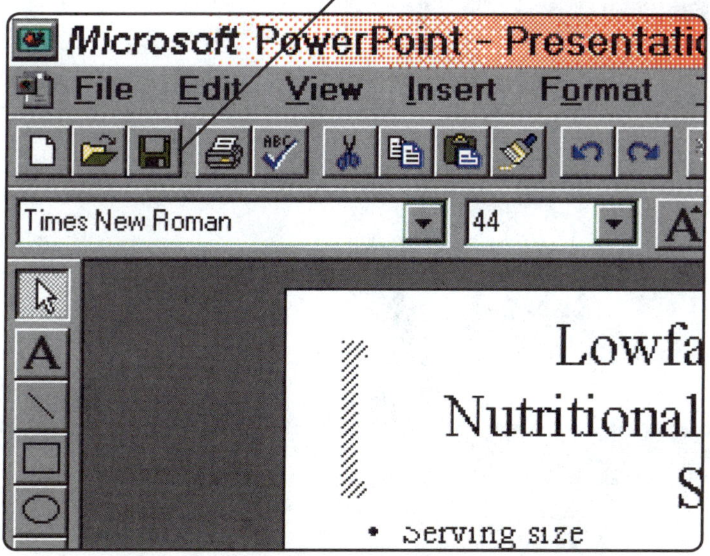

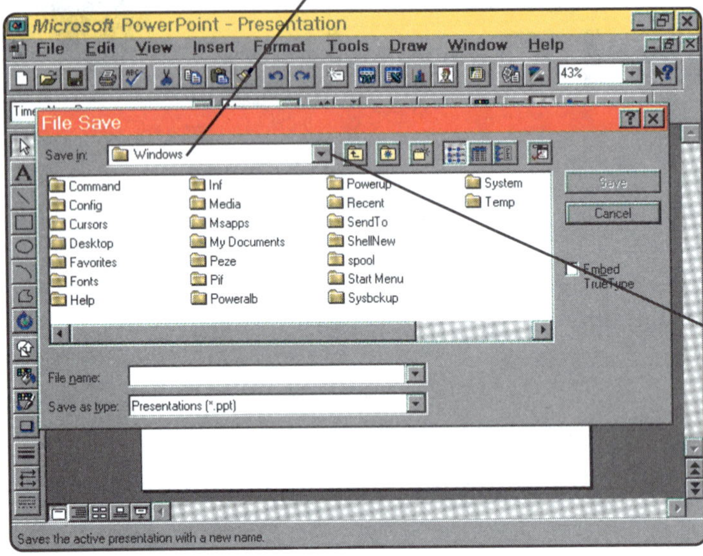

Notice that in this example the Windows file folder shows in the File Save in box. (Your Save in box may show something different.) This example will show you how to save your presentation to the Powerpnt file folder. If Powerpnt already appears in the Save in box, skip to step 6.

2. **Click** on the ▼ to the right of the Save in box. The Save in file folder menu will appear.

3. **Click** on **(C:).** If your PowerPoint program was installed on another drive, you should click on that drive.

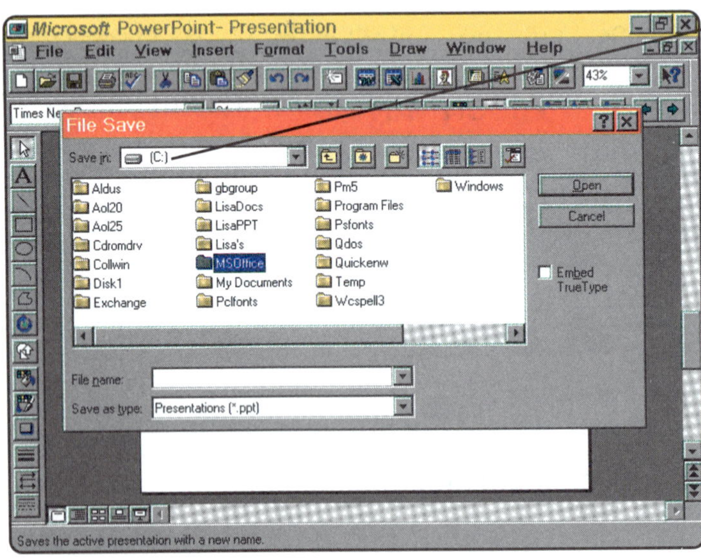

(C:) drive (or the drive you chose) will appear in the Save in box.

Notice that the program folders in drive (C:) appear in the window.

4. Click twice on **MSOffice** if you have it installed. (Click on Powerpnt if you have it installed as a separate program.)

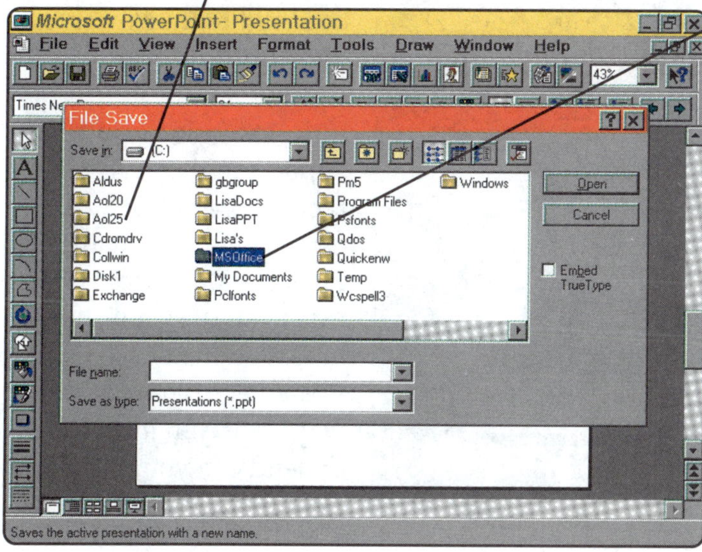

Notice that the Save in box now shows MSOffice. The program files found in MSOffice now show beneath the Save in box.

5. Click twice on **Powerpnt.**

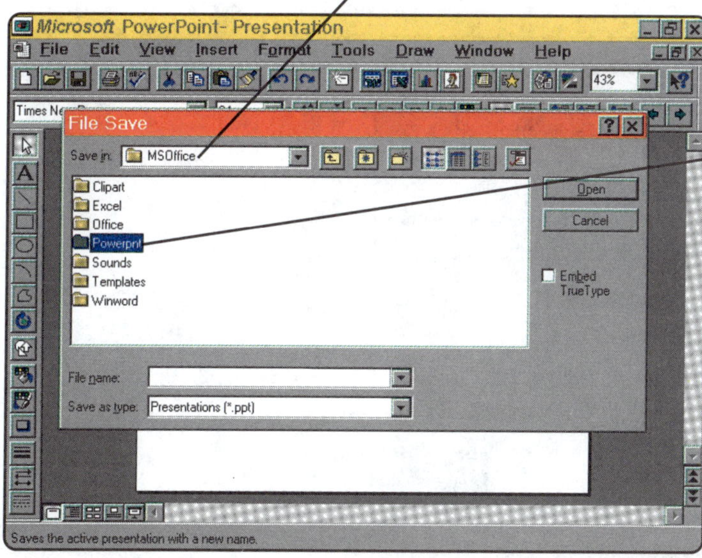

Powerpnt now shows in the Save in box. The open "Powerpnt" file folder indicates that the file will be saved in the Powerpnt directory.

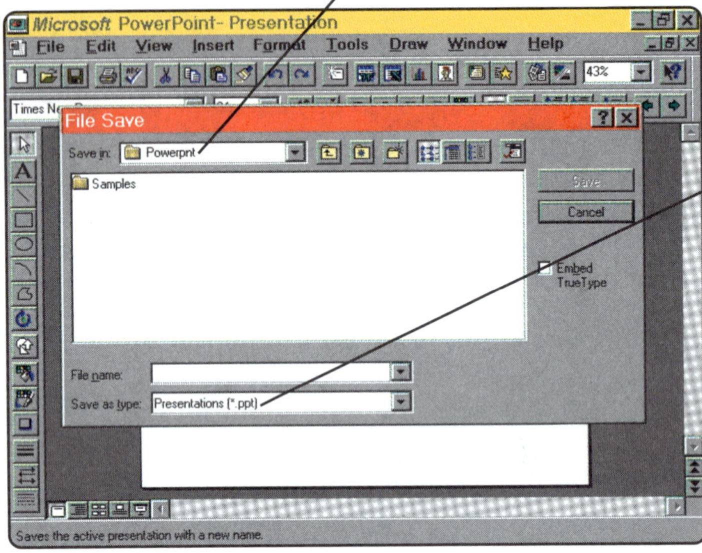

If the extension (.ppt) appears in the Save as type box, you'll see extensions on filenames in PowerPoint. If the extension does not show here, you won't see filename extensions. Either way is okay. It just depends on your system.

6. **Type slim** in the File name box.

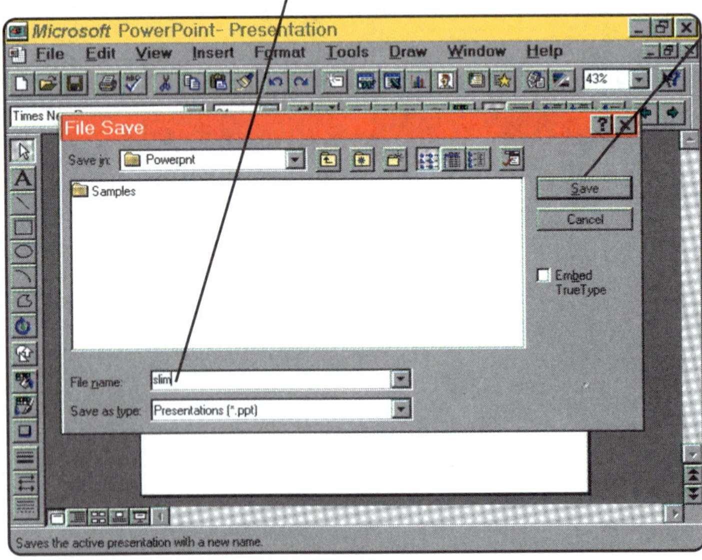

7. **Click** on **Save**. The slim.ppt Properties screen will appear.

Filling in the Summary Info

When you save a file for the first time, PowerPoint displays the Summary Info dialog box. Filling in this dialog box is optional. However, the information you add will be useful if you want to search for a file. If the Properties dialog box does not appear, you can access it after you save by clicking on File in the menu bar, then clicking on Properties.

Notice that the title has already been filled in from the first "title" slide you created in Chapter 1.

1. **Click** in the **Subject box** and **type Fat Content**.

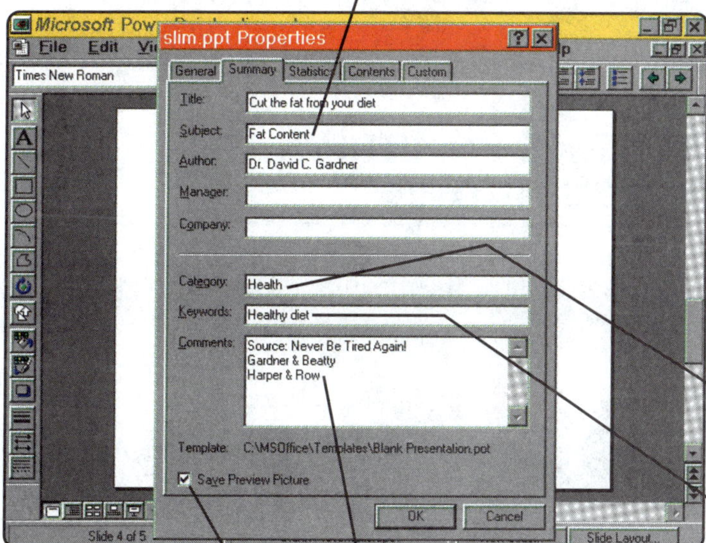

The Author's name is the name that was typed in during setup (in this example, Dr. David C. Gardner). You can change this by dragging the mouse pointer over the name and highlighting it. Then type the name you want.

2. **Click** in the **Category box. Type Health**.

3. **Click** in the **Keywords box. Type Healthy diet.**

4. **Press Tab** to move to the Comments box and **type** the following: **Source: Never Be Tired Again!**
Gardner and Beatty
Harper & Row

5. **Click** on **Save Preview Picture** to put a ✔ in the box.

6. **Click** on **OK.** The dialog box will disappear.

CLOSING A FILE

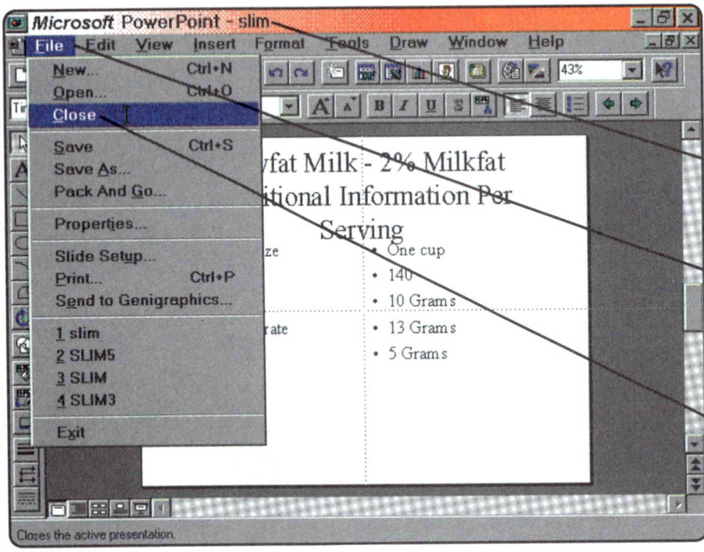

In this section you will close the slim.ppt file you created in Chapter 1.

Notice the file name in the title bar.

1. **Click** on **File** in the menu bar. The File menu will appear.

2. **Click** on **Close**. The slim.ppt file will close, and you will see a blank PowerPoint screen.

CLOSING POWERPOINT FOR WINDOWS

1. **Click** on **File** in the menu bar. The File menu will appear.

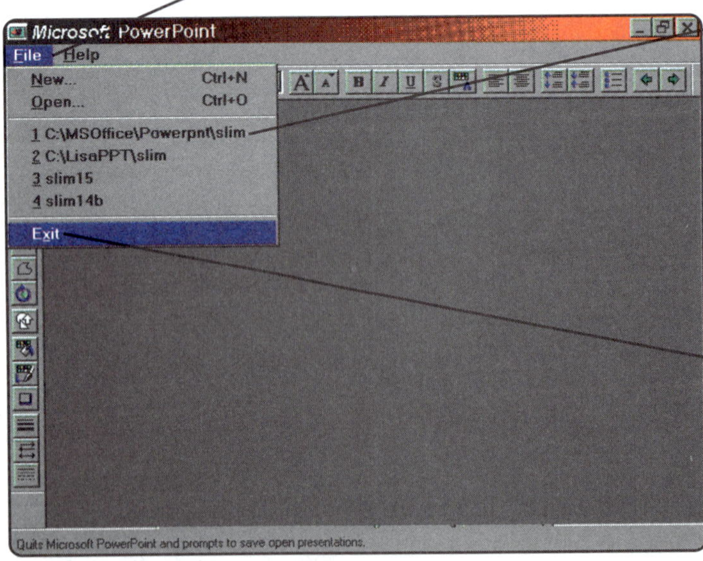

Notice that the file you just saved is listed on the File pull-down menu. This menu lists the four most recent files on which you have worked. You can open a file by clicking on its name on this menu.

2. **Click** on **Exit**. PowerPoint will close, and you will be back at the desktop.

OPENING AN EXISTING PRESENTATION

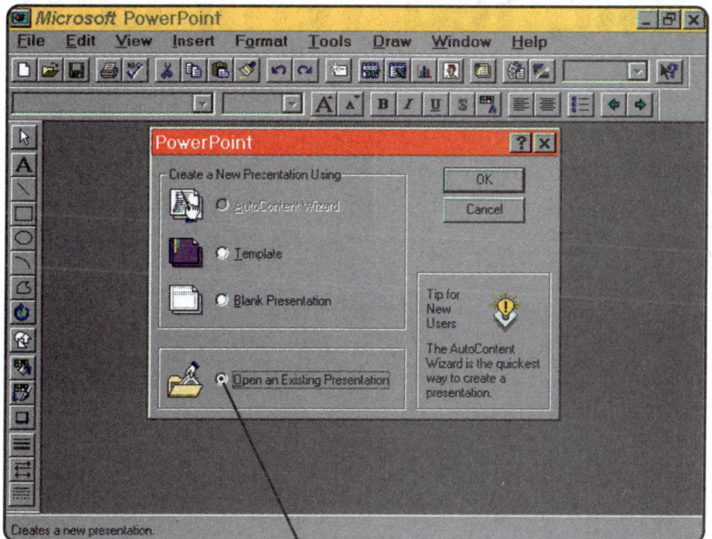

There are two ways to open an existing presentation. You can click on the name on the File menu, or you can use the PowerPoint dialog box, which you will do in this example.

1. **Open** PowerPoint 7.0 as described at the beginning of Chapter 1. The Tip of the Day dialog box will appear if you did not turn it off.

2. **Click** on **OK**. The PowerPoint dialog box will appear.

3. **Click** on **Open an Existing Presentation** to place a dot in the circle.

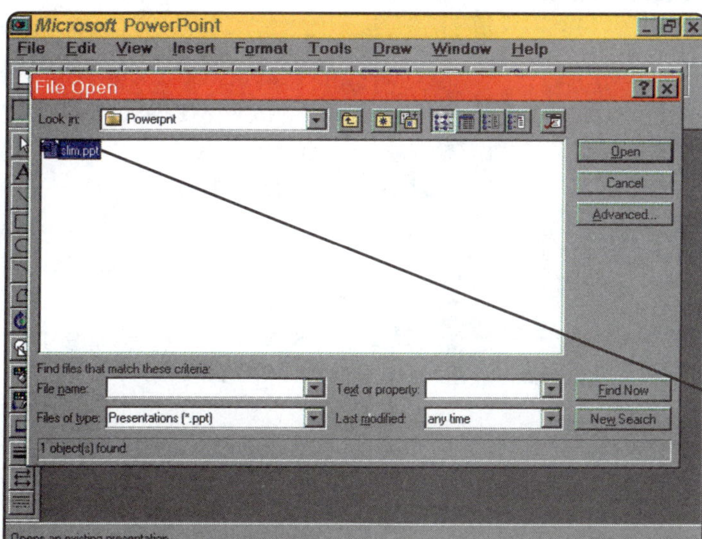

4. **Click** on **OK.** The Open dialog box will appear.

5. If Powerpnt does not appear in the Look in box, **repeat steps 2-5** in "Naming and Saving a File," on page 2, to go to the Powerpnt folder.

6. **Click** on **slim.**

7. **Click** on **Open.** A PowerPoint screen will appear.

CHAPTER 3

Choosing a Predesigned Template

You can dress up your presentation by choosing from a collection of predesigned templates. These templates include standard and custom color schemes. You can also add supplementary materials such as speaker's notes, handouts, and an outline to your presentation materials. You can customize each of these with your company name (or other identifying text), as well as the date, and page number. In this chapter you will do the following:

- ✔ Choose and apply a presentation template
- ✔ Determine the optional text to be included on slides, notes, handouts, and outlines
- ✔ Remove a predesigned template

OPENING A PRESENTATION TEMPLATE

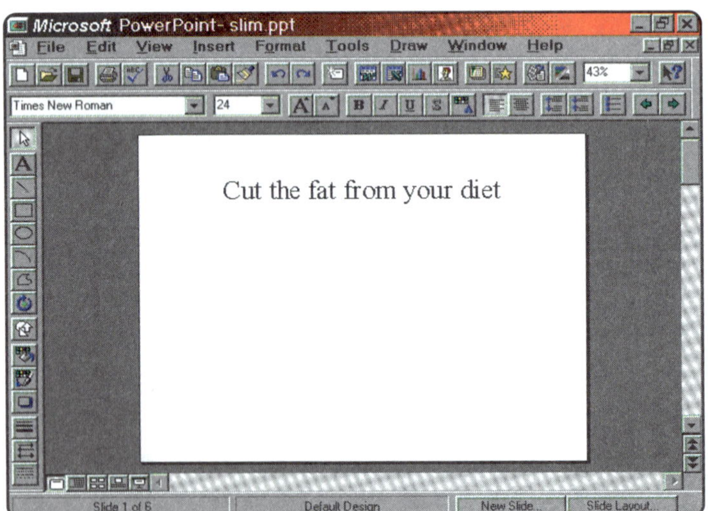

You can choose a design template using the Create a New Presentation option from the opening dialog box when you first boot up PowerPoint. Or, you can enter text first, then apply a template as you will do in this chapter.

1. **Open slim.ppt** if it is not already open. (Your version may not show the .ppt extension.)

2. **Click twice** on the **design format button** at the bottom of the screen, which says Default Design. The Apply Design Template box will appear.

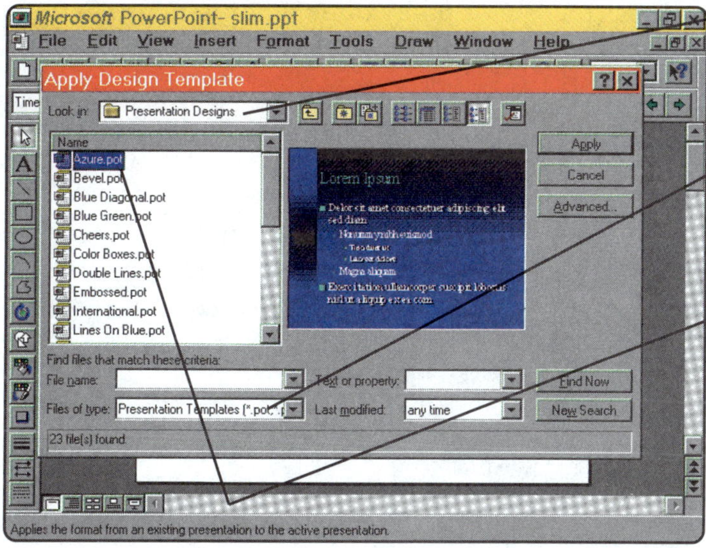

3. Confirm that **Presentation Designs** is in the Look in box.

4. Confirm that **Presentation Templates** is in the Files of type box.

Notice that the first presentation design, Azure, is highlighted. The Preview box shows the design that is highlighted. You may have different presentation templates than those listed here.

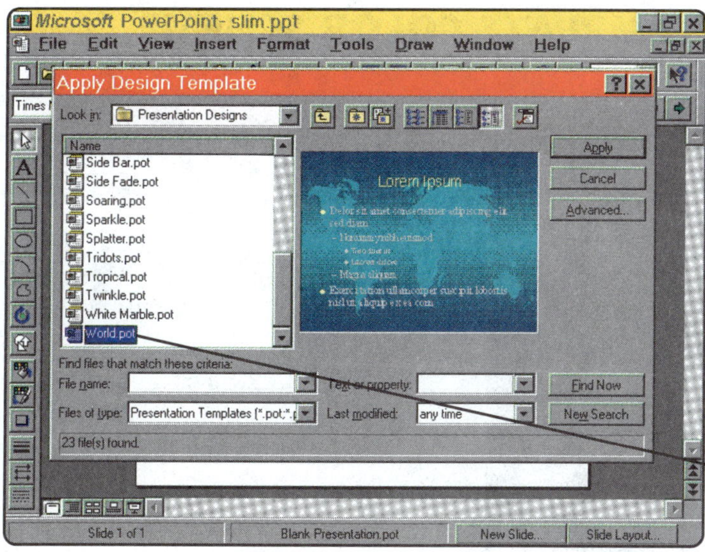

5. Click once on a **template** to see the design. (Be sure to click only once. If you click twice, the highlighted template will be applied to your presentation.) If this happens, repeat step 2 to get back to the Apply Design Template dialog box.

In this example, the World template appears in the preview box.

6. **Press** the **Page Up key three times** to return to the top of the presentation list.

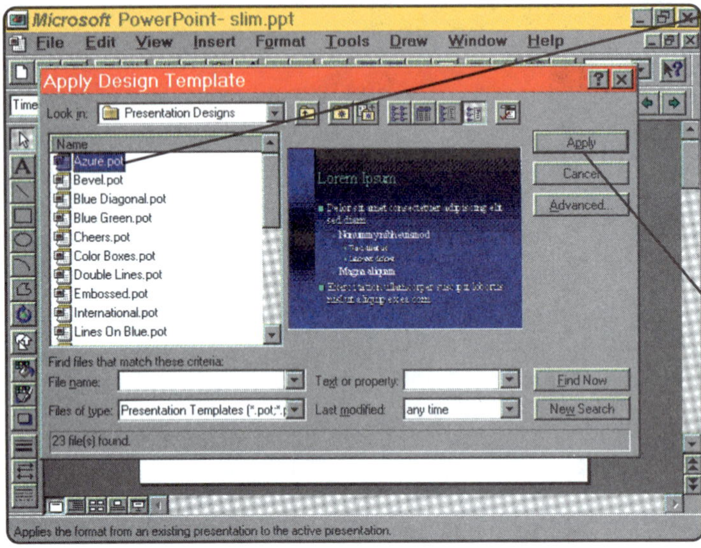

7. **Click** on **Azure** if it is not already highlighted.

If you don't have this presentation design template, choose another one.

8. **Click** on **Apply**. The Apply Design Template box will disappear, and the new template will be applied to your slides.

CUSTOMIZING THE DESIGN TEMPLATE COLOR SCHEME

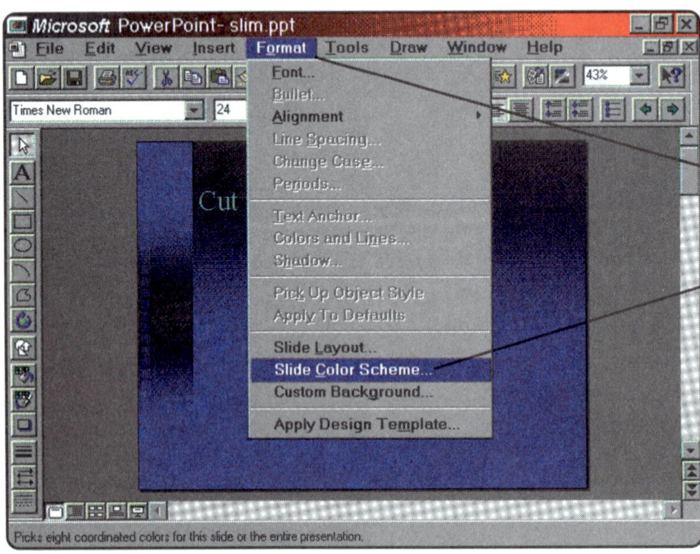

You can change the color scheme of the predesigned presentation templates.

1. **Click** on **Format**. The Format menu will appear.

2. **Click** on **Slide Color Scheme**. The Color Scheme dialog box will appear.

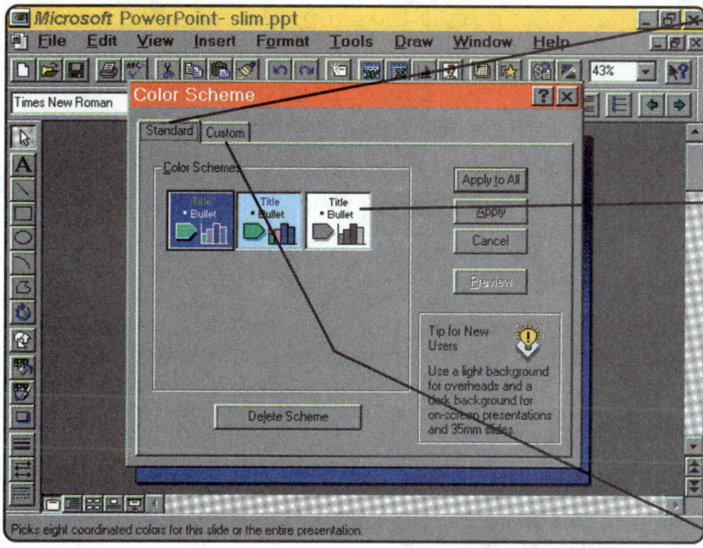

Notice that there are two tabs available in the Color Scheme box—Standard and Custom.

The Standard options for this template include three predesigned color schemes to choose from. We will skip the Standard options and change our color scheme using the Custom options.

3. **Click** on **Custom** to view its color options. The Custom options box will appear.

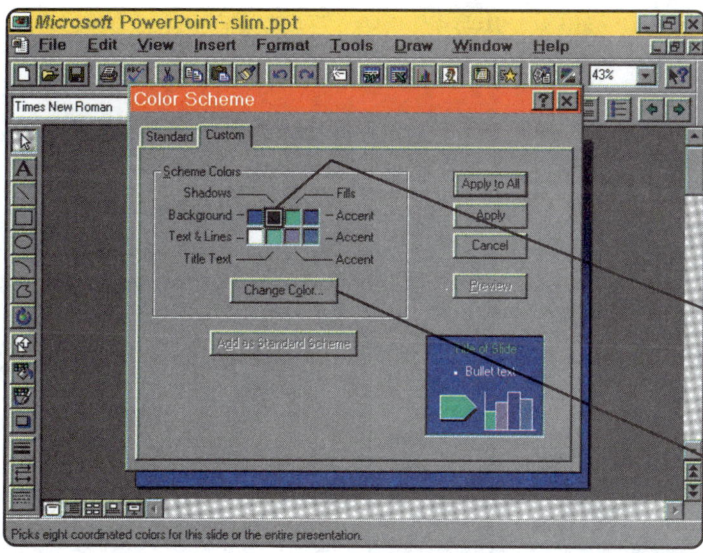

Notice there are eight different slide elements which can be recolored using the Custom options. We will change the template shadow color from black to purple.

4. **Click** on the **Shadows box.** The border will be highlighted.

5. **Click** on **Change Color.** The Shadow Color dialog box will appear.

6. **Click** on the **purple hexagon.** On our screen, it was the third one down from the top right corner. It may be different on your screen. The border of the purple hexagon will be highlighted.

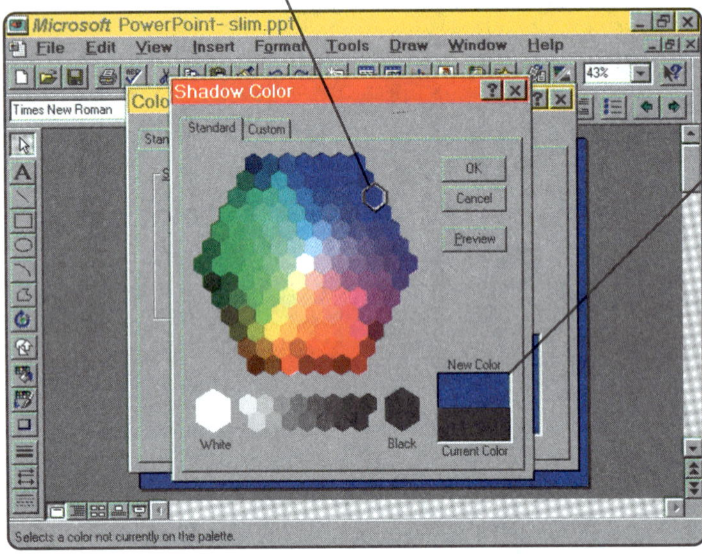

The highlighted color choice appears in the top of the Current Color box.

7. **Click** on **OK**. The Custom Color Scheme box will reappear.

Notice that the new shadow color appears in the Shadow selection box.

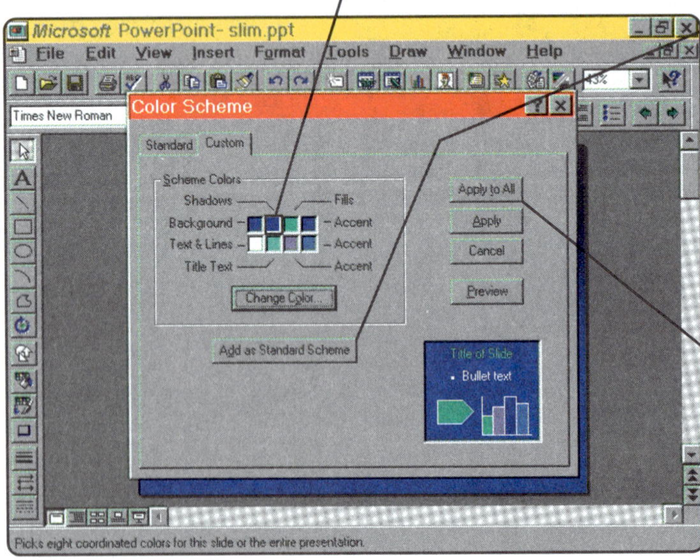

8. If you want to save this customized color scheme, **click** on **Add as Standard Scheme**. It will appear as the first option in the Standard Color Schemes box that you saw back on page 29.

9. **Click** on **Apply to all.** The Color Scheme dialog box will disappear, and your entire presentation will be changed to the new color scheme.

ADDING HEADERS AND FOOTERS TO YOUR PRESENTATION

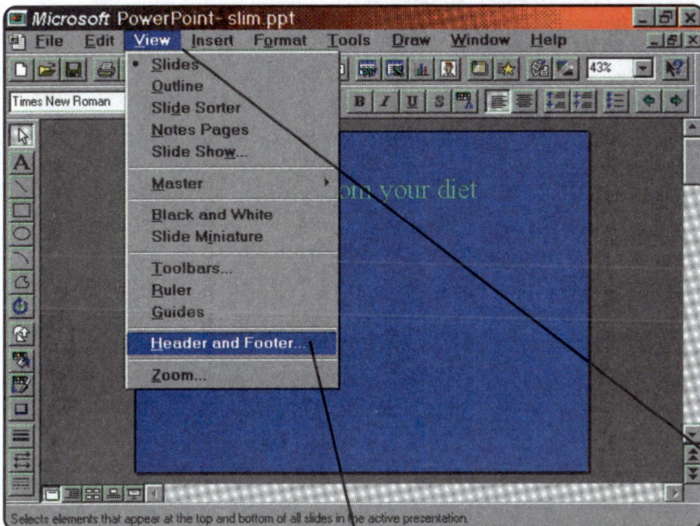

PowerPoint can add your company name (or other text), the date and time, and page numbers to slides. It can also add supplementary materials such as speaker's notes, handout slide copies and outline pages. Here we will add page numbers and a company name.

1. **Click** on **View**. The View menu will appear.

2. **Click** on **Header and Footer.** The Header and Footer dialog box will appear.

3. **Click** on the **Slide tab** to bring it to the front if it is not already there.

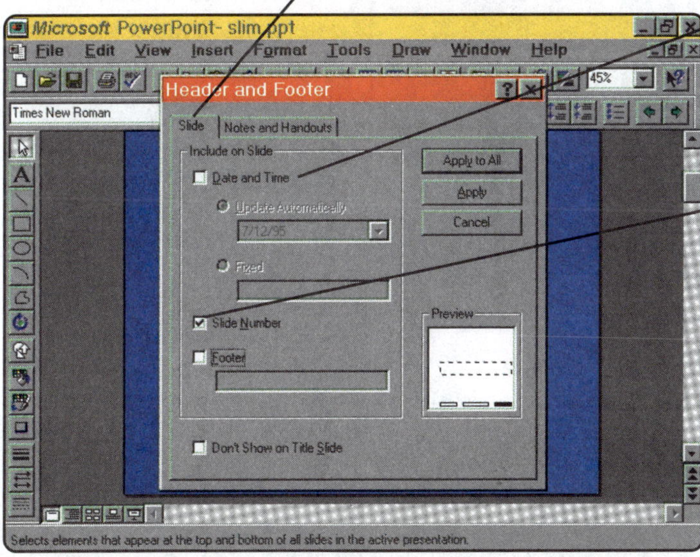

4. **Click** on **Date and Time** to *remove* the ✔ if you don't want the date and time to show.

5. **Click** on **Slide Number** to put a ✔ in the box.

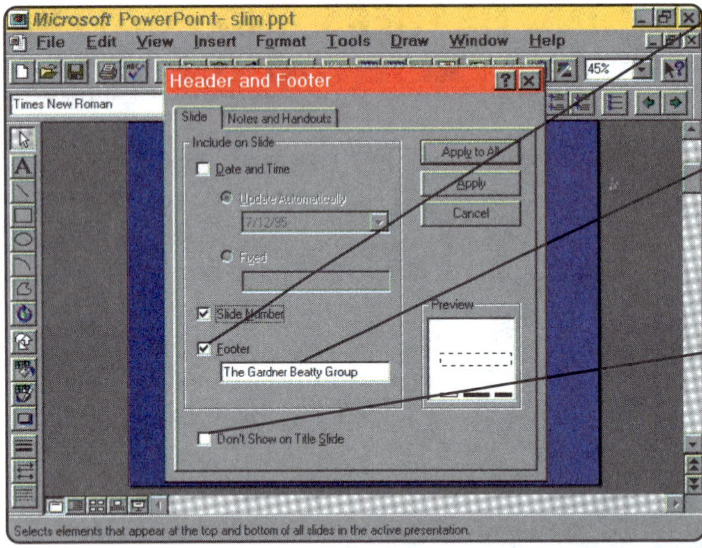

6. **Click on Footer** to put a ✔ in the box next to Footer.

7. **Type The Gardner Beatty Group,** or text of your choice, in the Footer box.

8. **Click** on **Don't Show on Title Slide** to put a ✔ in the box if you don't want the information you checked to show on the title slide.

9. **Click** on **Notes and Handouts** to bring up the Notes and Handouts dialog box.

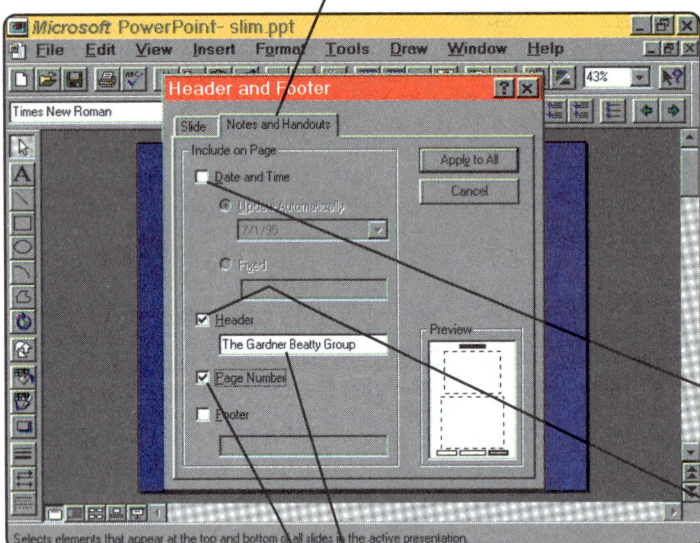

Under Notes and Handouts you can add the date and time, a header, page numbers and a footer. Notice that when you click on one of the option categories, the Preview box highlights the location of the selected option.

10. **Click** on **Date and Time** to *remove* the ✔.

11. **Click** to put a ✔ in the box next to Header.

12. **Type The Gardner Beatty Group.**

13. **Click** to put a ✔ in the box next to Page Number.

14. **Click** on **Footer** to *remove* the ✔.

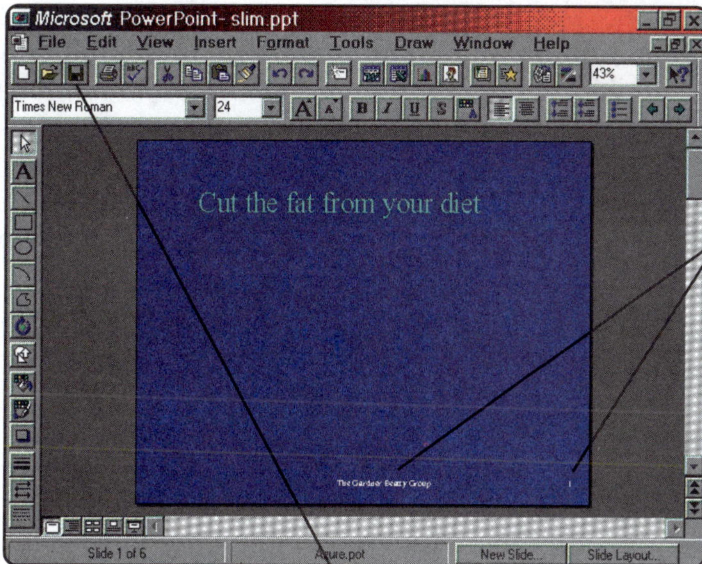

15. Click on **Apply to All.** The Header and Footer box will disappear, and your selected options will be added to the entire slide presentation.

Notice that if you didn't check the Don't Show on Title Slide box in the Header and Footer dialog box, the page number and company name appear at the bottom of slide 1.

SAVING THE FILE

1. Click on the **Save button**. The slim file is now ready for Chapter 5 "Editing and Styling Text."

REMOVING A DESIGN TEMPLATE

To remove a design template, follow these steps:

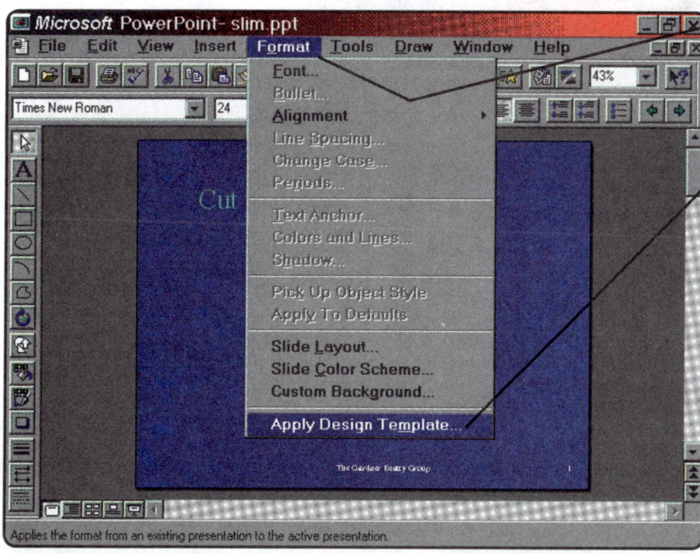

1. Click on **Format** in the menu bar. The Format menu will appear.

2. Click on **Apply Design Template.** The Apply Design Template dialog box will appear. (You can also click on the design format button at the bottom of the screen to get to the Apply Design Template dialog box. See the beginning of this chapter for details.) The Presentation Designs file folder will be in the Look in box.

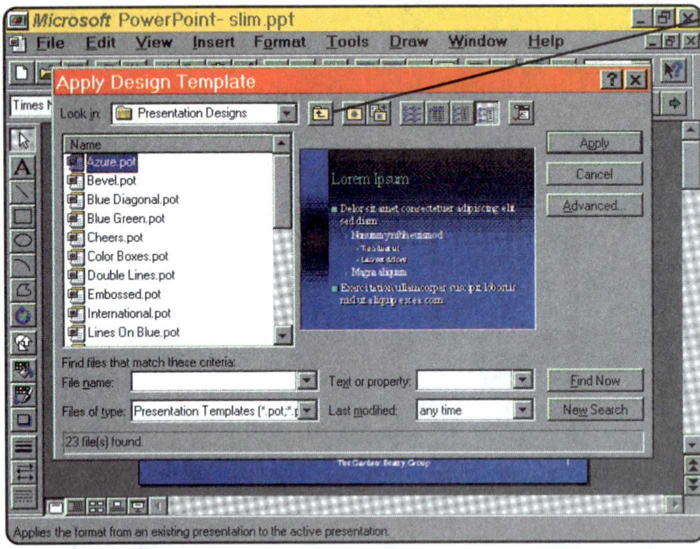

3. **Click** on the **Up One Level button** to the right of the Look in box. The Templates file folder will appear in the Look in box.

Notice that the Blank Presentation template, at the end of the list of templates, is highlighted.

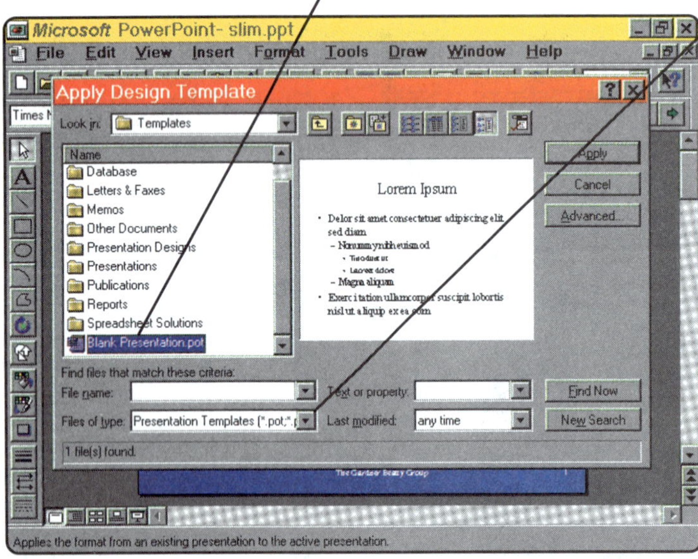

If Blank Presentation is not there, be sure that Presentation Templates is selected in the Files of type box.

4. **Click** on **Apply**. The Apply Design Template box will disappear, and the previous design template will be replaced with the Blank template.

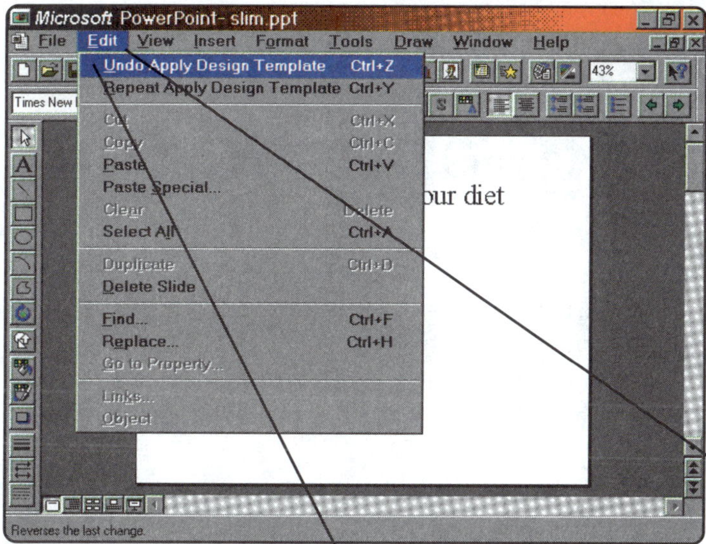

Because we will use the template design chosen for the presentation earlier in this book, we will undo the Blank presentation design we just applied. Feel free to go back into the Apply Design Template box at any time and apply the design template that you like best.

5. **Click** on **Edit**. The Edit menu will appear.

6. **Click** on **Undo Apply Design Template.** The Blank template format will be replaced with the design you applied earlier. Keep in mind that the undo feature will only work until another format change is made. If you don't undo immediately, you will need to go back and recreate your entire custom template.

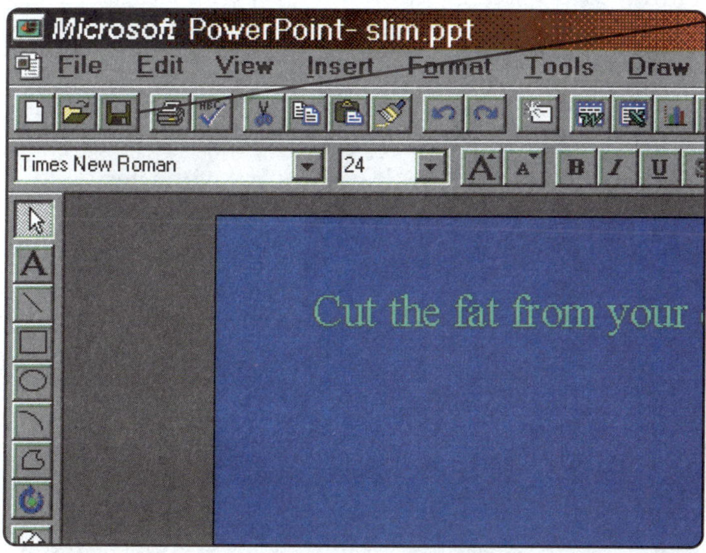

7. **Click** on **Save** before you continue on to Chapter 4.

CHAPTER

4

Viewing, Moving, Copying, and Adding Slides

You can move slides in PowerPoint almost as if you were using a slide tray. Copying and deleting slides is as easy as clicking your mouse. You can zoom in to see a close up of a slide or zoom out to see a number of slides at once. In this chapter, you will do the following:

✔ Change to different views
✔ Copy, move, and delete a slide
✔ Use the Zoom feature

CHANGING TO SLIDE SORTER VIEW

1. Open the Slim presentation if it is not already open. **Place** your **mouse arrow** over the **Slide Sorter View button**, which is the third button from the left at the bottom of your screen. Notice that a pop-up *tooltip* box tells you the name of the button. A description of the button's function appears in the status bar at the very bottom of your screen. (Try this with other buttons at the top and bottom of your screen.)

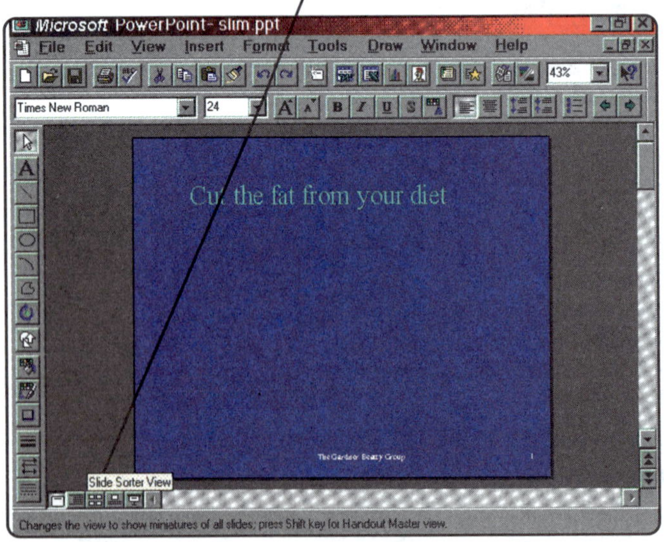

2. **Click** on the **Slide Sorter View button**. The slides in your presentation will be shown in bird's-eye view on the screen. It may take a few minutes for the color to fill in on all the slides.

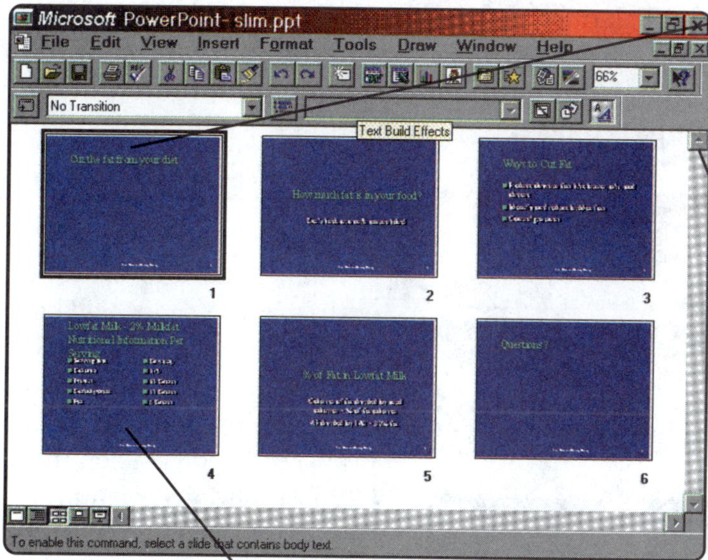

Notice that slide 1 has a bold border to show that it is the slide that is currently selected.

If you have more than six slides, you can view them by dragging the scroll button down the scroll bar.

COPYING A SLIDE WITH THE COPY BUTTON

There are several ways to copy a slide in PowerPoint. Here is one way.

1. **Click** on **Slide 4** to select it.

2. **Click** on the **Copy button**. (You can also click on Edit in the menu bar, then click on Copy on the pull-down menu.)

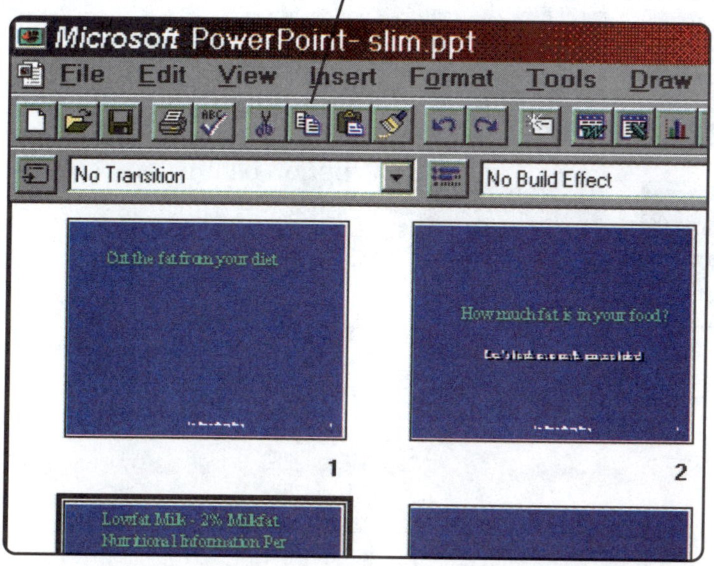

3. **Click once** to the **right** of **slide 4**. Notice the insertion line that appears between slides 4 and 5. Unless you click somewhere else, the copied slide will be pasted here.

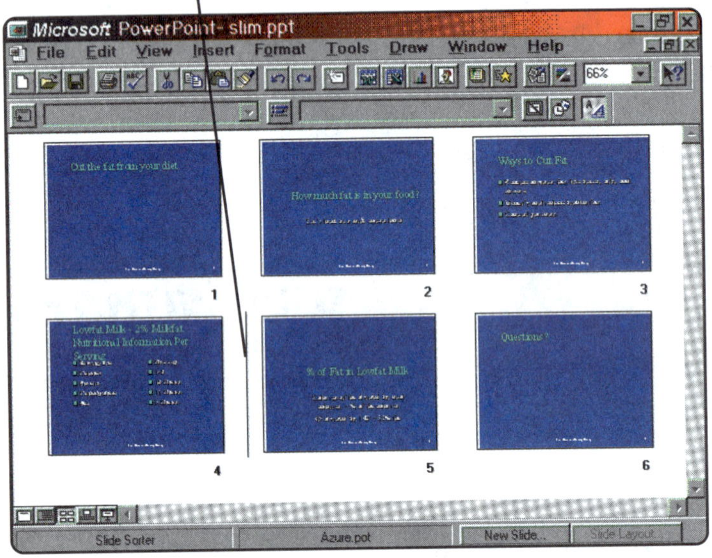

4. **Click** on the **Paste button**. A copy of slide 4 will be pasted to the left of slide 5. The slides will be renumbered to include the new slide as you see in the next example. (You can also click on Paste on the Edit pull-down menu.)

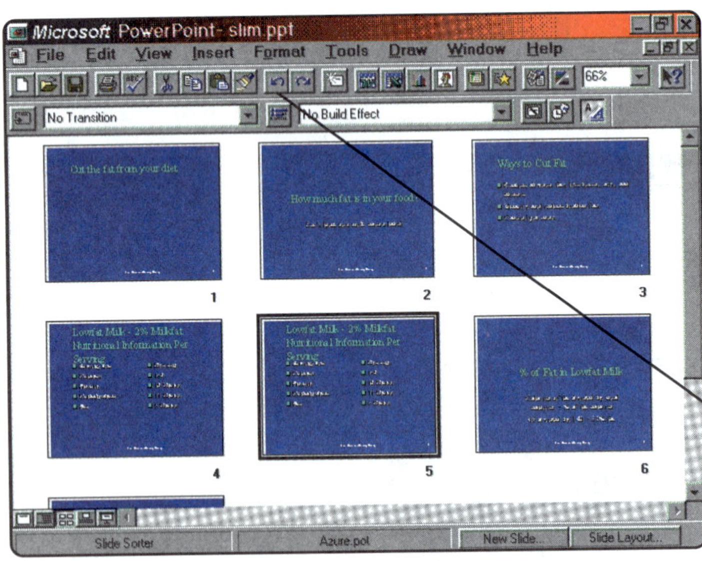

USING UNDO

Let's say you decided not to insert this copy of slide 4 after all. PowerPoint makes it easy to undo as long as you use the Undo option before you perform any other function.

1. **Click** on the **Undo button**. The slide will be deleted, and the other slides will be renumbered back to the way they were.

MOVING A SLIDE

The drag-and-drop feature of PowerPoint lets you move slides as if you were using a slide tray.

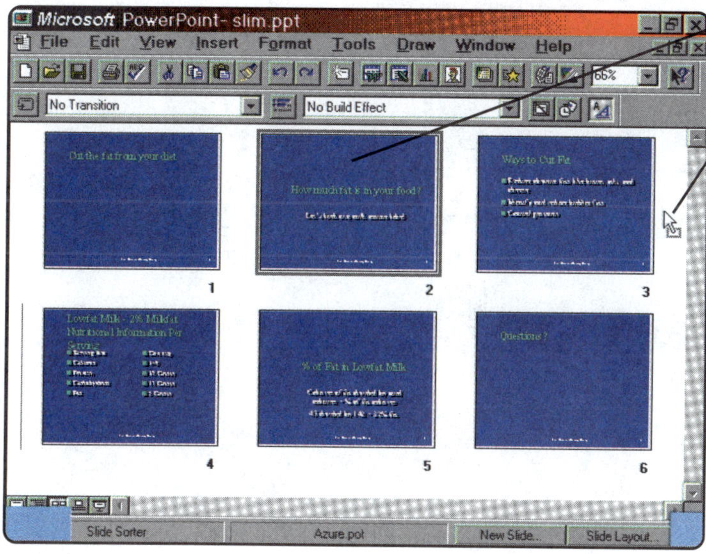

1. **Click** on **Slide 2** to select it.

2. **Press and hold** your **mouse button**. Then **drag** the mouse pointer to the right of slide 3. You will see a tiny slide being dragged.

3. **Release** the **mouse button**. Slide 2 will be in the slide 3 position and the slides will be renumbered accordingly.

INSERTING A SLIDE

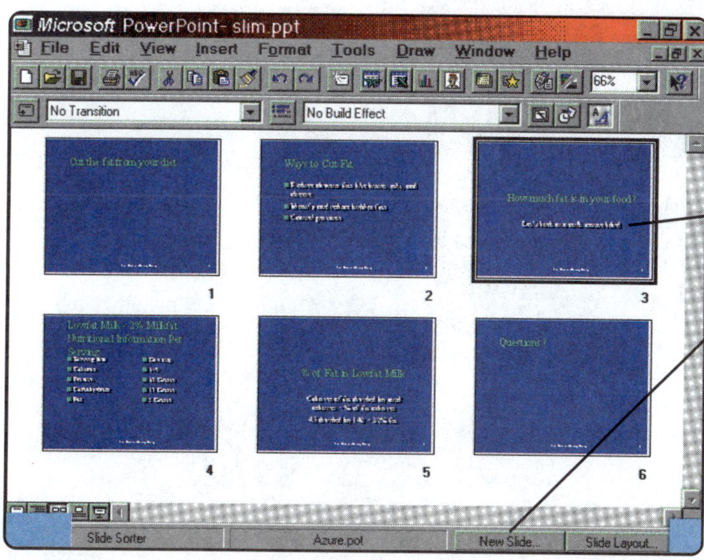

When you add a slide to a presentation, it is inserted to the right of whatever slide is already selected.

1. **Click** on **slide 3** if it is not currently selected.

2. **Click** on the **New Slide button**. The New Slide dialog box will appear.

3. **Drag** the **scroll button** to the top of the scroll bar if it is not already there.

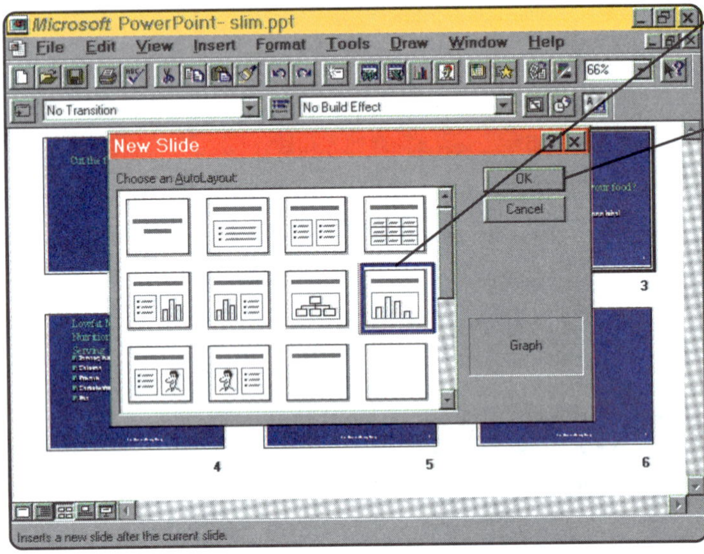

4. **Click** on the **Graph** slide.

5. **Click** on **OK**. The Slide Sorter view will appear with an empty slide as slide 4. The empty text blocks on this slide do not show in the Slide Sorter view. They show only in Slide view.

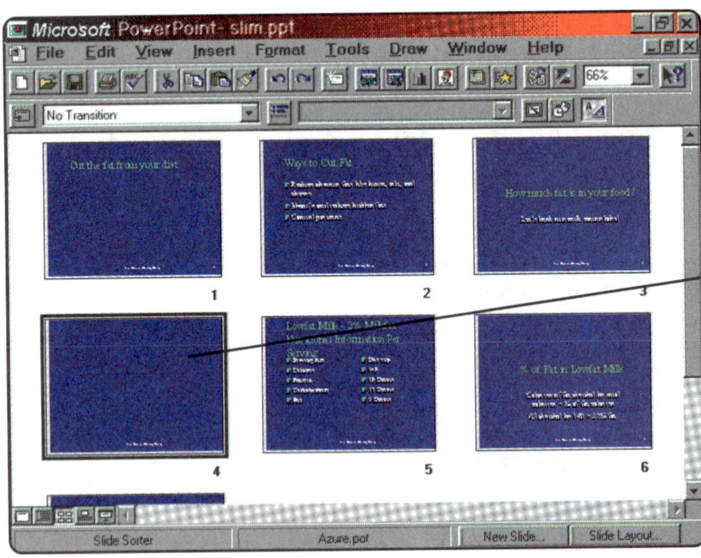

Your screen will look like the example to the left.

DELETING A SLIDE

1. **Click** on **slide 4** to select it if it is not already selected.

2. **Press** the **Delete key** (or Backspace key) to delete it. The slide will disappear instantly!

USING THE ZOOM FEATURE

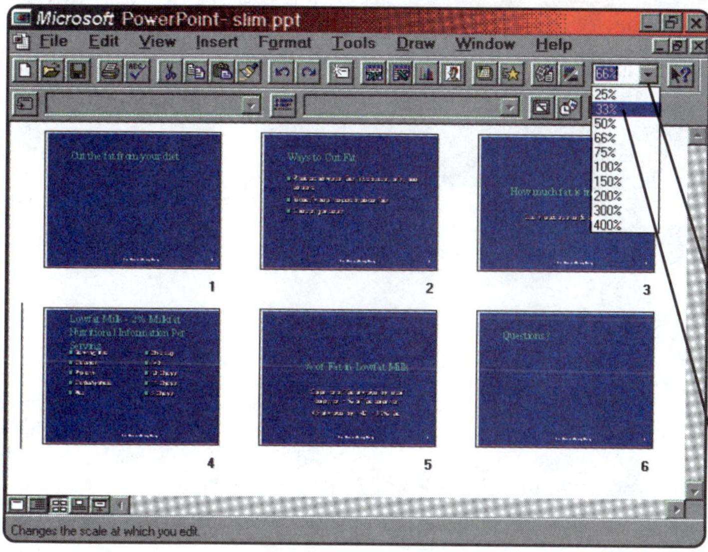

The standard Slide Sorter view shows six slides. If you have more than six slides in your presentation you can use the zoom feature to see more slides at the same time.

1. **Click** on the ▼ to the right of the zoom box in the toolbar.

2. **Click** on **33%**. The slides will appear in a 33% view.

You can also use the menu bar to zoom.

3. **Click** on **View** in the menu bar. The View menu will appear.

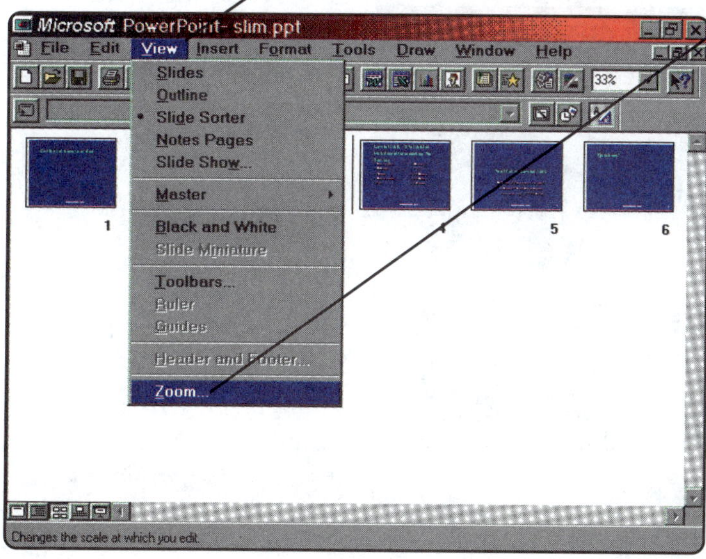

4. **Click** on **Zoom**. The Zoom dialog box will appear.

5. **Click** on **66%**.

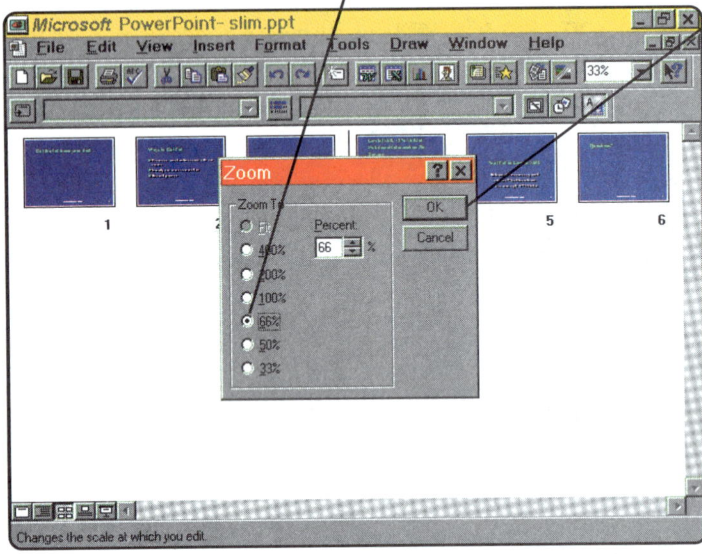

6. **Click** on **OK**. You will be returned to the default Slide Sorter view with six slides. It will take a while for the template colors to be applied.

CHANGING TO SLIDE SHOW VIEW

You can use your computer screen to practice your slide show or to run a slide show. You'll learn more about computer slide shows in Chapter 16. In this section, you will learn how to switch in and out of Slide Show view.

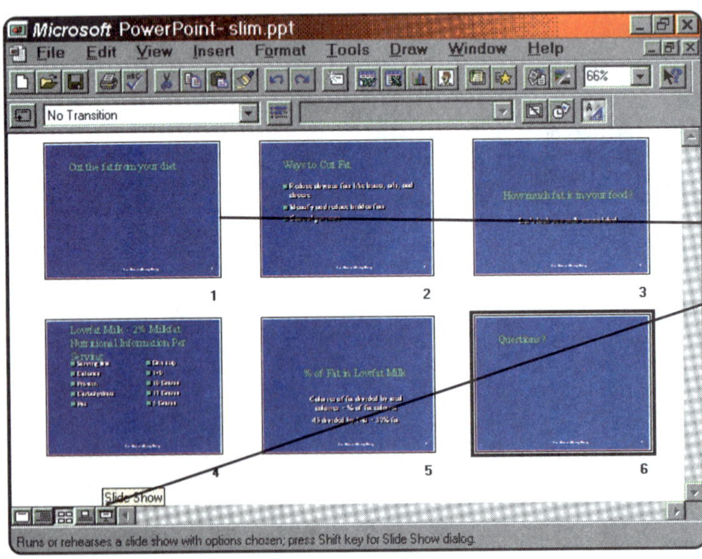

1. **Click** on **slide 1**.
2. **Click** on the **Slide Show button**, which is the fifth button from the left. Your screen will go blank for a few seconds. Then the Slide Show view will appear showing slide 1.

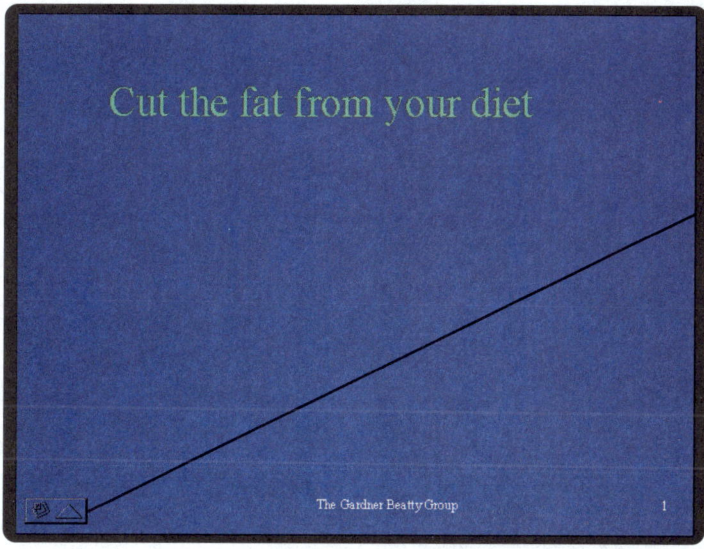

As soon as you move your mouse, an up arrow button will appear at the bottom left.

3. **Click** on the **up arrow**. A menu will appear.

CHANGING SLIDES IN SLIDE SHOW VIEW

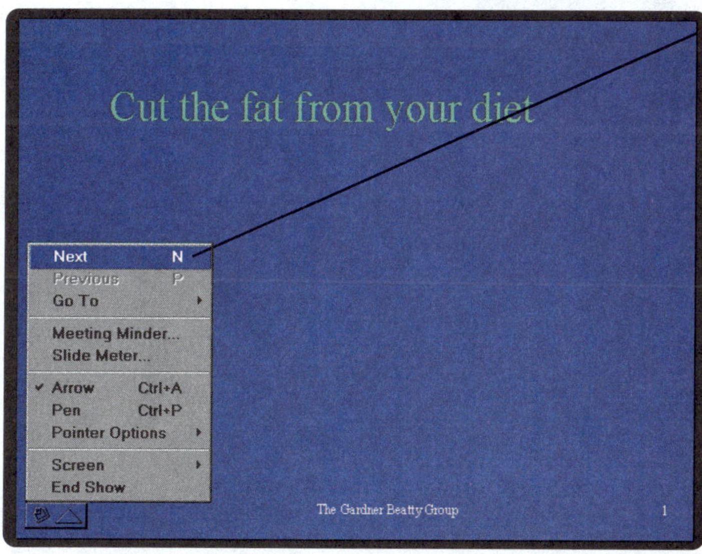

1. **Click** on **Next**. Slide 2 will appear.

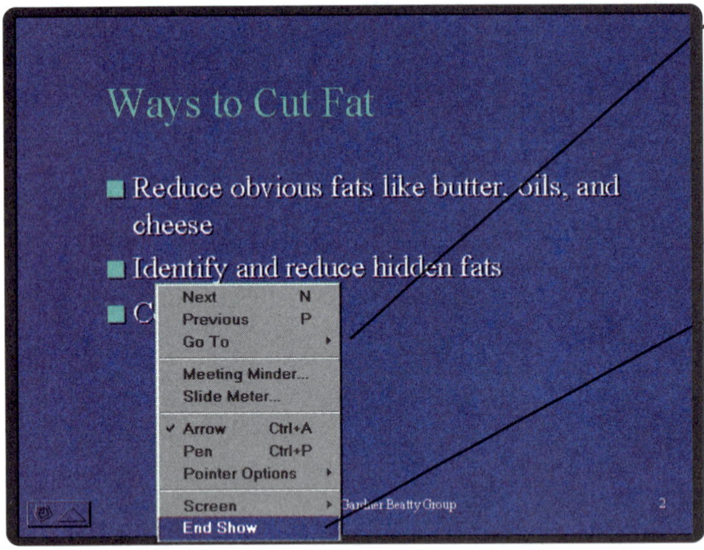

2. **Place** the **mouse arrow** anywhere on the slide background.

3. **Click** the **right mouse button**. The Slide Show menu will appear.

4. **Click** on **End Show.** You will be returned to the previous view, in this case Slide Sorter view.

CHANGING TO SLIDE VIEW

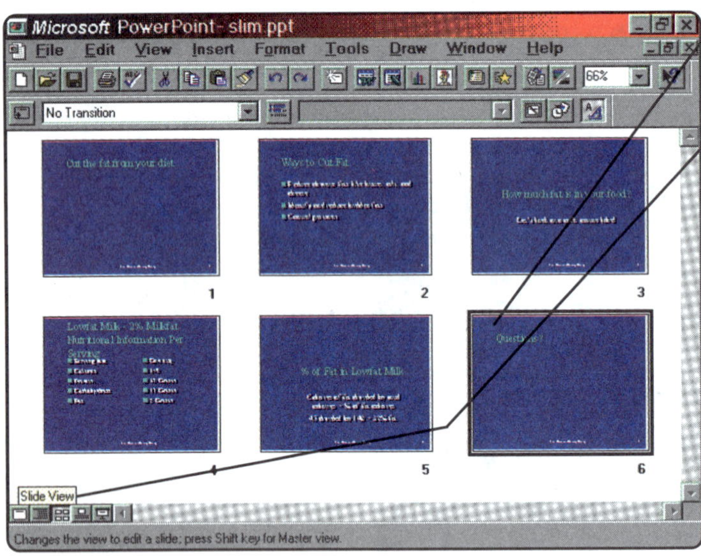

1. **Click** on **slide 6** to select it.

2. **Click** on the **Slide view** button. Slide 6 will appear in the Slide view format.

Changing the Size of the Slide in Slide View

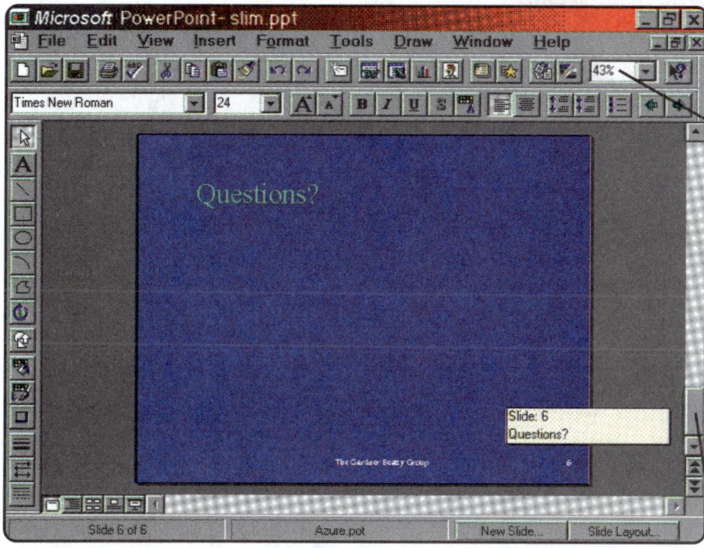

You can enlarge the slide that you see in Slide view.

1. **Click** in the **Zoom Control box**. The % will be highlighted. Your number may be different than this example.

2. **Type 43** and **press Enter**. The slide will be enlarged.

Moving Around in Slide View

1. **Place** the **mouse arrow** on the **scroll button**. Then **press and hold** the **mouse button**. Notice that the current slide number and title appears to the left.

2. **Drag** the **scroll button** up and down the scroll bar and release the button when the number of the slide you want to see appears in the box. Then drag the scroll button back down to slide 6.

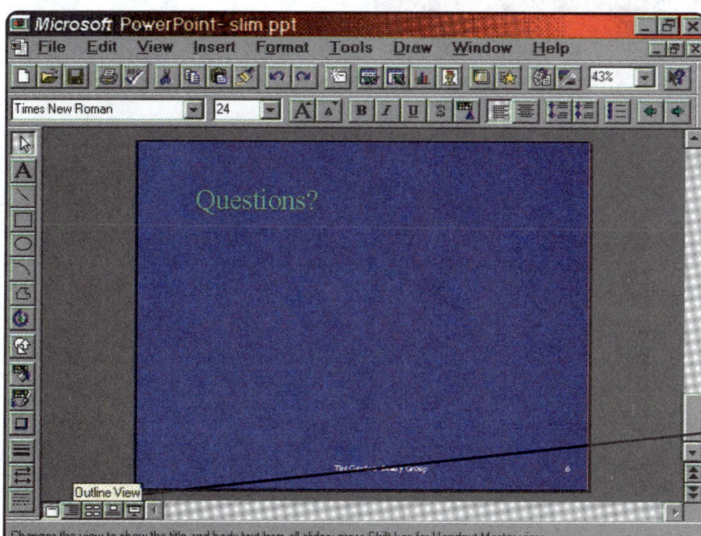

CHANGING TO OUTLINE VIEW

1. **Click** on the **Outline View button**, which is the second from the left at the bottom of your screen.

Notice you are at the bottom of the outline because slide six is the selected slide.

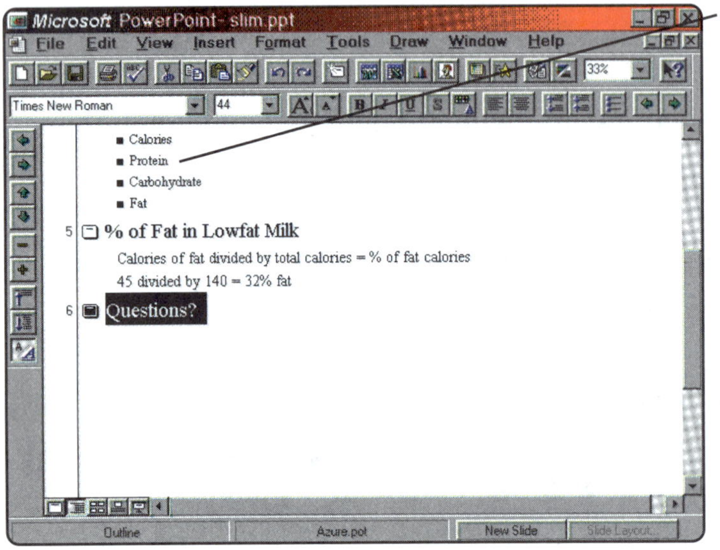

Also, notice on slide 4 the Outline view shows only the left bulleted list. (Strange, but Microsoft says this is the way it is.) If you want to edit the right bulleted list, you can do it in Slide view.

2. **Press** the **Page Up key** to move to the top of the outline.

3. **Click** on the **Save button** to save the change you made in the Slide view zoom size.

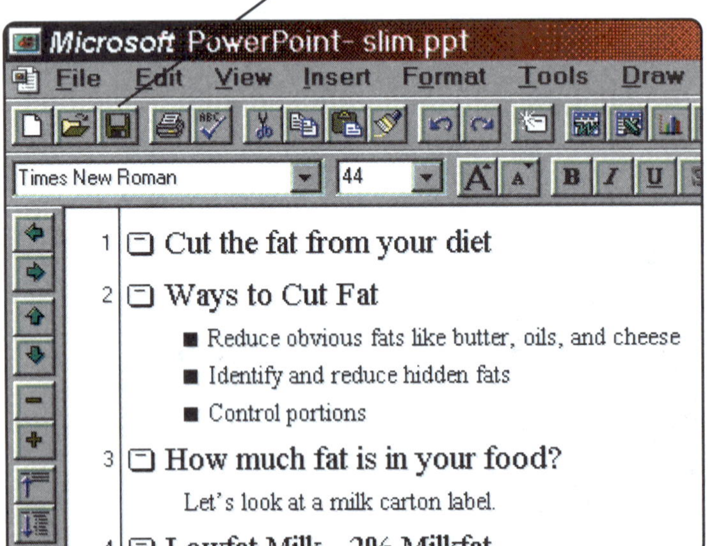

CHAPTER 5

Editing and Styling Text

You can edit and style text in both the Slide and Outline views. Anything you can do to text in a word processing program you can do in PowerPoint. There are additional styling features discussed in Chapter 6. In this chapter you will do the following:

- ✔ Edit bullets in Outline view
- ✔ Change the case
- ✔ Add periods
- ✔ Delete bullets in Slide view

EDITING TEXT IN OUTLINE VIEW

1. **Open** the **slim presentation**, if it is not already open. If you are not already in Outline view, see Chapter 4, "Changing to Outline View." In this section, you will change the bullets on the second slide to check marks. You can also do this in Slide view.

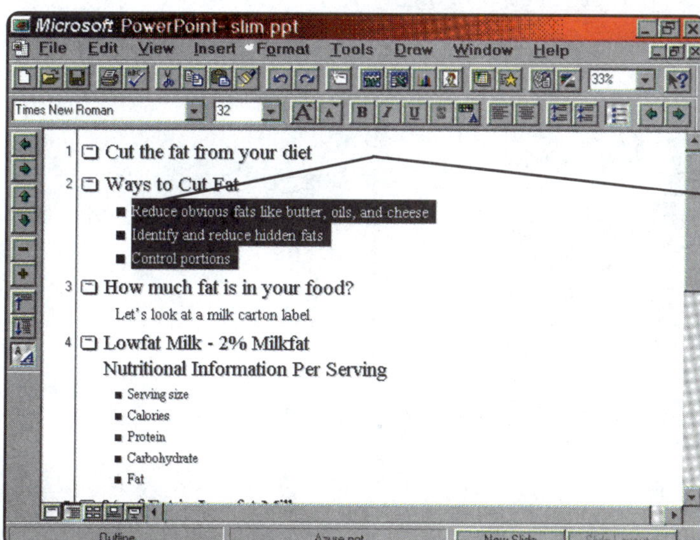

Changing Bullets to Check Marks

1. **Press and hold** the **mouse button** to the **left** of "**Reduce**" and **drag** the cursor to the end of "Control portions."

2. **Release** the **mouse button**. The text will be highlighted.

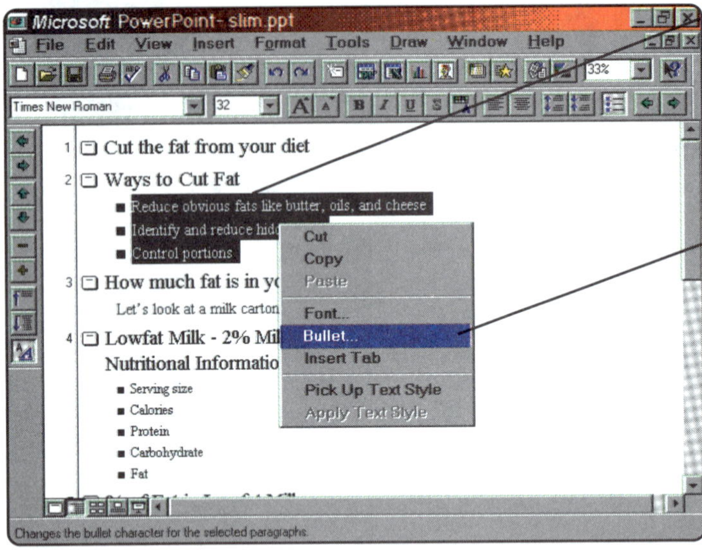

3. **Keeping** the **cursor** on the **highlighted text, click** the **right mouse button**. A menu will appear called a *quick* menu.

4. **Click** on **Bullet**. The Bullet dialog box will appear. (It may take a little while.)

Notice that the font is Monotype Sorts. Depending upon the version of monotype sorts you have, you may not have the exact symbol shown here. If you don't have the check mark, choose another symbol.

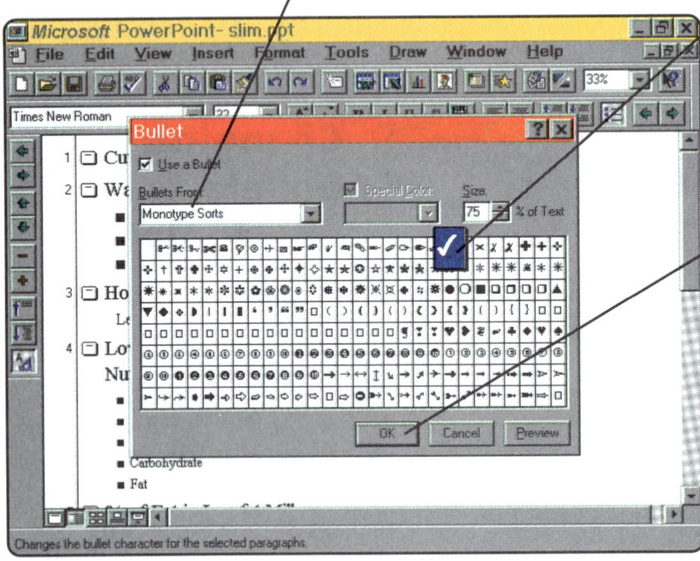

5. **Click** on the **bold check mark** in the top row, eighth from the right. The check mark will be enlarged.

6. **Click** on **OK**. The dialog box will disappear, and the bullets will be changed to check marks.

Switching to Slide View

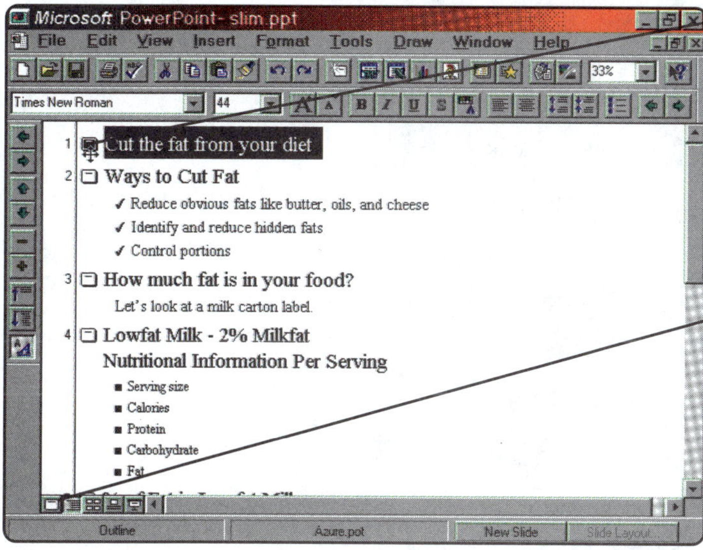

1. Click on the **small slide** to the **right** of **number 1** to highlight the text in slide 1. As you place the cursor on the slide icon, the cursor will change to a four-headed arrow.

2. Click on the **Slide View button** at the bottom of your screen. The Slide view screen will appear showing slide 1.

CHANGING THE CASE

You can change the capitalization of text to all uppercase, all lowercase, or use a feature which puts in the correct capitalization for a title. In this section you will correct the capitalization on the title slide.

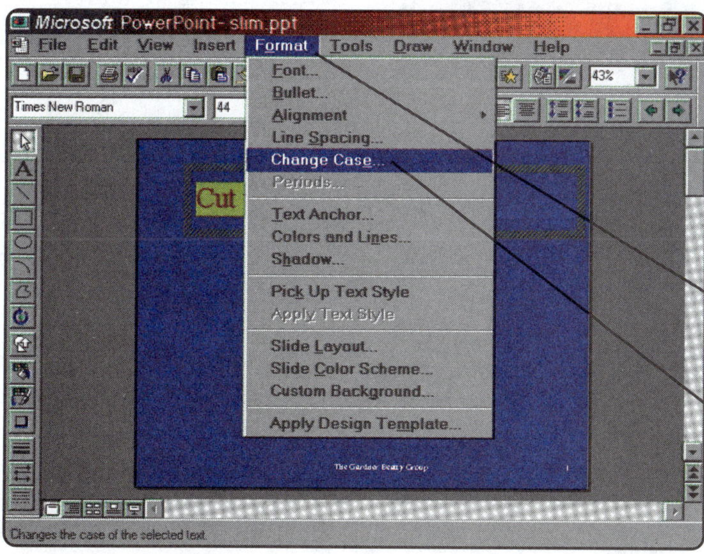

1. Click and **drag** the I-beam over the text to highlight it.

2. Click on **Format.** The Format menu will appear.

3. Click on **Change Case.** The Change Case dialog box will appear.

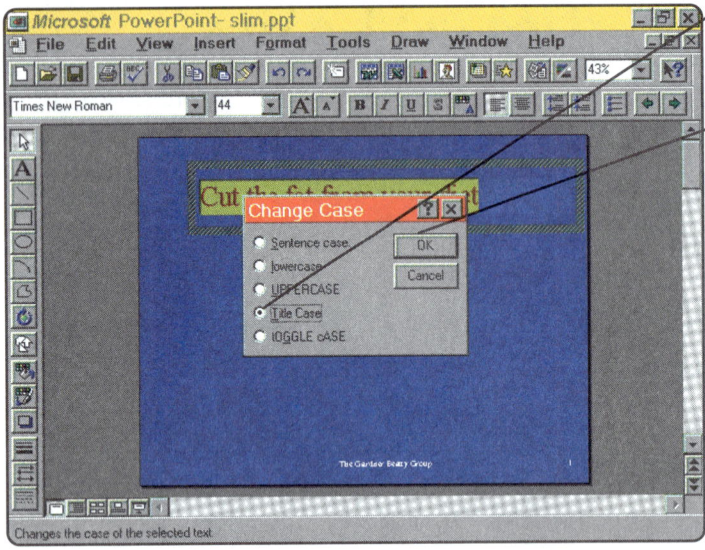

4. **Click** on **Title Case** to place a dot in the circle.

5. **Click** on **OK.** Slide 1 will appear with the title slide capitalized.

6. **Click anywhere** to remove the highlighting.

MAKING TEXT BOLD

Before you can format text, you must first highlight, or select, it.

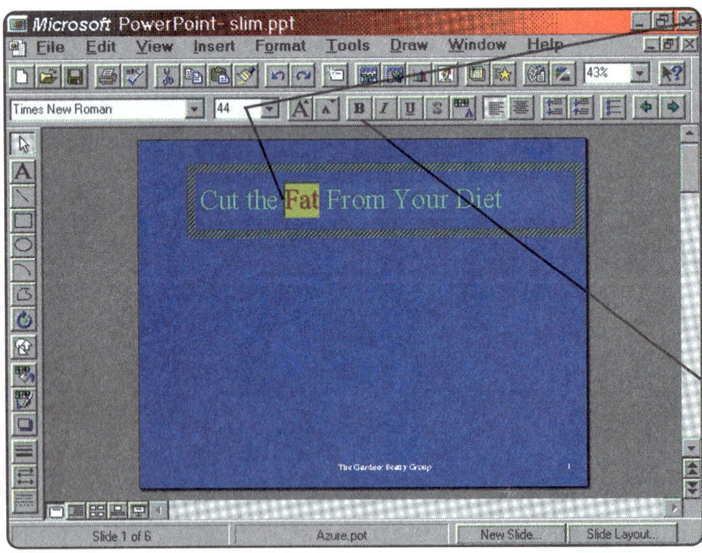

1. **Click** to the **left** of the word "**Fat**." The mouse pointer changes to an I-beam when it is in a text block.

2. **Drag** the **I-beam** over the word "Fat" to highlight it.

3. **Click** on the **Bold Button.**

4. **Click outside** the text block to remove the highlighting and deselect the text block.

ADDING PERIODS TO TEXT

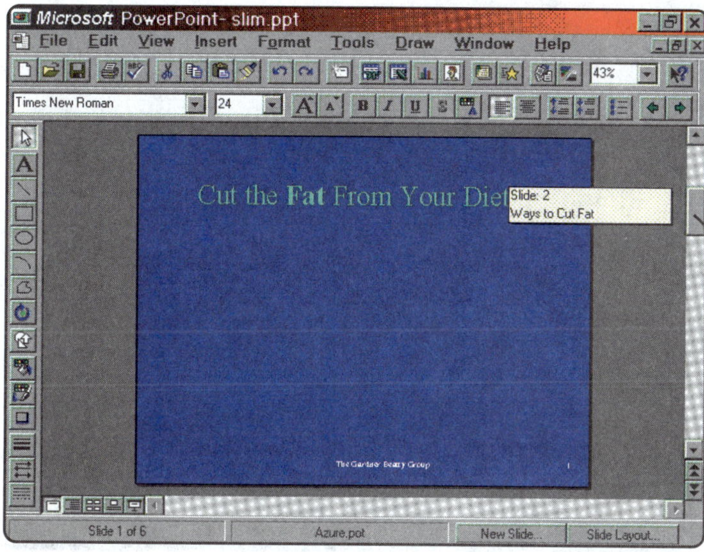

It's easy to be inconsistent in the use of periods on slides. Use the Periods feature to solve that problem.

1. **Move** the **mouse arrow** to the scroll button.

2. **Press and hold** the **mouse button** as you **drag** the scroll button down. When the slide 2 indicator appears, **release** the **mouse button.** Slide 2 will appear.

3. **Press and drag** the **I-beam** over the check marked text to highlight it.

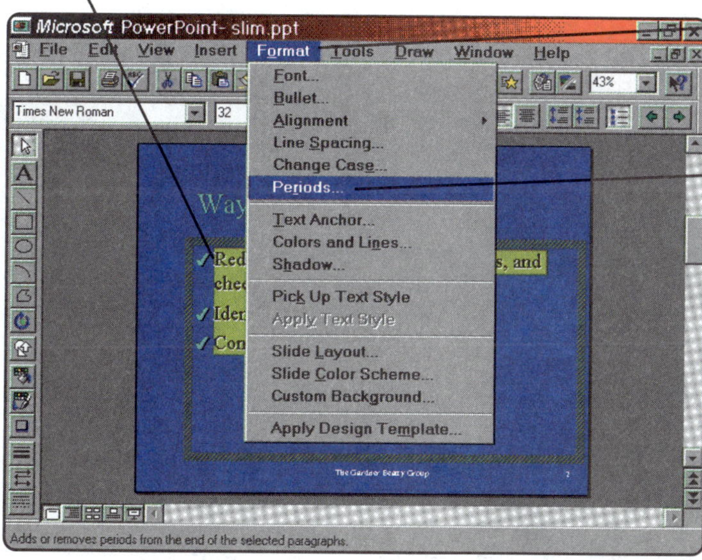

4. **Click** on **Format** in the menu bar. The Format menu will appear.

5. **Click** on **Periods**. The Periods dialog box will appear.

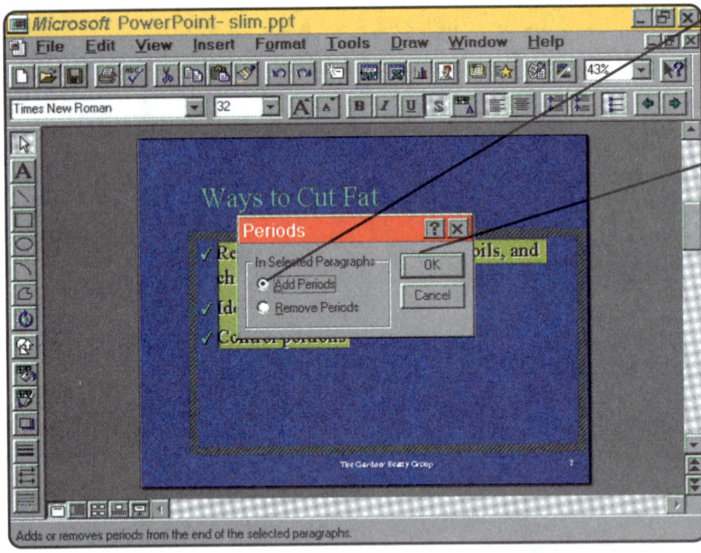

6. **Click** on **Add Periods** to place a dot in the circle, if one is not already there.

7. **Click** on **OK**. Slide 2 will appear with the added periods.

CHANGING TEXT SIZE

You can change the font or type size just as you do in word processing programs. In this example, we won't change the font. We will change the size of the font. You can change the font that is included with a specific template. It is best, however, to stick with True Type fonts so they can be embedded with the presentation when stored on disk.

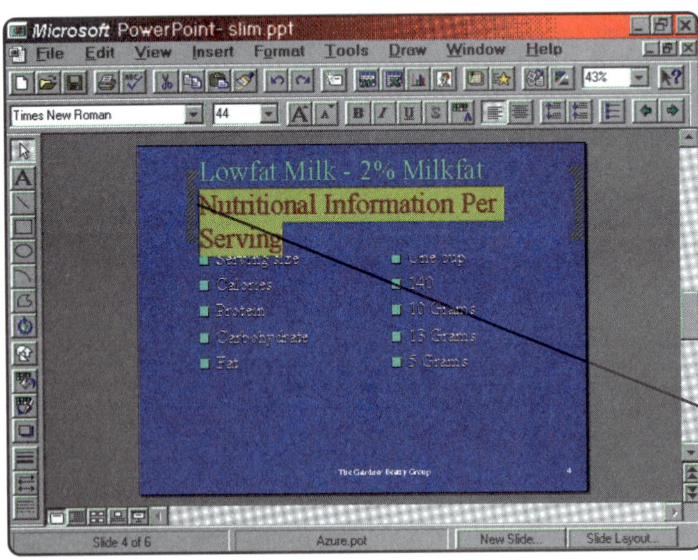

1. **Press** the **Page Down key** on the keyboard two times to move to slide 4.

2. **Click** to the **left** of "**Nutritional Information Per Serving**" and **drag** the I-beam over the text to highlight it.

3. **Click** on the ▼ to the right of the font size box. A pull-down menu will appear.

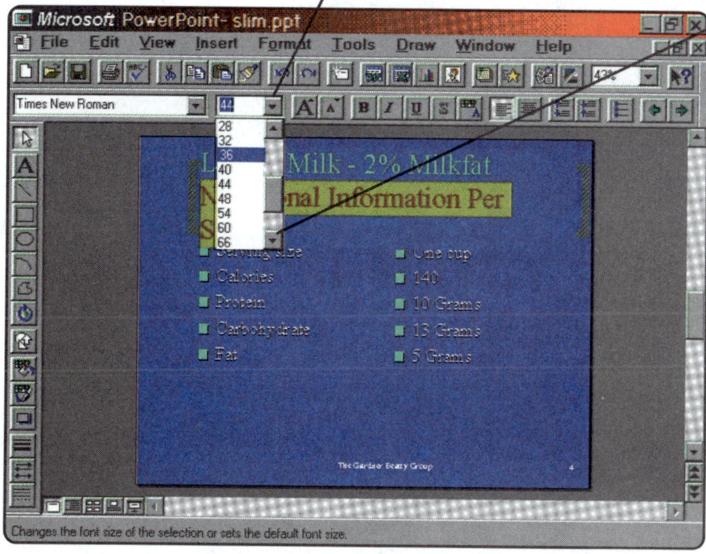

4. **Click** as many times as is necessary on the ▲ to show **36.**

5. **Click** on **36**. The highlighted text will be resized to 36 points.

6. **Click anywhere** outside the text block to remove the highlighting and deselect the text block.

DELETING BULLETS

There are two ways you can delete bullets.

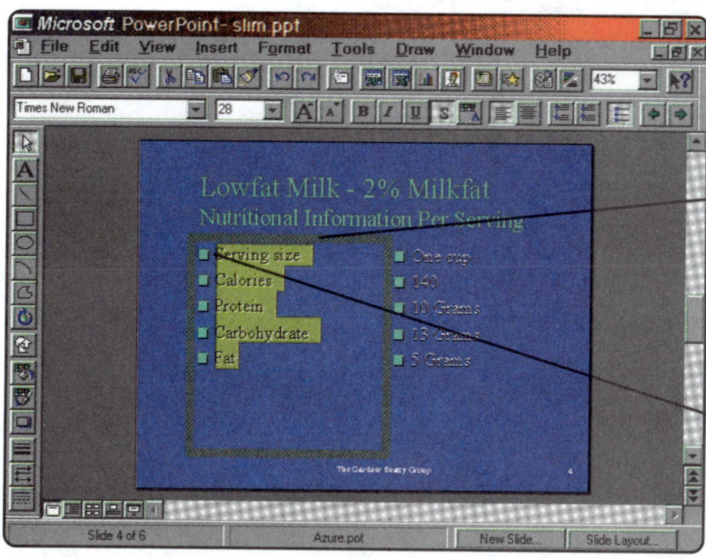

Deleting Bullets with the Format Menu

1. **Click** on the **text** in the left text block. A box will surround the text to show that the text block is selected.

2. **Click** to the **left** of "**Serving Size**" and **drag** the I-beam to the end of "Fat" to highlight the list.

3. **Click** on **Format** in the menu bar. The Format menu will appear.

4. **Click** on **Bullet**. The Bullet dialog box will appear.

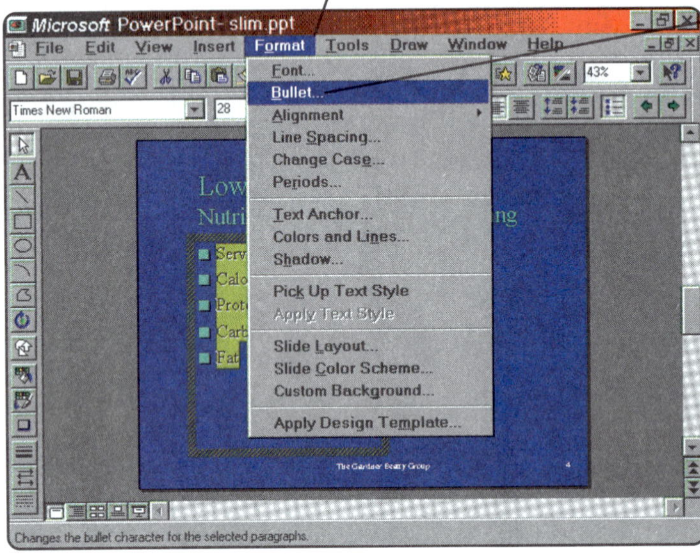

5. **Click** on **Use a Bullet** to *remove* the ✔ from the box.

6. **Click** on **OK**. The bullets will be removed from the list.

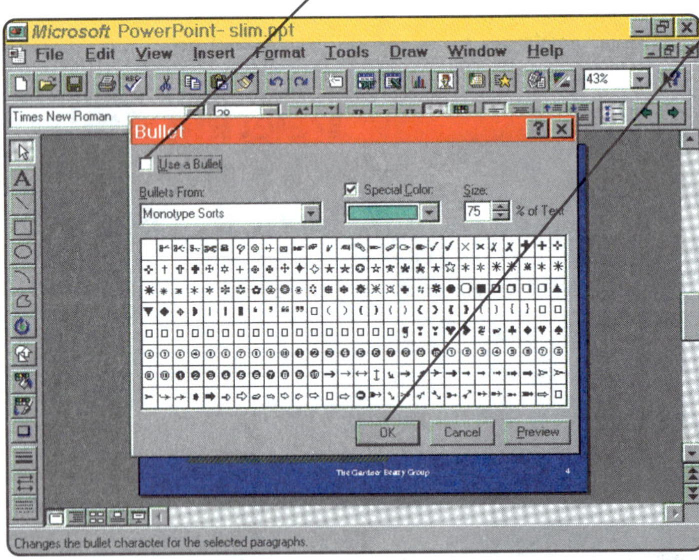

Deleting Bullets with the Bullet Button

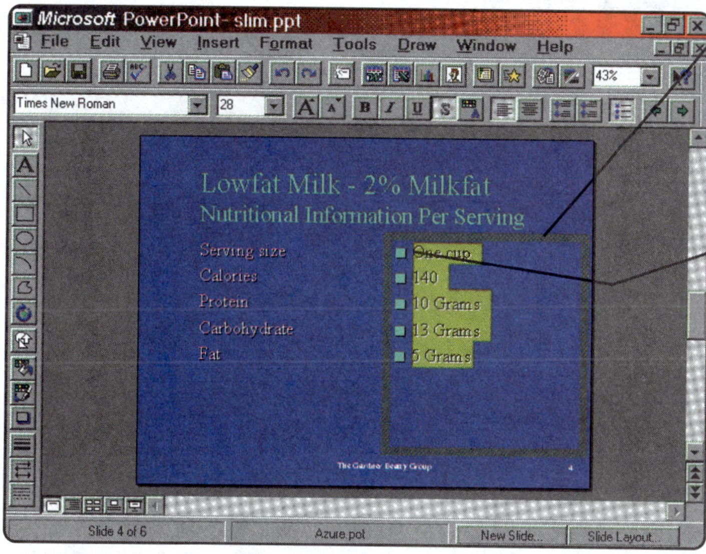

1. **Click** on the **text** in the right text block. A box will surround the text to show that the text block is selected.

2. **Click** to the **left** of "**One cup**" and **drag** the I-beam to the end of "5 Grams" to highlight the list.

Notice that the Bullet button is lighter in color and looks pressed in to show that the highlighted text has bullets.

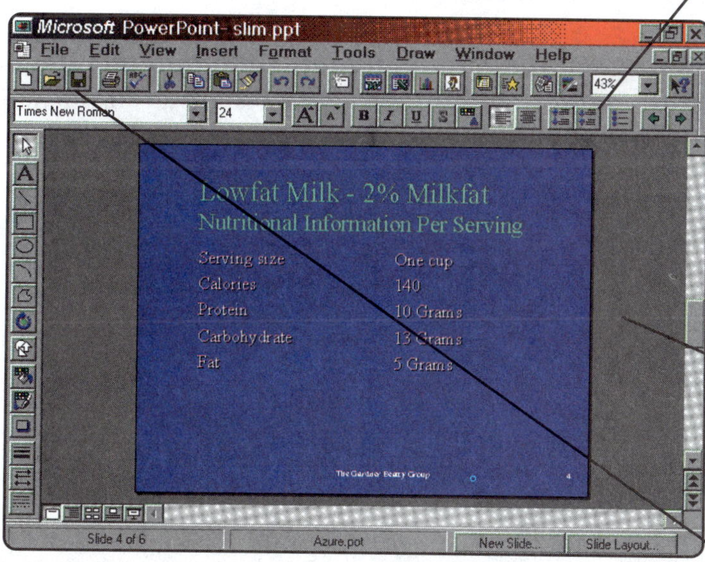

3. **Click** on the **Bullet button** in the toolbar. The bullets will disappear, and the Bullet button will no longer be pressed in and lighter in color.

If you want to add bullets, the steps are exactly the same.

4. **Click anywhere** outside the text block to remove the highlighting and deselect the text block.

5. **Click** on the **Save button** in the toolbar.

CHAPTER 6

Working with Text Blocks

In PowerPoint, text is contained in a space called a *text block*. You can have multiple text blocks on a single slide. Each text block can be formatted and moved independently of other text blocks. *Placement Guides* help align and center text blocks. This gives you tremendous control over the layout of your slide. In this chapter, you will do the following:

- ✔ Add Placement Guides
- ✔ Move and resize text blocks
- ✔ Add a text block to a slide
- ✔ Color, shadow, and realign text

ADDING PLACEMENT GUIDES

You can move text anywhere on a slide by moving the text block that holds the text. In this section you will add Placement Guides to help with exact positioning.

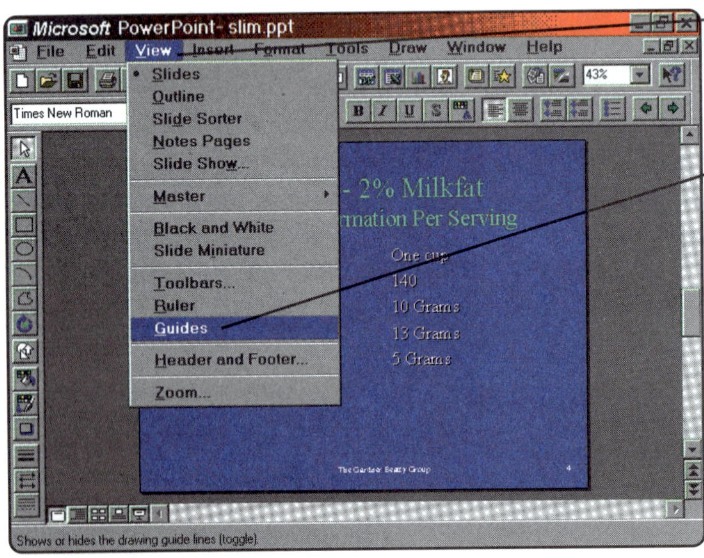

1. **Click** on **View** in the menu bar. The View menu will appear.
2. **Click** on **Guides.** Dotted guide lines will appear at the vertical and horizontal centers of the slide.

CENTERING TEXT BLOCKS

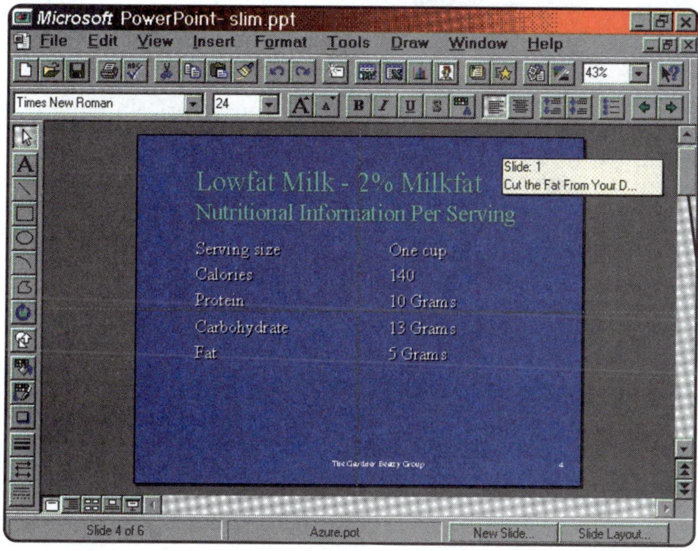

To center a text block you must physically move the block to the center of the slide.

Centering the Slide 1 Text Block

1. **Move** the **mouse arrow** to the scroll button.

2. **Press and hold** the **mouse button** as you **drag** the scroll button to the top of the scroll bar.

3. **Release** the **mouse button**. Slide 1 will be on your screen.

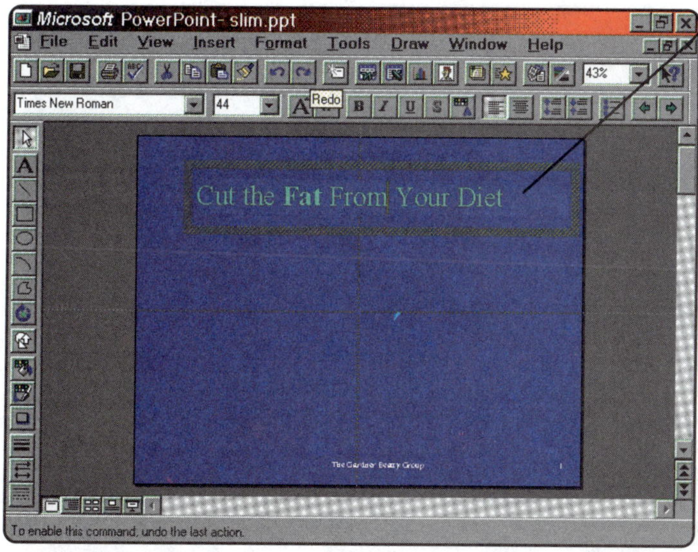

4. **Click anywhere** on the text. A box will surround the text and show the size and position of the text block.

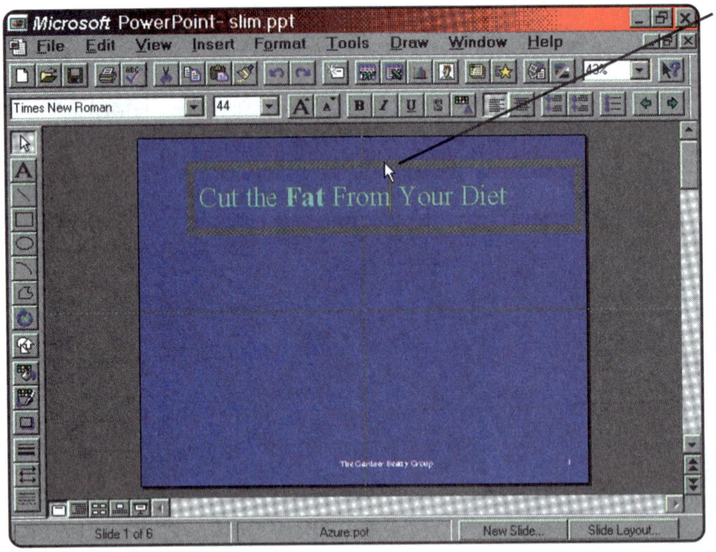

5. **Place** the **I-beam** on the **border** of the text block, *but not on the center guide.* The cursor will become an arrow. You may have to fiddle with the placement of the cursor to get it to change into an arrow.

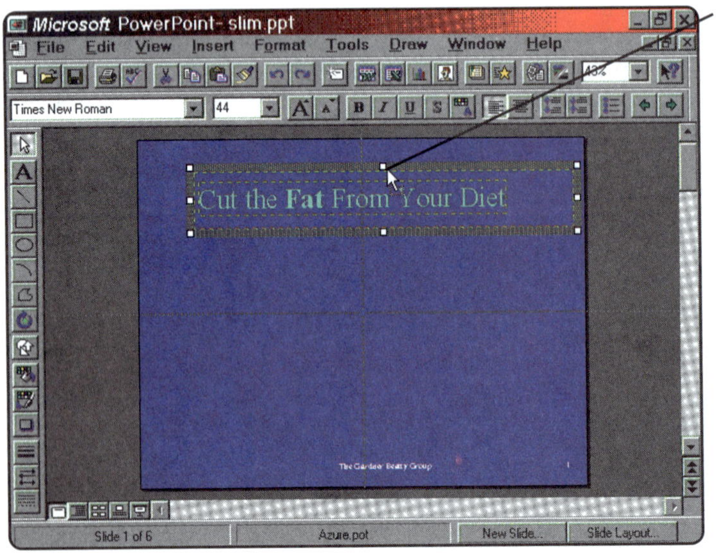

6. **Press and hold** the **mouse button**. Solid squares, or handles, will appear on the border of the text block. A dotted-line box will surround the text. Another dotted-line box will appear just inside the text block border. Before you go to the next step, make certain that the mouse arrow *is not* on one of the handles.

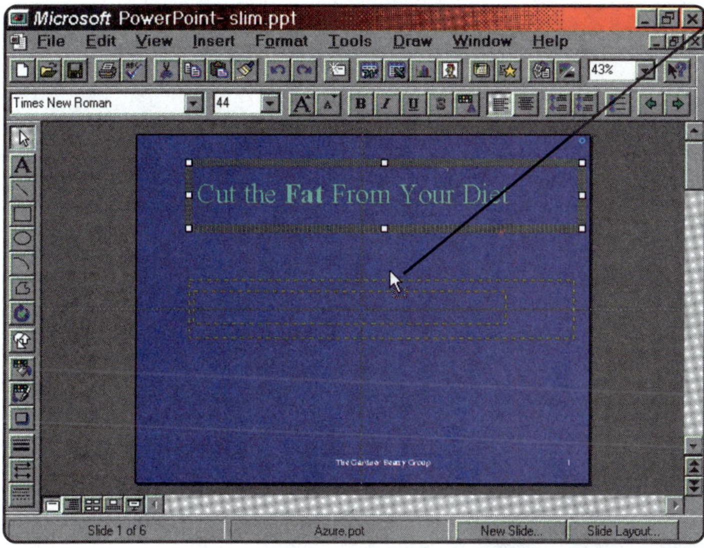

7. Continue to hold the **mouse button** down and **drag** the cursor down to the horizontal guide line. As you drag, the dotted outlines of the text and the text block will move with the cursor. When the middle of the text is close to the center guide, it will "jump" into place. Magic! Placement Guides act like magnets, pulling the text block into place automatically.

8. Release the **mouse button.** The text will be centered on the slide.

Centering the Slide 6 Text Block

1. Place the **mouse arrow** on the scroll button.

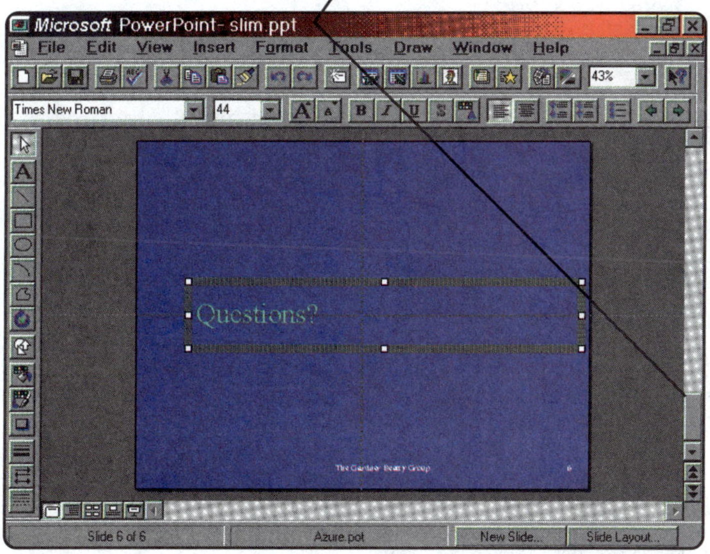

2. Press and **hold** the **mouse button** as you **drag** the scroll button to the bottom of the scroll bar.

3. Release the **mouse button**. Slide 6 will be on your screen.

4. Repeat steps 4 to 8 in the previous section to center the "Questions?" text block on slide 6.

RESIZING TEXT BLOCKS

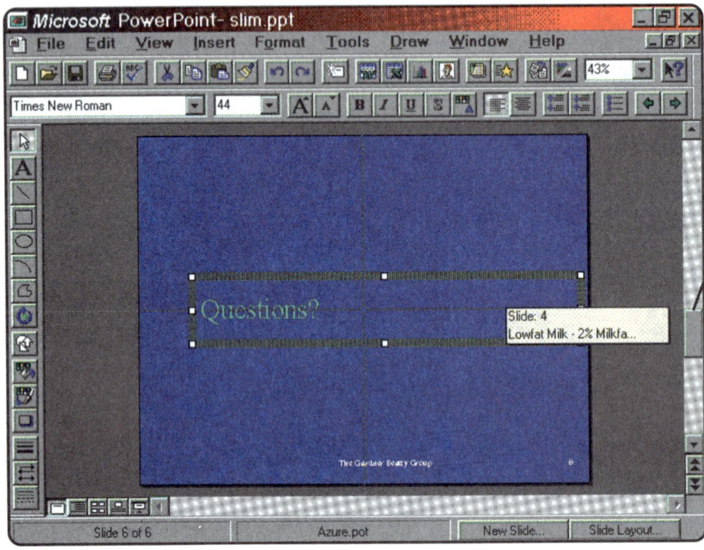

In this section, you will make the bulleted lists text blocks on slide 4 smaller so you can later add text to the bottom of the slide.

1. **Place** the **mouse arrow** on the **scroll button.**

2. **Press and hold** the **mouse button** as you **drag** the scroll button up until slide 4 appears to the left of the scroll bar.

3. **Release** the **mouse button**. Slide 4 will be on your screen.

4. **Click** on the **right text block** to select it if it is not already selected.

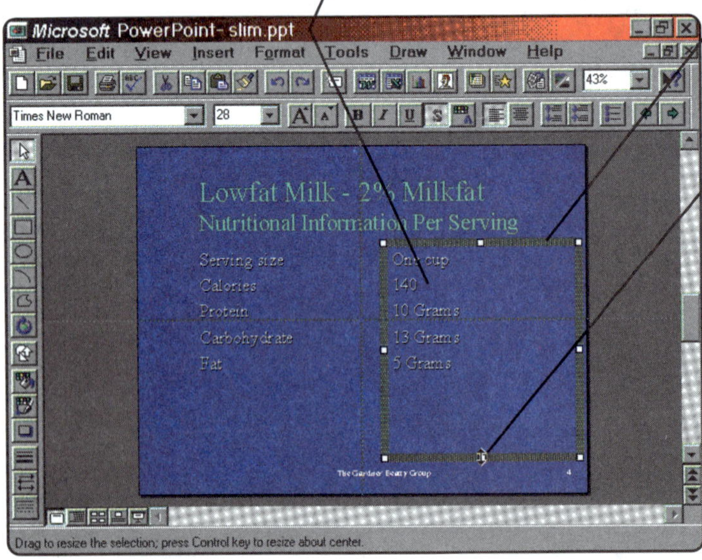

5. **Click** on the **border** of the text block. Handles will appear on the border.

6. **Place** the **cursor** on the **bottom middle handle**. The cursor will become a double-headed arrow.

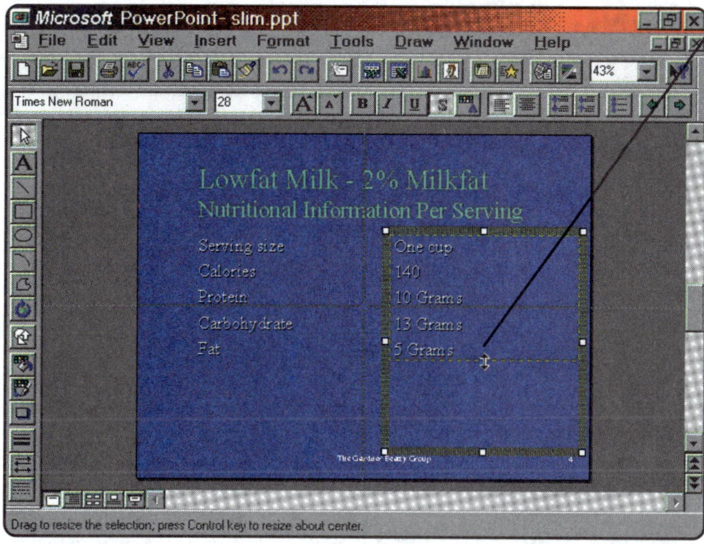

7. **Press and hold** the **mouse button**.

8. **Drag** the **double-headed arrow** to just below the last word in the list. **Release** the **mouse button**. It's okay if it seems to "stick" as you drag up. Simply continue to press and hold the mouse button as you drag the line up to where you want it.

9. **Repeat** steps **4 through 8** to resize the **left text block.**

ALIGNING TEXT WITHIN A BLOCK

In this example, you will right-align text so that it lines up on the last letter in each line.

1. **Click** on the **right text block** to select it.

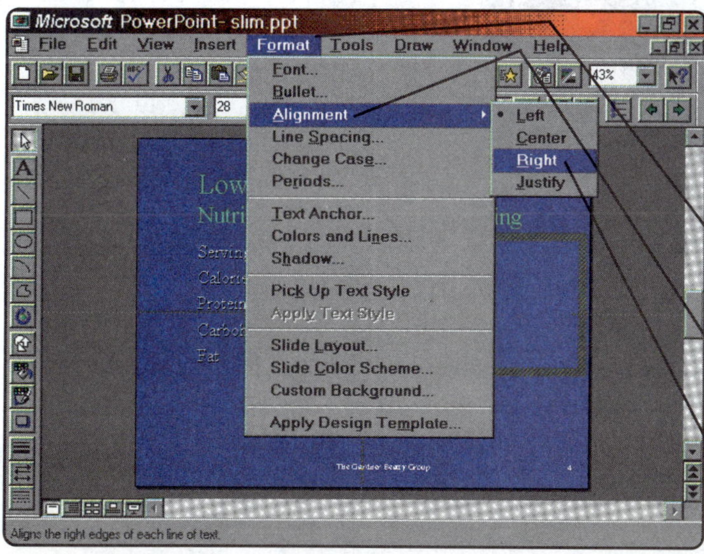

2. **Click** to the **left** of "**One cup**" and **drag** the **I-beam** to the bottom of the list. The text will be highlighted.

3. **Click** on **Format**. A menu will appear.

4. **Click** on **Alignment**. A second menu will appear.

5. **Click** on **Right**. The text of the list will appear aligned to the right.

USING GUIDES WHEN MOVING AND ALIGNING TEXT BLOCKS

In the previous section you aligned text within a text block. You can also move and align text blocks themselves. When you do this, guides can help with the exact placement of a text block. In the following sections you will move the vertical guide then use it as a placement guide for a text block.

Moving Guides to Help with Alignment

Guides can do more than show the center of the slide. A guide can be moved to an exact spot, then used as a placement guide.

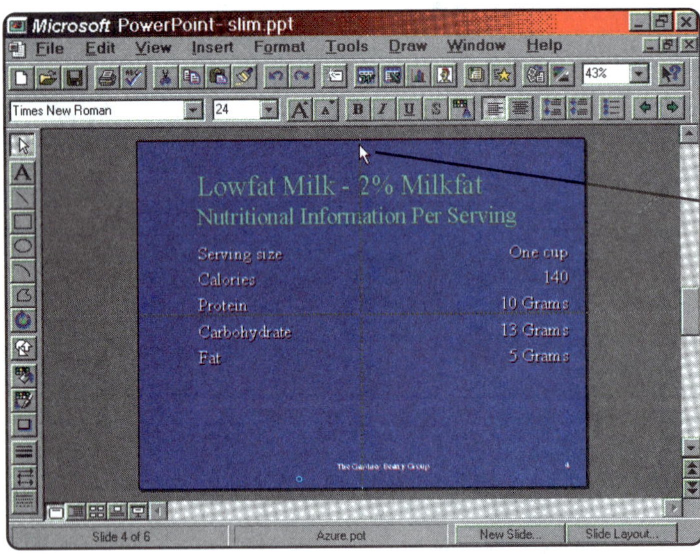

1. If the right text block is still selected, **click** on the **slide background** to deselect it.

2. **Move** the **cursor** onto the top outside frame of the slide. It will become an arrow. (Note: If you move the cursor inside the text block it will turn into an I-beam. In that case, it won't let you click on the vertical guide in step 3 below.)

3. **Place** the **arrow** on the vertical guide line and **press and hold** the **mouse button.** The arrow will change to a white box with numbers inside.

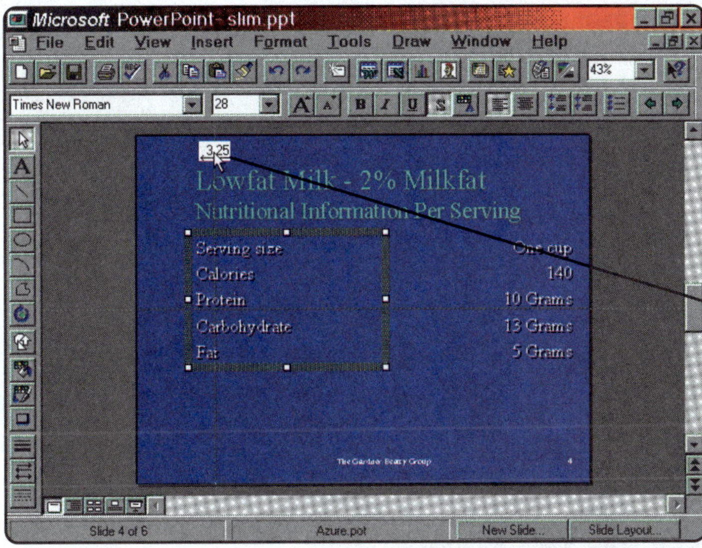

When the guide is at the center, the number is 0.00. As you move the guide line, the numbers change, showing how many inches away from center you have moved.

4. **Drag** the **guide line** to **the left** until the number 3.25 shows in the box. Then **release** the **mouse button.**

Aligning a Text Block with a Guide

1. **Press and hold** the **Shift key** and **click** on the **left block.** This is a shortcut way to select the text block and make handles appear.

2. **Press and hold anywhere** on the border *except on a handle box*, and **drag** the block to the right until the left hand edge "jumps " to the guide line. Notice that it's the *inside edge of the shaded text block border* that snaps to the guide line. You will need to take that into account when trying to align text.

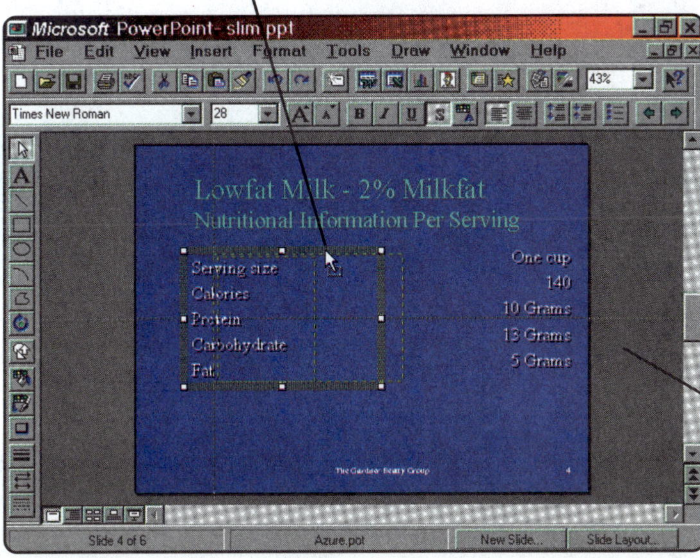

3. **Release** the **mouse button** when the text block is positioned.

4. **Click** on the **slide background** to deselect the text box.

5. **Repeat steps 1 to 4** in the "Moving Guides to Help with Alignment" section to move the vertical guide line right to 3.25.

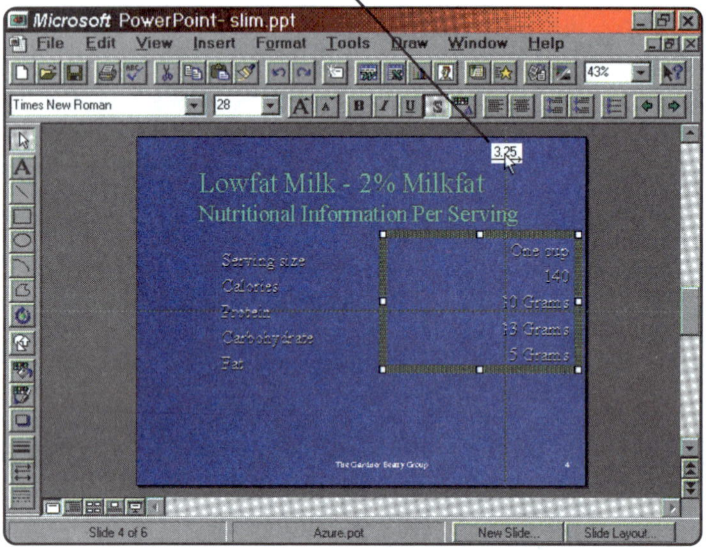

6. **Press and hold** the **Shift key** and **click** on the **right text block** if it is not already selected.

7. **Click anywhere** on the border *except on a handle box*, and **hold and drag** the block to the left, until the edge "jumps " to the guide line.

8. **Release** the **mouse button**.

Aligning Two Text Blocks with Each Other

In this section you will align the tops of the two text blocks you just moved so that the text in the left block is perfectly aligned with the text in the right block.

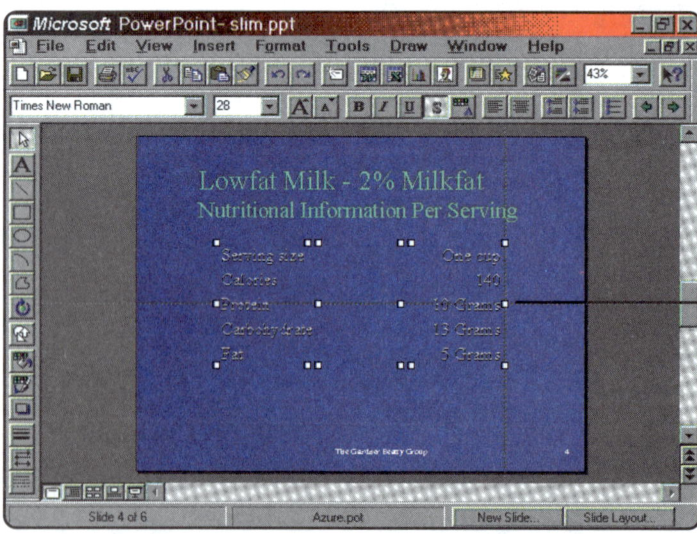

1. **Press and hold** the **Shift key** and **click** on the **right text block** if it is not already selected.

2. **Press and hold** the **Shift key** and **click** on the **left text block.** This will select *both* text blocks at the same time. You will see a border of handles.

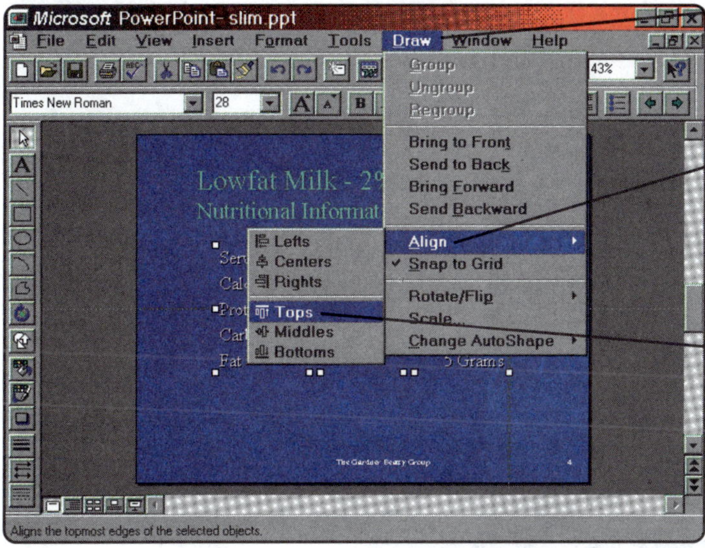

3. **Click** on **Draw** in the toolbar. A pull-down menu will appear.

4. **Click** on **Align**. A second menu will appear. It may appear to the left or right of the first menu.

5. **Click** on **Tops**. The tops of the selected text boxes will now be evenly aligned.

6. **Click** on the **slide background** to deselect the text boxes.

ADDING A TEXT BLOCK

You add text to an *existing* text block simply by typing in the additional text. In this section, you will add text *outside* of an existing text block. This requires you to use the text tool to create another text block. First, you will move the guides to help you align the new text block with existing text.

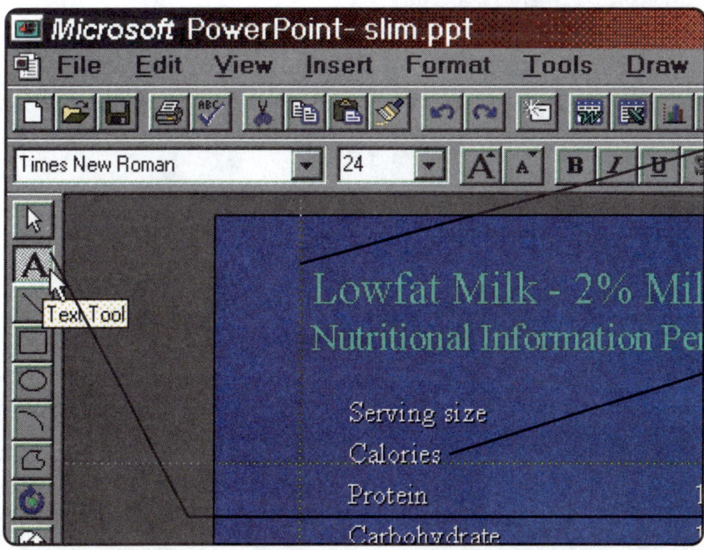

1. **Move** the **vertical guide left** to **3.83**. See "Adding Placement Guides" earlier in this chapter, on page 56, if you need help.

2. **Move** the **horizontal guide up** to just below "Calories".

3. **Click** on the **Text Tool**.

4. **Move** the **cursor onto the slide.** It will become a vertical line with a cross bar at the bottom.

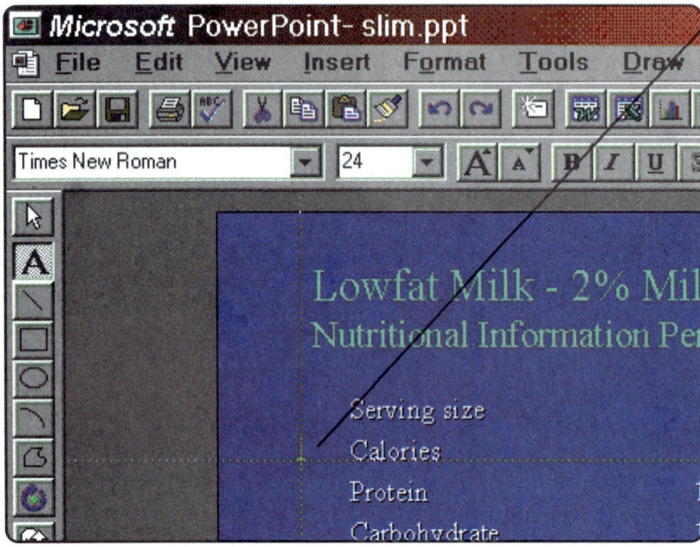

5. **Place** the **cursor** on top of the **vertical guide line** and **place** the **cross bar** on the **horizontal guide line** to the **left** of the word **"Calories."**

6. **Click** to set the cursor. A small, empty text block will appear.

7. **Type #1**. You have now created a text block containing text. In the next section you will color and add a shadow to this text.

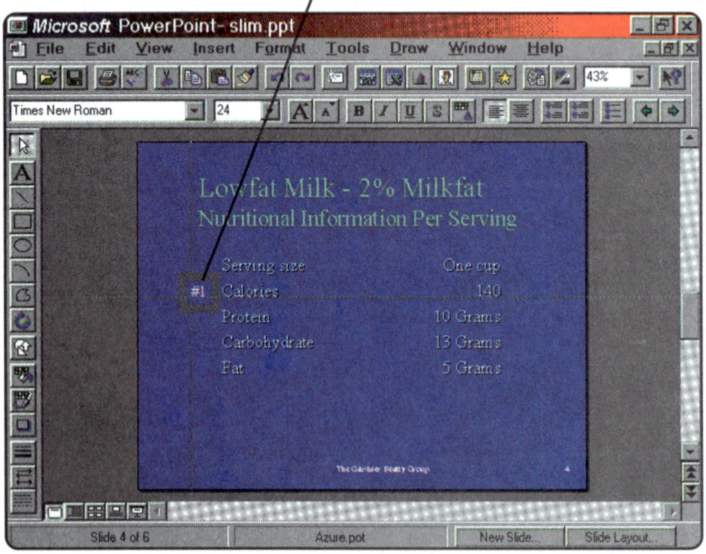

COLORING TEXT AND ADDING A SHADOW

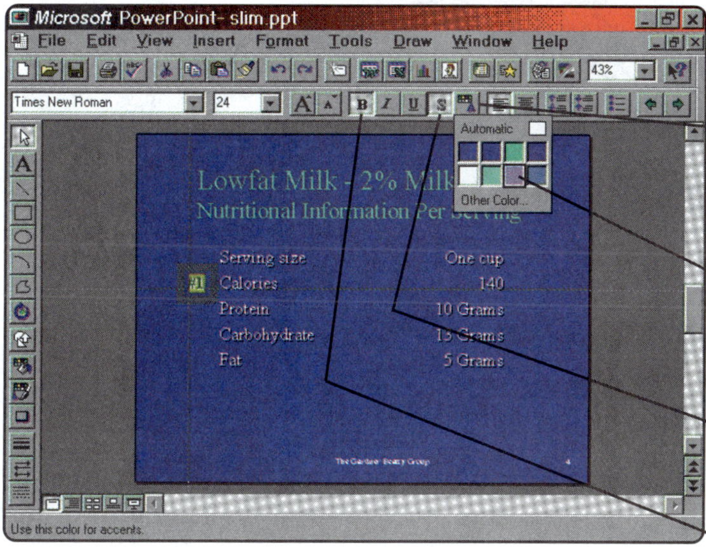

1. **Drag** the **I-beam** over "#1" to highlight it.
2. **Click** on the **Text Color button**. A color menu will appear in the toolbar.
3. **Click** on the **lavender** square. The color menu will disappear.
4. **Click** on the **Text Shadow button** (the S).
5. **Click** on the **Bold button.**
6. **Click off** the **text block** so you can see the text.

COPYING A TEXT BLOCK WITH DRAG-AND-DROP

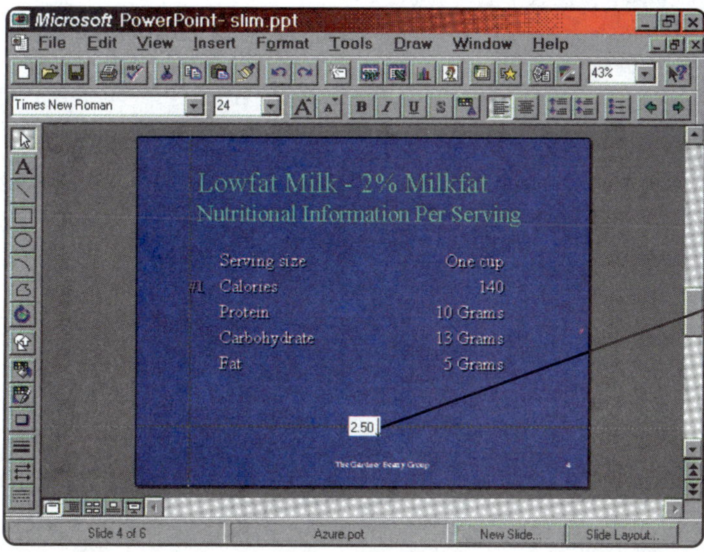

1. **Move** the **horizontal guide** down to 2.50. See "Moving Guides to Help with Alignment," on page 62, if you need help.

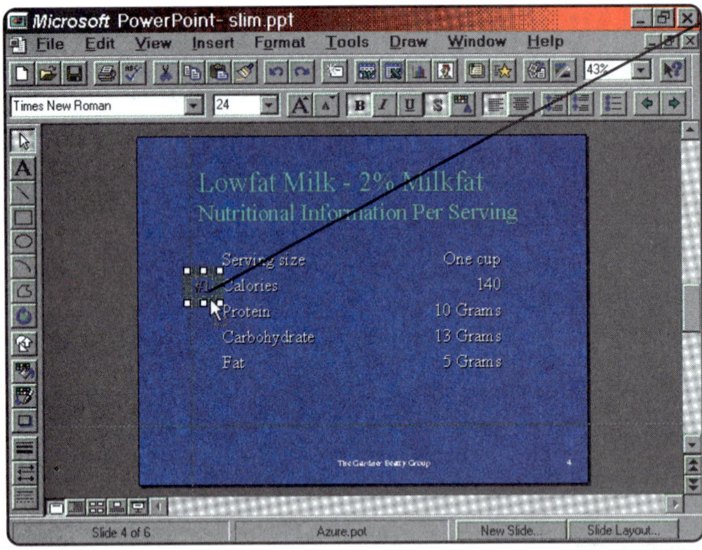

2. **Click** on **#1**. The text block will appear around the text.

3. **Press and hold** the **Control key**.

4. **Move** the **mouse arrow** onto the border of the text block. **Press and hold** the **mouse button**. A small cross will appear beside the arrow.

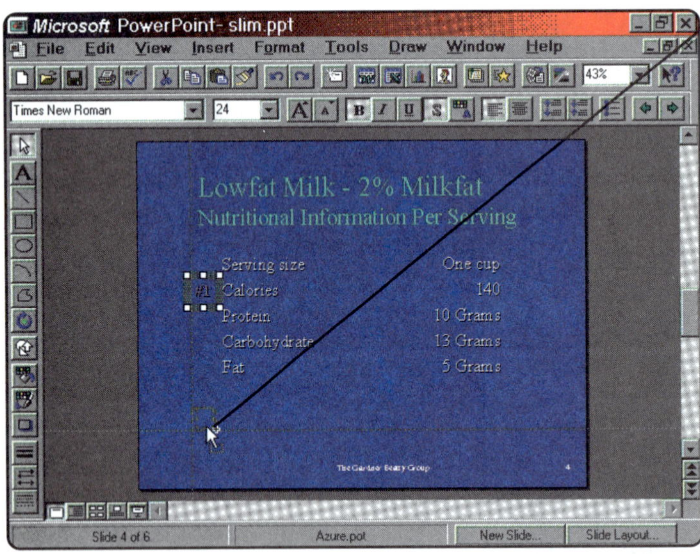

5. **Continue** to **hold** the **Control key**. **Continue** to **press and hold** the **mouse button** and **drag** the mouse pointer down to the guide lines. As you drag, keep the mouse pointer inside the vertical guide line. An outline of the text block will "jump" to the guide lines as shown in this example.

6. **Release** the **mouse button first.** Then **release** the **Control key**. Notice that the inside edges of the text block border are aligned with the guide lines.

ADDING TEXT TO A TEXT BLOCK

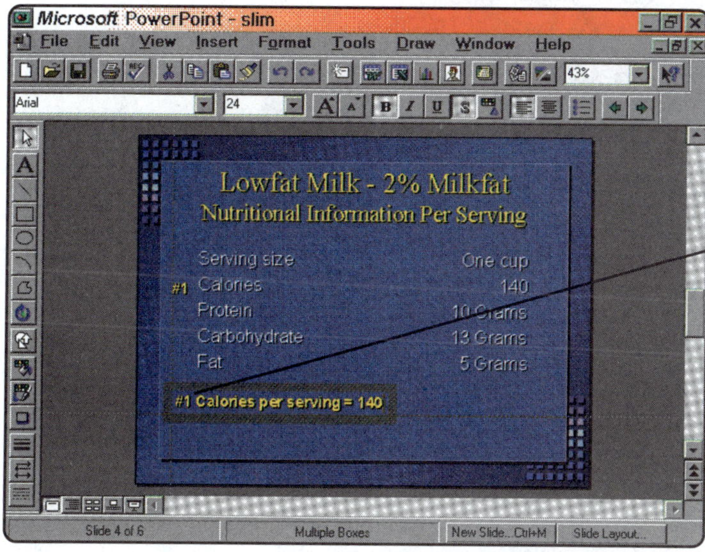

Now that you have a text block at the bottom of the slide, you can add text to it simply by typing it into the block.

1. **Place** the cursor **after** the **#1** in the text block.

2. **Press** the **Spacebar** and **type Calories per serving = 140.**

CENTERING TEXT IN A TEXT BLOCK

Because this new text block is not part of the predesigned slide, it does not contain any formatting commands. You have to provide them. In this section, you will center the text within the text block, then center the text block on the slide.

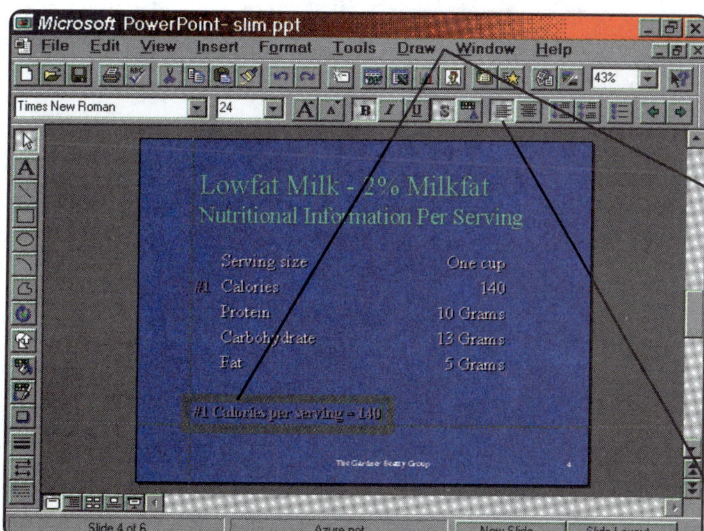

1. **Drag** the **I-beam** over the **text** to select it. Notice that the Left Alignment button in the toolbar is pressed in to show that this text is left-aligned.

2. **Click** on the **Center Button**.

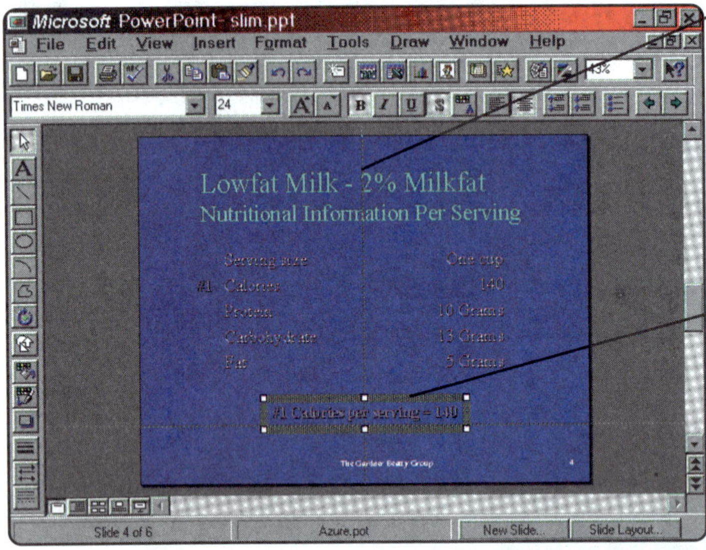

3. **Move** the **vertical guide line** to 0.00.

4. With the cursor as an arrow, **click** on the **border** of the text block to see the selection handles.

5. **Press and hold** on the **text border,** *not a handle*, and **drag** the text box to the middle guide line. When you release the mouse button, the center handles should be aligned with the vertical guide.

COLORING A TEXT BLOCK

Previously in this chapter, you colored text. In this section you will color the text block itself and put a colored line around the text block.

Adding Fill to a Text Block

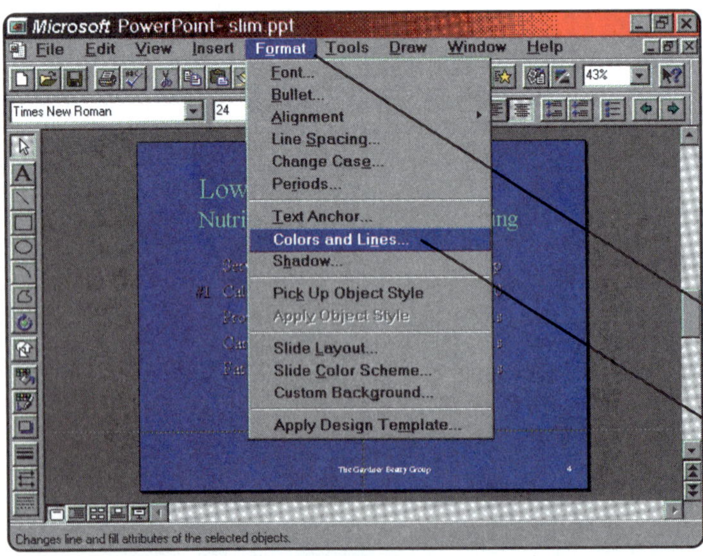

1. **Press** and **hold** the **Shift key** and **click** on the edge of the **Calories per Serving text block** (the one you just moved) to show handles, if it is not already selected.

2. **Click** on **Format** in the menu bar.

3. **Click** on **Colors and Lines.** The Colors and Lines dialog box will appear.

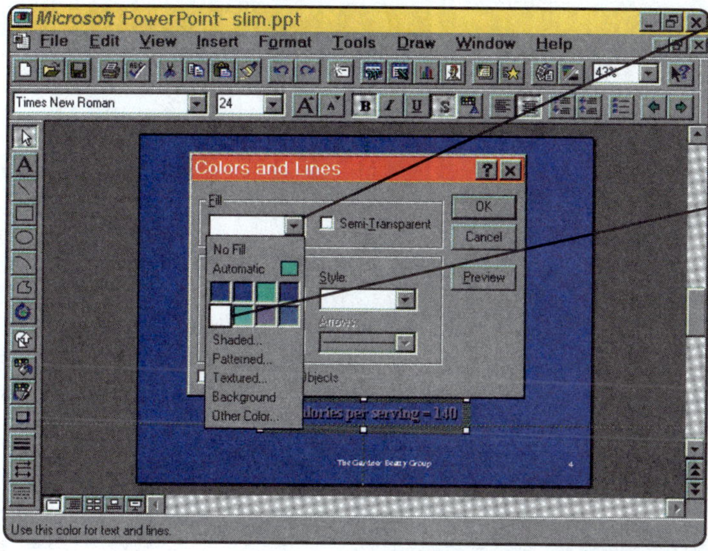

4. **Click** on the ▼ to the right of No Fill. A pull-down color menu will appear.

5. **Click** on the **white square** (first from the left in the second row). The pull-down menu will disappear and the Fill box will be white.

Note: Be careful not to place white text on a white background or you won't be able to see the text.

Adding a Line Around a Text Block

1. **Click** on the ▼ to the right of No Line. A pull-down color menu will appear.

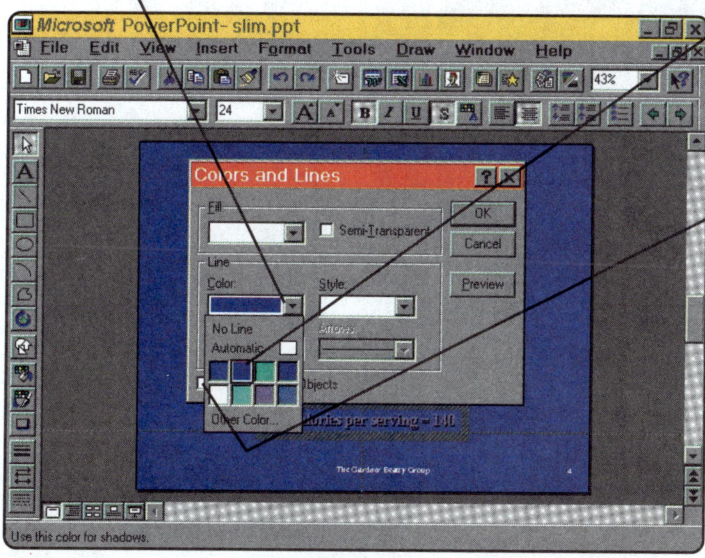

2. **Click** on the **dark purple square.** The pull-down menu will disappear.

3. **Click** in the **Default for New Objects box** to place a ✔ in it. This will cause all new text boxes in this presentation to have this formatting.

4. **Click** on **OK.**

5. **Click off** the **text block** to see what it looks like.

REMOVING PLACEMENT GUIDES

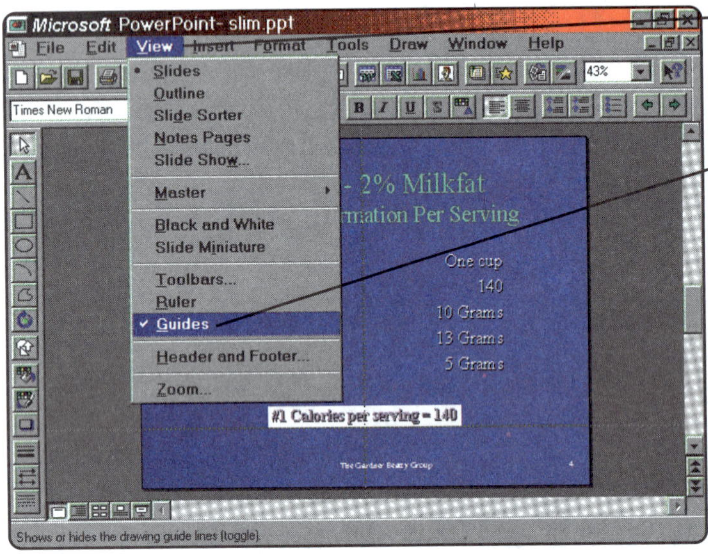

1. **Click** on **View** in the menu bar. The View menu will appear.
2. **Click** on **Guides** to remove the ✔.

Notice that the Placement Guides are no longer visible on the slides.

SAVING THE PRESENTATION

1. **Click** on the **Save Button** in the toolbar to save your work.

CHAPTER

7

Printing a Paper Copy

PowerPoint uses standard Windows-based commands to print. PowerPoint will print colors as shades of gray unless you have a color printer, or if you don't check the black and white print option when printing with a black and white printer. If you don't check the black and white option in the print dialog box, slide copies printed on a black and white printer may be difficult to read because gray does not show the differences in color. You can, however, choose to print all background and fill colors in white, and text and lines in black using the black and white print option. This makes for much faster printing. In this chapter, you will do the following:

✔ Print copies of your slides in color or shades of gray
✔ Eliminate background shading and print in pure black and white

PRINTING COPIES

You can print in color if you have a color printer. Here are the steps to use for printing slides in color on a color printer or in shades of gray on a black and white printer.

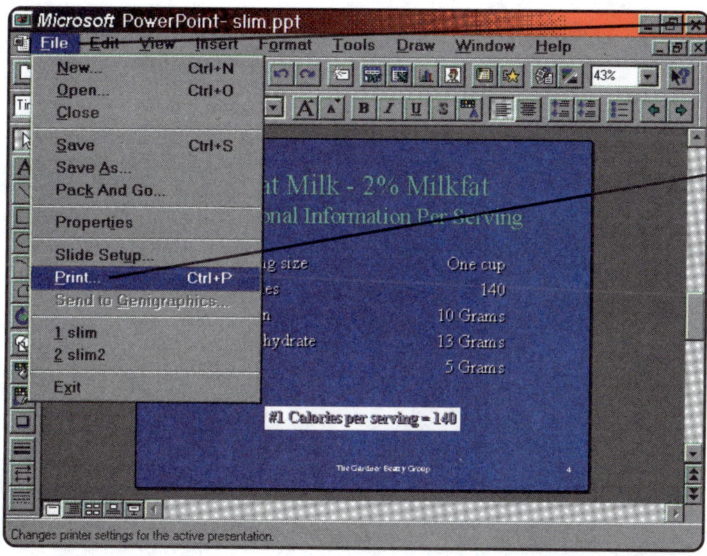

1. **Click** on **File** on the menu bar. The File menu will appear.

2. **Click** on **Print**. The Print dialog box will appear.

3. If there is a ✔ in the box to the left of Black & White, **click** in the **box** to deselect it.

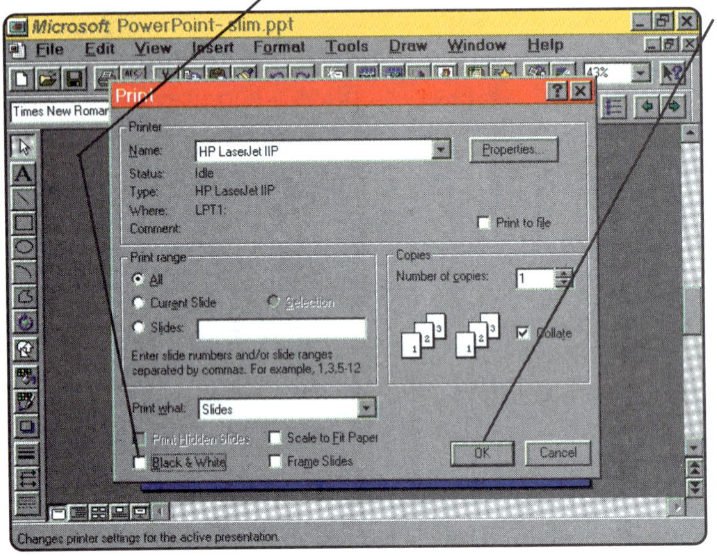

4. **Click** on **OK**. You will have a long wait because printing in color takes a long time. If you don't have a color printer, your printer will print colors in shades of gray, which also takes a long time. We recommend using the black and white printing option, described on the next page, when you print paper copies of your slides.

Printing Options: Multiple Copies and Selected Pages

1. Click on the ▲ or ▼ to indicate the number of copies to be printed. In the example above, you printed one copy of each slide.

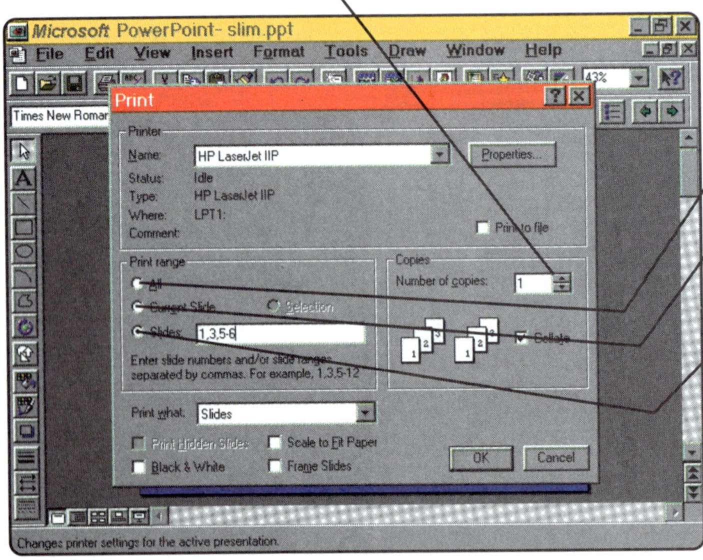

You have three options for printing selected slides:

- ❖ Printing all slides
- ❖ Printing the currently selected slide
- ❖ Printing a range such as 1,3,5-6 (this means you want to print pages 1, 3, and 5 to 6 and is currently selected).

Printing in Black and White

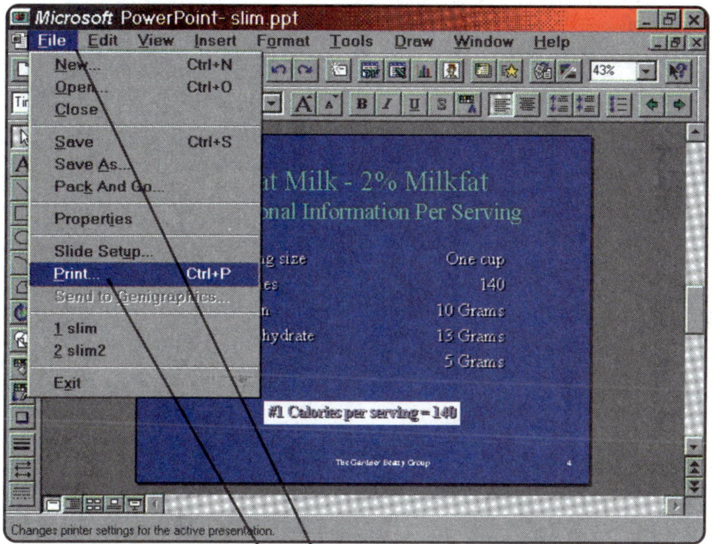

If you have a black and white printer, you can print your paper copies in shades of gray (by using the color printing option from the previous page) or in black and white. The option to print in black and white eliminates background colors. It is useful in printing drafts and crisp, clear copies of notes and handout pages.

1. **Click** on **File**. The File menu will appear.
2. **Click** on **Print.** The Print dialog box will appear.

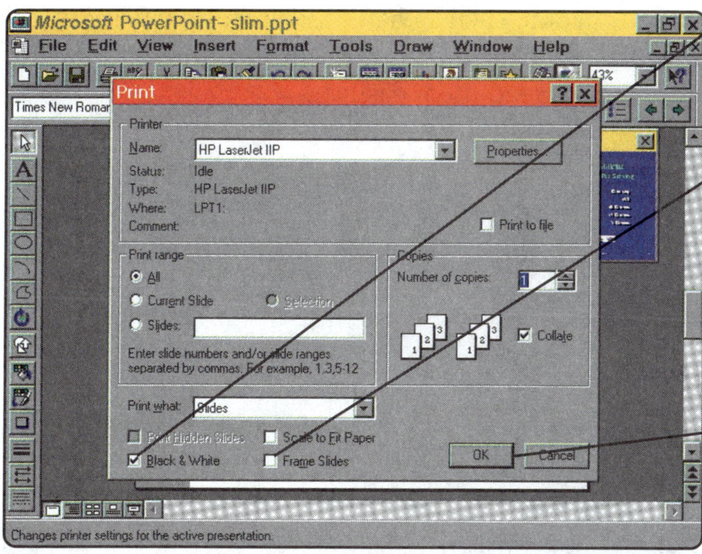

3. **Click** to place a ✔ in the Black & White box if there isn't one already in it.
4. **Click** to place a ✔ in the Frame Slides box only if you want your paper copies to print with a black border around them.
5. **Click** on **OK.**

CHAPTER

8

Creating and Printing Notes and Handouts

A note page shows a slide in the top half of the page and keeps the bottom half of the page free for text. You can print note pages for the speaker and different note pages for the audience. The master page for notes can be modified to have a larger font size. You can also print handout pages that contain two to six slides per page. In this chapter you will do the following:

✔ Create and print a page with speaker's notes
✔ Change the master page for notes and create and print audience note pages
✔ Print handout pages

MODIFYING THE NOTES MASTER

Speaker's notes can be anything from special comments the speaker wants to make about the contents of the slide to reminders to perform some specific action, such as handing out supplementary material. It helps to have the notes in large type so the speaker can read them easily.

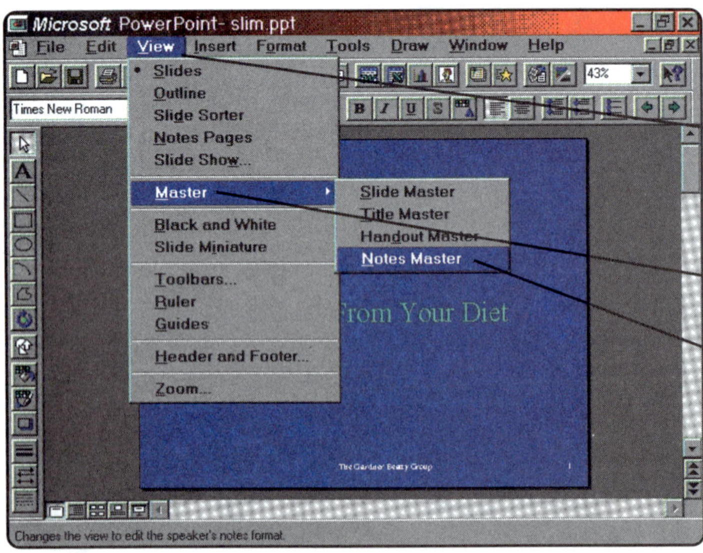

1. **Go to slide 1** if you are not already there.

2. **Click** on **View** in the menu bar. The View menu will appear.

3. **Click** on **Master**.

4. **Click** on **Notes Master**. Slide 4 will appear in Master view.

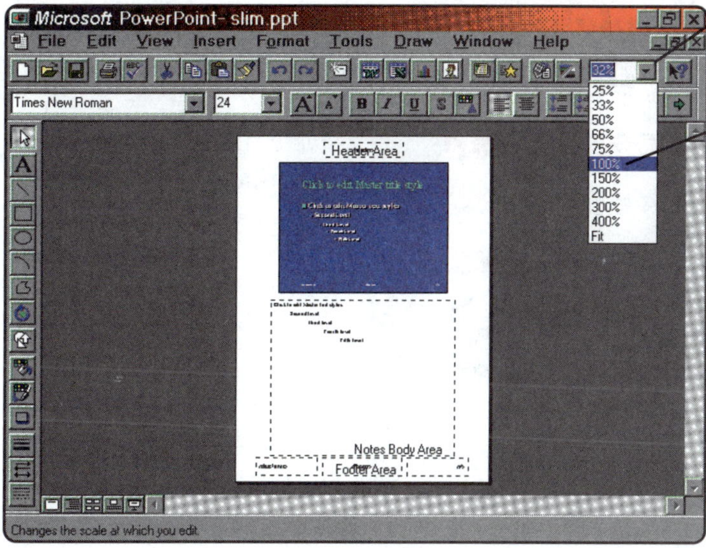

5. **Click** on ▼ to the right of the Zoom Control box.

6. **Click** on **100%**. The Notes Page view will be magnified.

7. **Click** to the **left** of the word **"Click"** in the notes text block at the bottom of the slide.

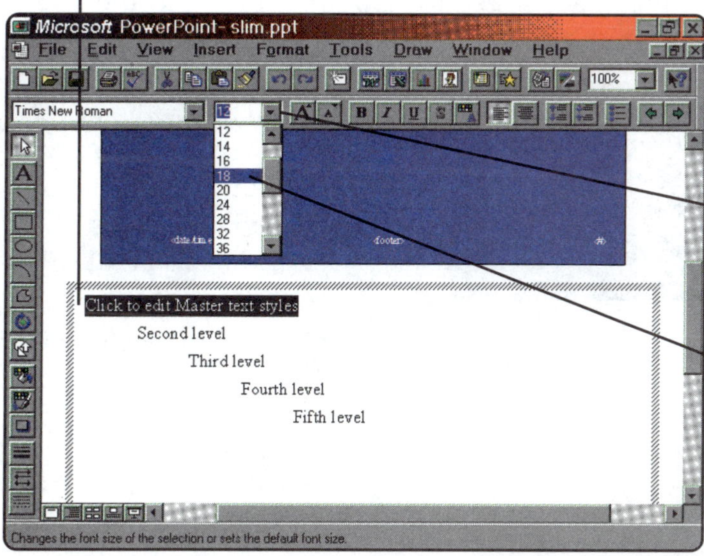

8. **Press and hold** the **mouse button** and **drag** the I-beam over the first line of text to highlight it.

9. **Click** on ▼ to the right of the font size box. A pull-down list will appear.

10. **Click** on **18**. The highlighted text will change to 18-point text.

Applying a Master Page Change to the Entire Presentation

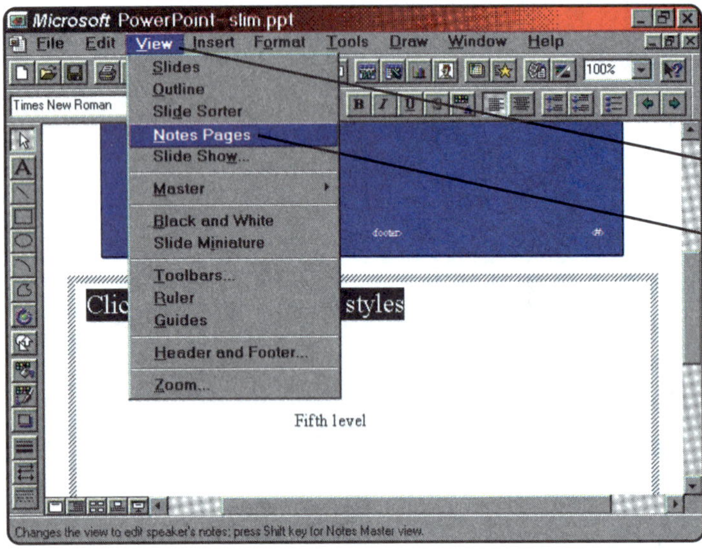

Master page changes can be applied to the entire presentation. Here's how:

1. **Click** on View.
2. **Click** on **Notes Pages**. The presentation will appear in Notes Pages view.

Your first line of type may still be in 12-point type or it may be changed to 18-point type. We couldn't get any consistency on this issue. In any event, you need to apply the master page change to the entire presentation, which you will do in the steps below. This is because the master changes haven't yet been applied.

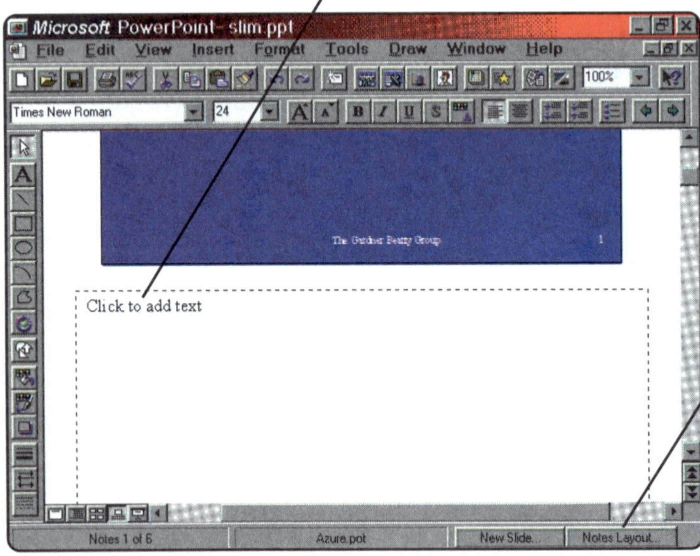

3. **Click** on the **Notes Layout button.** The Notes Layout dialog box will appear.

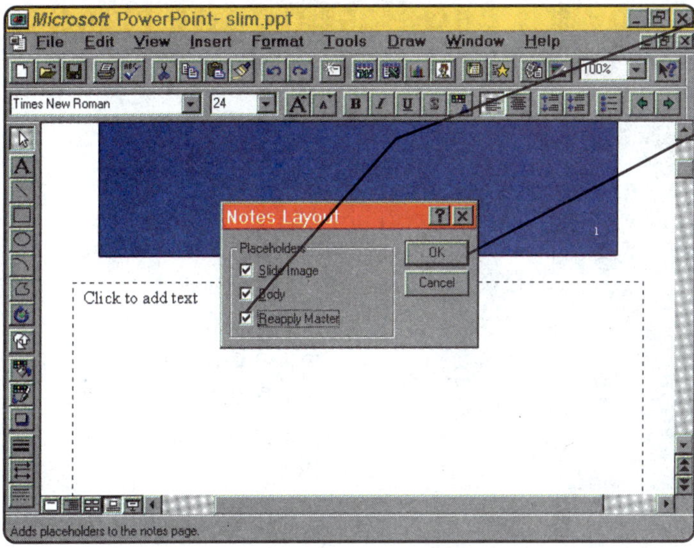

4. **Click** on **Reapply Master.**

5. **Click** on **OK.** The text will change to 18-point text.

CREATING AND PRINTING NOTES PAGES

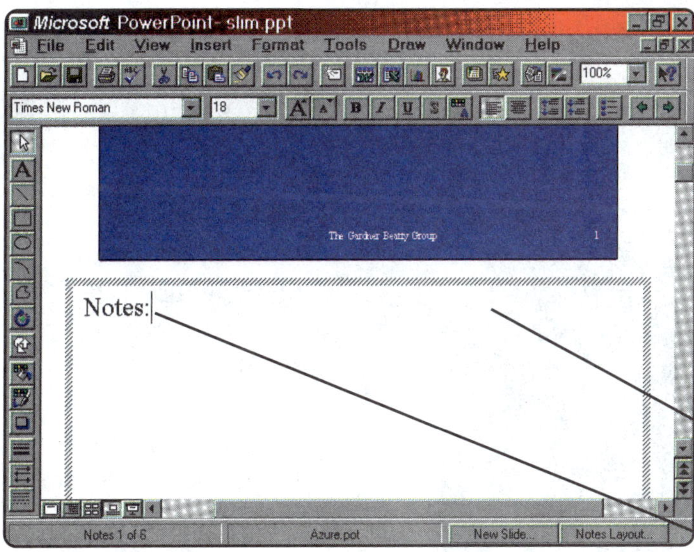

You can make notes pages for the speaker and/or for the audience. If you want to give your audience an impressive package that contains a copy of each slide and room to make notes, customize the Notes Pages with the steps below.

1. **Click inside** the **notes text block.**

2. **Type Notes:**. It will appear in 18-point type.

Copying and Pasting the Header Between Notes Pages

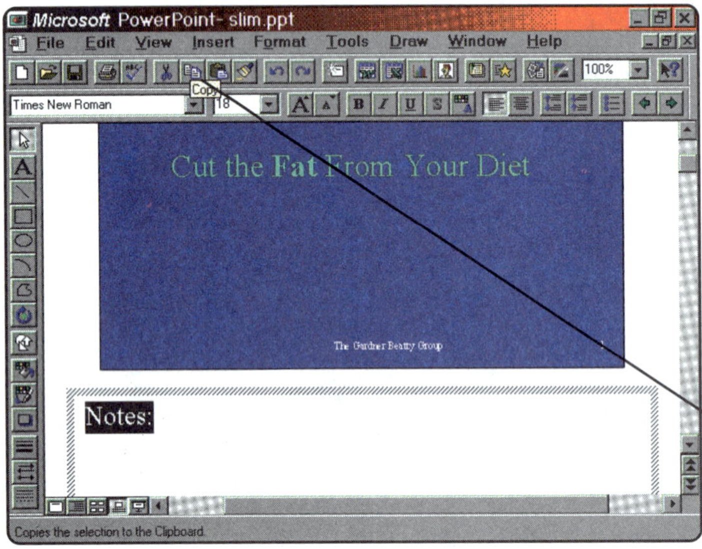

In this section, you will copy "Notes:" from page 1 and paste it into the remaining note pages.

1. **Press and hold** the **mouse button** as you **drag** the **I-beam** over "Notes:" to highlight the word and the colon.

2. **Click** on the **Copy button** in the toolbar. The text will be copied to the Clipboard.

3. **Press** the **Page Down key** on your keyboard to move to slide 2.

4. **Click inside** the text block at the bottom of the page to set the cursor.

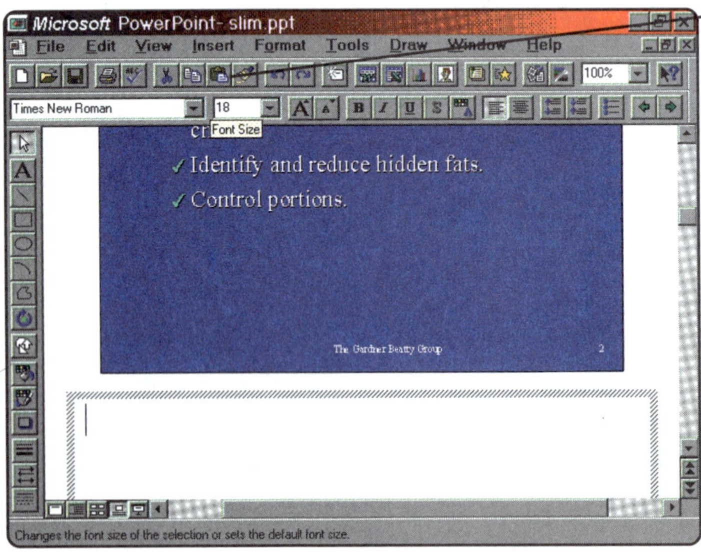

5. **Click** on the **Paste button** on the toolbar. "Notes:" will be pasted into the slide in an 18-point type size.

6. **Repeat steps 3 to 5** to copy the text onto slides 3 to 6. You don't have to copy the text again. You can continue to paste it onto successive pages until it is replaced in the Clipboard by another copy or cut command.

Printing Notes or Handouts

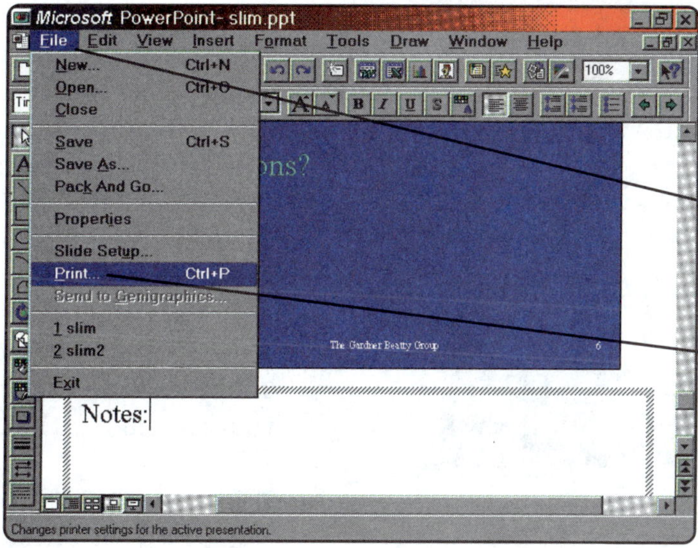

Printing copies of your slides with a note taking area can be very useful for your audience.

1. **Click** on **File** in the menu bar. The File menu will appear.
2. **Click** on **Print**. The Print dialog box will appear.
3. **Click** on the ▼ to the right of the Print What box. A pull-down list will appear.

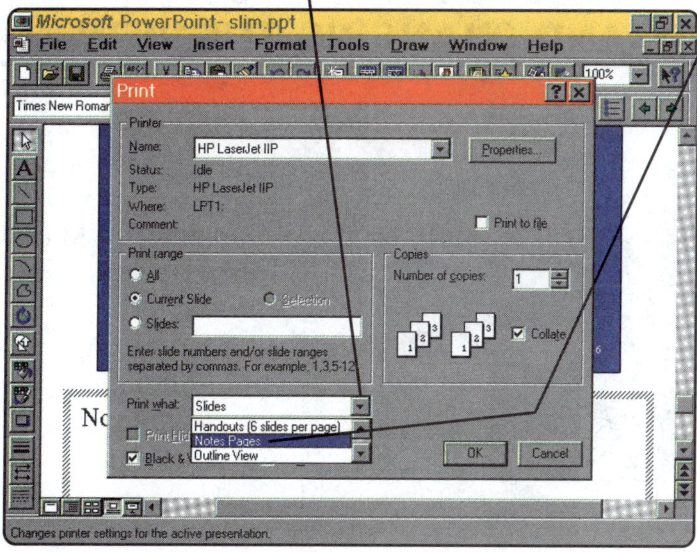

4. **Click** on **Notes Pages** to highlight it. It will replace the text in the box. (You may have to scroll down the list to see Notes Pages.)

Notice that this list also has choices for printing handouts. Handouts can be useful when you are designing your slides. You can see up to six slides per page and it gives you a good overview of your presentation.

5. **Click** on **All** to put a dot in the circle.

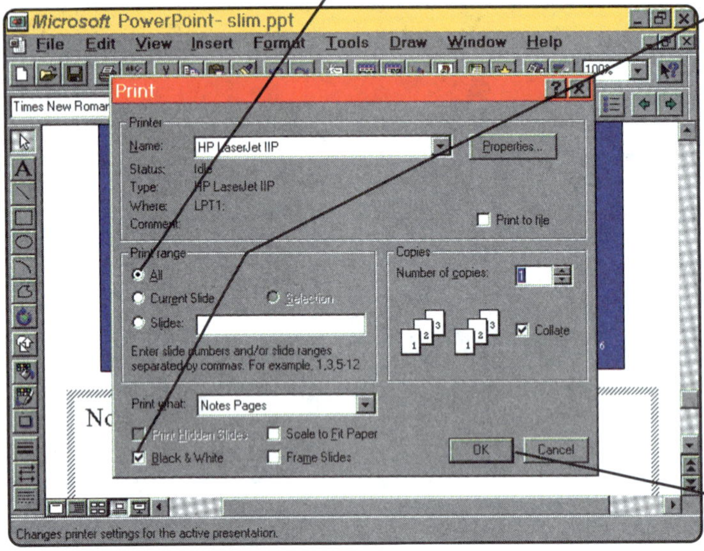

6. **Click** to **place** a ✔ in the **Black & White box** if it is not already there.

The Print dialog box remembers the selections you had in effect the last time you printed. Therefore, you need to check all the options to see if they are appropriate for your current print job.

7. **Click** on **OK**. The Print Status message box will appear briefly. The audience notes will be printed.

SAVING THE NOTES AND CHANGING THE VIEW

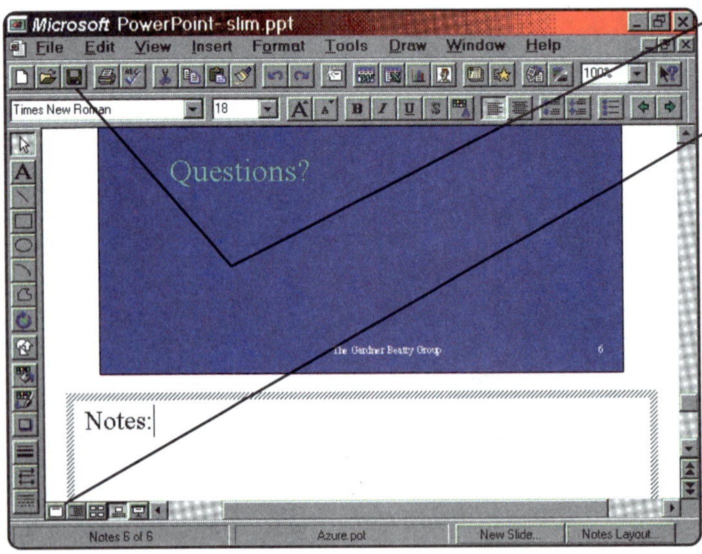

1. **Click** on the **Save button** to save your work.

2. **Click** on the **Slide View button.**

CHAPTER 9

Producing Slides through a Service Bureau

After you've designed your presentation, the next step is to produce it. You can send your PowerPoint file to a service bureau and it will produce slides, overheads, and other products for you (overnight, if you like). PowerPoint includes a special feature that will send your file to Genigraphics, a leading service bureau. In this chapter, you will do the following:

- ✔ Send a file to Genigraphics
- ✔ Save a file to a disk in drive A so you can send it to another service bureau

SENDING A FILE TO GENIGRAPHICS

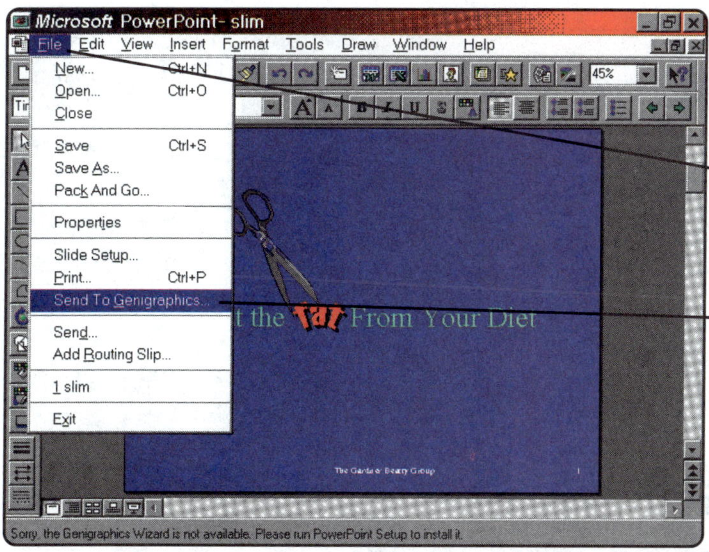

Sending a file to Geni-graphics couldn't be easier.

1. **Click** on **File** in the menu bar. The File menu will appear.

2. **Click** on **Send To Genigraphics**. The Genigraphics Wizard will appear.

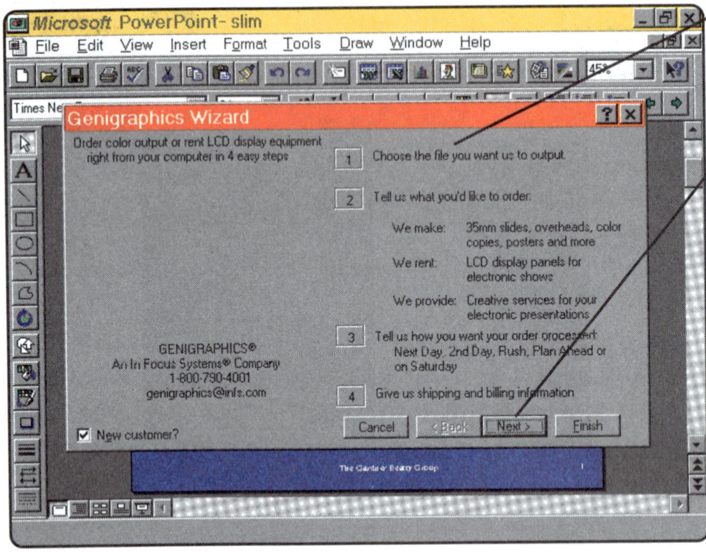

Genigraphics has included a summary of the Wizard process that you can read.

3. **Click** on **Next** to go to the next step.

Choosing the Products and Services You Want

Call Genigraphics at 1-800-790-4001 to get a description of their exciting new services. The LCD device rental (toward the end of the list shown here) is an especially cool option, allowing you to display whatever is on your computer screen through an overhead projector.

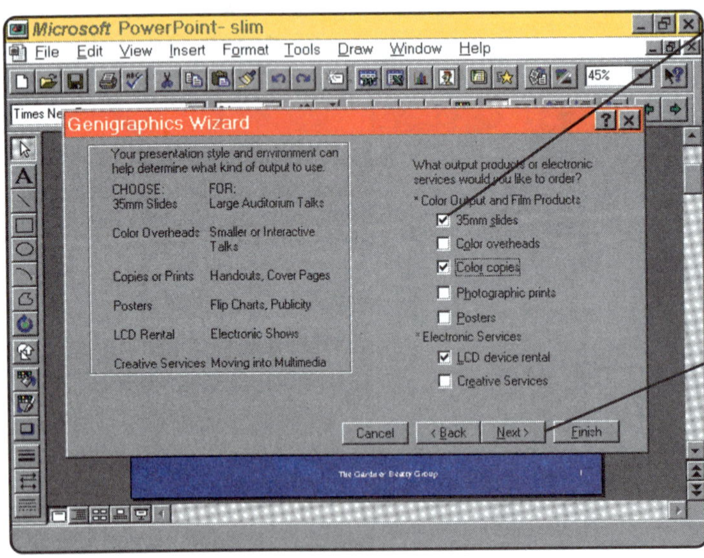

1. **Click** on each **option** you want. This will put a ✔ in its box. In this example, three options are selected. The specific options you choose determine which screens you see later in the Wizard.

2. **Click** on **Next** to go to the next step.

Selecting the File and the Method

If you have a modem, you can send the file directly to Genigraphics.

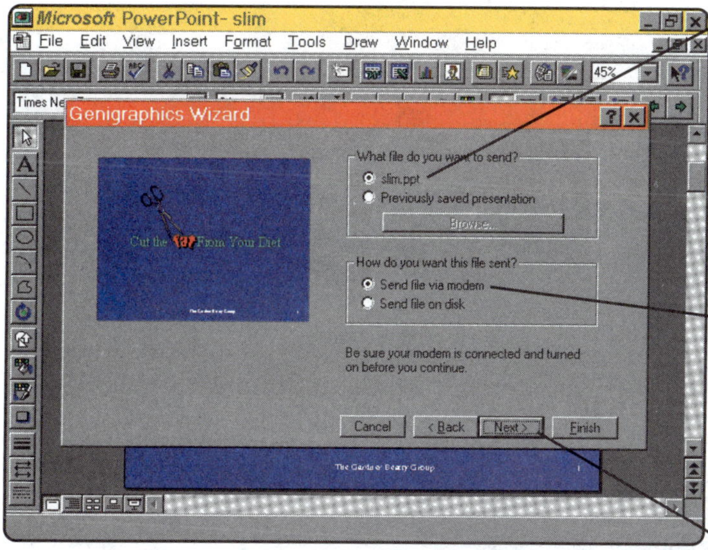

1. **Confirm** that the file you want to send is listed here. If you want another file, click on Previously saved presentation, then click on the Browse button to get the file you want to send.
2. If you want to send the file by modem, **click** on **Send file via modem** to put a dot in the circle if one is not already there.
3. **Click** on **Next**.

Mounting Your Slides

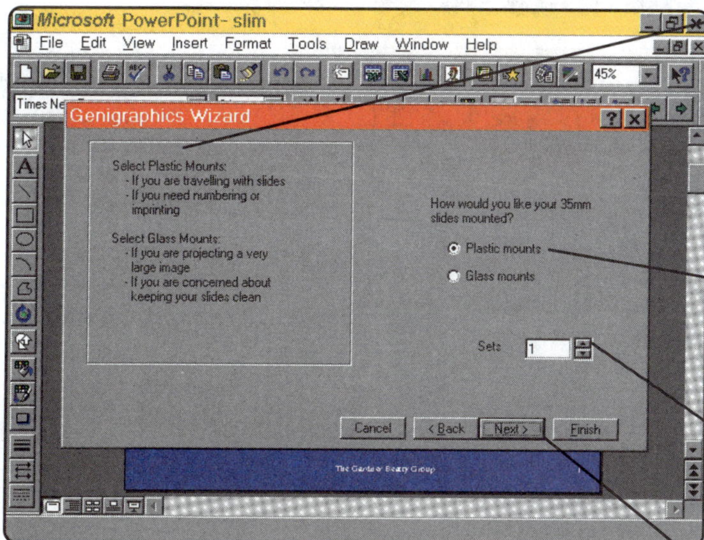

1. **Review** the **description** of plastic and glass mounts if you're not sure which you want. A *mount* is the frame around the slide.
2. **Click** on the **option** you prefer to put a dot in the circle.
3. **Click** on the ▲ to get more than one set of slides.
4. **Click** on **Next**.

Getting Color Copies of Your Presentation

If you selected the color copies option, you'll see this screen. If you change your mind about the options you want, click on Back until you're back at the options screen.

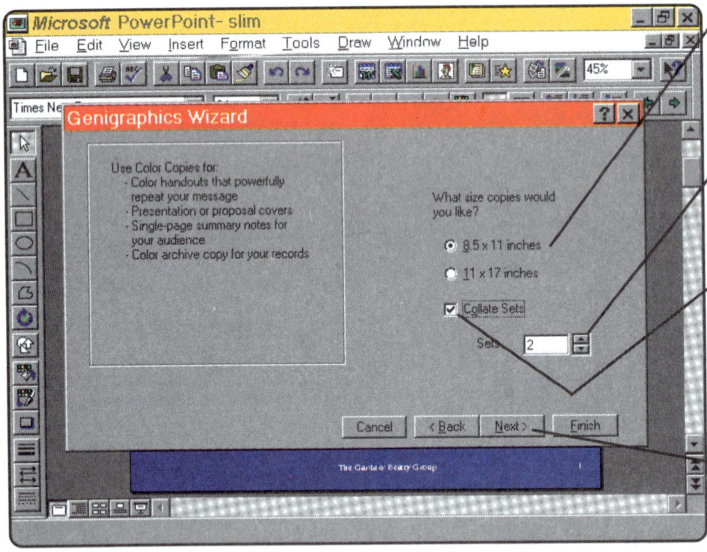

1. **Click** on the **size** you want to put a dot in the circle.
2. **Click** on the ▲ to get more than one set.
3. If you did step 2, **click** on **Collate Sets** to put a ✔ in the box if you want the sets collated.
4. **Click** on **Next**.

Choosing an LCD Display

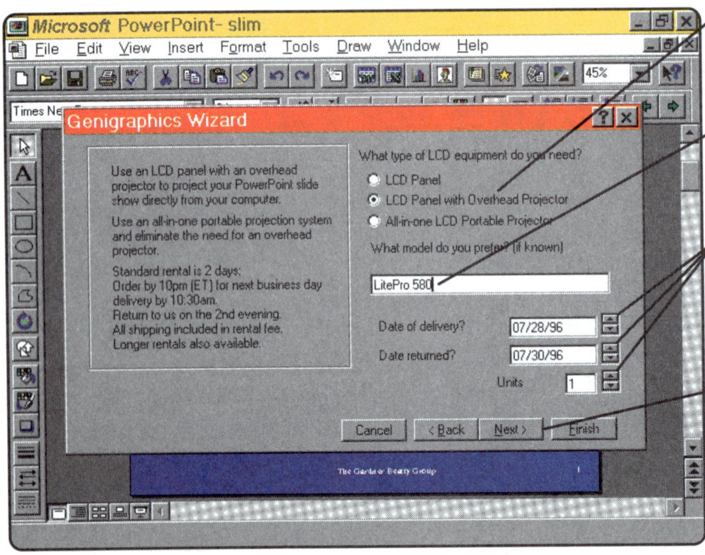

1. **Click** on the **type** of LCD equipment you want.
2. **Type** the **name** of any preferred equipment.
3. **Click** on the ▲ to set the delivery and return dates and the number of units.
4. **Click** on **Next**.

Correcting Trouble Spots

The Genigraphics Wizard will automatically detect such potential trouble spots as: (1) You chose an unusual font that Genigraphics doesn't use; or (2) You didn't format your file as a 35mm slide presentation.

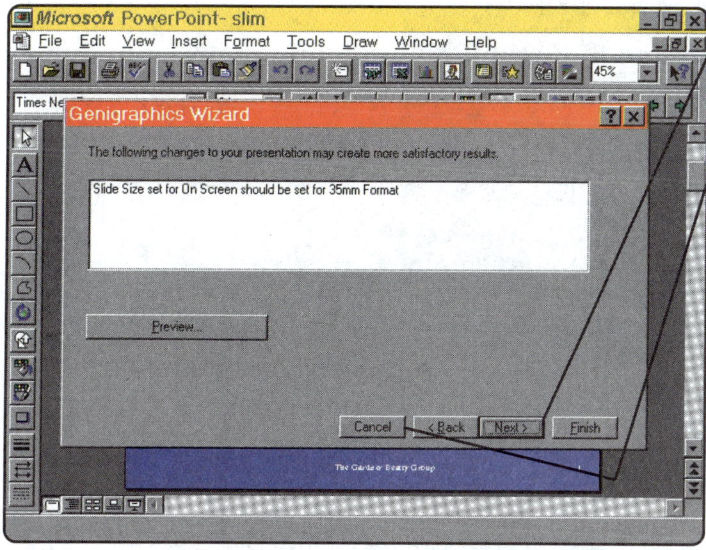

1. If there is no message here, **click** on **Next**.

2. If there is a message and you want to fix the problem, **click** on **Cancel** to close the Wizard.

To format your presentation for 35mm slides:

❖ Click on File in the menu bar, then click on Slide Setup.

❖ In the Slide Setup dialog box, click on the ▼ under "Slides Sized for" and choose 35mm Slides from the list. Click on OK. Check your presentation to make sure everything looks the way you want.

❖ Open the Wizard again and click on Next until you come back to this screen.

If you chose an unsupported font, you can make a global change while the file is open on your screen. Click on Tools in the menu bar, then click on Replace Font. See page 236 in Chapter 19 for an example of the process. Check your presentation to make sure everything looks the way you want.

Specifying Processing Directions and Turnaround Time

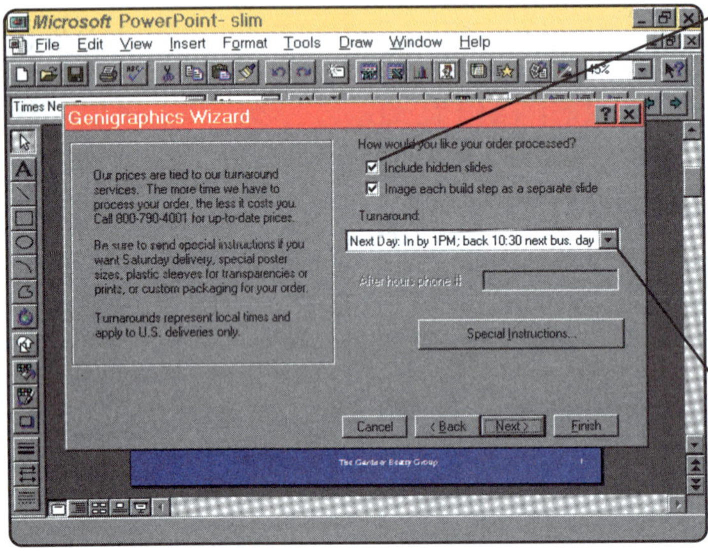

1. If you have hidden slides or build slides, click on the appropriate box to put a ✔ beside the option.

Standard turnaround time is next day. There are several other options from which you can choose.

2. **Click** on the ▼ to the right of the Turnaround text box. A pull-down list will appear (not shown in this example).

3. **Click** on the **turnaround time** you prefer.

Special instructions can be included by clicking on the Special Instructions button.

4. **Click** on **Next**.

Including "Ship To" Information

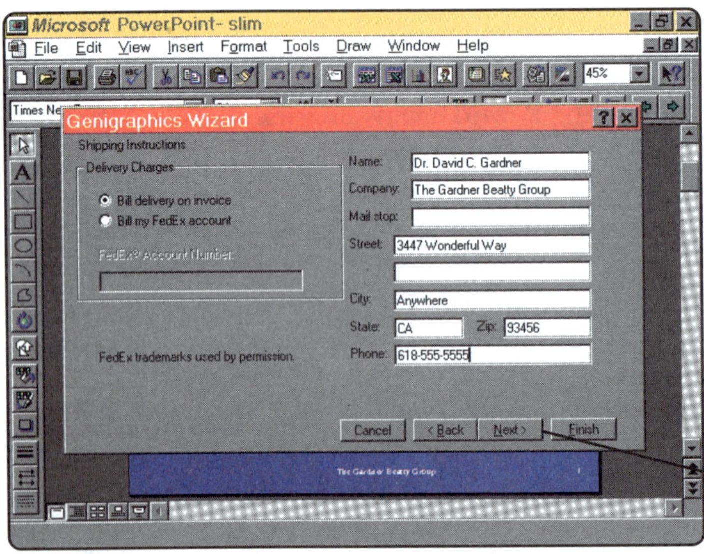

1. **Type** the appropriate **"ship to"** information in the spaces provided.

The Genigraphics Wizard will remember this information for future orders.

2. **Click** on **Next**.

Including "Bill To" Information

Be sure to include the "bill to" information even if it is the same as the "ship to" information. The Genigraphics Wizard will remember this information so you won't have to type it on your next order.

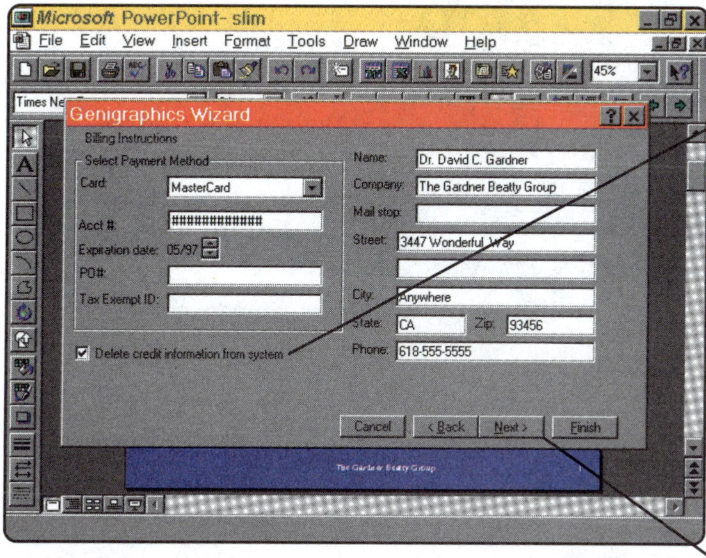

1. **Type** the appropriate **billing** information.
2. Genigraphics will normally delete the credit information from this screen after every transaction to protect your credit security. If you want Genigraphics to keep your credit information on the screen, **click** on **Delete credit information from system** to *remove* the ✔.
3. **Click** on **Next**.

Sending the File to Genigraphics

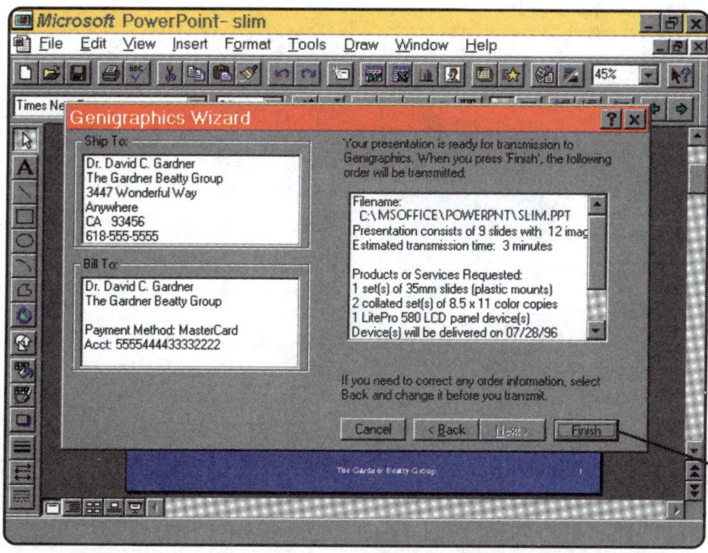

1. **Confirm** that the information shown is correct.
2. If you want to make any changes, **click** on **Back** to go to the appropriate screen.
3. If the information is correct, **click** on **Finish**. After a pause, the Send Status dialog box will appear.

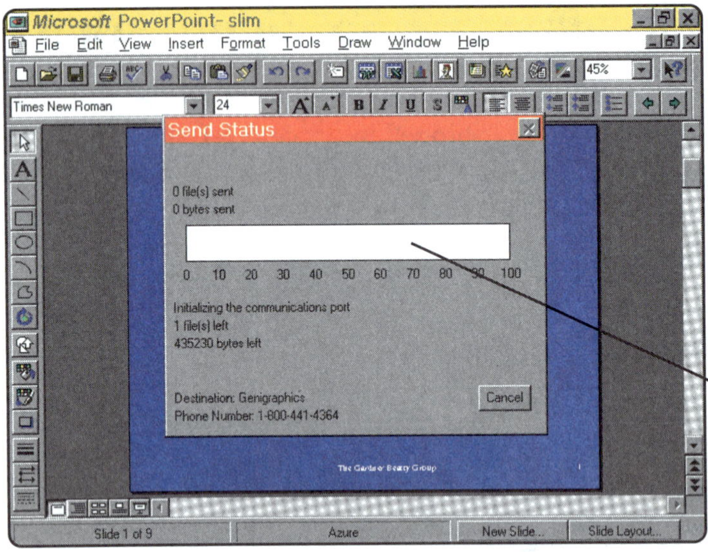

Depending on the size of your file, it may take a little while for any apparent activity to take place. Genigraphics is actually making a compressed copy of your file. Your original file will be left intact.

As the file is sent to Genigraphics, you'll see a bar informing you of the progress.

You can cancel at any time.

When the file is successfully transferred, you'll see the Transmission Summary dialog box and, behind it, the Graphics Link dialog box.

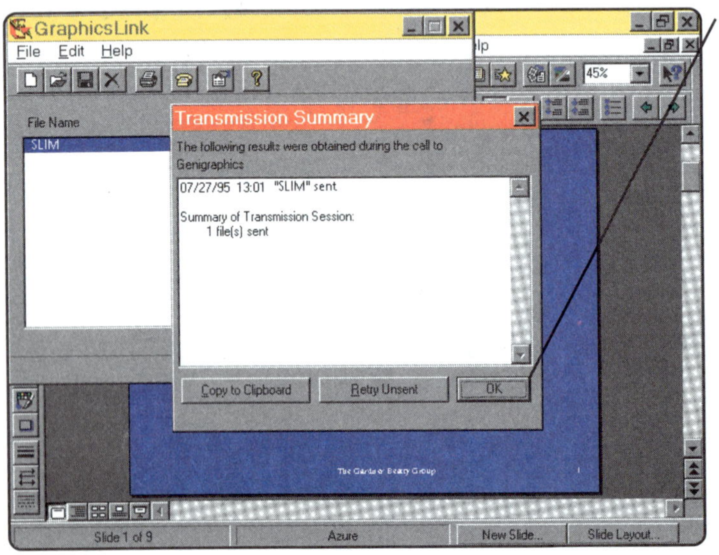

4. **Click** on **OK** to close the Transmission Summary dialog box.

5. **Click** on the **Close button** (☒) to close the Graphics Link dialog box.

Your presentation is now at Genigraphics! Isn't this great?

SENDING A FILE TO OTHER SERVICE BUREAUS

Feel free to call other bureaus to shop prices. Some bureaus require only that you send them your PowerPoint file on a disk. They do the rest! Other bureaus need special information to process your file. Call and ask.

The best way to put your file on a disk is to use the Pack and Go Wizard described in Chapter 17.

1. **Click** on **File**. The File menu will appear.

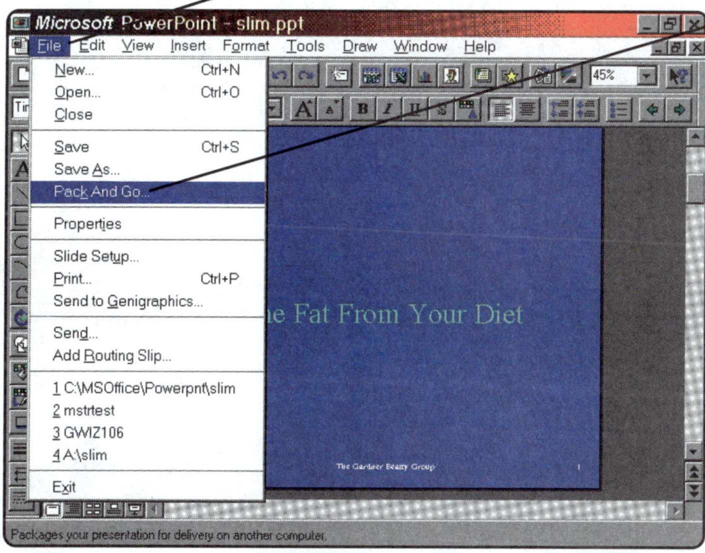

2. **Click** on **Pack and Go**. The Save As dialog box will appear.

3. **Go** to **Chapter 17**, "Taking Your Show on the Road," for detailed directions on using the Wizard.

Part II: Creating a Customized Presentation

CHAPTER

10

Drawing

PowerPoint has a very versatile drawing program that includes a number of predesigned shapes. You can layer text blocks and drawn items by sending one element to the back or bringing an element to the front. You can group layered elements so that they become one element and can be moved together. In this chapter you will do the following:

- ✔ Draw a rectangle
- ✔ Layer and group elements
- ✔ Duplicate a slide
- ✔ Edit and move a grouped element
- ✔ Enhance text blocks
- ✔ Create AutoShapes

DRAWING A RECTANGLE

Showing Guides

Unless you have an eagle eye (like our editor), use guides to help place drawn items.

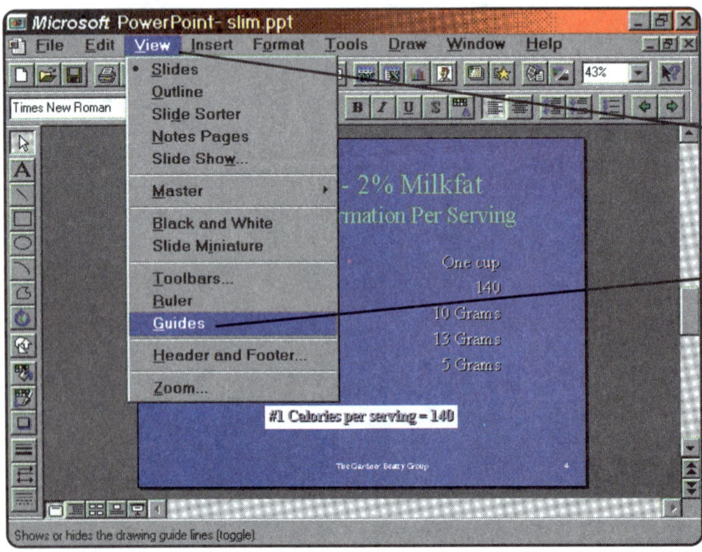

1. **Go** to **slide 4** in the slim presentation.
2. **Click** on **View** in the menu bar. The View menu will appear.
3. **Click** on **Guides**. Dotted lines will appear at the horizontal and vertical centers of the slide. If you used the guides in Chapter 6, they will appear in the position they were in when you last used them.

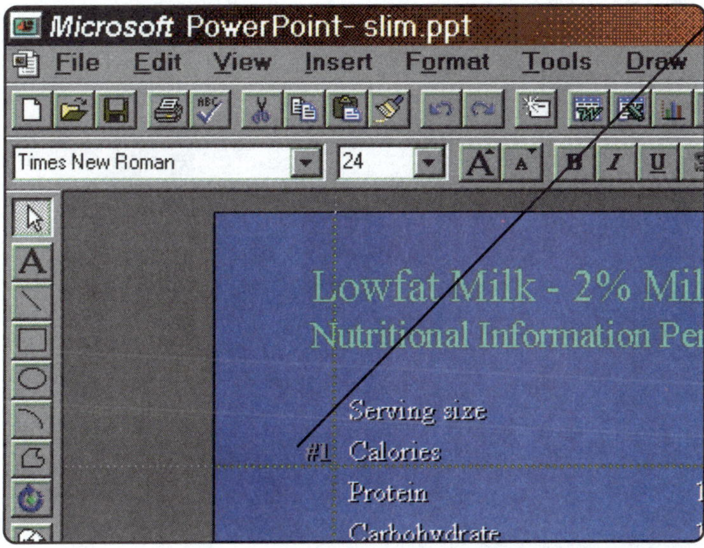

4. **Move** the **vertical and horizontal guides** so that they look like this example. On our computer, we placed the vertical guide at 3.33 to the left of center. The horizontal guide should be a little under the word "Calories." Your numerical positions may be different depending on your video driver. If you need help, see the section entitled "Moving Guides to Help with Alignment," in Chapter 6.

Zooming in for Close-Up Work

1. **Click** on "**#1**". The text block will appear. This tells the Zoom Control where to focus when it zooms in.

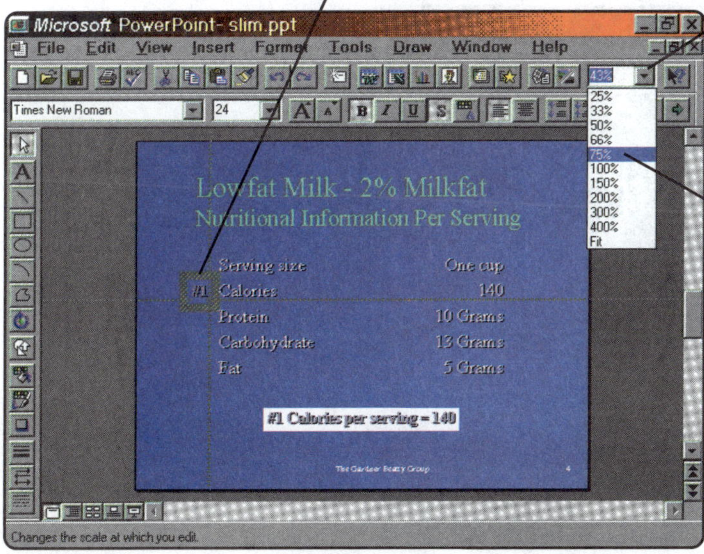

2. **Click** on ▼ to the right of the Zoom Control box. A pull-down list will appear.

3. **Click** on **75%**. The view will be magnified.

Drawing the Rectangle

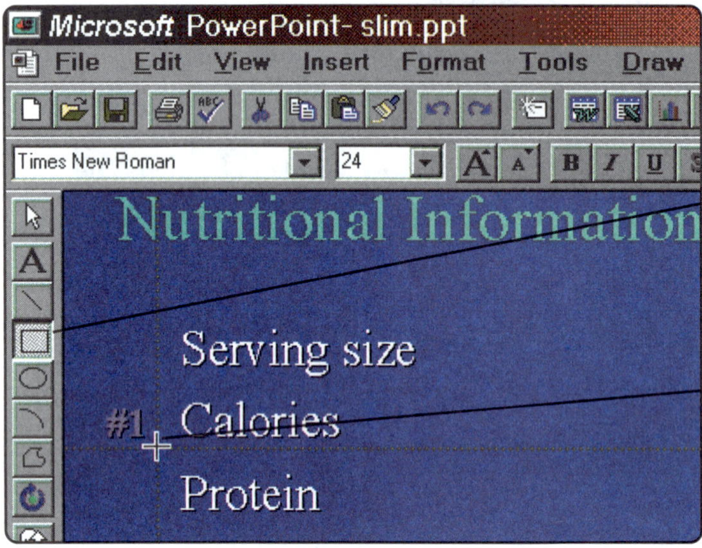

In this section you will use the rectangle tool. Notice that there are many shapes from which to choose.

1. **Click** on the **Rectangle tool** in the drawing toolbar at the left of your screen.

2. **Place** the **cursor** at the intersection of the vertical and horizontal guides. The cursor will be in the shape of a plus sign.

3. **Press and hold** the **mouse button** and **drag** the cursor up and to the left. A rectangle will form like the one you see in this example. As long as you continue to hold the mouse button, you can fiddle with the size and shape of the rectangle.

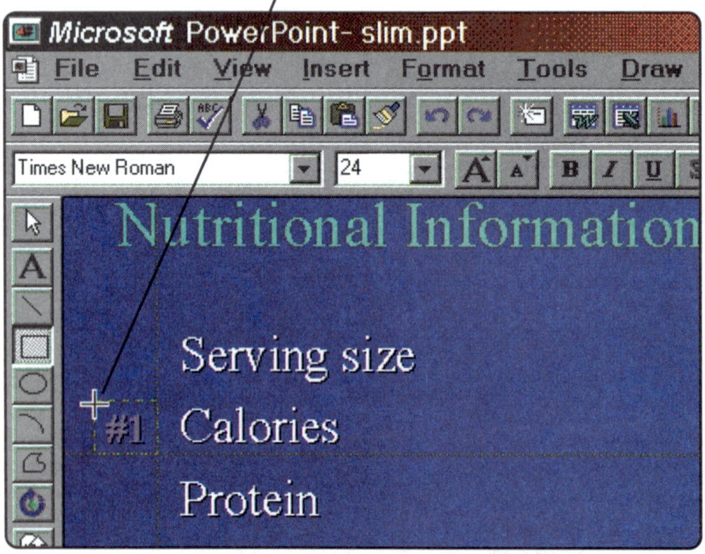

4. **Release** the **mouse button** when the rectangle is the size and shape you want.

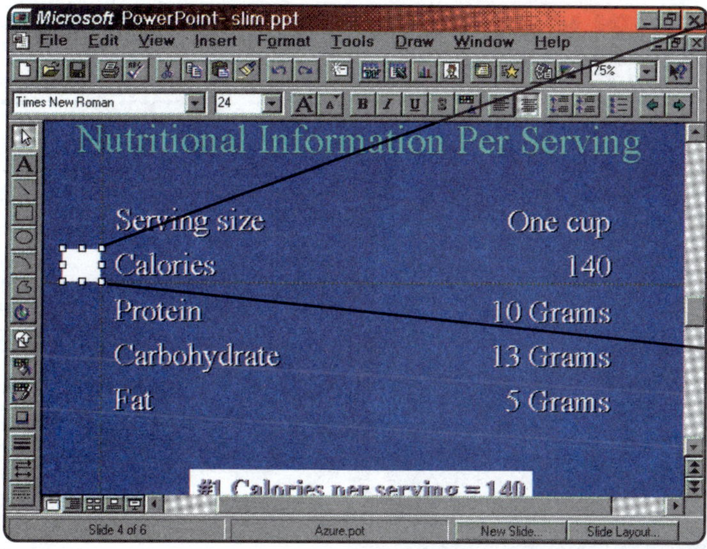

Notice that if you checked the Default for New Objects box the last time you used lines and fills in Chapter 6, the rectangle appears with the default fill color and line that you selected then.

Notice also that the rectangle appears on top of the text block and completely blocks it from view. You'll fix that in the next section.

SENDING AN ELEMENT TO THE BACK

When you placed the rectangle over the "#1" text block, PowerPoint automatically placed it on top. You can tell PowerPoint to place it behind the text.

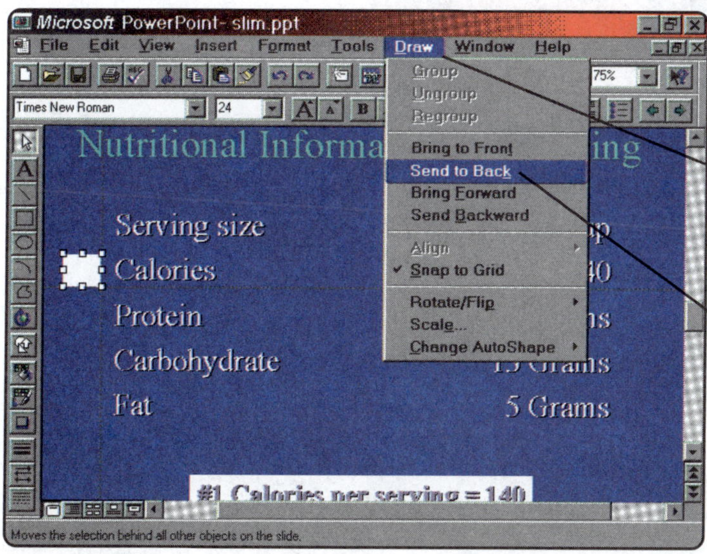

1. **Click** on the **rectangle** if it does not already have handles on its border.
2. **Click** on **Draw** in the menu bar. The Draw menu will appear.
3. **Click** on **Send to Back**. The rectangle will be sent to the back and the "#1" text block will appear in the front.

DUPLICATING A SLIDE WITH THE EDIT MENU

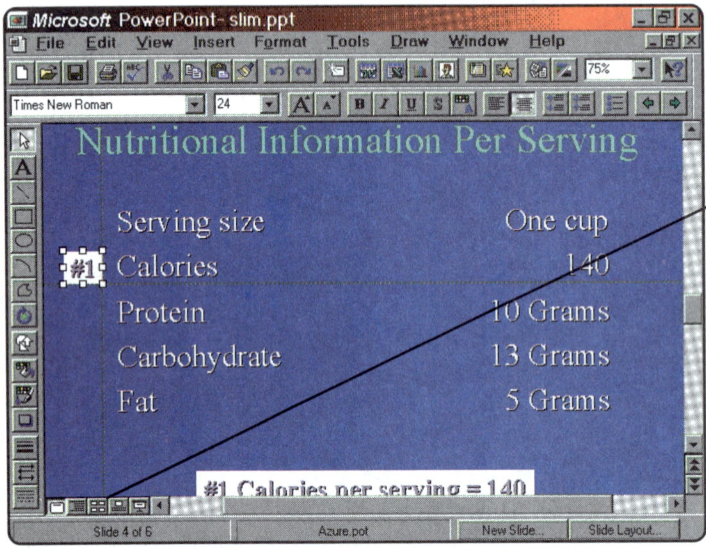

In this section you will duplicate slide 4. First you have to change to Slide Sorter view.

1. **Click** on the **Slide Sorter view button** at the bottom of your screen. The Slide Sorter view will appear.

2. **Click** on **slide 4** below, if it doesn't already have a selection border.

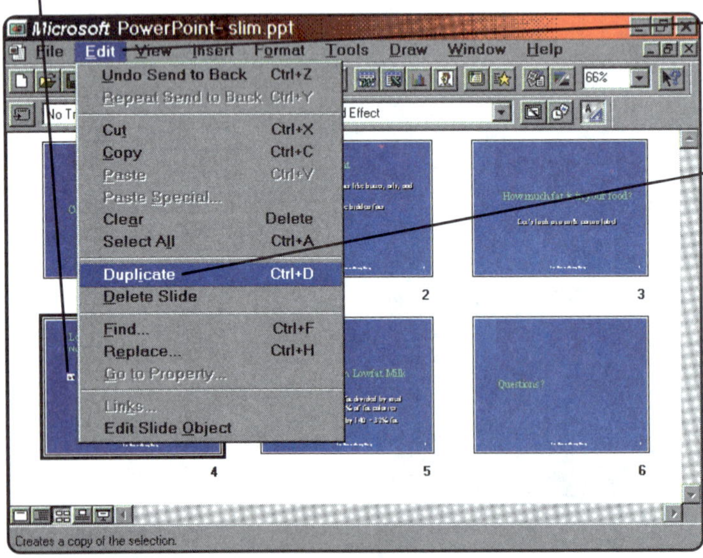

3. **Click** on **Edit** in the menu bar. The Edit menu will appear.

4. **Click** on **Duplicate**. A duplicate slide will appear as slide 5.

5. **Click twice** on the **new slide 5** to move to Slide View.

Notice that PowerPoint duplicated the slide exactly, including the 75% zoom view.

GROUPING ELEMENTS

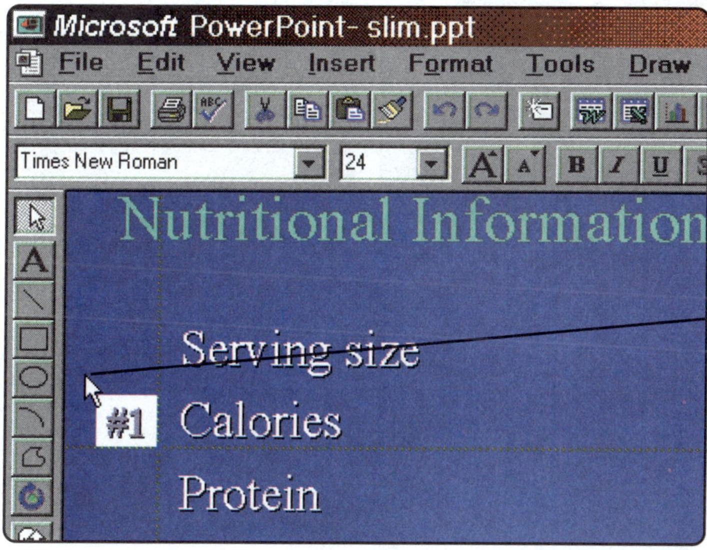

In this section, you will combine the rectangle and "#1" into a single element so they always stay together. First, you will use the mouse arrow to lasso them together.

1. **Place** the **mouse arrow** above and to the left of the rectangle as you see in this example.

2. **Press and hold** the **mouse button** and **drag** the arrow down and to the right. As you drag, you will see a dotted rectangle form a lasso around the rectangle and text block.

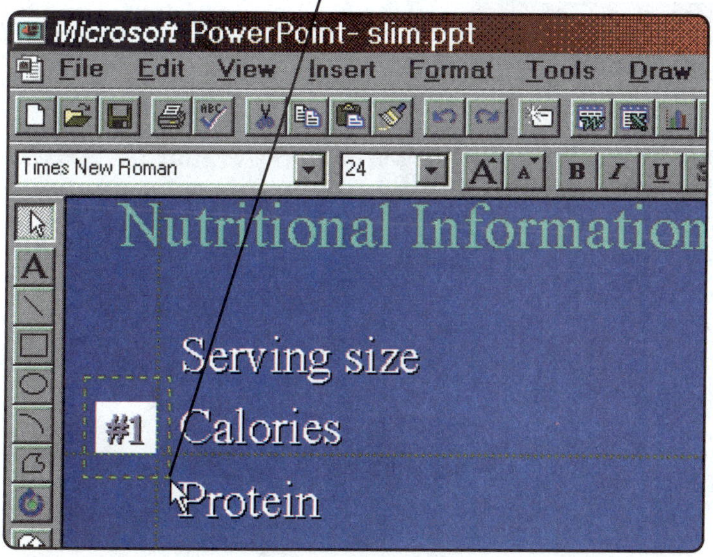

3. **Release** the **mouse button** when you have *completely* enclosed the elements within the lasso. The lasso will disappear.

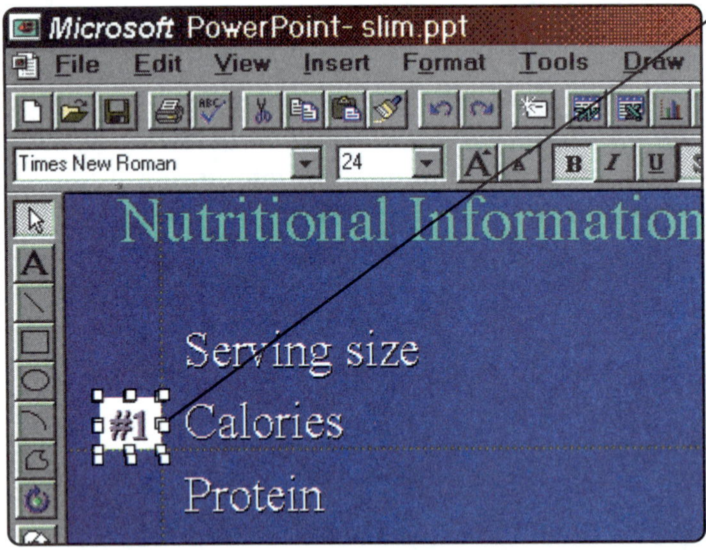

Notice that the lassoed block now has double handles. The double handles show that you have selected two elements. (If you get more than two sets of handles, try reselecting the text box with a smaller lasso.)

4. **Click** on **Draw** in the menu bar. The Draw menu will appear.

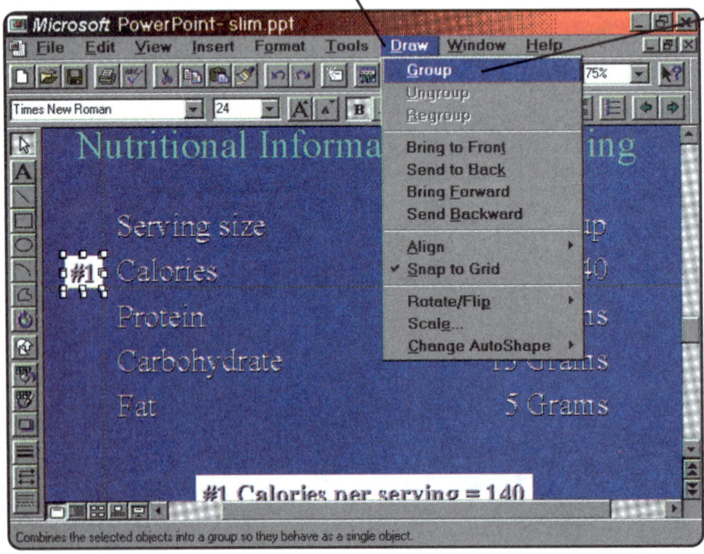

5. **Click** on **Group**. The menu will disappear, and there will be a single set of handles. The two blocks are now grouped. *Grouped* means that the two blocks will be treated as a single unit when you move or edit them. In the next section you will move the grouped block.

MOVING A GROUPED ELEMENT

Once an element has been grouped, you move it just like any other element.

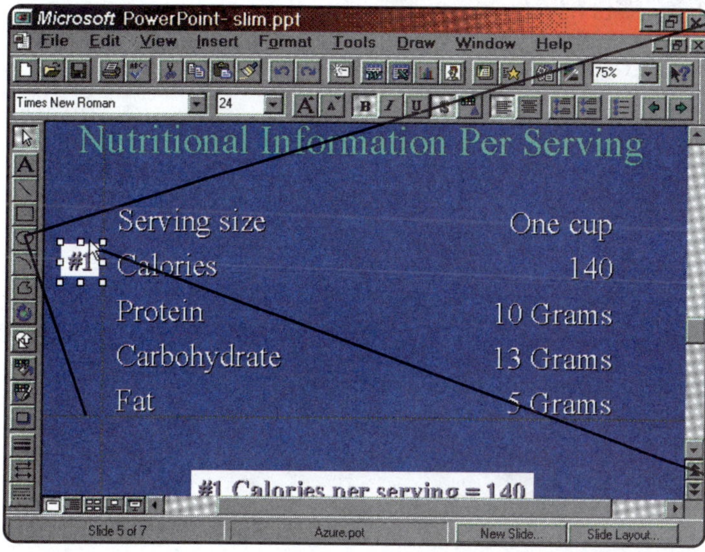

1. **Move** the **horizontal guide** so that it is a little beneath the word "Fat." On our screen, the line was at 1.33 below the center point. Your number may be different.

2. **Press and hold** the **Shift key** and **click** on the "#1" **square** if it doesn't already have selection handles.

3. **Place** the tip of the **arrow** on the border *not* on a handle.

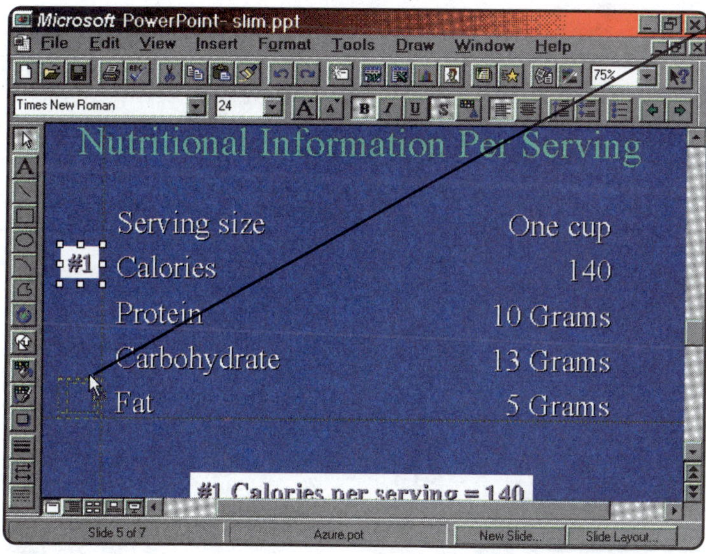

4. **Press and hold** the **mouse button** and **drag** the dotted square to the intersection of the guides you placed by "Fat." If you have trouble moving the square, be sure you placed just the tip of the arrow on the border.

5. **Release** the **mouse button.** The "#1" block will snap to the guides next to the word "Fat." (If you find it's difficult to place the square exactly, click on Draw in the menu bar, then click on Snap to Grid if it doesn't have a ✔ in front of it.)

EDITING TEXT IN A GROUPED ELEMENT

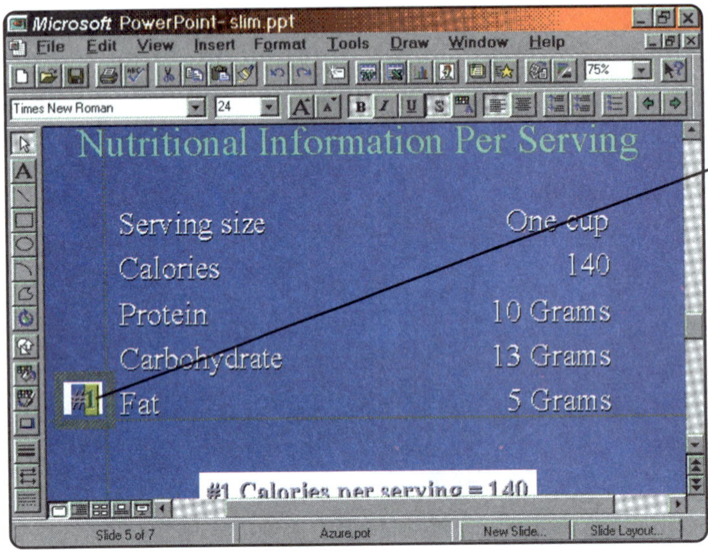

This process is exactly the same as editing text that isn't grouped.

1. **Drag** the **I-beam** over the "**1**", but not over the # sign.

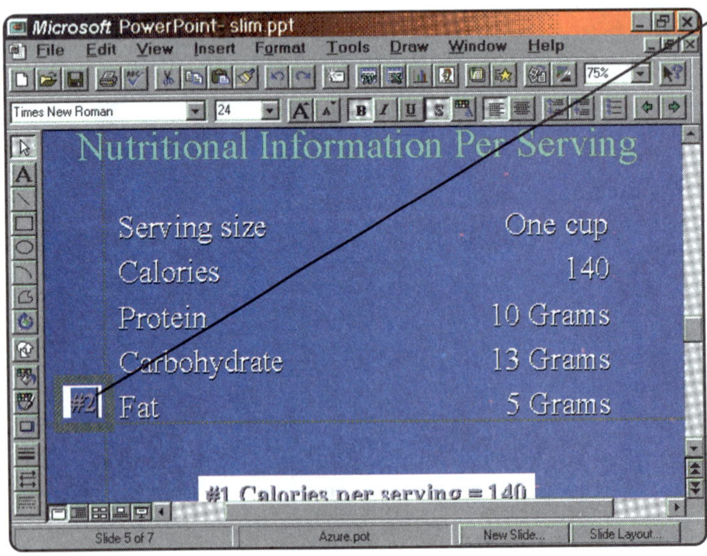

2. **Type 2**.

3. **Click anywhere** off the text block to deselect it.

Changing the View

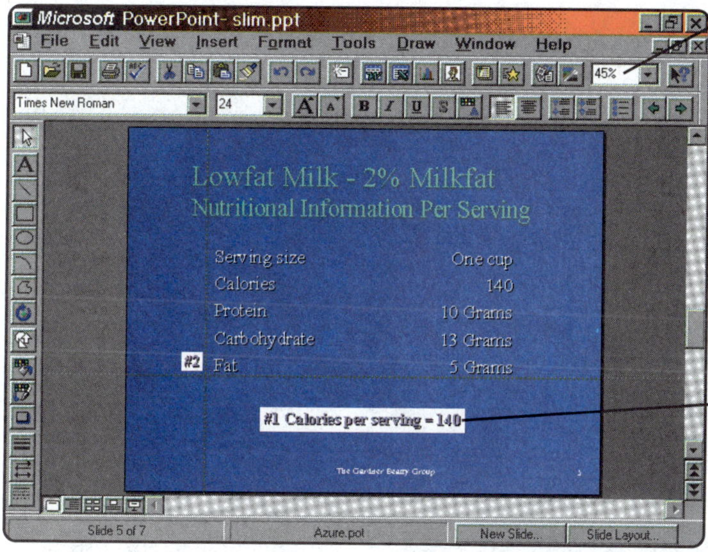

1. **Click once** in the **Zoom box** to **highlight 75%.**

2. **Type 45** and **press Enter**. Your view will change back to 45%.

Adding Text to a Text Block

1. **Drag** the **I-beam over "1 Calories per serving = 140"** to select it. You don't have to highlight the # sign because you're not going to change it.

2. **Type 2 Multiply fat grams by 9**. Don't type the period.

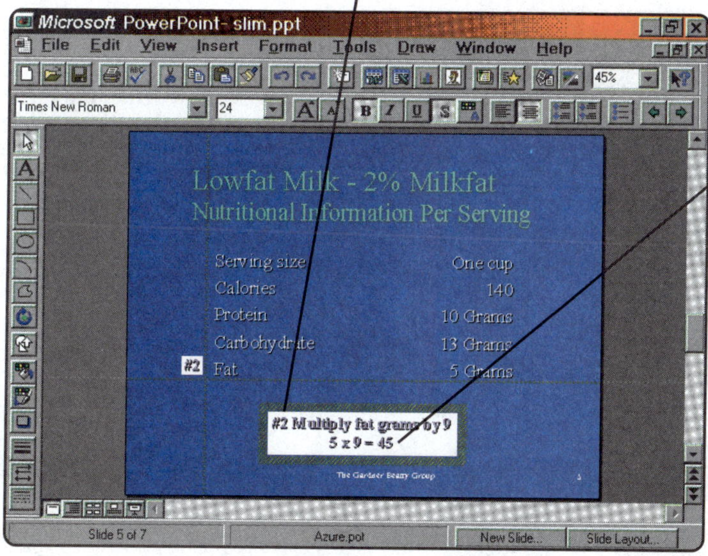

3. **Press Enter** to expand the text block to a second line.

4. **Type 5 x 9 = 45**. (Don't type the period.) It will be centered on the next line because you centered text in this block in "Centering Text in a Text Block," on page 69, in Chapter 6.

USING RULERS

In this section you will use the rulers as guides for changing the size of the "Questions?" text block. You are changing the size of the text block in preparation for changing its shape in the next section.

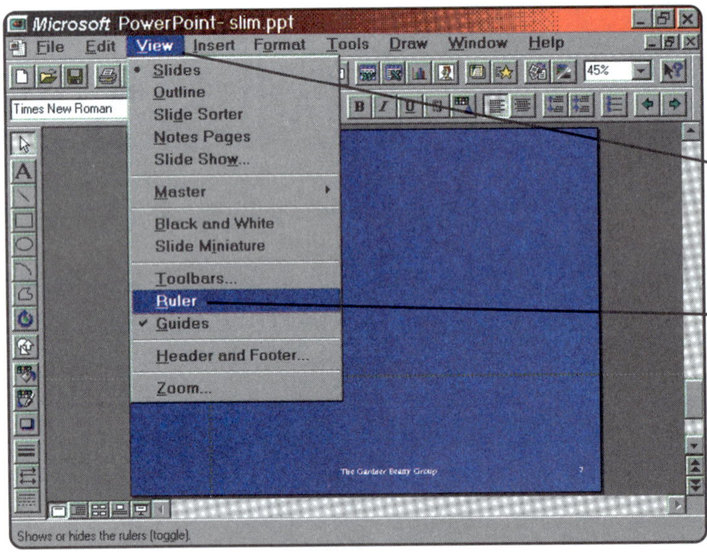

1. **Press** the **Page Down key** on your keyboard **twice** to move to slide 7.
2. **Click** on **View** in the menu bar. The View menu will appear.
3. **Click** on **Ruler.** Rulers will appear at the top and left of the slide.

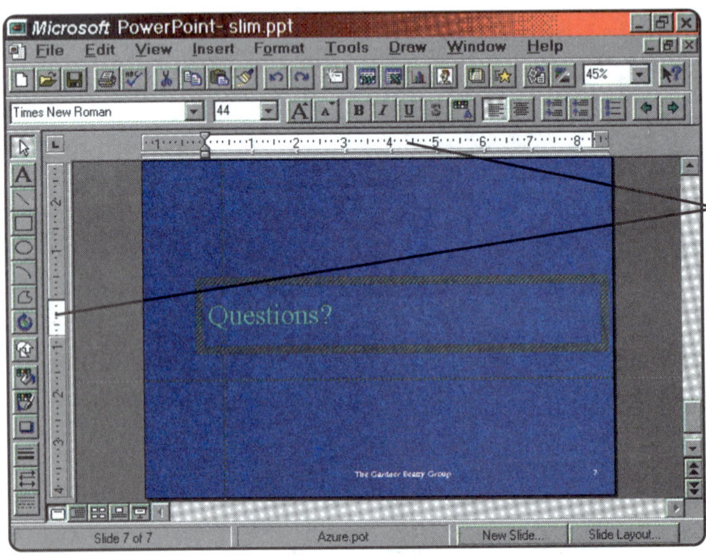

4. **Click** on "**Questions?**" to select it. The text block will be surrounded by a border.

Notice that the highlighted portions of the rulers show the size of the selected text block.

5. **Click off** the **text block** to deselect it in preparation for doing the next step.

6. **Move** your **mouse pointer** around the slide. Notice that the pointer's exact location is shown by dotted lines in the rulers. As you move the mouse pointer, the dotted lines move.

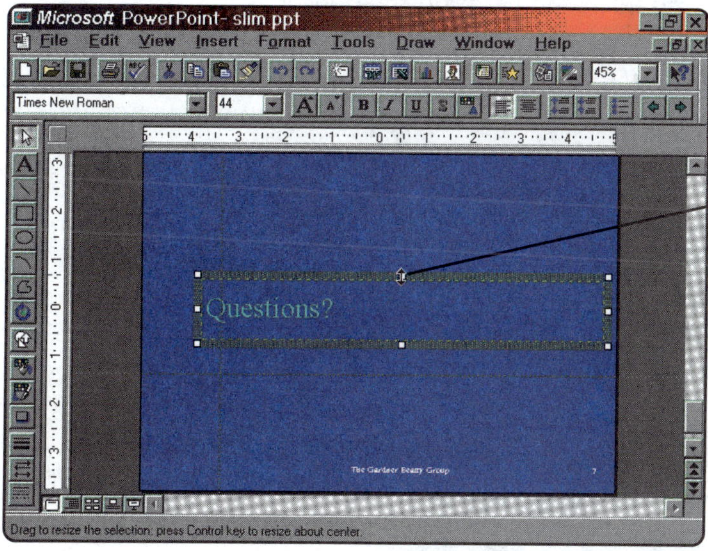

7. **Press and hold** the **Shift key** and **click** on the text to select the text block with handles.

8. **Place** the **cursor** on the **top middle handle**. The cursor becomes a double-headed arrow.

9. **Press** and **hold** the **mouse button.** A dotted line will appear around the inside of the text block.

10. **Continue** to **hold** the **mouse button** as you **drag** the cursor up until it reaches the 1.5″ mark on the side ruler.

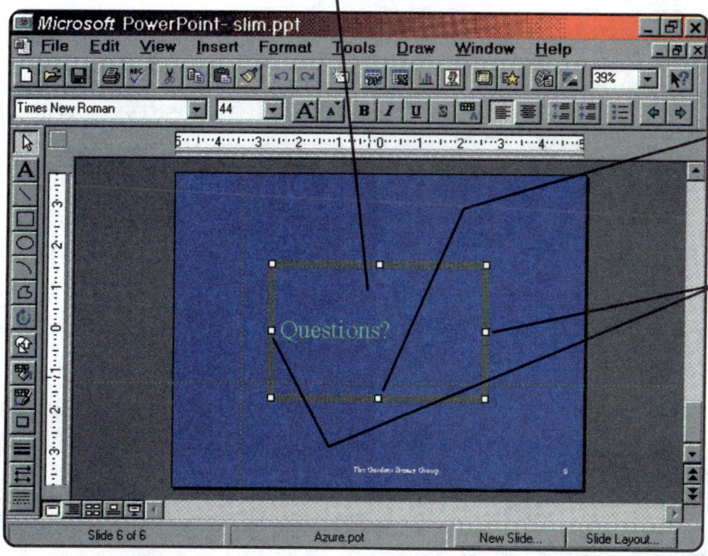

11. **Release** the **mouse button**.

12. **Repeat steps 8 to 11** to move the **bottom edge** of the text block down to 1.5″.

13. **Repeat steps 8 to 11**, to ***decrease*** the width of the text box to 2.5″ on the right and left sides. Use the top ruler to measure. The text will not get lost as you change the left side of the text block. The text will move with the text block.

USING CHANGE AUTOSHAPE

In this section you will change the shape of the text block. Then you will fill in the text block with color and add a line around the border.

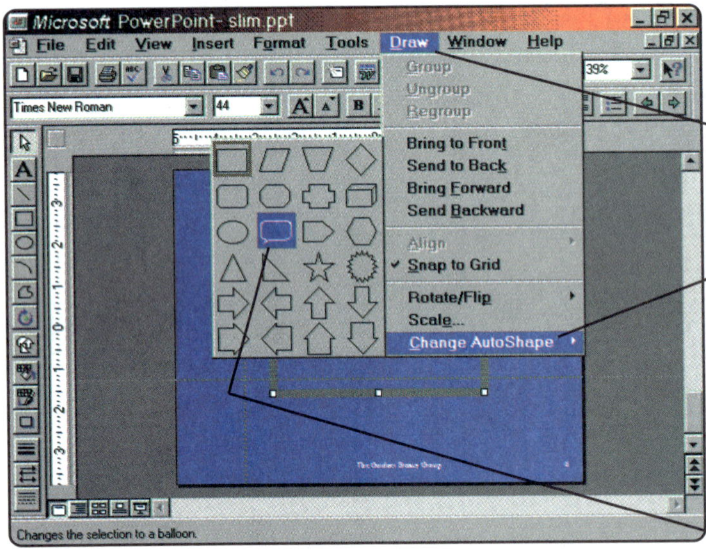

1. **Click** on the **text block**, if it is not already selected.
2. **Click** on **Draw** in the menu bar. The Draw menu will appear.
3. **Click** on **Change AutoShape**. An AutoShape box will appear. It may appear in a different spot than you see here.
4. **Click** on the dialog **balloon shape**, in the third row.

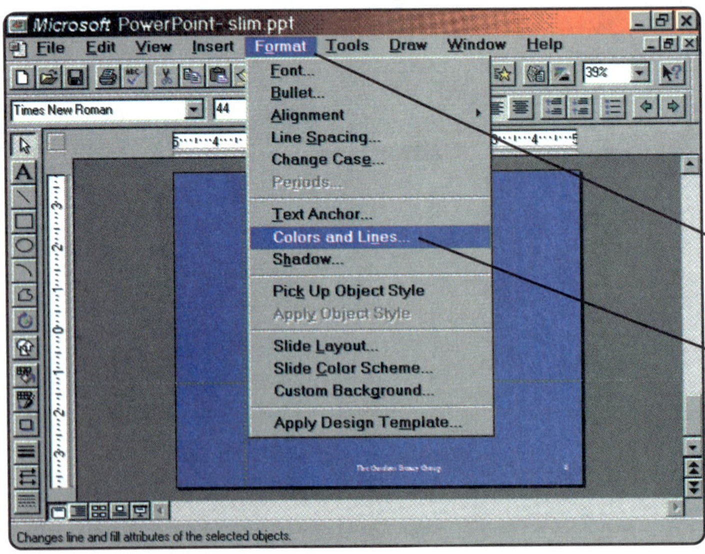

Notice that nothing *seems* to have changed. The new shape really is there, you just need to format it with fill and line color.

5. **Click** on **Format** in the menu bar.
6. **Click** on **Colors and Lines**. A Colors and Lines dialog box will appear.

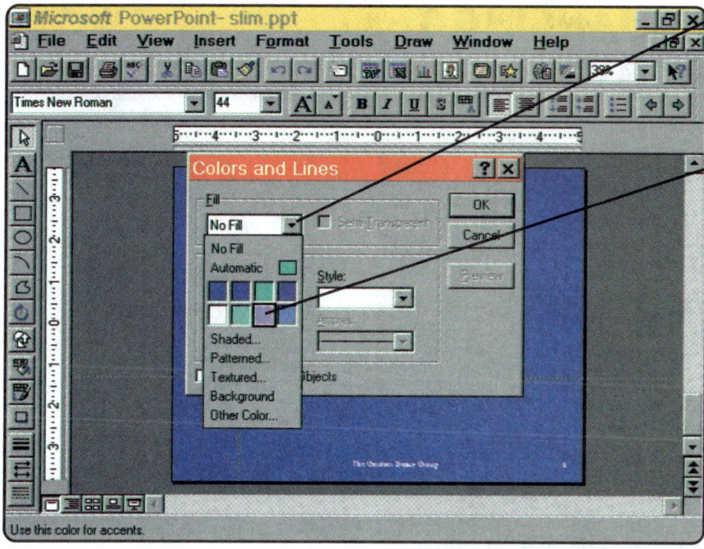

7. **Click** on the ▼ to the right of No Fill. A color menu will appear.

8. **Click** on the **lavender box**. In our example, it's the third box from the left in the bottom row. It may be in a different spot on your screen. If you are using a different template design, you may have completely different colors. If so, choose another color.

9. **Click** on the ▼ to the right of the Line text box. A color menu will appear.

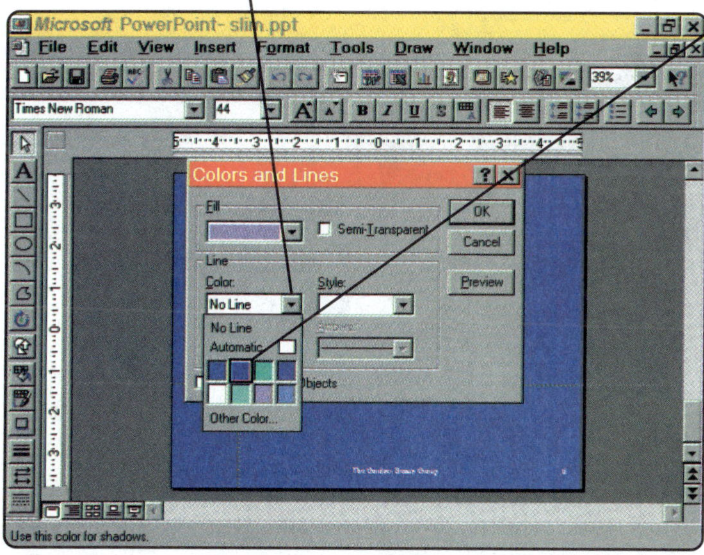

10. **Click** on the **black square**. The line box will become black. Depending on the template design you chose for your slides, the black square may be in a different spot or you may have completely different colors. If you don't see a black square, click on Other Colors to see additional choices.

11. **Click** on **OK**. The text block will appear with the new shape and colors.

ENHANCING TEXT IN AUTOSHAPE TEXT BLOCKS

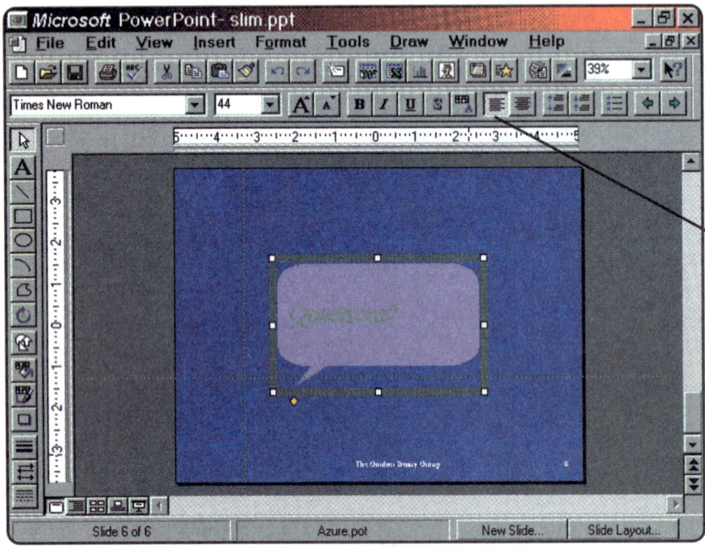

It is easy to enhance text in autoshape. Here's how:

1. **Click** on the **text block** if it isn't already selected.

2. **Click** on the **center alignment button**.

3. **Click** on the **text shadow tool** in the menu bar.

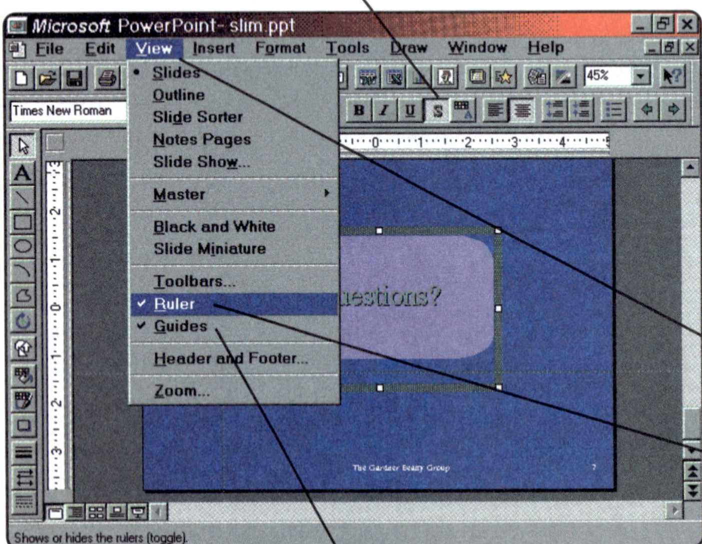

4. **Click anywhere** off the text block to see the results.

Turning off Rulers and Guides

1. **Click** on **View** in the menu bar.

2. **Click** on **Ruler** to *remove* the check mark and turn off the rulers.

3. **Repeat steps 1 and 2,** clicking on Guides instead.

CREATING AN AUTO SHAPE

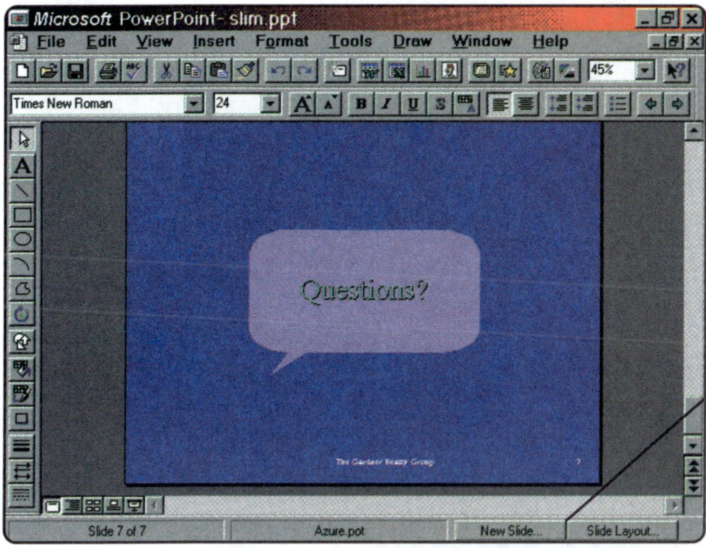

Now it's time to play! In this section you will create a new slide so that you can play with making and changing auto shapes. If you are following along with this presentation, you will not save this new slide to the slim file.

1. **Click** on **New Slide.** The New Slide dialog box will appear.

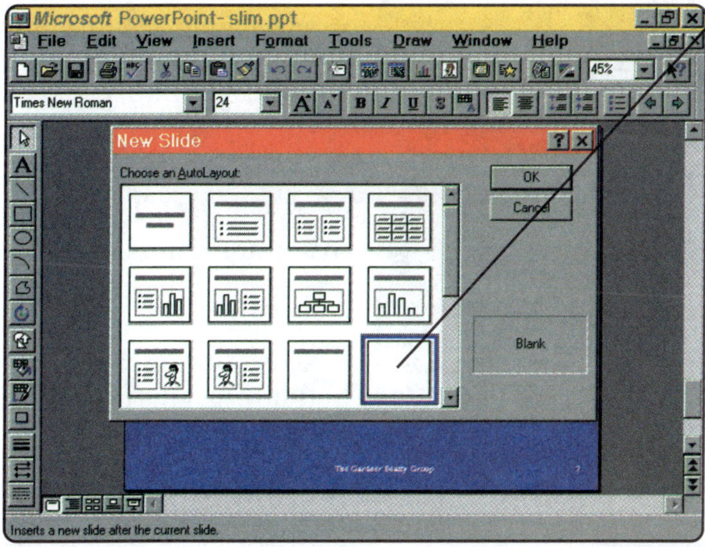

2. **Click twice** on the **blank slide** at the end of the third row. A blank slide will appear.

3. **Click** on the **AutoShapes tool**, which is the seventh from the bottom on the drawing toolbar. A pop-up box of shapes will appear. It may be a different size than you see in this example.

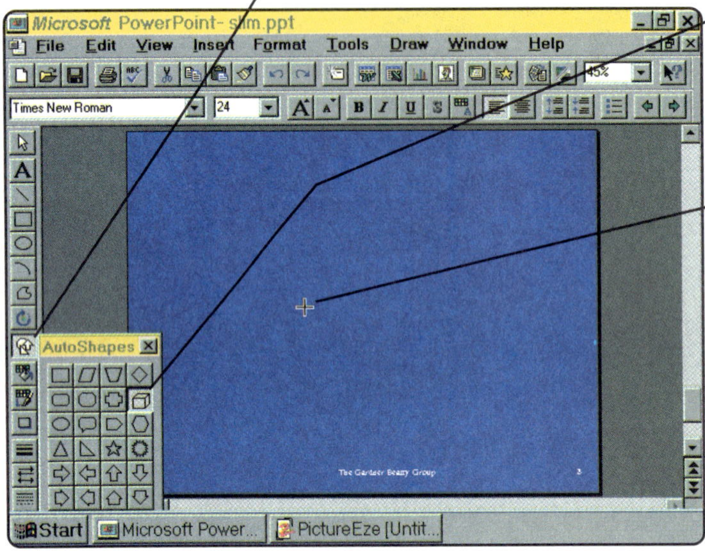

4. **Click** on any shape you would like. In this example we chose the **cube tool**.

5. **Place** the **mouse pointer** on the slide. Notice that the pointer turns into a cross.

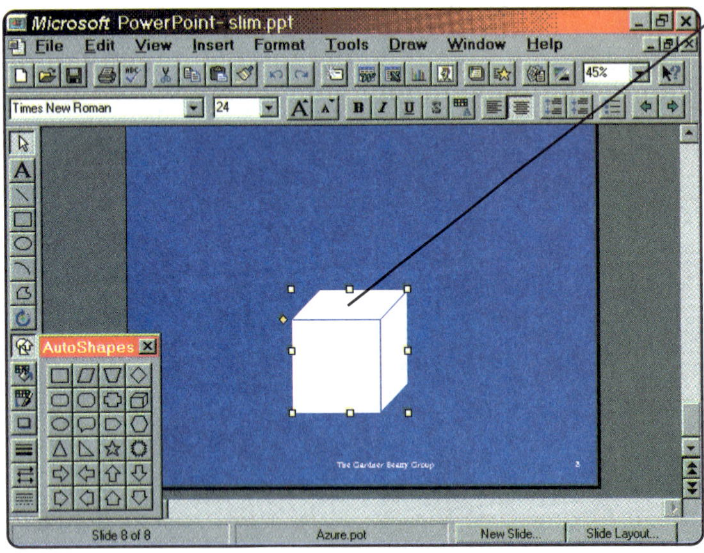

6. **Press and hold** the **mouse button** and **drag** it diagonally up or down to draw the cube. Notice that as long as you hold the mouse button you can drag up, down and sideways to change the shape and orientation of the object.

7. **Release** the **mouse button** when the cube is the shape you want. Remember, the cube's color is based on the default color changes you made in Chapter 6, "Working with Text Blocks," on page 56.

Changing AutoShapes

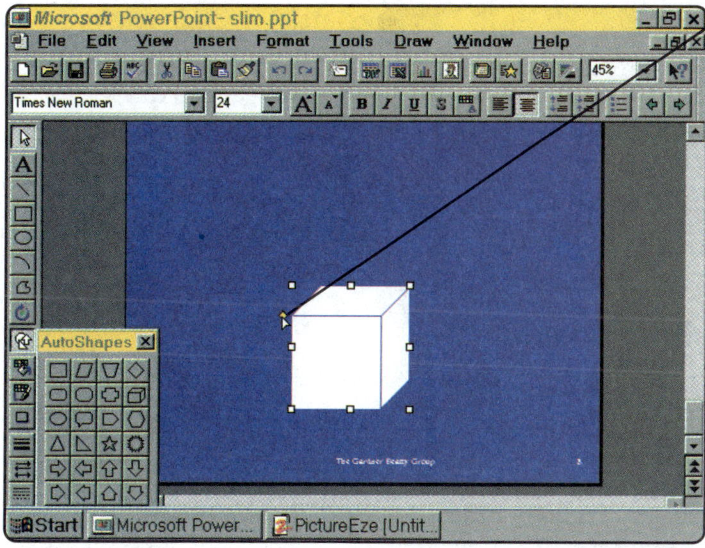

1. **Place** the **mouse pointer** on the **small diamond shaped handle**. The mouse pointer will change into an arrow head.

2. **Press and hold** the **mouse button** as you **drag** it down and to the right to change the dimension of the cube. Notice how easily you can change the shape of the object by moving the cursor back and forth. Notice also that you can change the shape of the object only within the parameters of the original shape. You cannot use the diamond to make the new shape bigger than the original. Use the square handles to change the size of an object.

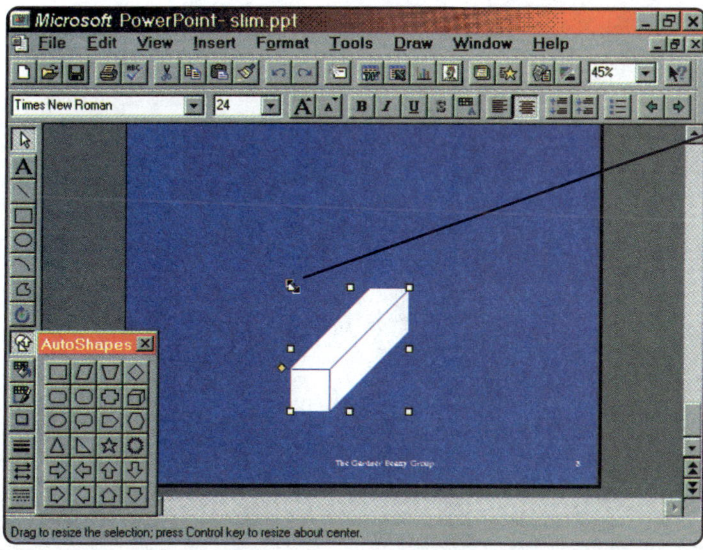

3. **Place** the **mouse pointer** on the **upper left square handle** of the object.

4. **Press and hold** the **mouse button** as you **drag** it to the left to change the size of the cube.

5. **Release** the **mouse button** when you find the right shape.

Deleting a Slide

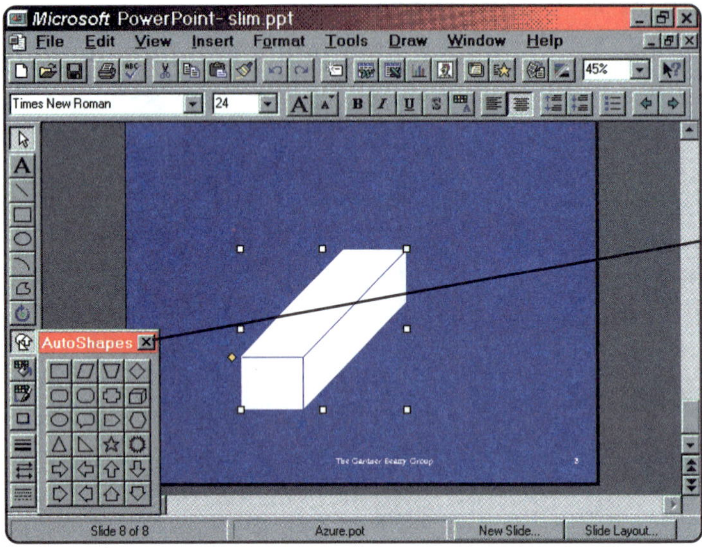

Since this slide was created simply so you could practice drawing shapes, please delete it from the presentation.

1. **Click** on the **Close button** (☒) on the AutoShapes menu bar. The box will disappear.

2. **Click** on **Edit** in the menu bar.

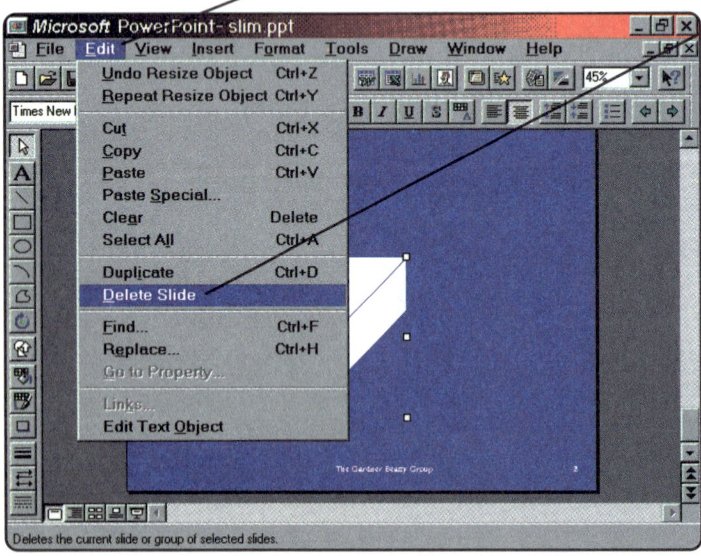

3. **Click** on **Delete Slide.** The newly created Slide 8 will disappear, and Slide 7 will appear on your screen.

Remember to save your work if you are continuing on to the next chapter.

CHAPTER 11

Working with Clip Art

Pictures can do wonderful things for your presentation. PowerPoint has a wide selection of color clip art images especially designed for use in a presentation. In this chapter you will do the following:

✔ Learn two ways to add clip art to slides
✔ Move, size, and color clip art
✔ Rotate an object

CHANGING SLIDE LAYOUT

In this section you will change the layout of a slide, then add clip art to the slide.

1. **Press and hold** the **mouse button** and **drag** the scroll button towards the top of the scroll bar.

2. **Release** the **mouse button** when slide 3 appears to the left of the scroll bar. Slide 3 will appear on your screen.

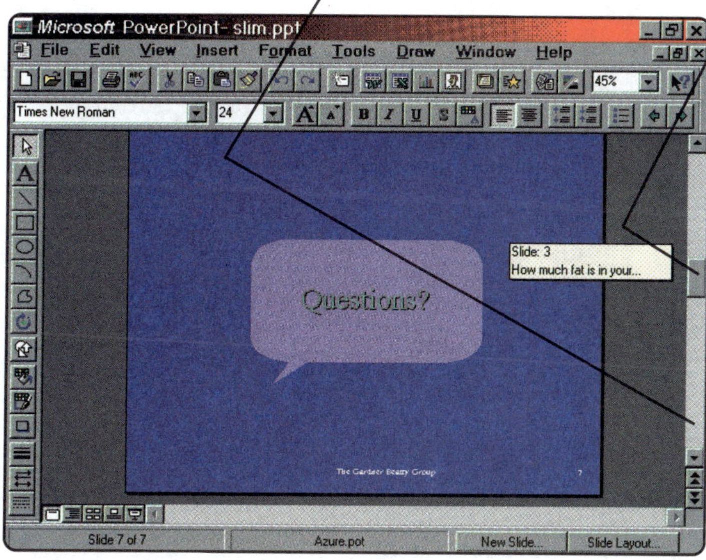

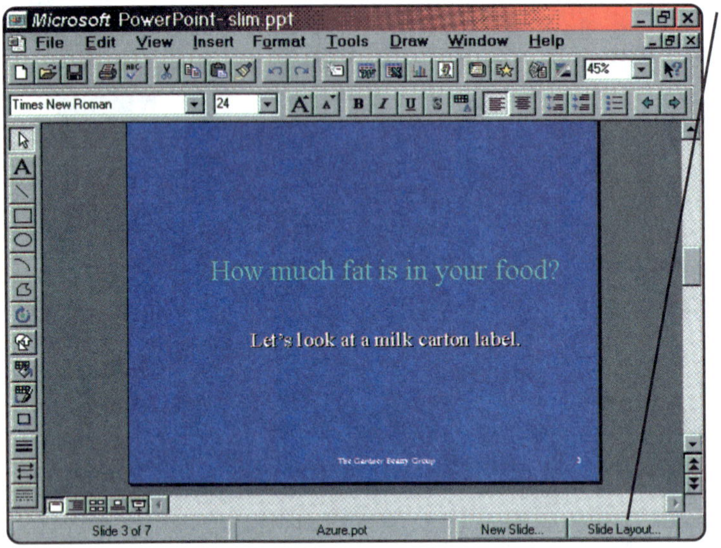

3. **Click** on **Slide Layout.** The Slide Layout dialog box will appear.

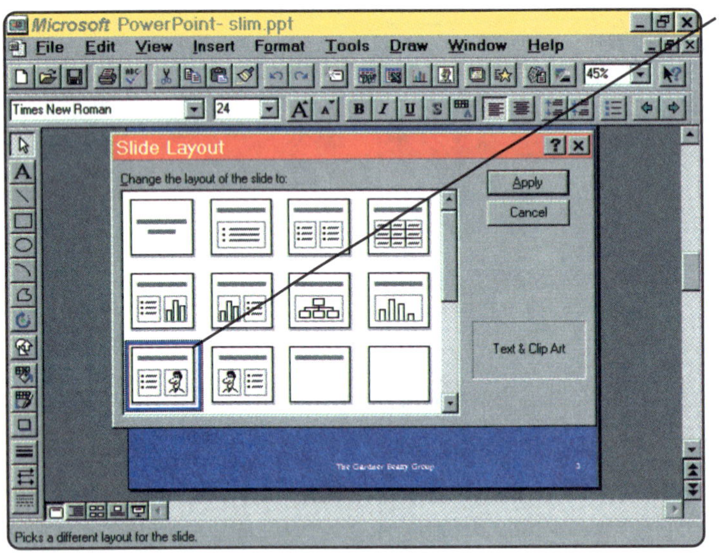

4. **Click** on the **Text and Clip Art slide** in the first column of the third row.

5. **Click** on **Apply**. The layout of slide 3 will be changed.

ADDING CLIP ART

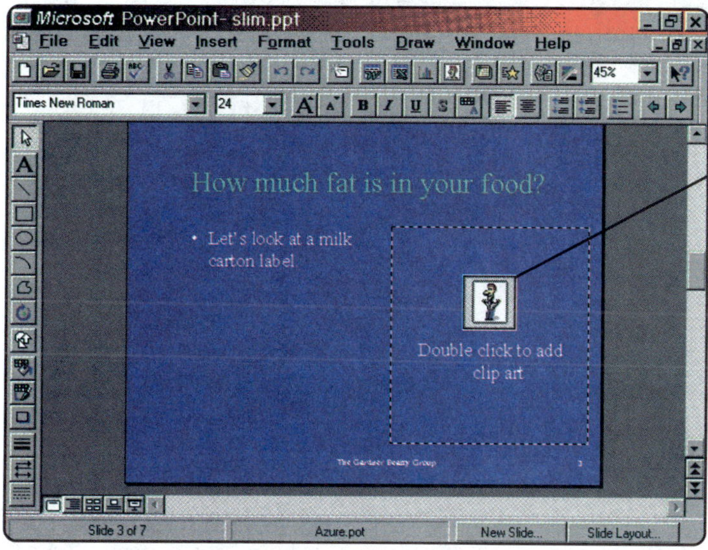

In this section, you'll use a piece of clip art to create a label.

1. **Click twice** on the **ClipArt Gallery button**.

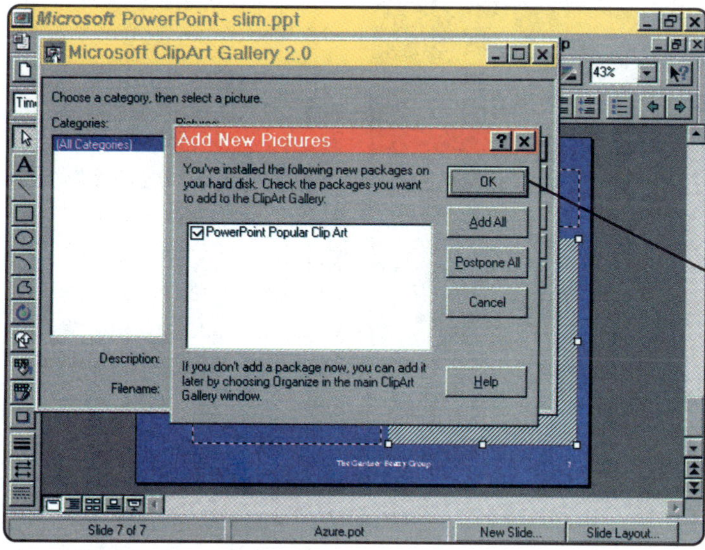

If you are opening up the clip art library for the first time, do step 2 to load the clip art. If the clip art is already loaded, go to step 3.

2. **Click** on **OK.** Be patient; it will take a few minutes to load in the new clip art.

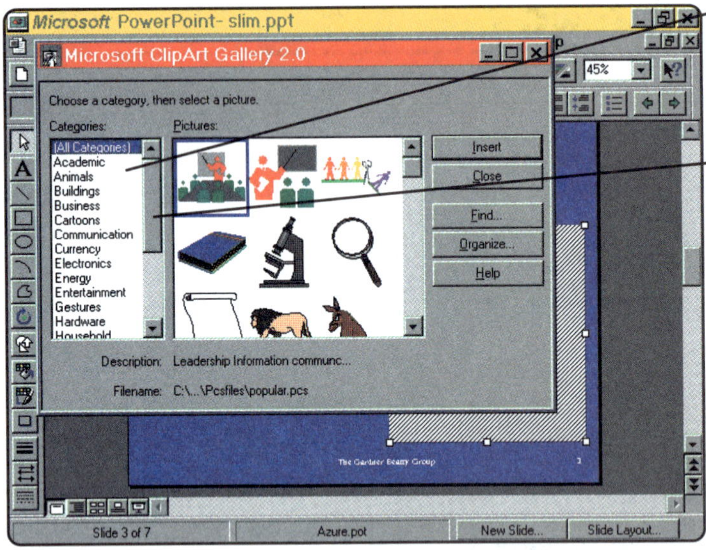

Notice there are many different categories of clip art from which to choose.

In each category you can see the selection of clip art by clicking on the scroll bar arrows to the right of the pictures.

3. **Press and hold** the **mouse button** and **drag** the scroll bar button down until you see Shapes on the list.

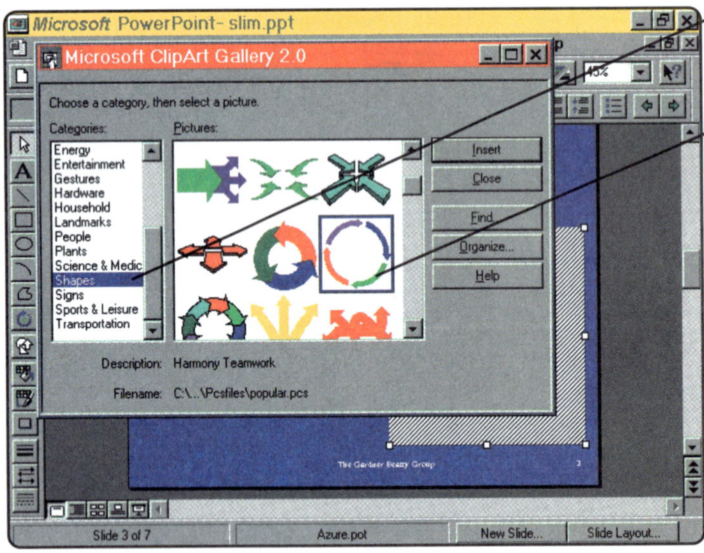

4. **Click** on **Shapes** to highlight it.

5. **Click** on the **Harmony Teamwork circle**. It will be surrounded by a thick selection border. (Our version of PowerPoint had two of these shapes listed. Only the second shape near the bottom of the list worked.)

6. **Click** on **OK**. Slide 3 will appear with the new clip art that was selected.

SIZING CLIP ART

In this section you will fine-tune the clip art by making it slightly larger.

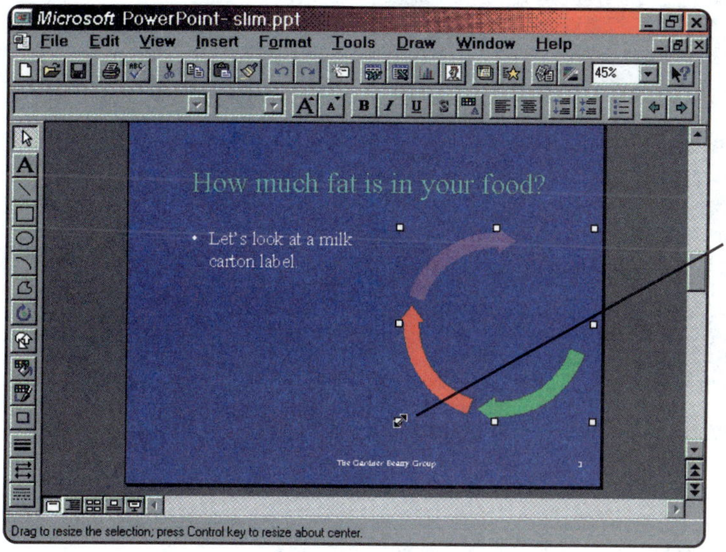

1. **Click** on the **clip art**, if it is not already selected. Solid squares, or *handles*, will appear on the border of the clip art.

2. **Place** the **mouse arrow** on the **bottom left handle**. The mouse pointer will become a two-headed arrow.

3. **Press and hold** the **mouse button.** The two-headed arrow will change into a plus sign and a dotted rectangle will appear around the clip art. **Drag** the **plus sign** diagonally down and to the left to size the circle proportionally.

Note: Depending on exactly where your clip art was placed, you may want to place the mouse pointer on the upper left handle and drag diagonally up to increase the size of the clip art.

4. **Release** the **mouse button** when you have the desired size. You may have to fiddle with the other corner handles of the clip art until it is sized the way you want it.

MOVING CLIP ART

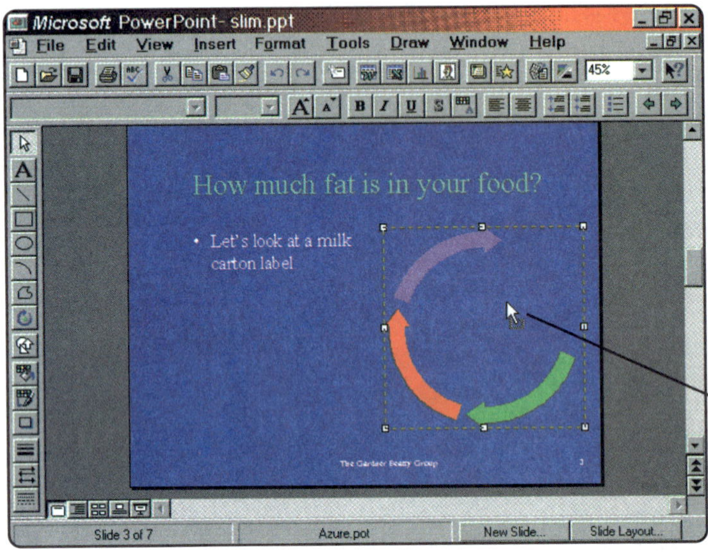

There are two ways to move clip art.

Dragging Clip Art

1. **Click anywhere** on the circle, if it isn't already selected.

2. **Press and hold** the **mouse button** and **drag** the cursor to reposition the circle to the left.

3. **Release** the **mouse button.**

Moving Clip Art with the Arrow Keys

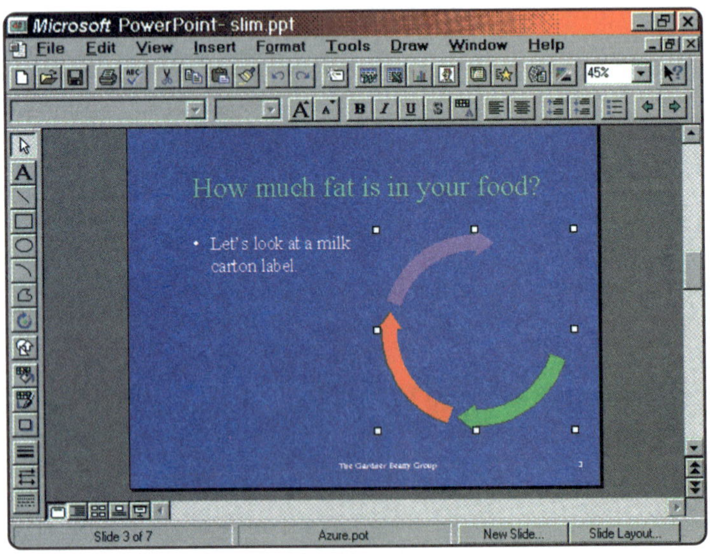

You can fine-tune the placement of graphics (and text blocks) by using the arrow keys to "nudge" the graphic in a specific direction.

1. **Click** on the **circle,** if it does not already have section handles.

2. **Press** the **" key** on your keyboard. The graphic will move slightly to the right. Experiment with the other arrow keys.

RECOLORING CLIP ART

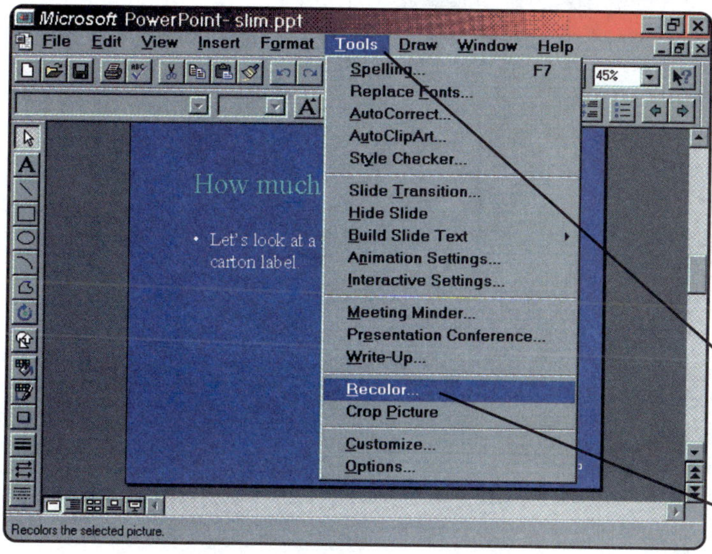

In this section you will change the blue color in the clip art to another color.

1. **Click** on the **clip art** if it does not already have handles.

2. **Click** on **Tools** in the menu bar. The Tools menu will appear.

3. **Click** on **Recolor**. The Recolor Picture dialog box will appear.

4. **Click** on the ▼ beside the top blue color block. A pull-down list will appear.

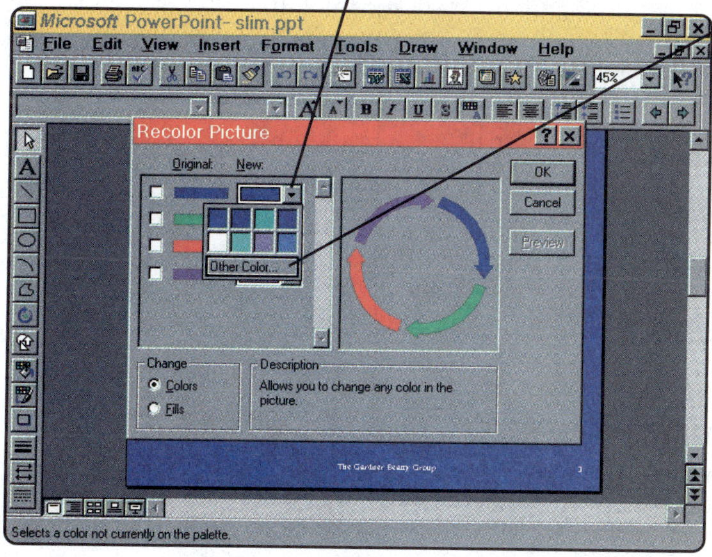

5. **Click** on **Other Color**. The Other Color dialog box will appear.

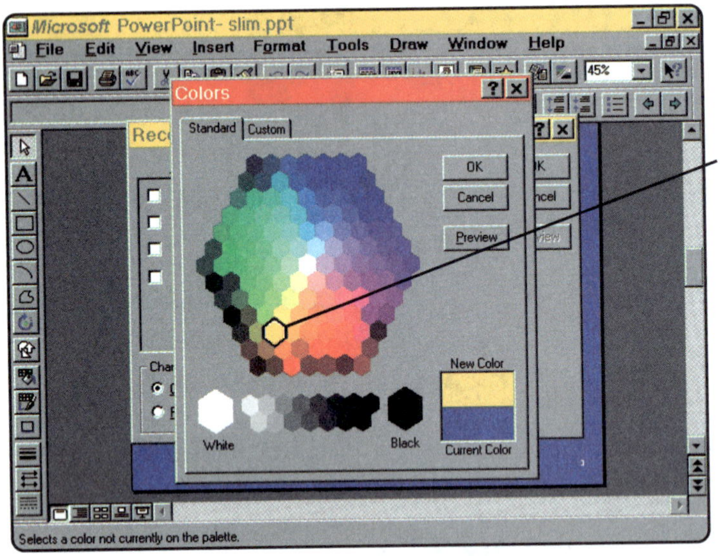

6. **Click** on the **Standard tab** to bring that box to the front.

7. **Click** on the **bright yellow hexagon**.

8. **Click** on **OK**. The Recolor Picture dialog box will appear.

9. If the new color selection is not already showing in the Preview box, **click** on **Preview** to see how the object will look with the new color.

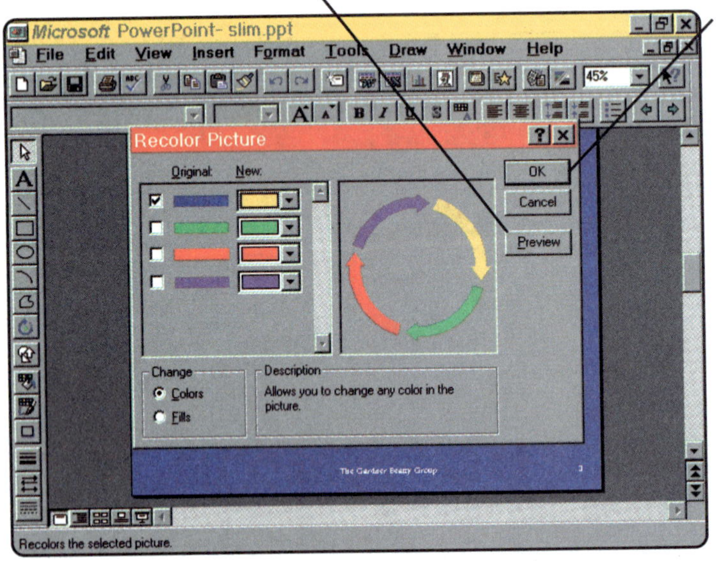

10. **Click** on **OK**. Slide 3 will reappear with the new color selection.

You'll create special text to put inside this symbol in Chapter 12, "Creating Special Effects with WordArt."

You'll learn more about working with clip art in the following sections of this chapter.

ADDING CLIP ART WITH THE INSERT MENU

In this section you will add clip art to a slide using the Insert menu.

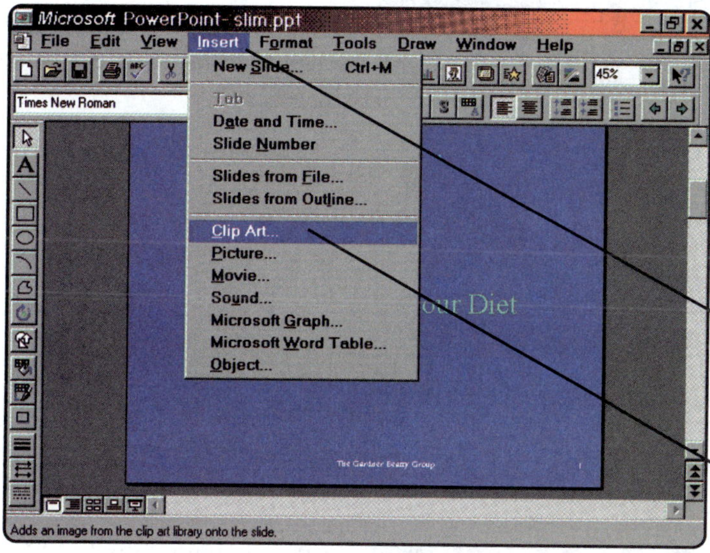

1. **Press** the **Page Up key two times** to change the view to slide 1.

2. **Click** on **Insert** in the menu bar. The Insert menu will appear.

3. **Click** on **Clip Art.** The Microsoft ClipArt Gallery will appear.

4. **Click** on the ▼ at the bottom of the Categories scroll bar.

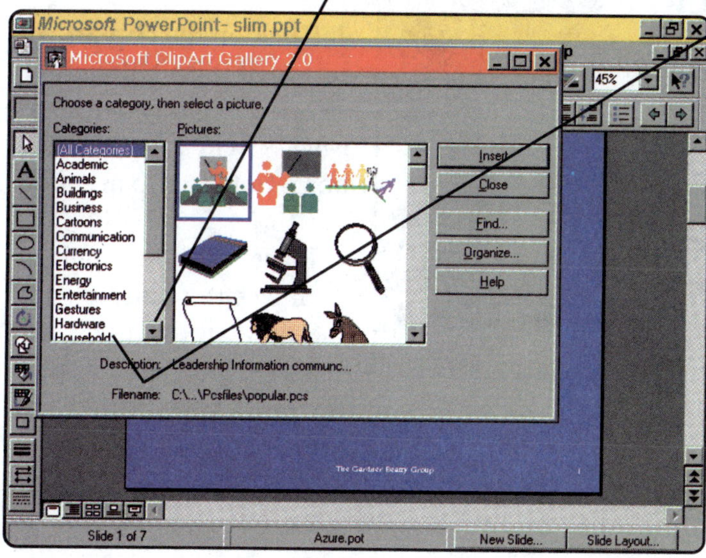

5. **Click** on the **Household** category.

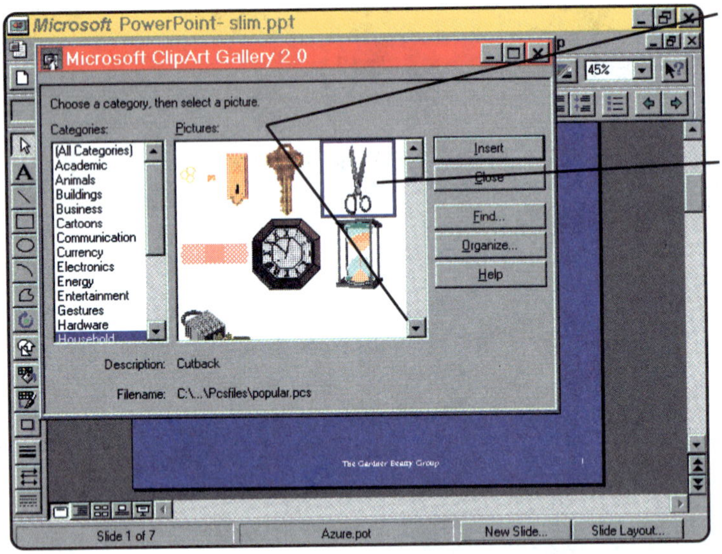

6. **Click** on the ▼ on the Pictures scroll bar until you see the scissors.

7. **Click twice** on the **scissors** to insert them into the slide.

CHANGING CLIP ART WIDTH

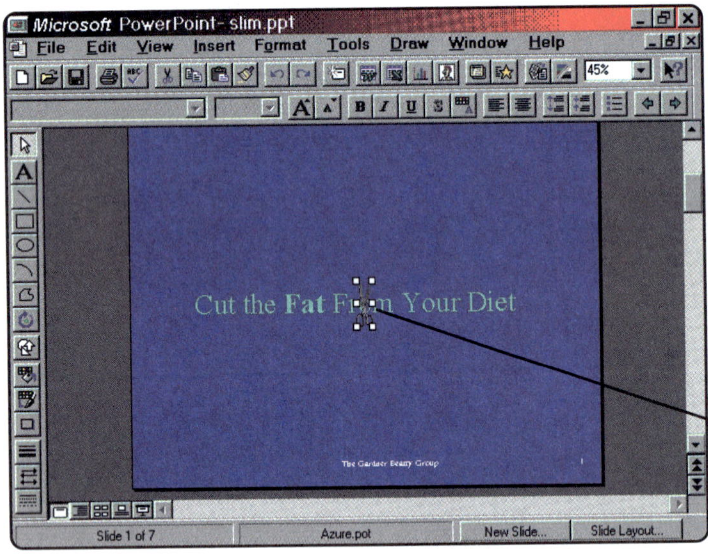

You can change just the width of clip art by using the center handle on the left or right of the clip art.

1. **Click** on the **clip art image**, if it isn't already selected. Solid squares, or *handles*, will appear on the border of the clip art.

2. **Place** the **mouse pointer** on the **center handle** on the **right side** of the scissors. The pointer will become a two-headed arrow.

3. **Press and hold** the **mouse button**.

4. **Drag** the **handle** to the **right** to widen the scissors and then **release** the **mouse button.**

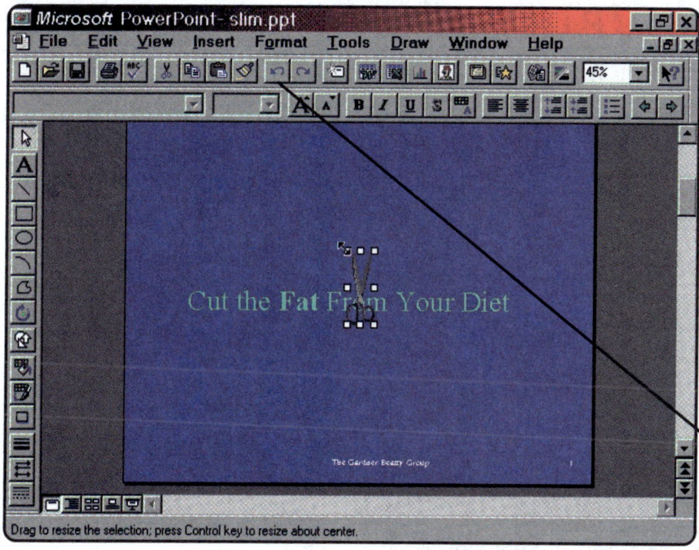

Undoing a Change

In this example, you don't want the scissors to be extra wide. You can use the Undo feature to undo or reverse a change if you use it before you do any other function.

1. **Click** on the **Undo button** in the toolbar. The picture will be returned to the size it was before you widened it.

Changing the Overall Size of Clip Art

1. **Place** the **mouse arrow** on the **top left handle.** It will turn into a two-headed arrow.

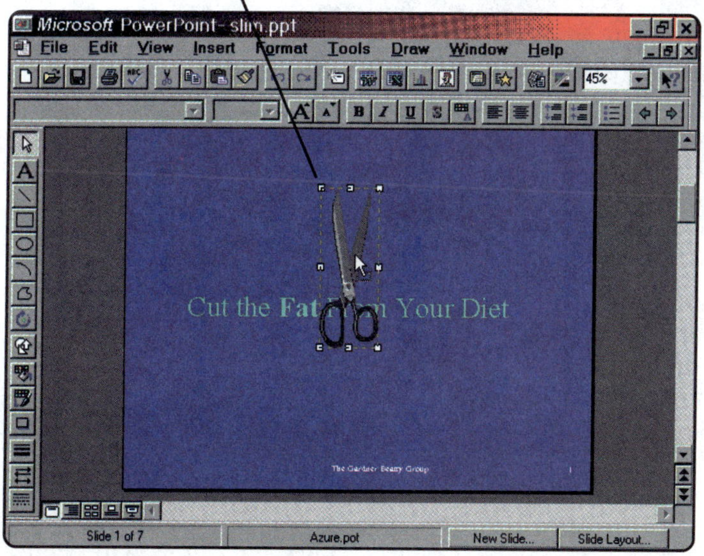

2. **Press and hold** the **mouse button** as you **drag** the arrow diagonally up and to the left to increase the size of the scissors proportionally.

3. **Release** the **mouse button** when you have the desired size. You may have to repeat steps 1 and 2 until the scissors are sized the way you want them.

ROTATING AN OBJECT

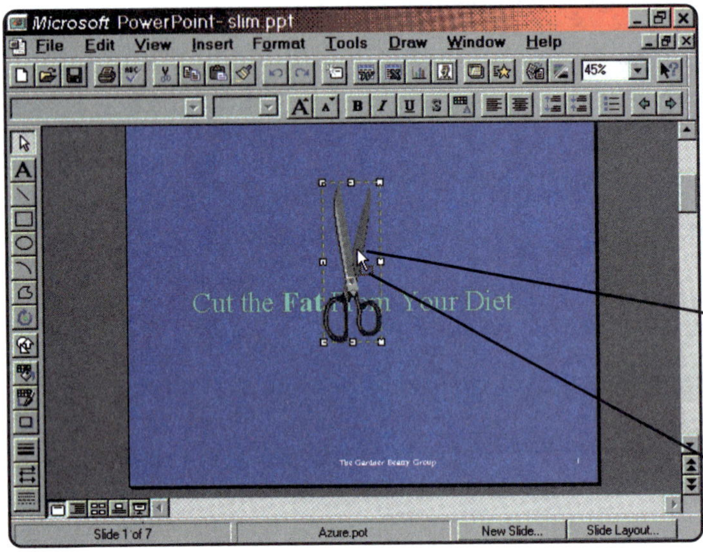

Before you rotate the scissors, you'll move them to the top half of the slide and convert them to a PowerPoint object.

Moving Clip Art

1. **Click** on the **scissors** if they don't already have handles.
2. **Place** the **mouse arrow** on the scissors.
3. **Press and hold** the **mouse button** and **drag** the cursor to move the scissors to a position above the text block, as in the next example. Then **release** the **mouse button.**

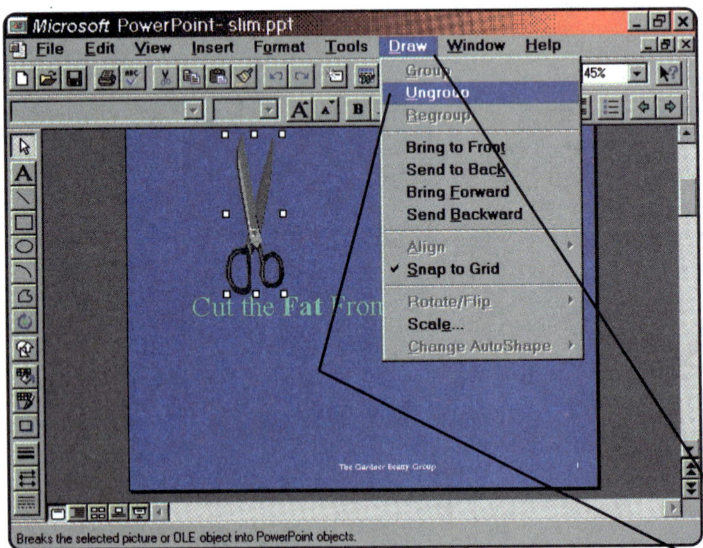

Converting Clip Art to a PowerPoint Object

Normally, only objects that are drawn in PowerPoint can be rotated. To rotate clip art, you must complete the following steps:

1. **Click** on **Draw**.
2. **Click** on **Ungroup**. A Microsoft PowerPoint message box will appear.

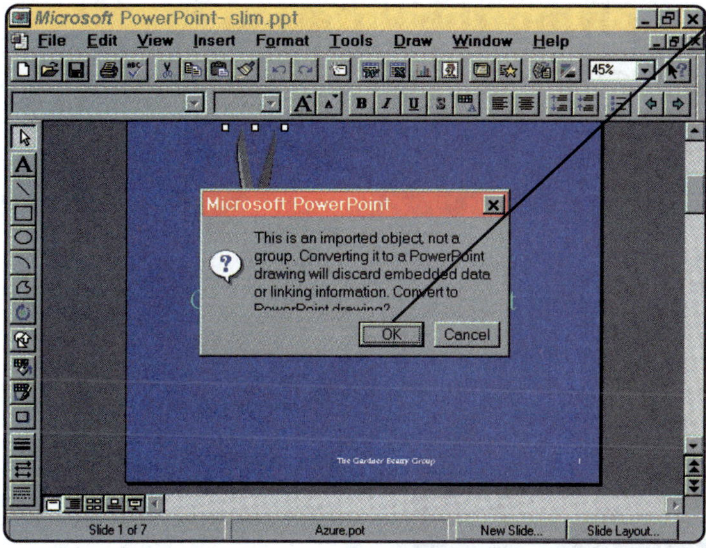

3. Click on **OK.** The scissors, with lots of selection handles, will appear in the window. In the next step, you will group the scissors as a PowerPoint object.

4. Click on **Draw** in the menu bar. The Draw menu will appear.

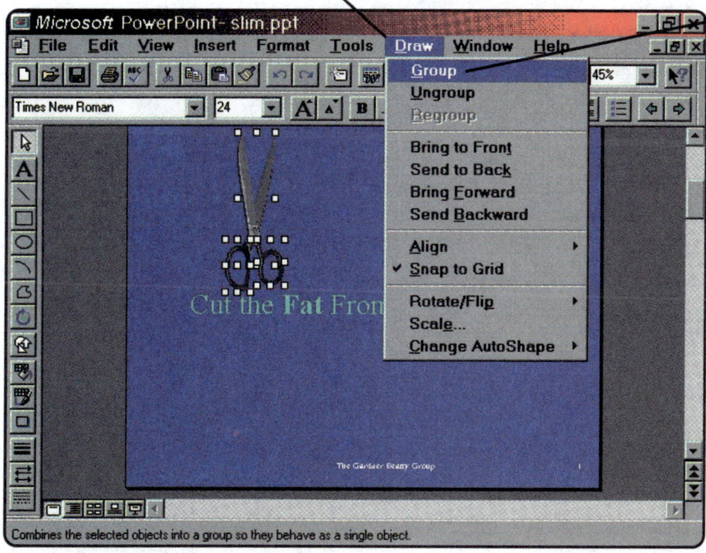

5. Click on **Group**. The scissors are now considered a PowerPoint object and can be rotated.

Applying the Rotation

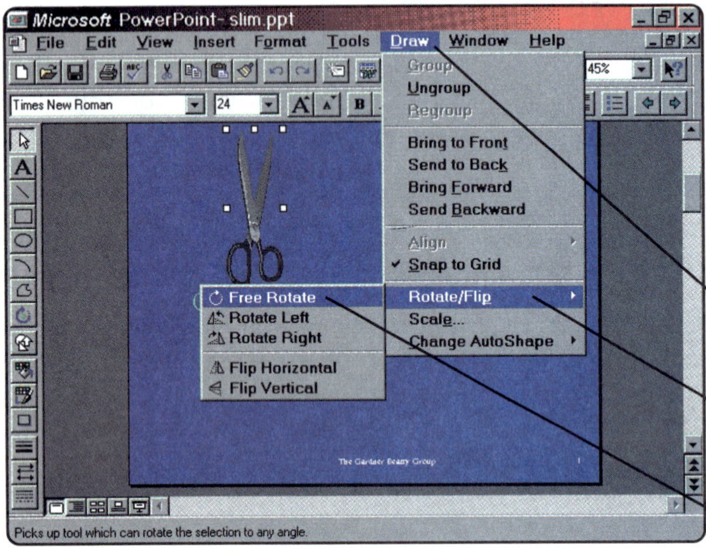

In this section you will change the orientation of the clip art.

1. **Click** on the **scissors** if they are not already selected.

2. **Click** on **Draw**. The Draw menu will appear.

3. **Click on Rotate/Flip.** A second menu will appear.

4. **Click** on **Free Rotate.** The mouse arrow will turn into a circular design.

5. **Click** and **hold** on the **upper-right section handle**. The cursor will change to the shape you see here.

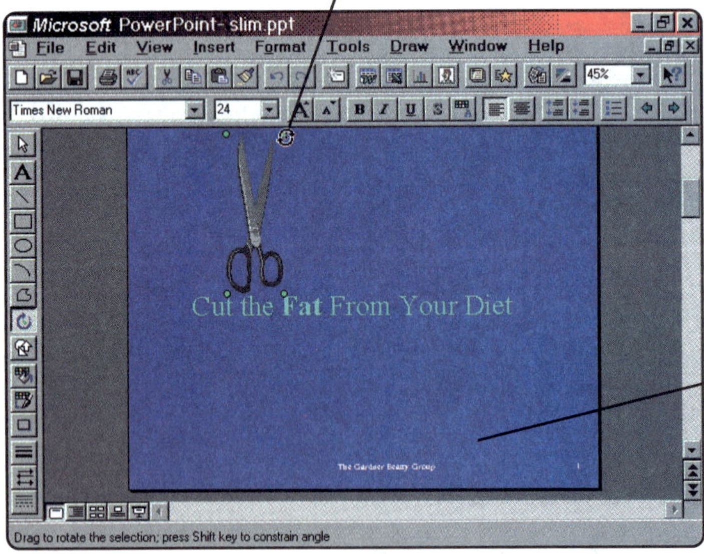

6. **Drag** the **selection handle down** towards "Fat." An outline of the scissors will rotate as you drag.

7. **Release** the **mouse button** when the scissors point towards "Fat."

8. **Click** on the **background** to release the rotation tool.

9. **Click** on the **scissors** and **use** the mouse pointer to move the scissors to the position you see in the next example.

Adding a Shadow to Clip Art

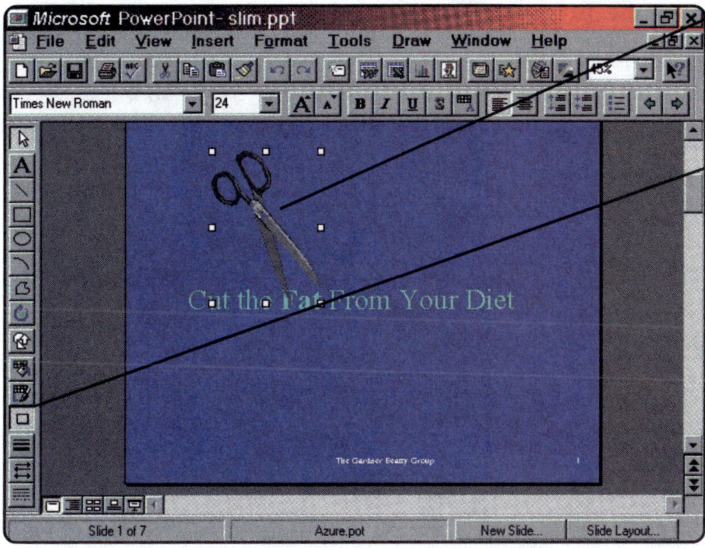

1. **Click** on the **scissors** if they are not already selected.

2. **Click** on the **Shadow button** in the drawing toolbar. A shadow will be added to the scissors.

Sending an Object to the Back

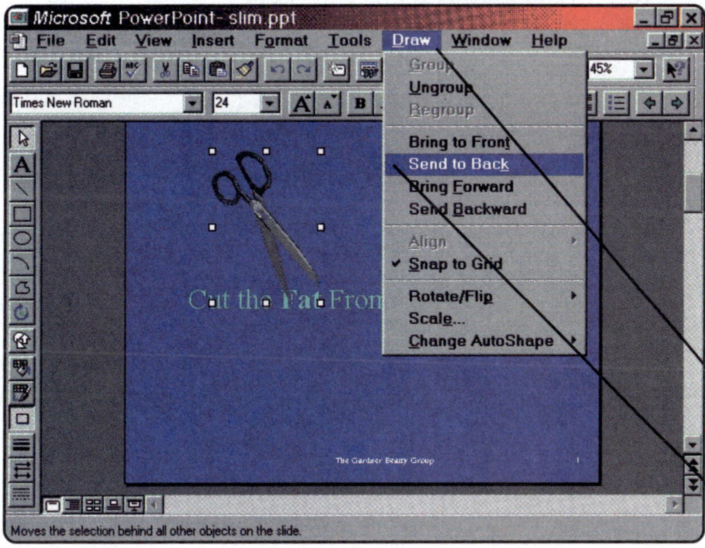

It is necessary to send the object to the back of the slide so that the scissors will not print on top of the text.

1. **Click** on the **scissors** if they are not already selected.

2. **Click** on **Draw**. The Draw menu will appear.

3. **Click** on **Send to Back.**

4. **Click anywhere** on the slide to deselect the object.

Saving the Slide

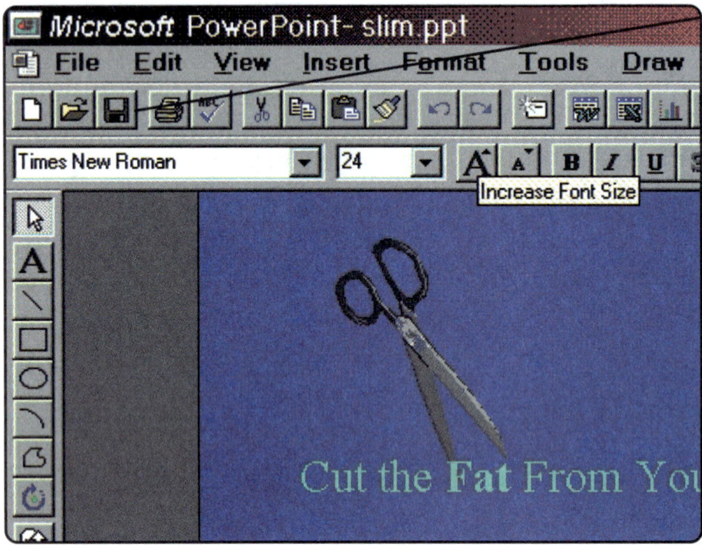

1. **Click** on the **Save button** in the toolbar. The clip art that has been added to your slides will now be saved to the slim file.

You are now ready to work with WordArt in the next chapter.

CHAPTER

12

Creating Special Effects with WordArt

Sometimes a slide just needs that little extra pizzazz. PowerPoint allows you to access a special subprogram, WordArt 2, to help you embellish your presentations. If you didn't do a custom install for PowerPoint (or MicrosoftOffice) in which you added the WordArt 2 option, you may not have WordArt 2 available. In that case, you will need to go back and install it in order to do this chapter.

WordArt 2 uses the TrueType fonts you have loaded on your system. In this chapter you will do the following:

✔ Create a special effect using WordArt 2
✔ Insert a symbol in WordArt text

USING WORDART 2

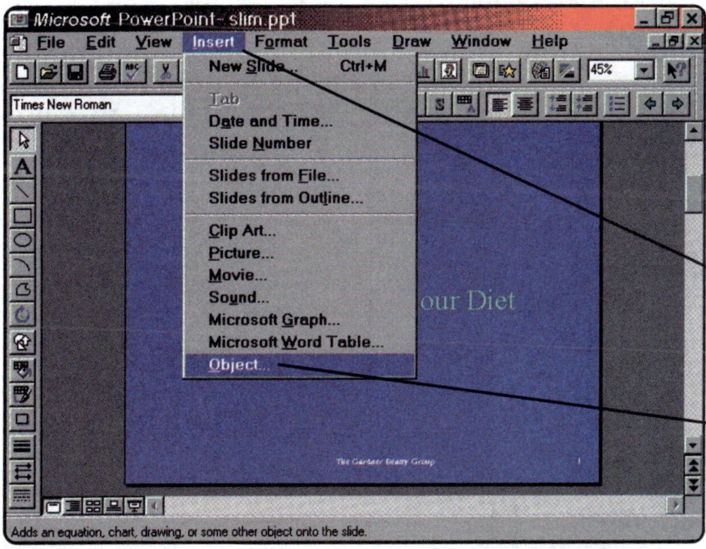

In this section, you will embellish the title on slide 1.

1. **Open slim** to **slide 1** if it isn't already open.

2. **Click** on **Insert** in the menu bar. The Insert menu will appear.

3. **Click** on **Object**. The Insert Object dialog box will appear.

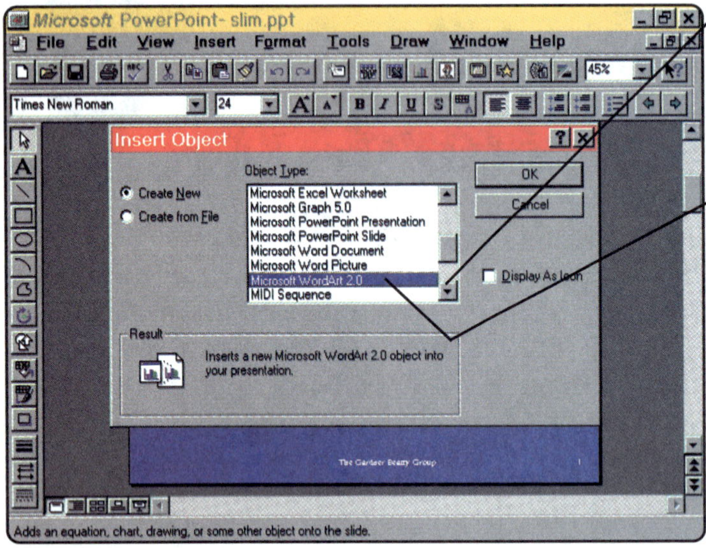

4. **Click repeatedly** on the ▼ to scroll through the programs available on your system.

5. **Click** on **Microsoft WordArt 2.0** to select it.

6. **Click** on **OK**. A Microsoft WordArt dialog box will appear.

Notice that the menu bar now shows the WordArt command buttons.

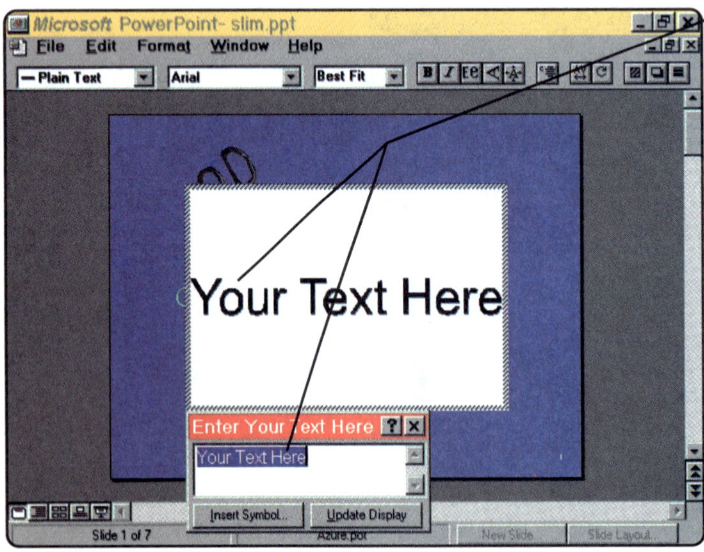

Notice also that "Your Text Here" is already highlighted and can be seen in the Preview box.

ENTERING AND STYLING TEXT IN WORDART 2

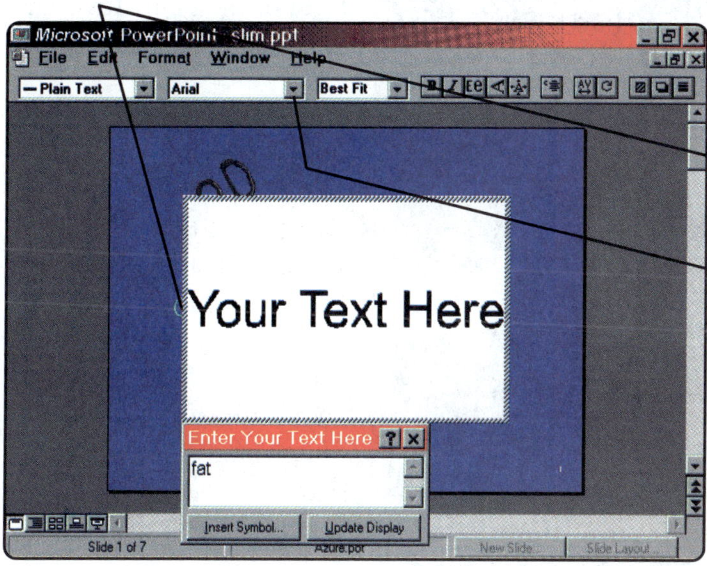

Changing the Font

1. **Type fat** in the text entry box.

2. **Click** on the ▼ to the right of the Font box.

The word fat will appear in the preview box.

3. **Click repeatedly** on the ▼ at the bottom of the scroll bar, to scroll down to GeoSlab703 XBd Bt.

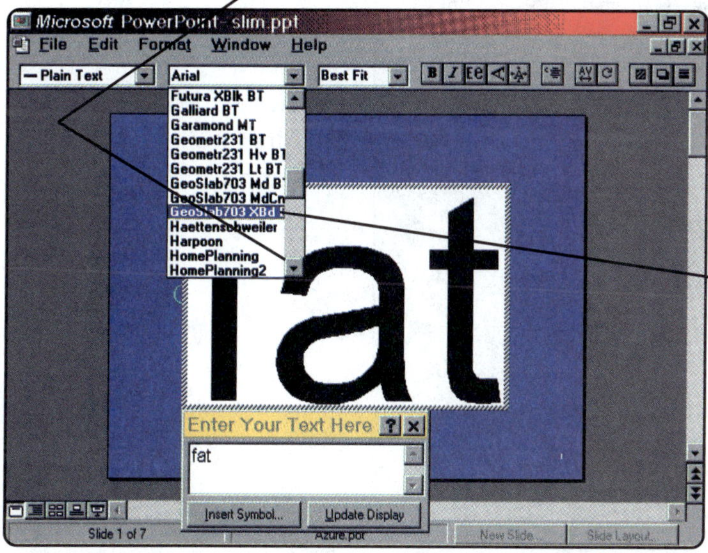

4. **Press** the ▼ key on your keyboard to move through the list of fonts. Wait a few seconds for each highlighted font to be reflected in the example.

5. **Click** on **GeoSlab703 XBd Bt**. (If you don't have this font, choose another one.)

Notice that the word "fat" in the Preview box changes from Arial to GeoSlab703 XBd Bt. The new font name appears in the Font box.

Changing the Font Shape

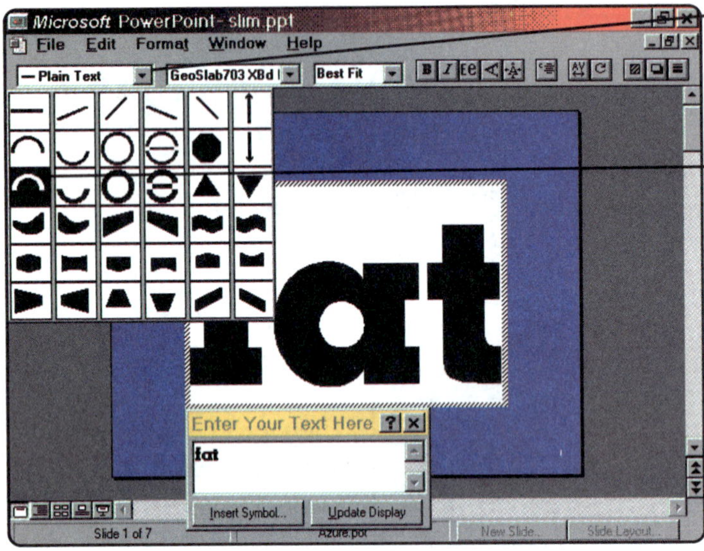

1. **Click** on the ▼ to the right of the Plain Text. The Shape menu will appear.
2. **Click** on the **Arch Up (pour)** shape.

Notice that the new font shape will show in the Preview box.

The name of the new font shape appears in the Shape box.

Changing the Fill Color and Adding a Shadow

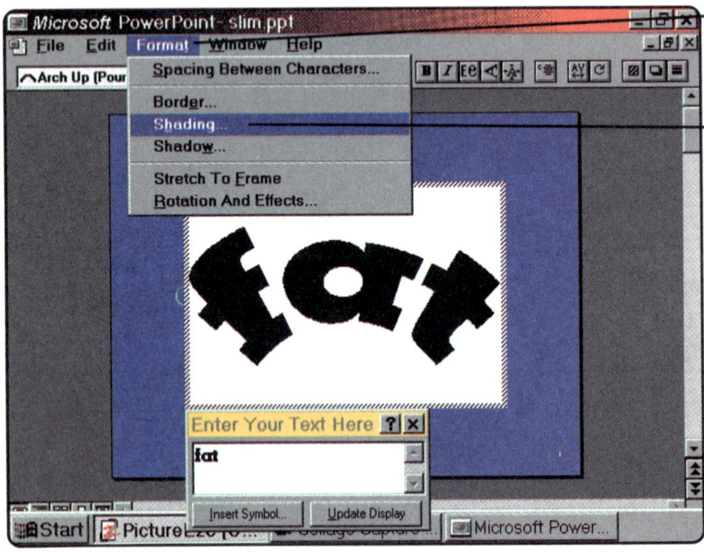

1. **Click** on **Format**. The format menu will appear.
2. **Click** on **Shading**. The Shading dialog box will appear.

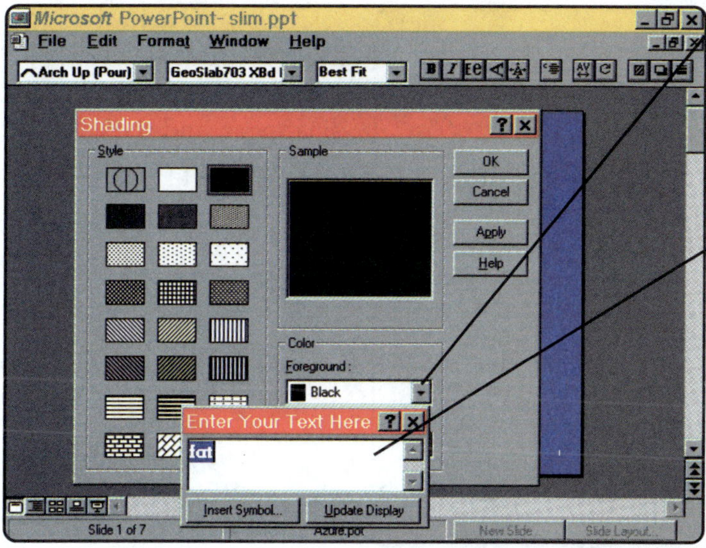

3. **Click** on the ▼ to the right of Black below Color Foreground. The Color Foreground box will appear.

The WordArt text entry dialog box will disappear.

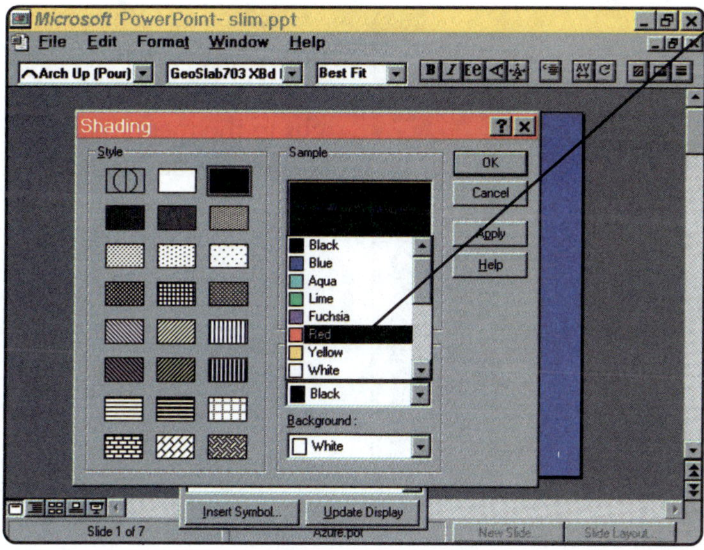

4. **Click** on **Red** in the Color Foreground selection box. The sample color will now be red.

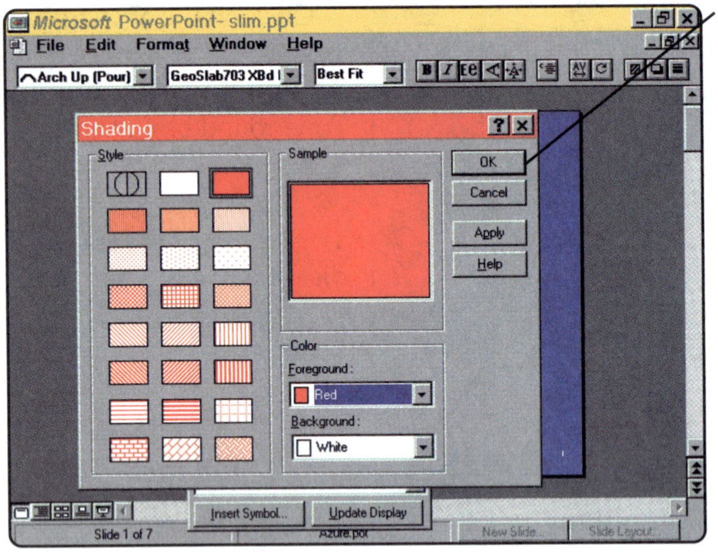

5. **Click** on **OK** to change the WordArt fill color to red. The Shading box will disappear, and the word "fat" will appear in red.

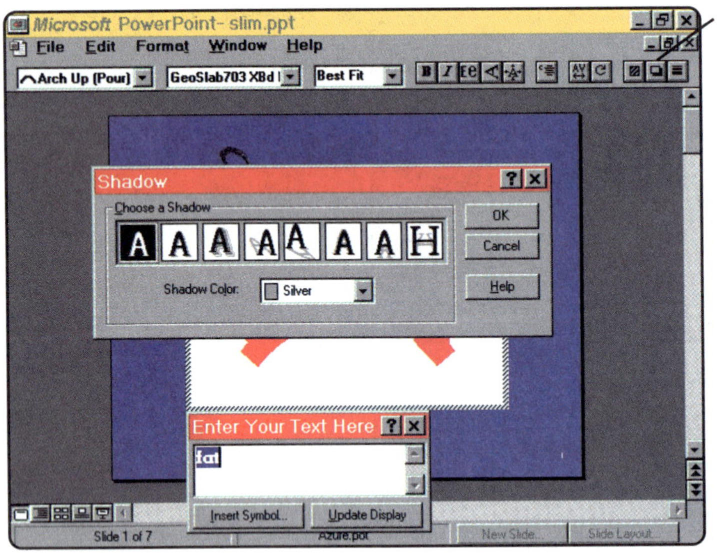

6. **Click** on the **Shadow button**, which is the second button from the right in the menu bar. The Shadow dialog box will appear.

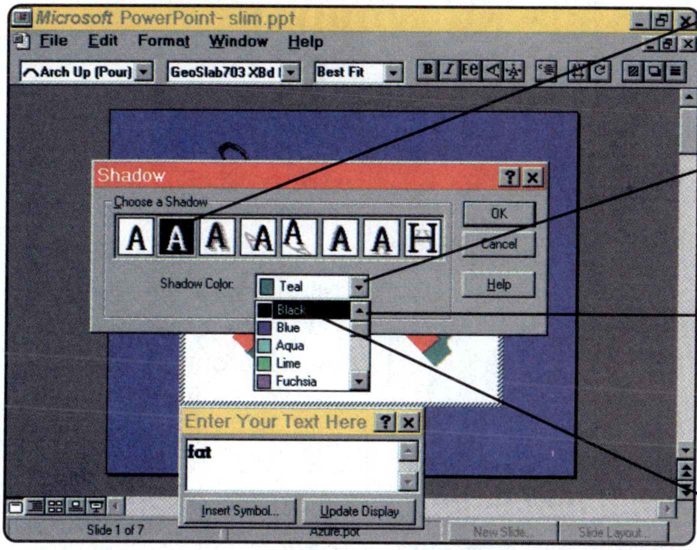

7. **Click** on the **second shadow type box** to select it.

8. **Click** on the ▼ to the right of Shadow Color. A color menu will appear.

9. **Click repeatedly** on the ▲ at the top of the Shadow Color scroll bar to scroll to the top of the list.

10. **Click** on **Black**.

11. **Click** on **OK**. The Shadow dialog box will disappear.

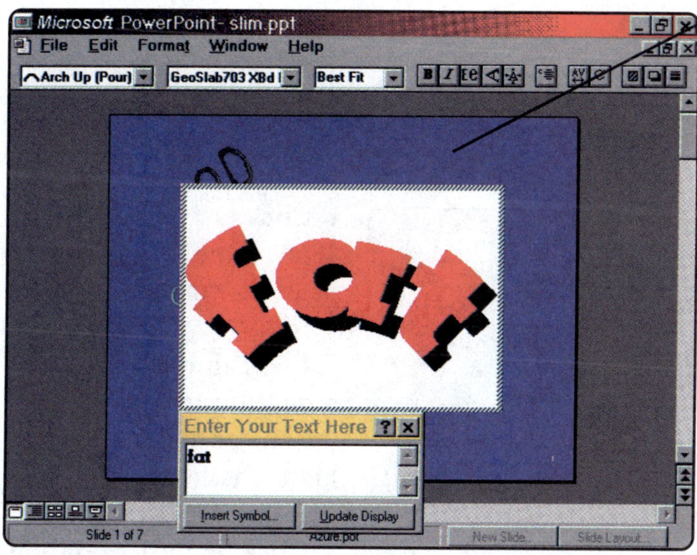

12. **Click anywhere** on the slide background. The WordArt text entry and preview boxes will disappear. The WordArt object will be placed in the middle of your slide, ready to be sized and placed into position.

COMBINING WORDART WITH A TEXT LINE

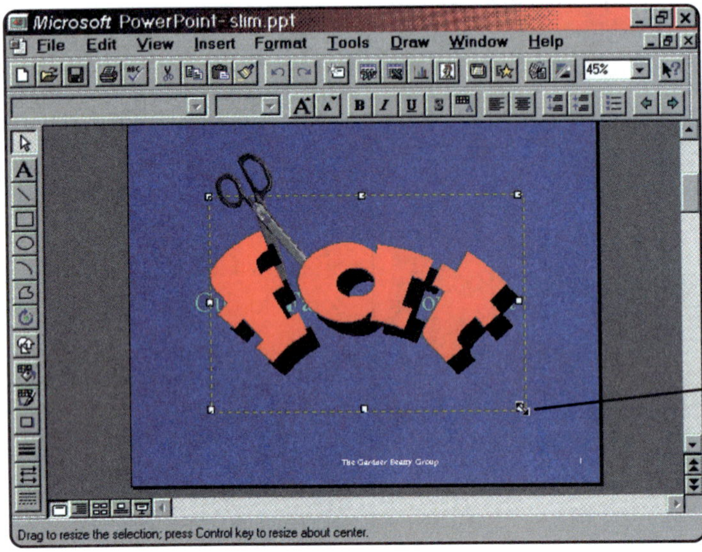

Because WordArt is created as an object, PowerPoint won't allow you to combine it with regular text in a text line. But, with a slightly fussy "work-around," you can make it look as though it all fits together.

1. **Click** and **hold** the **bottom right corner handle** of the WordArt and **drag** up and to the left to resize it smaller. This is only to get it out of the way for now, so the exact size doesn't matter. If you need help with this, refer to Chapter 11, "Working with Clip Art."

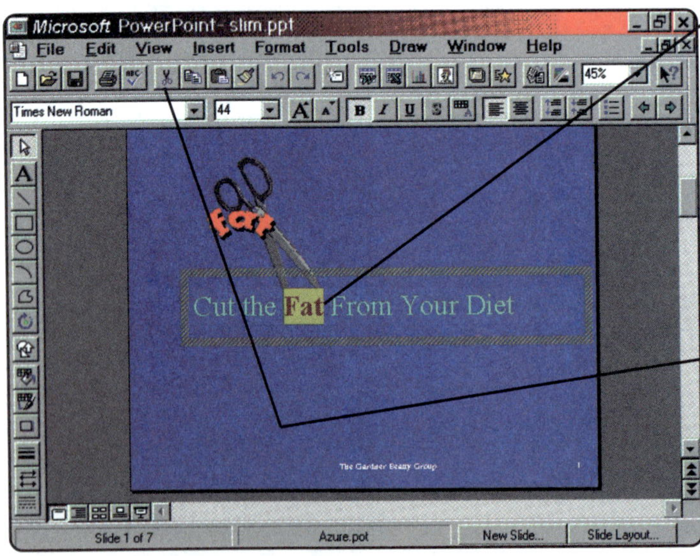

2. **Click** just after the **t** in **"Fat"** in the text block to place the cursor.

3. **Press and hold** the **mouse button** and **drag** the cursor to the left to highlight the word "**Fat**."

4. **Click** on the **Cut button** in the toolbar. "Fat" will disappear. (We should all be so lucky.)

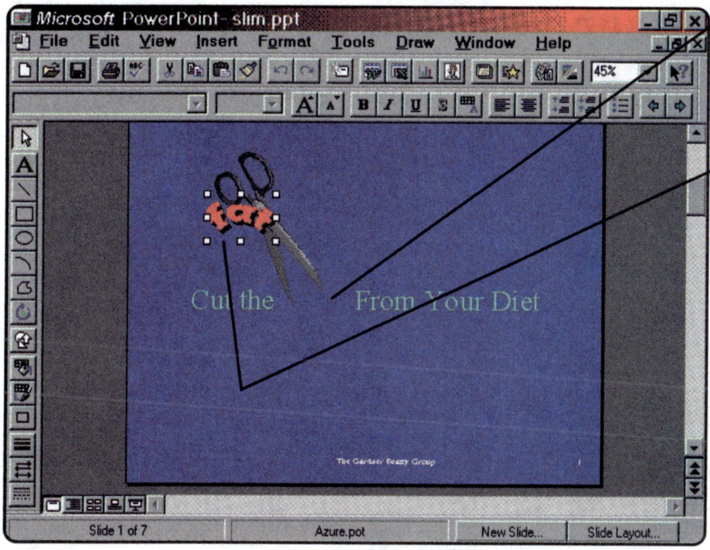

5. **Press** the **Spacebar repeatedly** until you make room for the WordArt.

6. **Click** on the "**fat**" **Word Art** to get the selection handles.

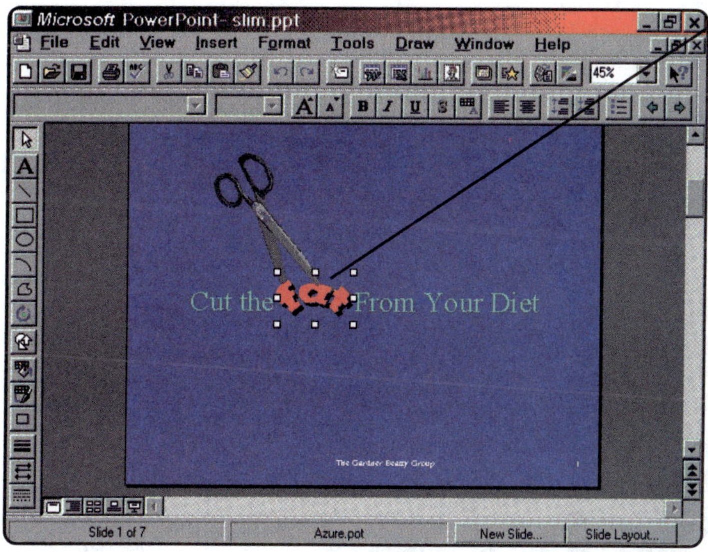

7. **Press and hold** the **mouse button** and **drag** the WordArt into the space between "the" and "From".

8. **Click**, **hold**, and **drag** a **corner handle** to **resize** the WordArt to fit the space as you see in this example. If you need help with this, refer to Chapter 11 "Working with Clip Art," on page 113. Remember that you can use the arrow keys to make fine adjustments in the position of the WordArt.

Grouping WordArt and Text

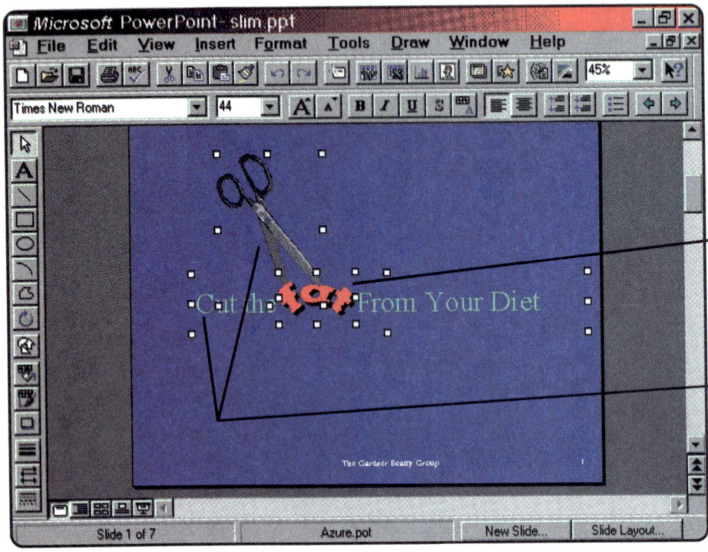

In this section, you will learn to group WordArt with text and graphics so they can be moved together as a single unit.

1. **Click** on the **WordArt** if it doesn't already have selection handles.
2. **Press and hold** the **Shift key** and **click** on the **text block** and the **scissors** to select all three items at the same time.
3. **Release** the **Shift key**.
4. **Press and hold** the **mouse arrow** anywhere on the three items and drag the grouped objects to a different part of the slide, if you like.

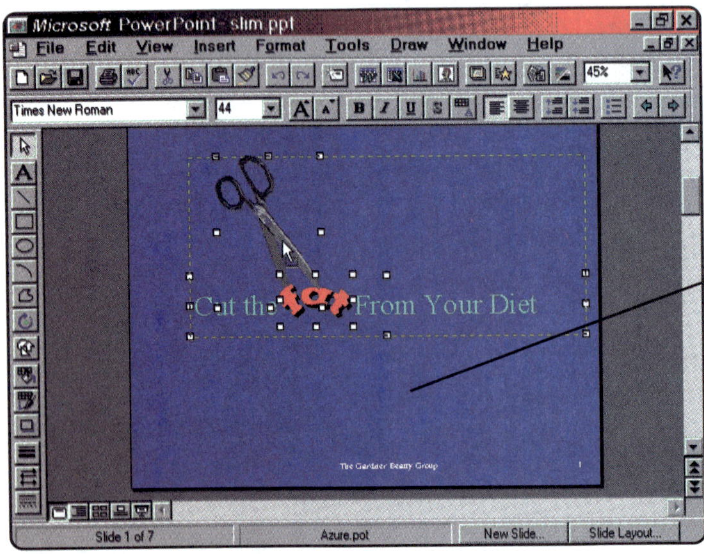

5. **Release** the **mouse button**.

You may need to try steps 3 and 4 more than once to get the hang of it.

6. **Click anywhere** on the slide background to deselect the three objects. They will no longer be grouped. (In order to regroup these objects, you need to repeat the above steps.)

Inserting a Symbol in WordArt Text

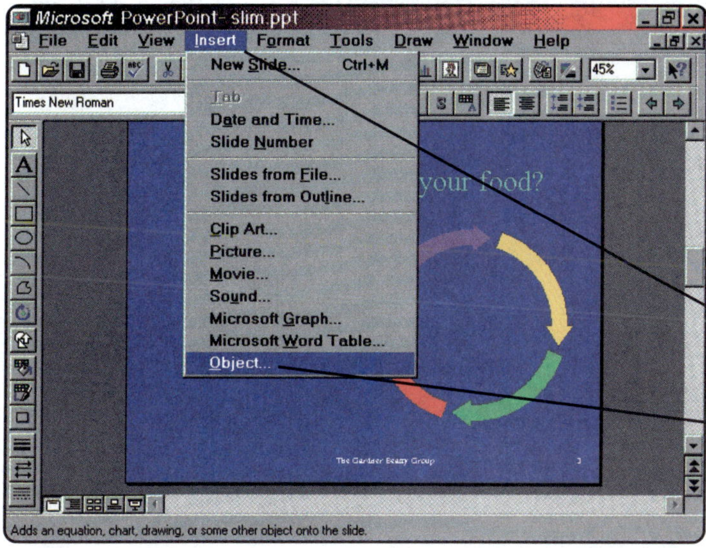

In this section you will create a milk carton logo for slide 3.

1. **Press** the **Page Down key twice** to move to slide 3 in slim.

2. **Click** on **Insert**. The Insert menu will appear.

3. **Click** on **Object**. The Insert Object dialog box will appear.

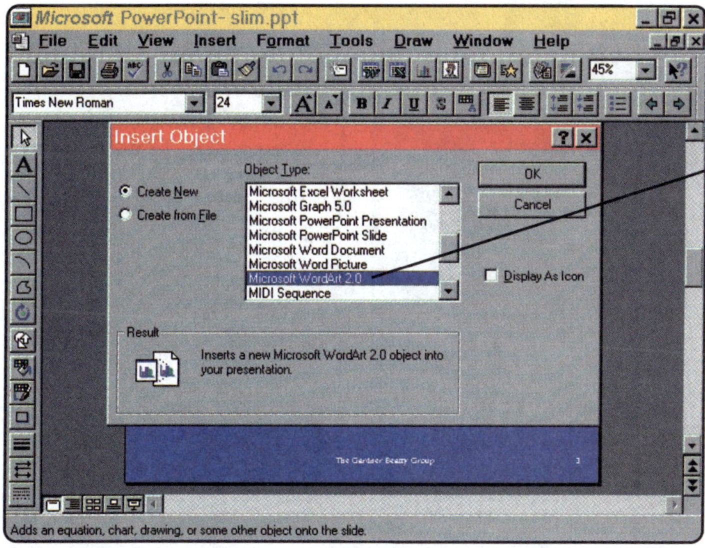

4. **Click repeatedly** on the ▼ to scroll through the available programs.

5. **Click** on **Microsoft WordArt 2.0** to select it.

6. **Click** on **OK.**

The WordArt 2.0 dialog box will appear.

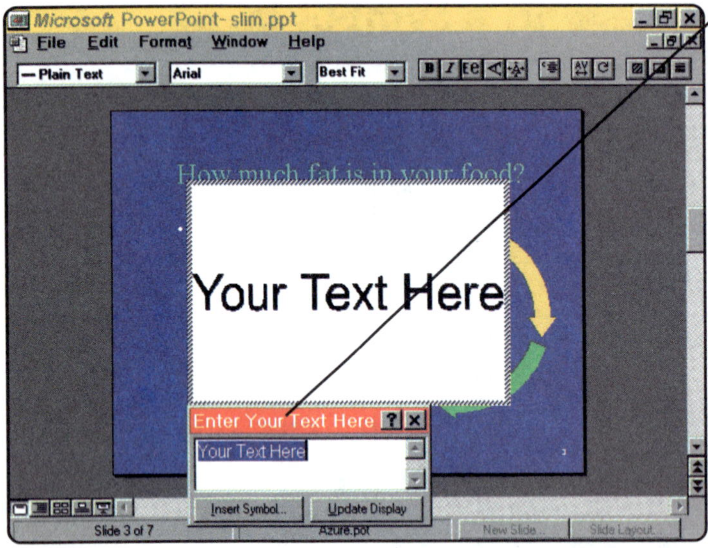

The text entry box can be moved by placing the arrow on the title bar. Then press, hold, and drag to a more convenient position.

7. **Type Blue Sky** in the text entry box. **Press Enter.**

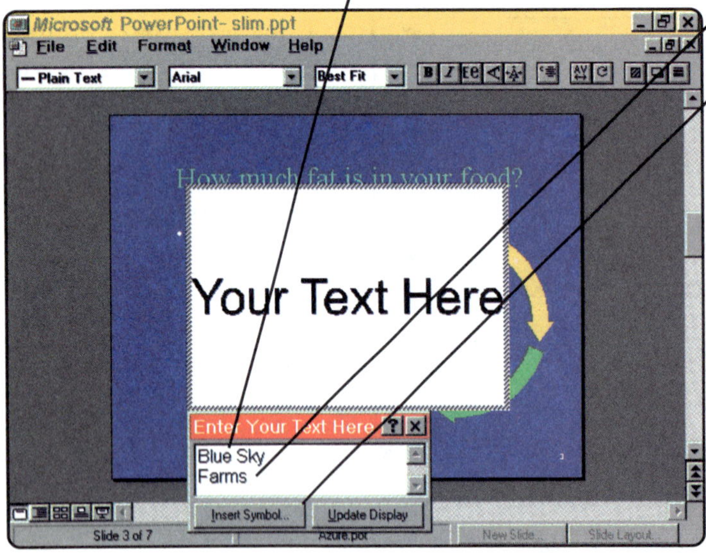

8. **Type Farms.**

9. With the cursor placed just after "Farms," **click** on **Insert Symbol.** The Insert Symbol dialog box will appear.

10. **Click** on the ® in the middle of the fifth row.

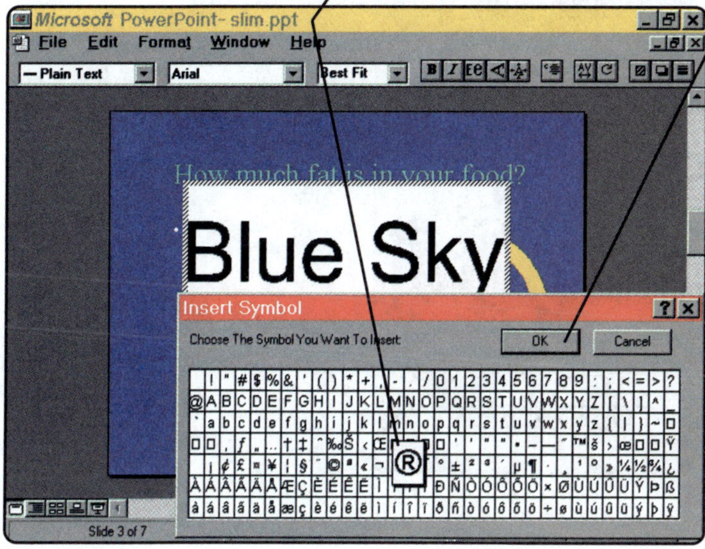

11. **Click** on **OK**. The Insert Symbol dialog box will disappear.

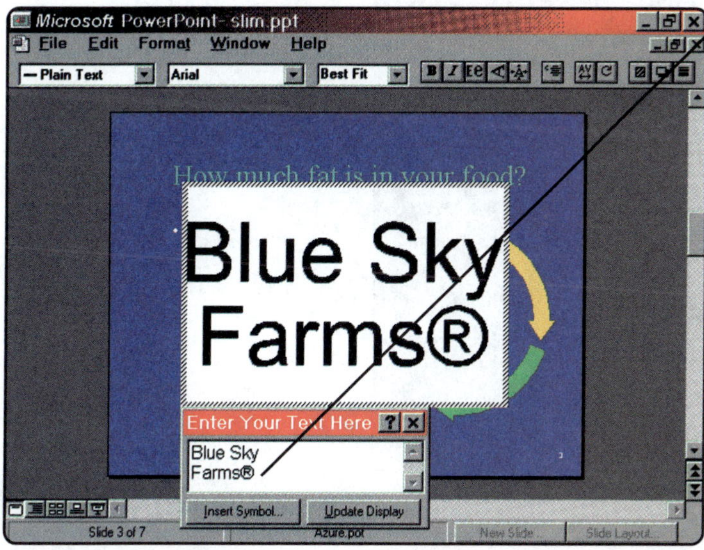

12. **Click** just after the **(R)** and **Press Enter.**

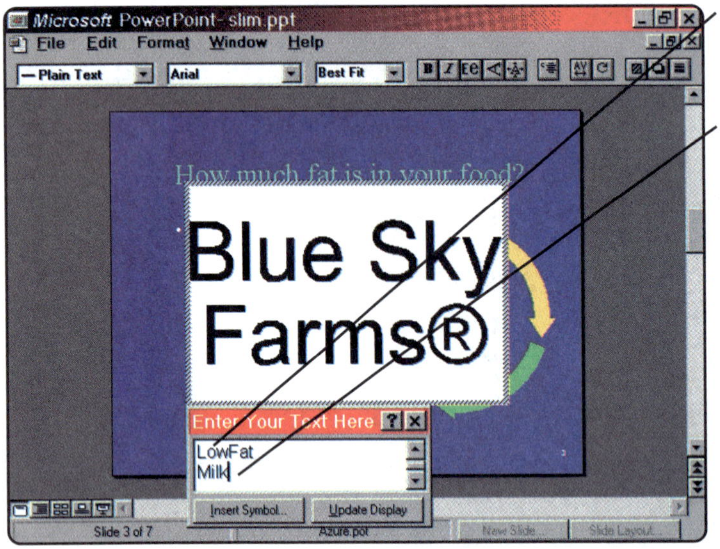

13. **Type LowFat. Press Enter.**

14. **Type Milk.**

15. Click on the **Bold button** to select it.

16. Click on the **Rotate button**, which is the fourth button from the right. A Special Effects dialog box will appear.

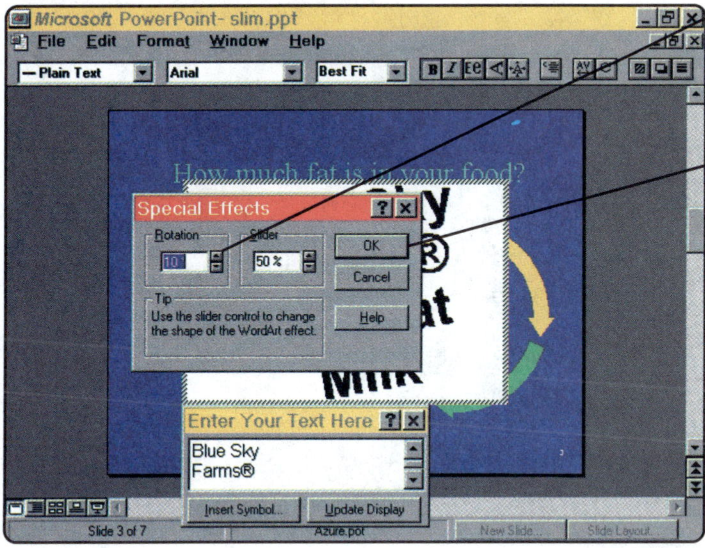

17. **Click twice** on the ▲ to the right of 0 to change the rotation angle to 10%.

18. **Click** on **OK.**

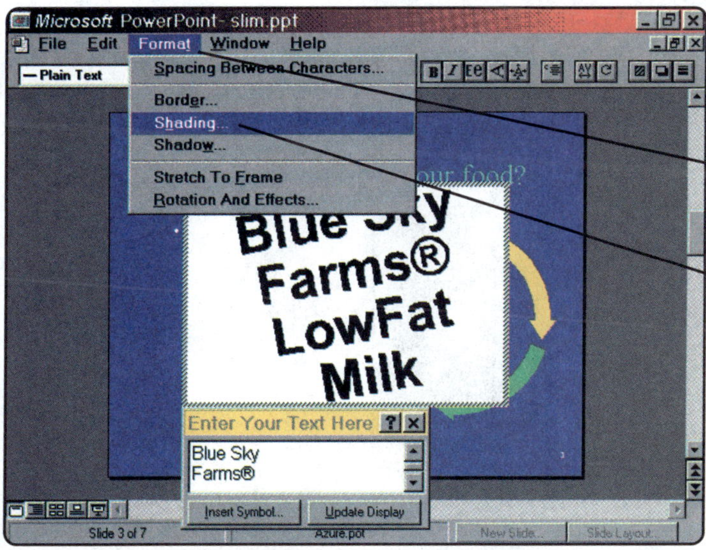

Notice that the type in the preview box has rotated 10°.

19. **Click** on **Format**. The Format menu will appear.

20. **Click** on **Shading**. The Shading dialog box will appear.

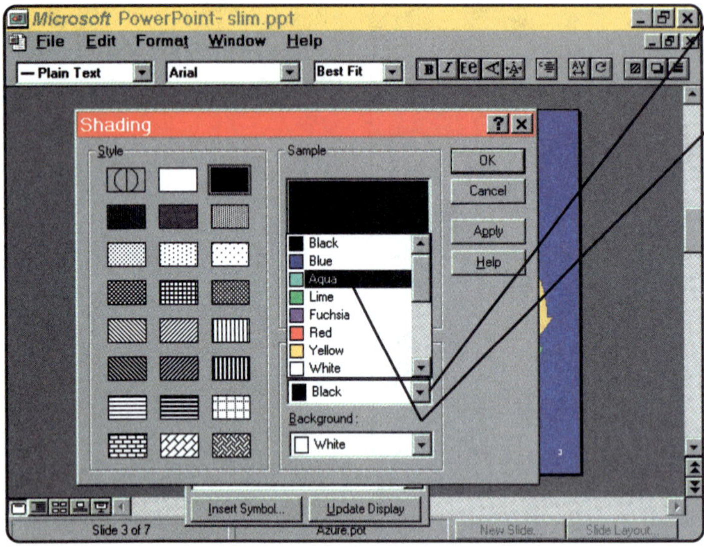

21. **Click** on the ▼ to the right of Black.

22. **Scroll up** and **click** on **Aqua**.

23. **Click** on **OK**. The Shading selection box will change to shades of aqua.

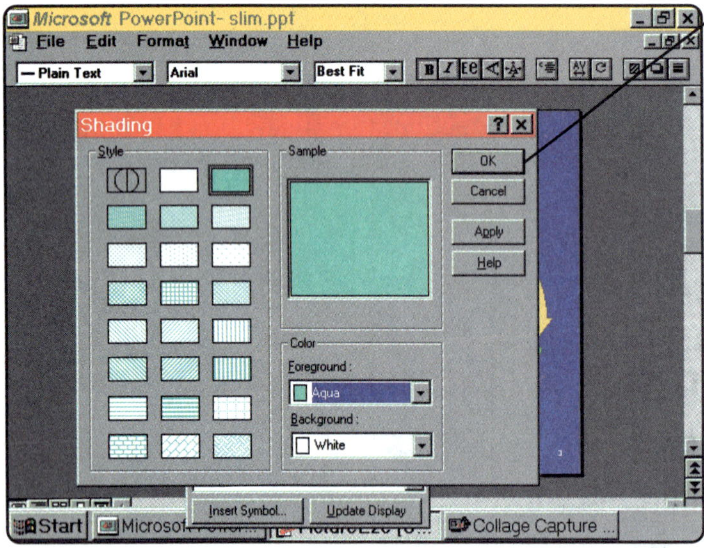

24. **Click** on **OK** to return to the Text Entry box. The text will change to an aqua color.

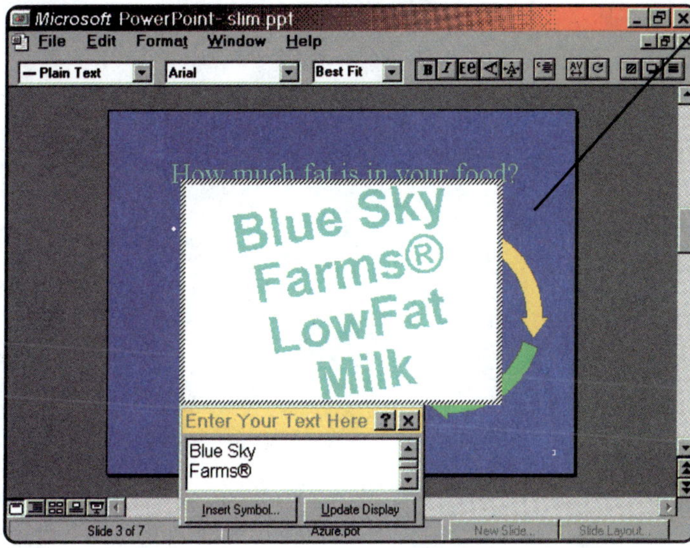

25. Click on the **slide background.** The WordArt text entry and preview boxes will disappear. The WordArt object will be placed in the middle of your slide, ready to be sized and placed into position.

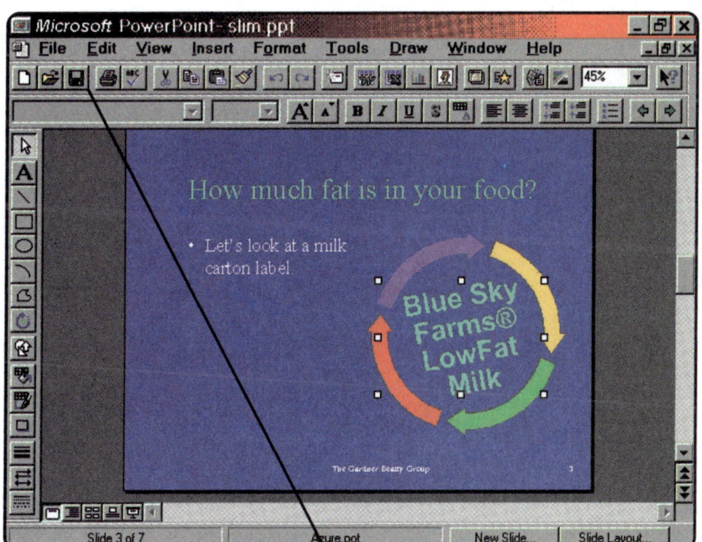

If you're using a WordArt picture as an independent graphic, treat it just like a piece of clip art or other object. Placement, moving, and sizing are done as shown in Chapter 11, "Working with Clip Art."

Fiddle to your heart's content with the rotation angle, sizing, colors, etc. As you can see, we have placed the WordArt here in the milk carton logo.

26. Remember to **click** on the **Save button** to save your work.

Part III: Graphs, Tables, and Charts

CHAPTER

13

Working with Graphs

In order to create a graph, you must first create a *datasheet*, or spreadsheet. You can create the datasheet in PowerPoint using a predesigned graph slide. If you already have a spreadsheet and graph in Excel, you can copy or link them into PowerPoint. You can also use a special toolbar button to take you into Excel. In this chapter you will do the following:

- ✔ Create a graph in PowerPoint
- ✔ Insert a graph from Excel into PowerPoint
- ✔ Use the Insert Microsoft Excel Worksheet button

CREATING A GRAPH IN POWERPOINT

In order to create a graph, you must first create a datasheet. PowerPoint has a predesigned slide that makes this task really easy. In this section, you will add the graph slide after slide 6.

1. **Go** to **slide 6**.
2. **Click** on **New Slide**. The New Slide dialog box will appear.

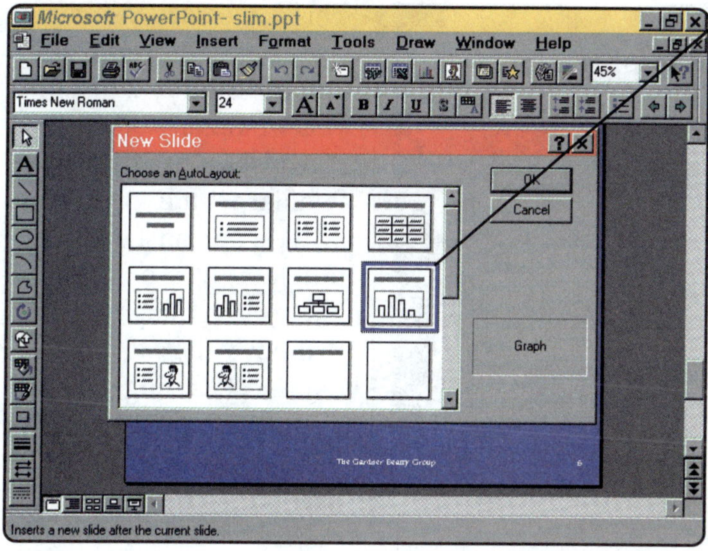

3. **Click twice** on the **Graph slide**, which is the last slide in the second row. The graph slide will appear in slide view.

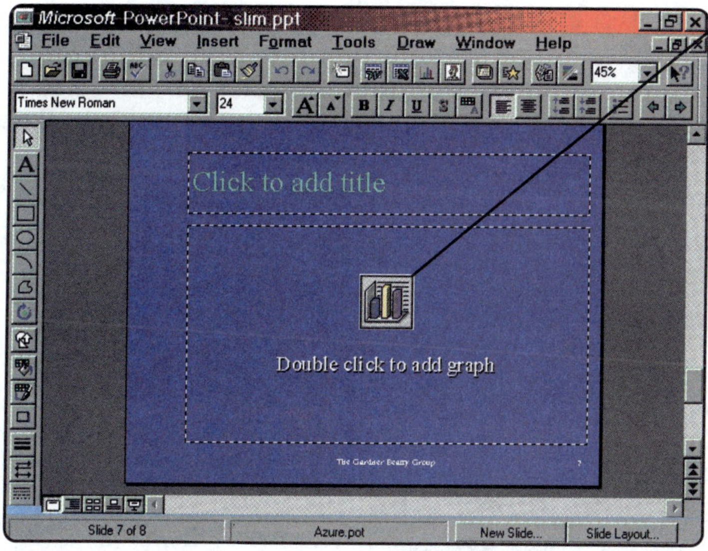

4. **Click twice** inside the **graph block**. It will take a while, but eventually you will see the PowerPoint datasheet, or spreadsheet.

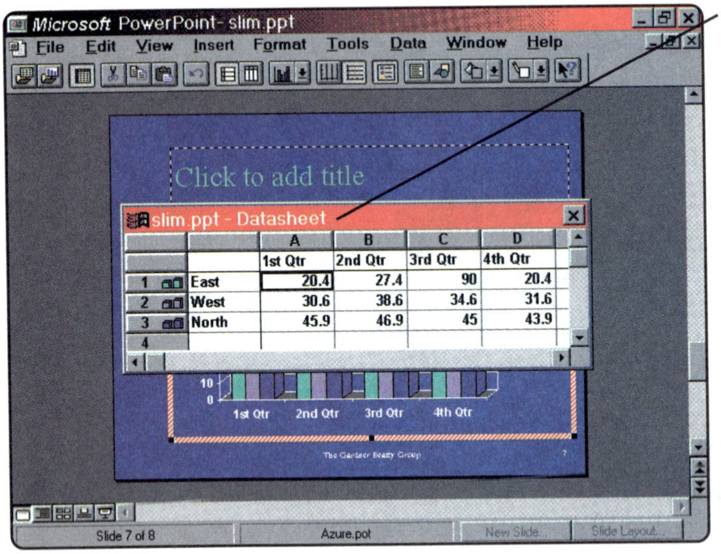

This is the datasheet that comes with PowerPoint. You can modify it just as you would any other spreadsheet. If you are familiar with Excel (or another spreadsheet program), you probably know everything you need to modify the existing datasheet. Giving step-by-step directions on working with spreadsheets is beyond the scope of this book, however. If you need help, refer to *Excel for Windows 95*, another book in the Visual Learning Guide series.

This section will use a datasheet that has been modified as you see here. Notice that we deleted the data in column D, increased the width of columns A and B, and changed the actual data. If you want to go through the steps in this process without changing the data, simply use the existing datasheet.

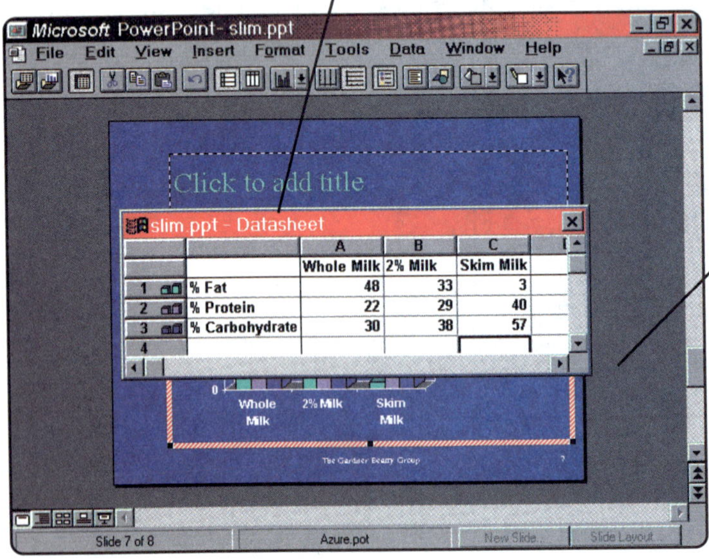

5. **Click anywhere** on the background. PowerPoint will automatically convert the datasheet into a graph and insert the graph into the slide. It couldn't be easier!

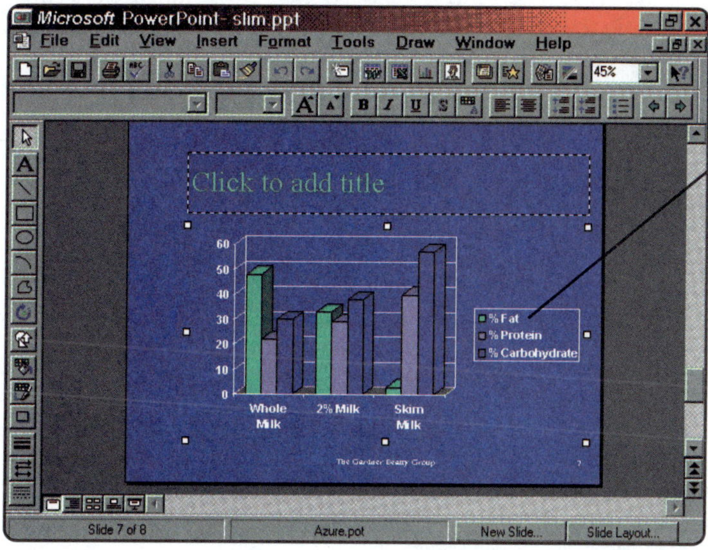

REMOVING THE LEGEND

If you want to remove the legend, complete the following steps.

1. **Click twice** on the **graph**. It will be surrounded by a candy-striped border.

Notice that the toolbar has changed to an Excel toolbar.

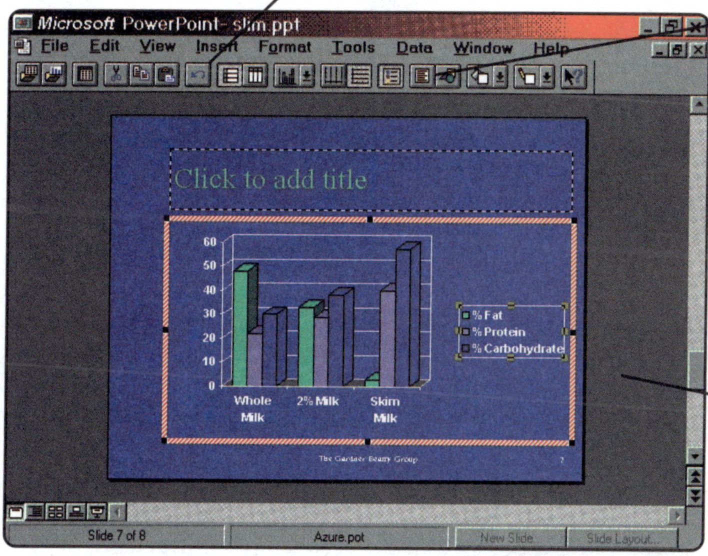

2. **Click** on the **Legend button** in the toolbar. The legend will be removed from the graph.

3. **Click** once again on the **Legend button**. The legend will be restored to the graph.

4. **Click** on the **background** to insert the graph into the slide.

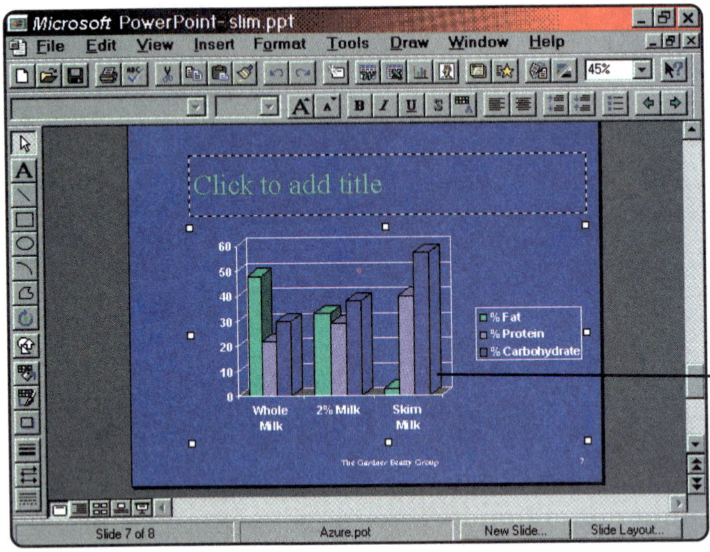

Isn't this terrific!

EDITING THE DATASHEET

You edit the contents of the graph by editing the datasheet.

1. **Click twice** on the **graph**. It will be surrounded by a candy-striped selection border. It is now the active element in the slide.

2. **Click** on **View** in the menu bar. The View menu will appear.

3. **Click** on **Datasheet**. The datasheet will appear.

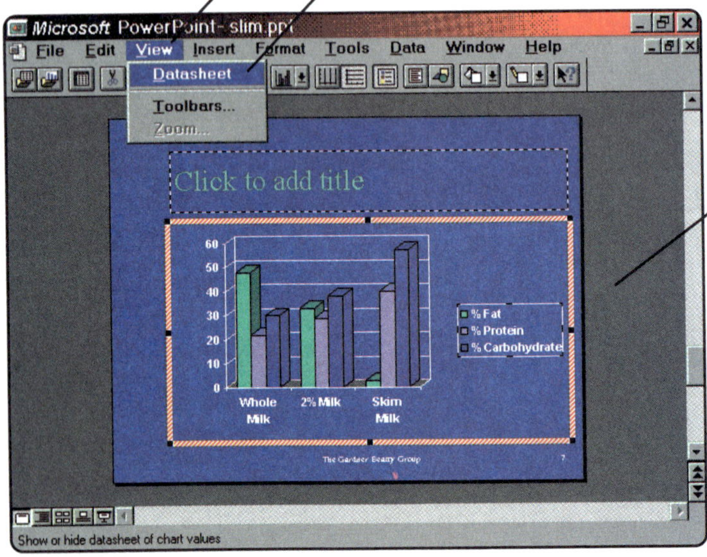

4. **Make** whatever **edits** you want. The changes will automatically be carried over to the graph.

5. **Click** on the **background** to insert the edited graph into the slide.

6. Once the graph is inserted into the slide, **click** on the **background** once again to remove the selection handles from the graph.

EDITING THE GRAPH

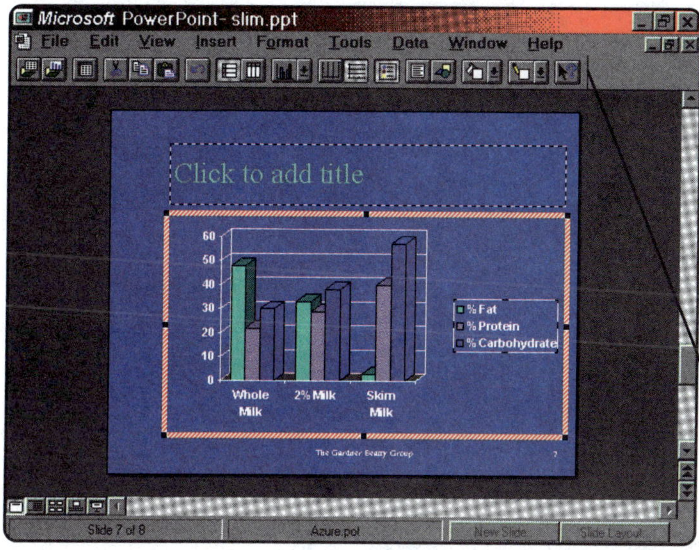

You can change the color and pattern of the bars. You can also change the grid behind the bars.

1. **Click twice** on the **graph**. It will be surrounded by a candy-striped selection border.

Notice that the buttons in the toolbar have changed to graph-related tools. Refer to *Excel for Windows 95: The Visual Learning Guide* on how to change a graph.

Changing the Format of the Graph

You can change the chart type with a click of your mouse.

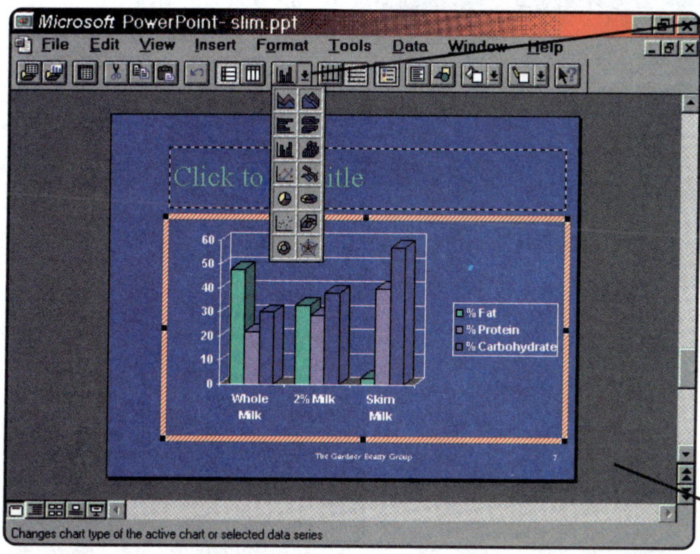

1. While the graph is surrounded by the selection border, **click** on the ▼ to the right of the Chart Type button in the toolbar. A list of chart types will appear.

2. **Click** on the **chart type** of your choice. The graph will be changed. Here, we decided to keep it the same.

3. **Click** on the **background** to insert the edited graph back into the slide.

DELETING A TEXT BLOCK FROM A PREDESIGNED SLIDE

Normally, you would add a title to the graph that explains what the graph is about. However, if you've been following along with this book, you already know how to add a title and the process wouldn't teach you anything new. So, instead, you will delete the title block that is part of this slide. Just because a text block is on a predesigned slide doesn't mean you have to use it. You can delete any text block you don't need.

1. **Click** on the **slide background** to remove the selection handles from the graph.

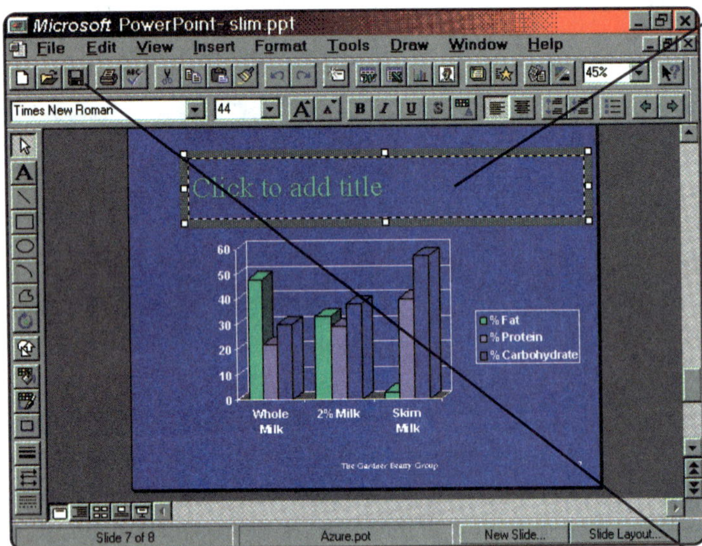

2. **Press and hold** the **Shift key** and **click** inside the title text block. This will select the block and add handles to the border. (Be sure you have not also selected the graph. It should not have handles.)

3. **Press** the **Delete** (or Backspace) **key** to delete the text block from the slide.

4. **Click** on the **Save button** in the toolbar to save your work.

IMPORTING AN EXISTING WORKSHEET

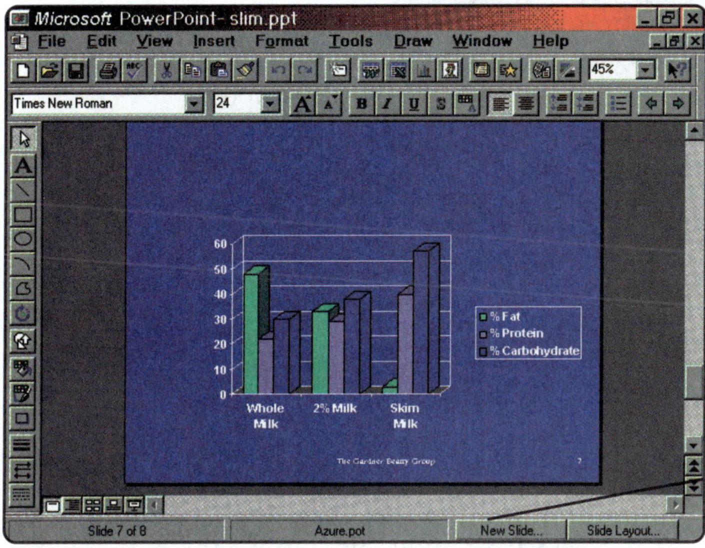

If you have a worksheet already created and saved in a spreadsheet program such as Excel or 1-2-3, you can import it into PowerPoint. In this section, you will import a worksheet from Excel.

Switching to Excel

1. **Click** on **New Slide** on the bottom selection bar.

2. **Click** on the **blank slide** at the end of the third row.

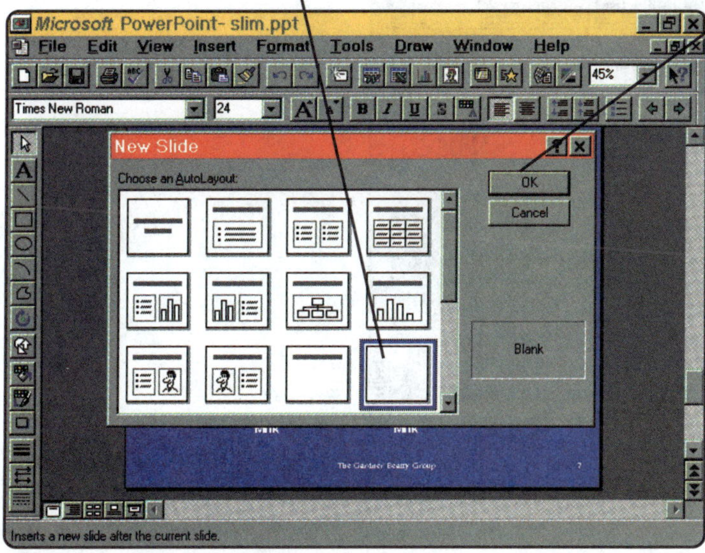

3. **Click** on **OK**. A blank slide will be inserted into your presentation. (You now have a spot to place a new graph object.)

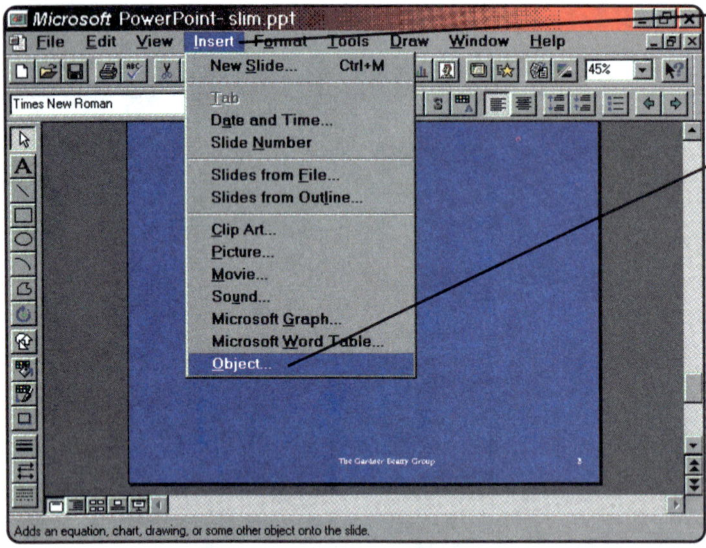

4. **Click** on **Insert** in the menu bar. The Insert menu will appear.

5. **Click** on **Object**. The Insert Object dialog box will appear.

6. **Click** on **Create from File** to put a dot in the circle. The dialog box will change to show a Browse button.

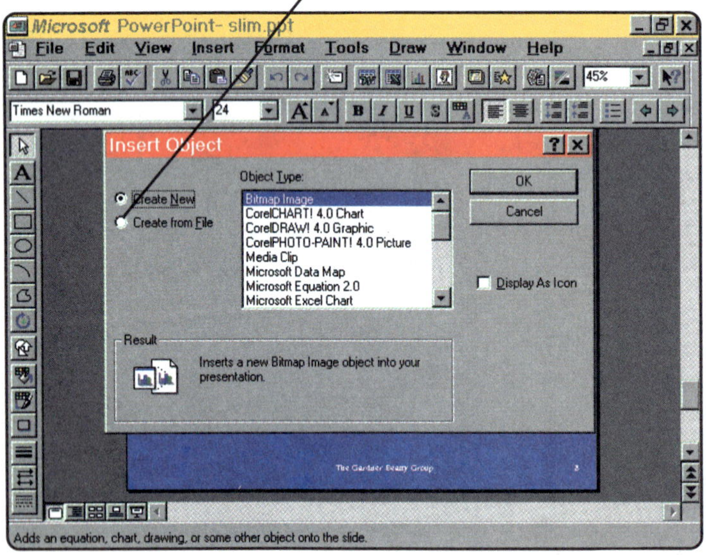

Your File directory box may say something different than what you see here. That's okay.

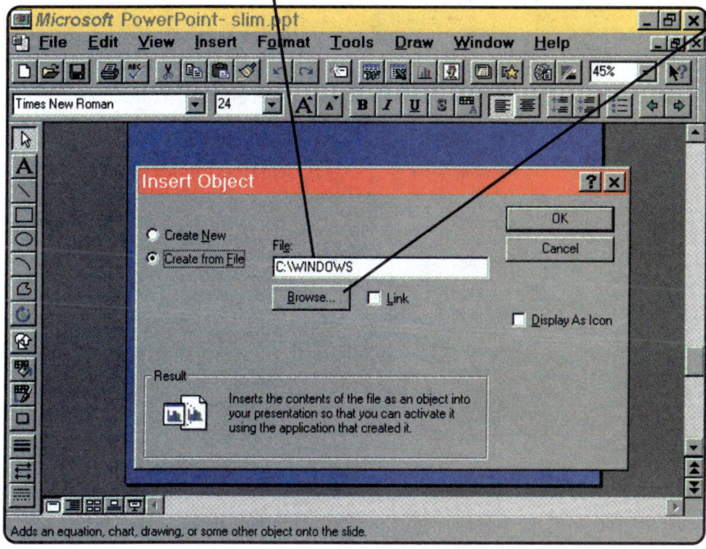

7. **Click** on **Browse** to look for the directory that has the file you will insert. The Browse dialog box will appear, but it may take a while for all of the subdirectories to load into the box.

Depending on what programs you have installed on your computer, there are several ways to get to the directory your spreadsheet is in. The following steps will work no matter what your setup is.

8. **Click** on the **Up One level button** until you see (C:).

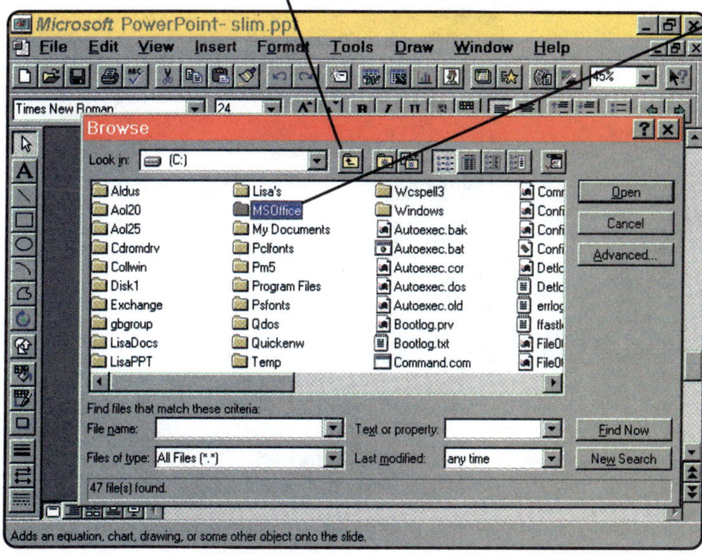

9. **Click twice** on the **directory** that contains the Excel file you want to import. In this example, it is MSOffice.

In this example, the spreadsheet is in Excel under MSOffice.

10. **Click twice** on **Excel** to open the Excel directory. (This step is not shown here.)

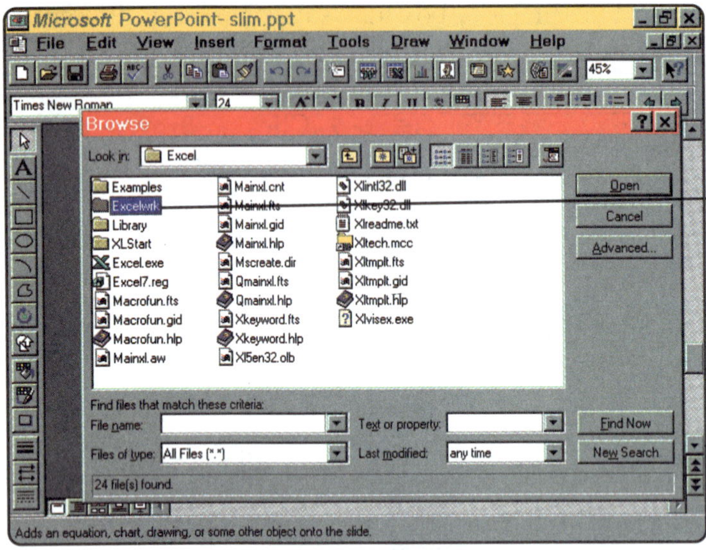

The spreadsheet in this example is in a subdirectory of Excel labeled "Excelwrk."

11. **Click twice** on the **subdirectory name** your file is in. It will appear in the Look in box. Its directories will appear below it.

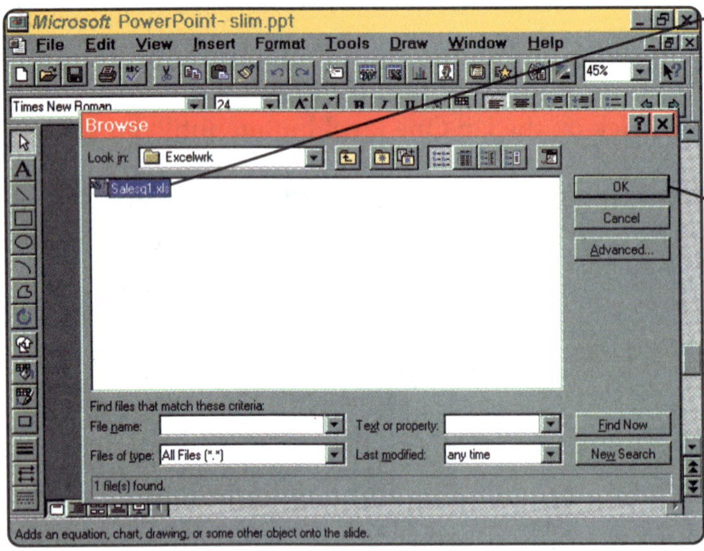

12. **Click** on the **name** of the **file** you want to import. (In this example, it is salesq1.xls.)

13. **Click** on **OK**. You will return to the browse box under Insert Object.

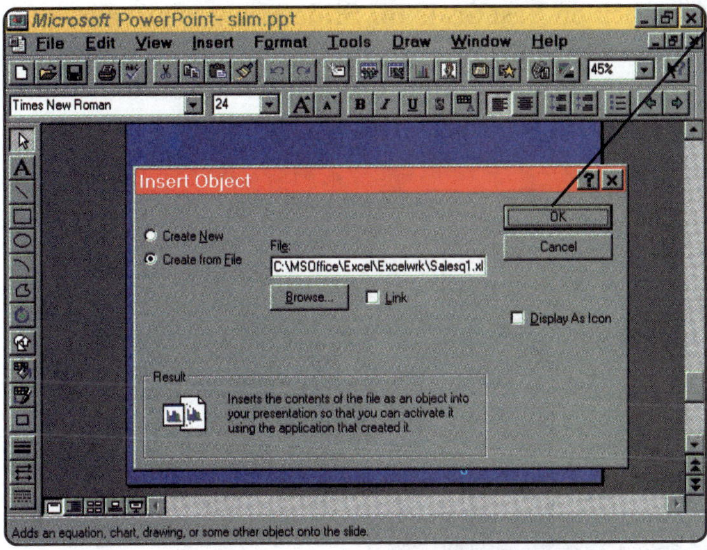

14. Click on **OK**.

You will see an hourglass flash on and off as PowerPoint imports the file into your slide presentation. (It will take a few minutes, so don't think you did anything wrong.)

SCALING AN OBJECT

As you can see, the miniaturization gremlins have been at work and messed up the size of the worksheet. Fortunately, it's easy to fix.

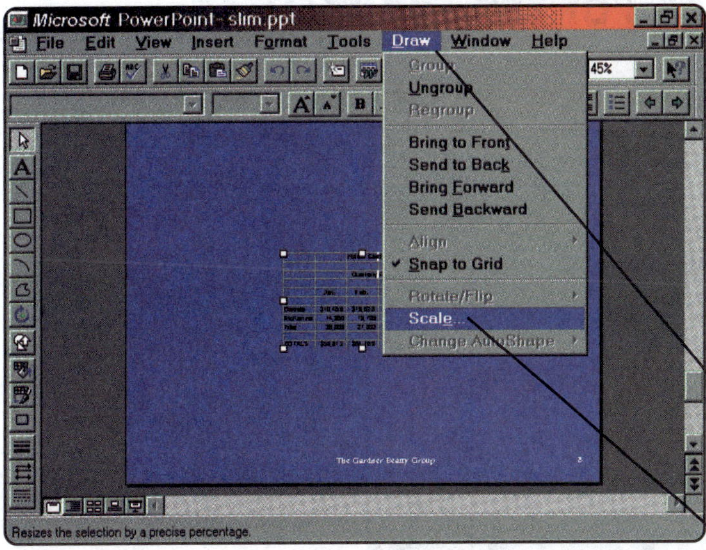

You can, of course, drag a corner handle to enlarge the worksheet, but there is another way to accomplish the same thing.

1. Click on the **worksheet** if it does not already have selection handles.

2. Click on **Draw** in the menu bar. The Draw menu will appear.

3. Click on **Scale**. The Scale dialog box will appear.

4. **Click** on **Best Scale for Slide Show** to put a ✔ in the box. The Relative to Original Picture Size option will be automatically selected as well. Notice that the Scale To figure changes.

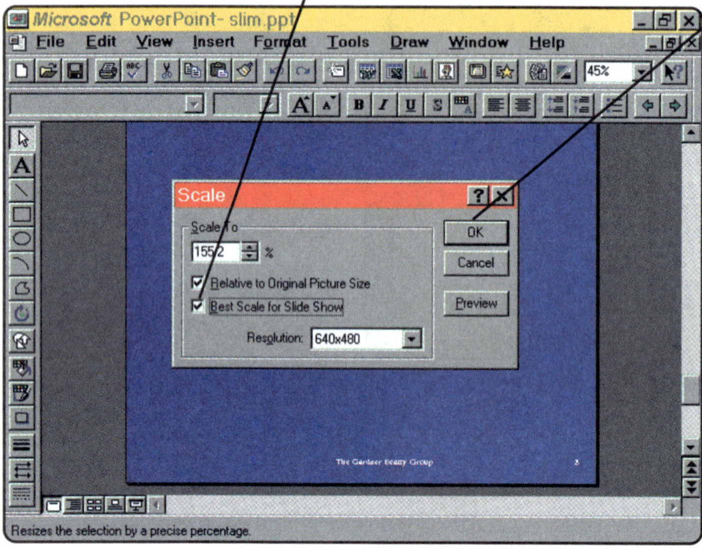

5. **Click** on **OK**. The worksheet will be resized proportionately.

If the slide background is too dark for the worksheet to show well, you can change the background fill color of the worksheet using the Color/Lines options under Format, as described in Chapter 10 in the section entitled "Using Change AutoShape" on page 106.

REMOVING GRIDLINES FROM AN IMPORTED WORKSHEET

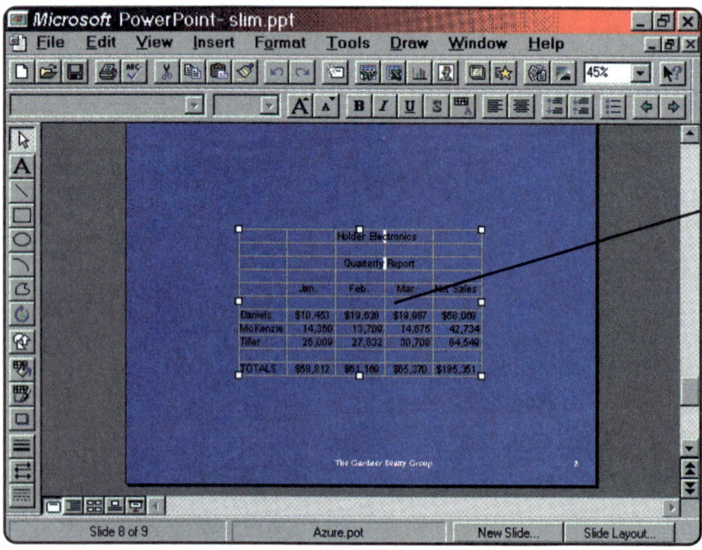

Notice that the gridlines on the chart are showing. If you don't want them, you can take them out.

1. **Click twice** on the **worksheet**. It will be surrounded by a candy-striped border and the toolbar will change to an Excel toolbar. It may take a while for this to happen.

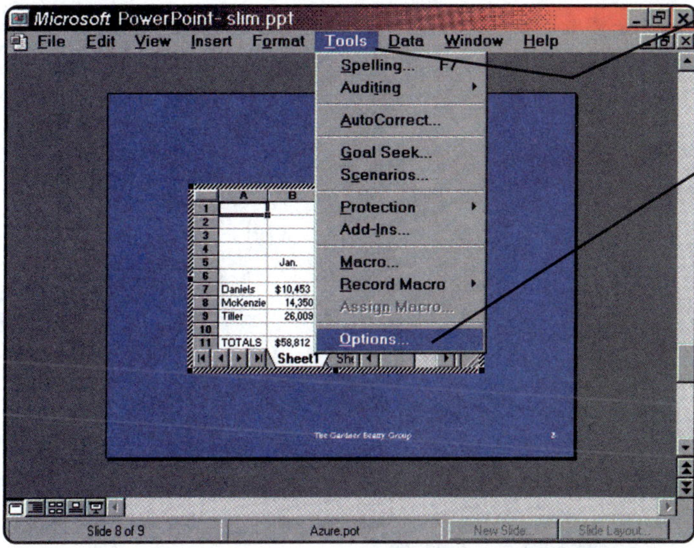

2. **Click** on **Tools** in the menu bar. The Tools menu will appear.

3. **Click** on **Options** to see the Options dialog box. It may take some time for this to happen, so be patient.

4. **Click** on the **View tab** if it is not in front in the dialog box.

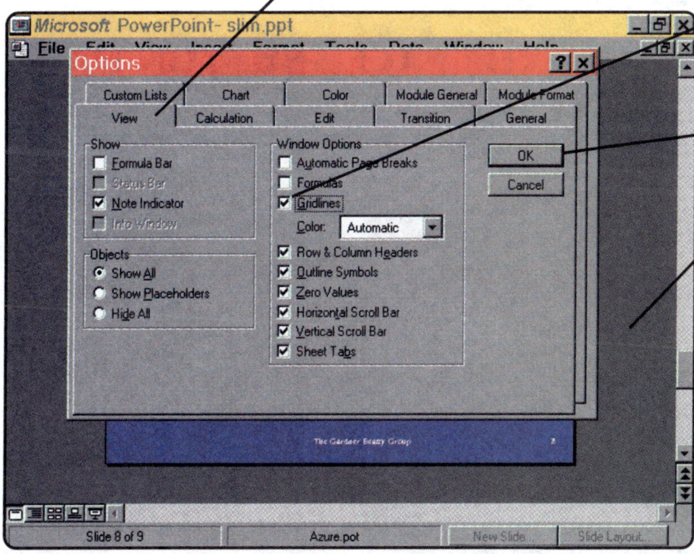

5. **Click** on **Gridlines** to *remove* the ✔ from the box.

6. **Click** on **OK**. The gridlines will disappear.

7. **Click** on the **slide background** to place the graph into the slide presentation.

DELETING A WORKSHEET OR GRAPH FROM A SLIDE

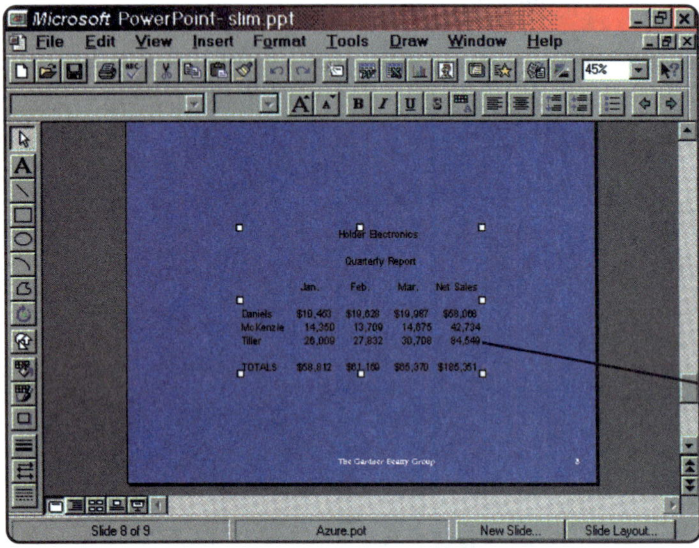

Remember, that if your worksheet does not show up well on a dark slide like this one, you can change the background fill color of the worksheet, as described in Chapter 10. Here, we will delete the graph from the slide.

1. **Click** on the **worksheet** if it is not selected.

2. **Press** the **Backspace** or **Delete key**. You may have to click on the slide for the change to register.

USING THE EXCEL BUTTON IN THE TOOLBAR

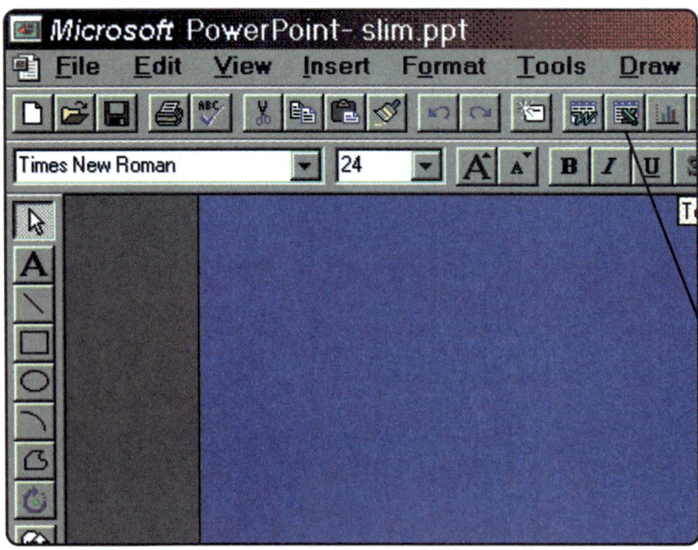

If you have Excel, you can call it up from within PowerPoint and create a new worksheet. Excel does not have to be running. This button will open it for you. Use a blank slide format for your slide.

1. **Click** on the **Insert Microsoft Excel Worksheet button** in the toolbar. A pull-down grid will appear.

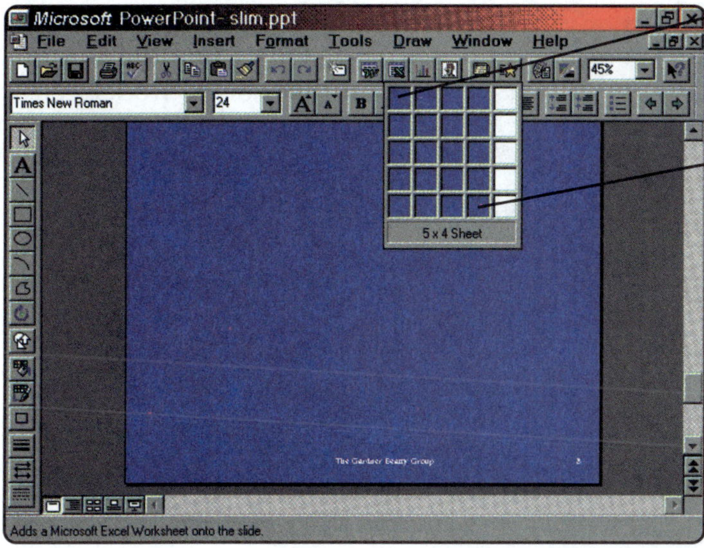

2. **Place** the **mouse pointer** on the **first square** in the grid.

3. **Press and hold** the **mouse button** and **drag** the pointer across and down to indicate how many columns and rows will be in your worksheet. The grid will expand as you drag. In this example there are four columns and five rows. **Release** the **mouse button** when you have finished.

This is the worksheet that will appear on your screen, and it is too small for you to enter data. You need to insert it into the slide before you can make it larger. Then you can edit it.

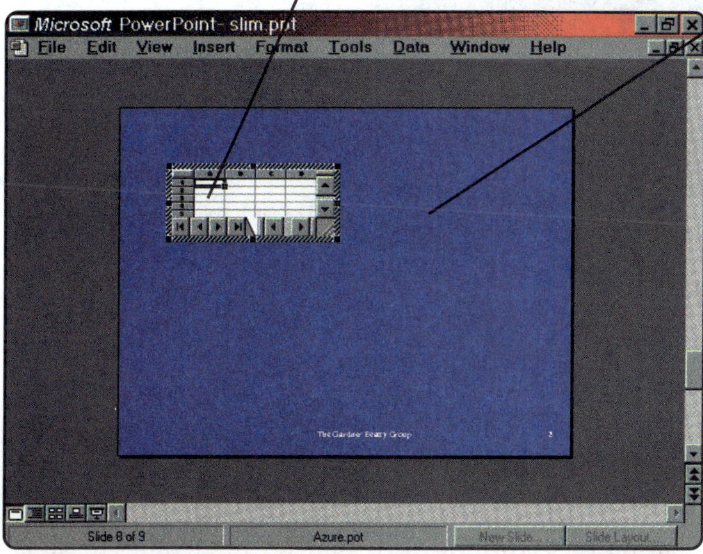

4. **Click** on the **slide background** to insert the miniature worksheet into the slide presentation.

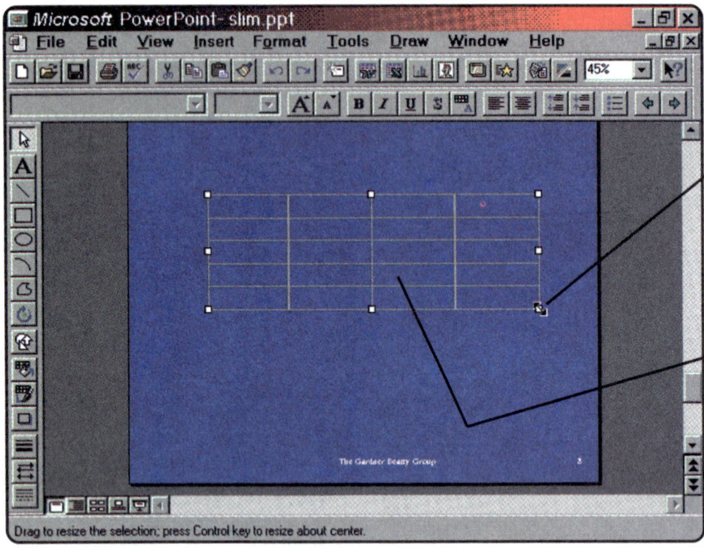

5. **Place** the **mouse button** on the **bottom right handle** of the worksheet.

6. **Press and hold** as you **drag** the corner handle down to the right to make the worksheet larger.

7. **Click twice** on the worksheet to edit it, as you did earlier in this chapter.

8. When you have completed the worksheet, **click anywhere** off the worksheet to insert it into the slide.

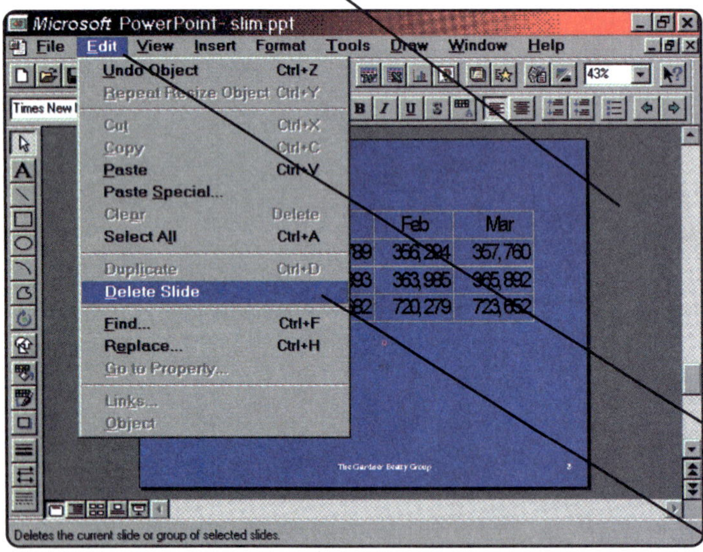

This slide was only created to teach you about inserting Excel worksheets. For the purposes of this book we will not include this exercise in our presentation, so you'll delete the slide in the two steps below.

9. **Click** on **Edit**. The Edit menu will appear.

10. **Click** on **Delete Slide**. The slide will disappear.

11. **Go to slide 1** so you will be ready for the next chapter on "Working with Tables." Remember to save your work.

CHAPTER

14

Working with Tables

PowerPoint has a predesigned slide that brings up a Word table. There is also a button in the toolbar that will boot you into Word. In this chapter you will do the following:

✔ Use the predesigned Table slide
✔ Use the Insert Microsoft Word Table button

USING THE TABLE SLIDE

PowerPoint has a predesigned table slide that opens Word and brings up a table. If you aren't familiar with Word tables, refer to *Word for Windows 95: The Visual Learning Guide* for a more detailed discussion of how to create a table. If you don't have Word installed on your computer, you will not be able to do these procedures.

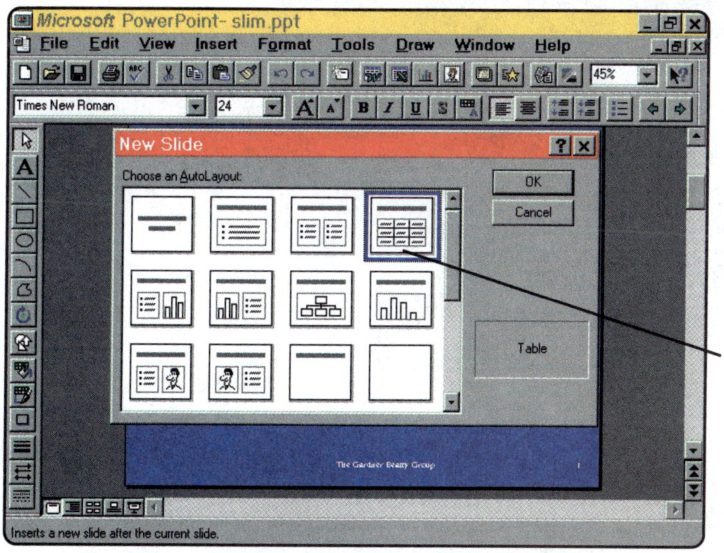

1. **Open slim** to **slide 1** if it isn't already open.

2. **Click** on the **New Slide button** at the bottom of your screen. This will bring up the New Slide dialog box you see here.

3. **Click twice** on the **Table slide**. It is the last slide in the first row. The Table slide will appear on your screen.

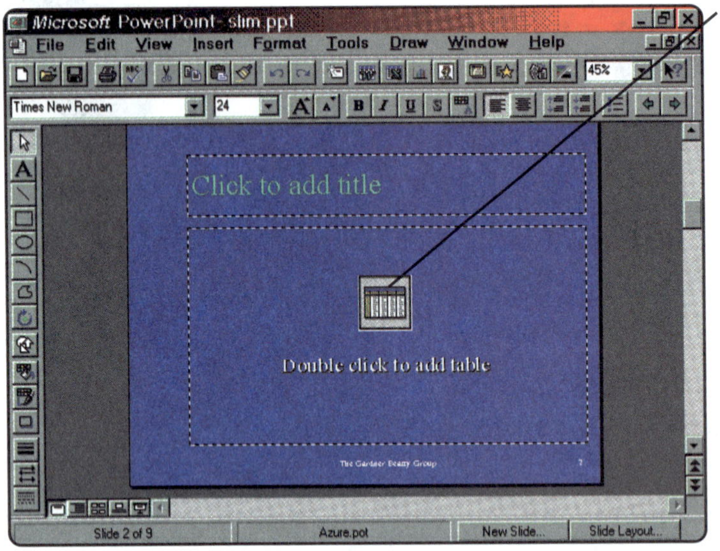

4. **Click twice** on the **table text block**. The Insert Word Table dialog box will appear.

Setting Up Columns and Rows

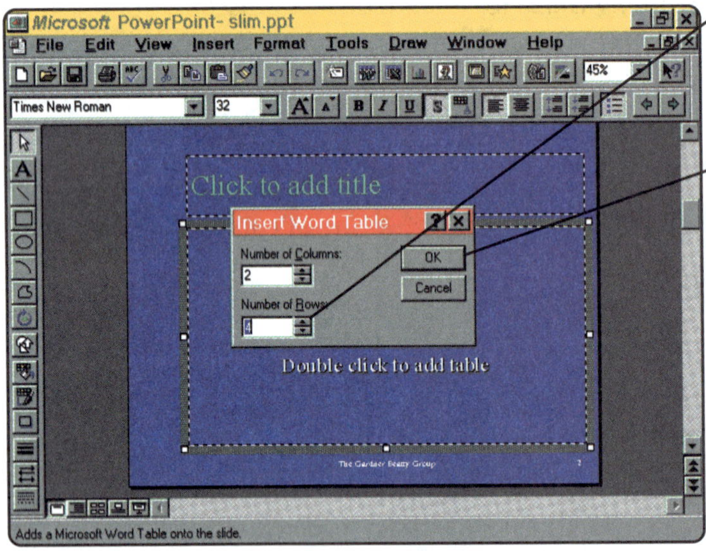

1. **Click twice** on ▲ to increase the number of rows to 4.
2. **Click** on **OK**.

After a considerable hourglass intermission, a Word table will appear with two columns and four rows.

ENTERING TEXT IN THE TABLE

1. **Click** in the **first cell** of the table.

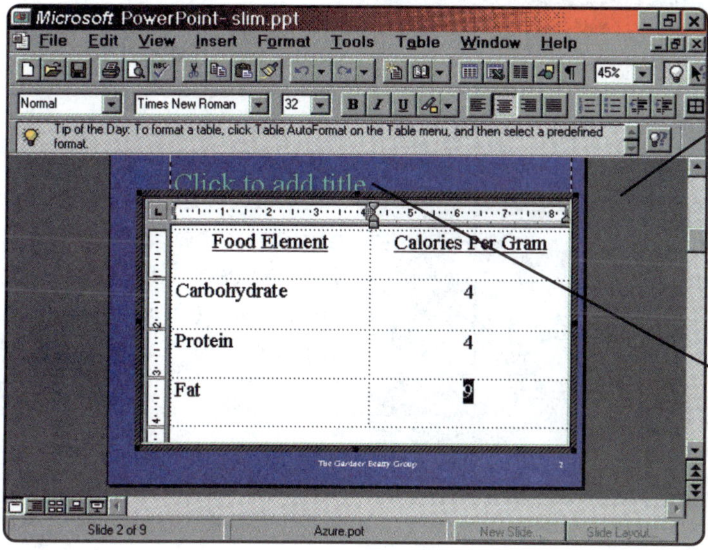

2. **Enter and format** the **text** as you would in Word.
3. **Click** on the **background** to insert the table into the slide. It will appear without gridlines because you have to add them in Word in order for them to show.
4. **Click** on the **title text block.**
5. **Type Comparison of Calories.**

EDITING A TABLE

1. **Click twice** on the **table** in the slide. This will boot you back into the table.

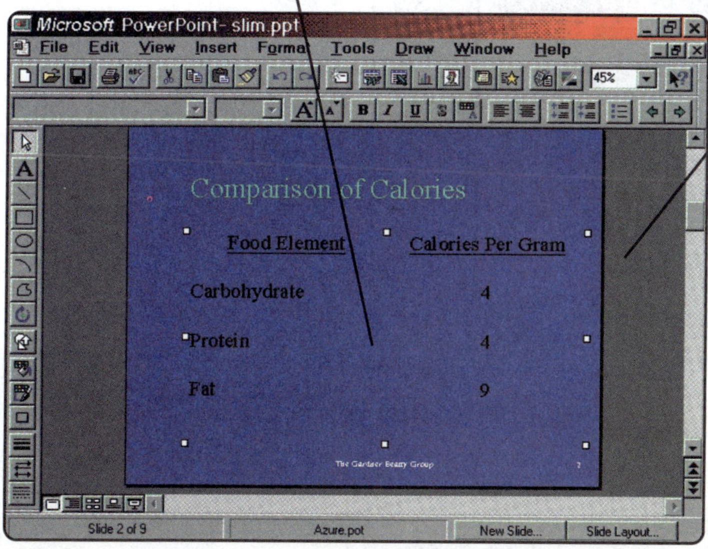

2. **Make** your **edits** as you would in Word.
3. **Click anywhere** on the background to insert the table back into the slide.

If the slide background is too dark for the table to show, you can change the background fill color of the table, as described in Chapter 10 in "Using Change AutoShape" on page 106.

USING THE WORD BUTTON

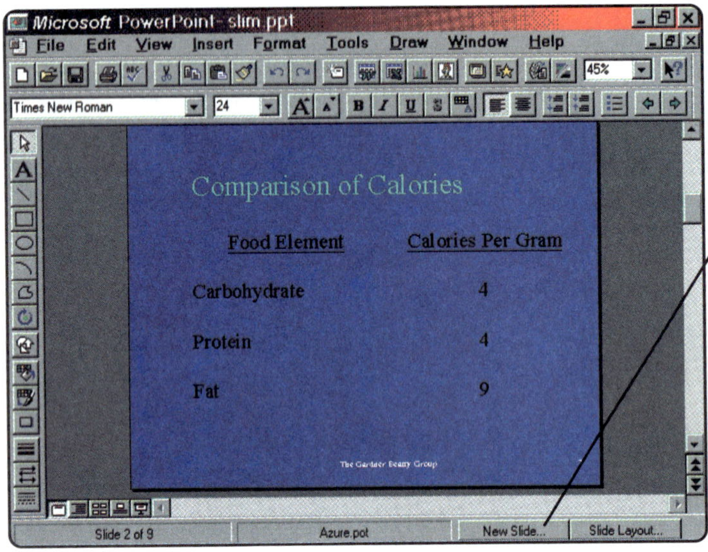

You have to have Word installed on your computer in order to do this next section. First, you will add a blank slide.

1. **Click** on the **New Slide button** at the bottom of your screen. The New Slide dialog box will appear.

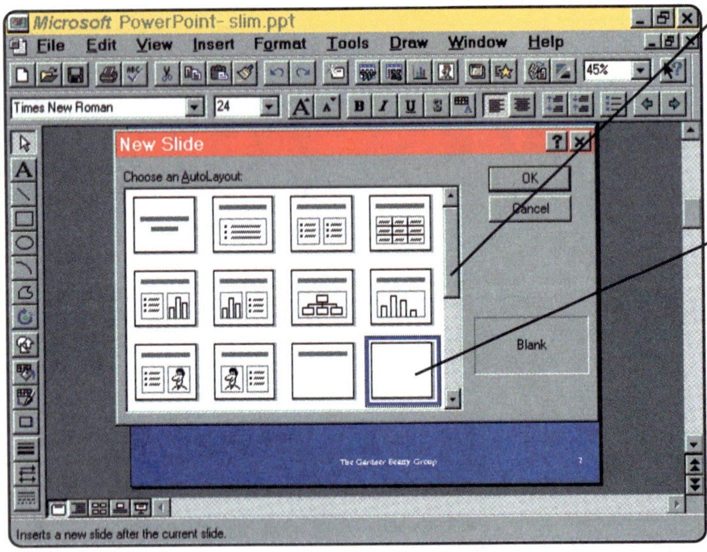

2. **Press and hold** the **mouse button** on the scroll button and **drag** it until you see the Blank slide layout.

3. **Click twice** on the **Blank slide**. A blank slide will appear on your screen.

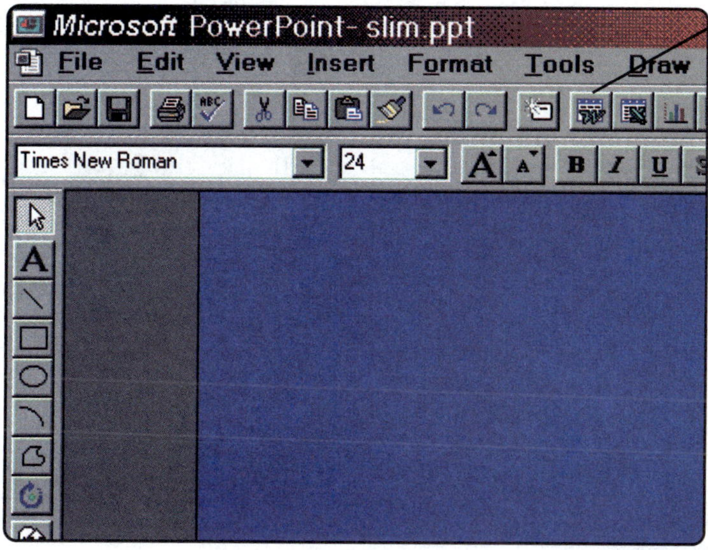

4. **Click** on the **Insert Microsoft Word Table button** in the toolbar. A pull-down grid will appear.

Setting Up the Table

1. **Place** the **mouse pointer** on the **first cell** of the grid.

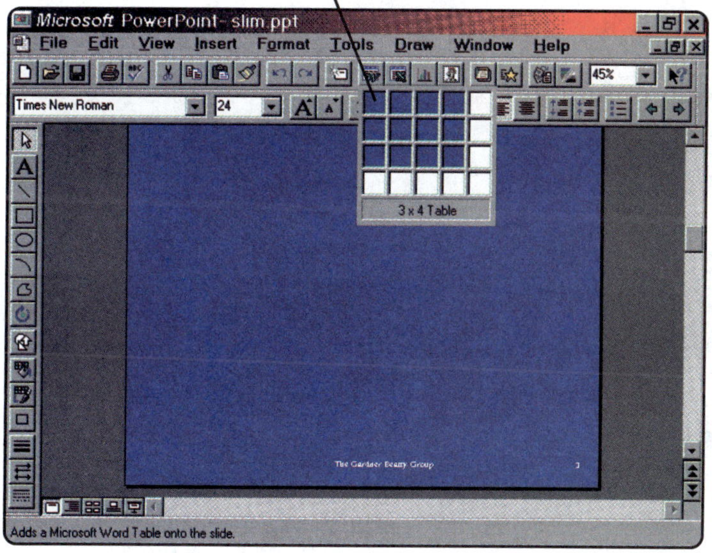

2. **Press and hold** the **mouse button** and **drag** the pointer across and down to highlight the number of columns and rows you want in the table. This example has four columns and three rows.

3. **Release** the **mouse button** when you have highlighted the appropriate number of squares. You will see the hourglass, then a table will appear on your screen.

In this example, you will not actually enter any data into the table.

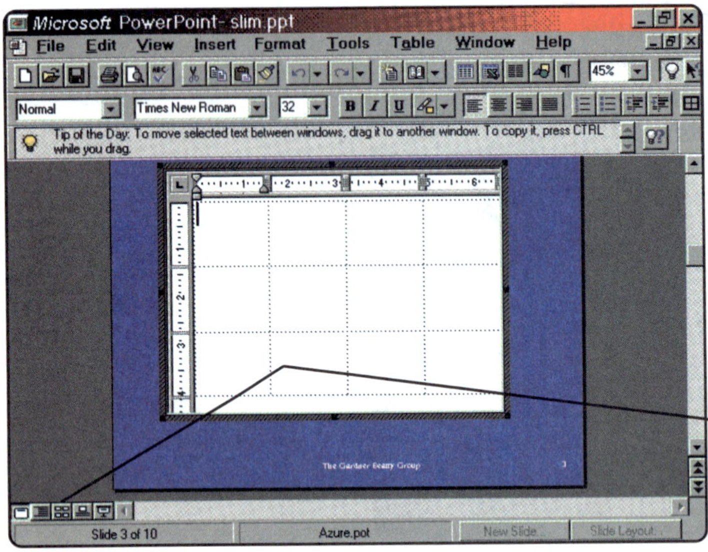

4. **Click anywhere** on the slide background to enter the table into the slide. Notice that the selection handles are the only thing you see on your screen. This is because you must add gridlines to a table in Word in order for them to show.

5. **Click** on the **Slide Sorter View button.**

We will now delete slides 2 and 3 since they will not be included in our final presentation.

6. **Click** on **Slide 2** to place a selection border around it.

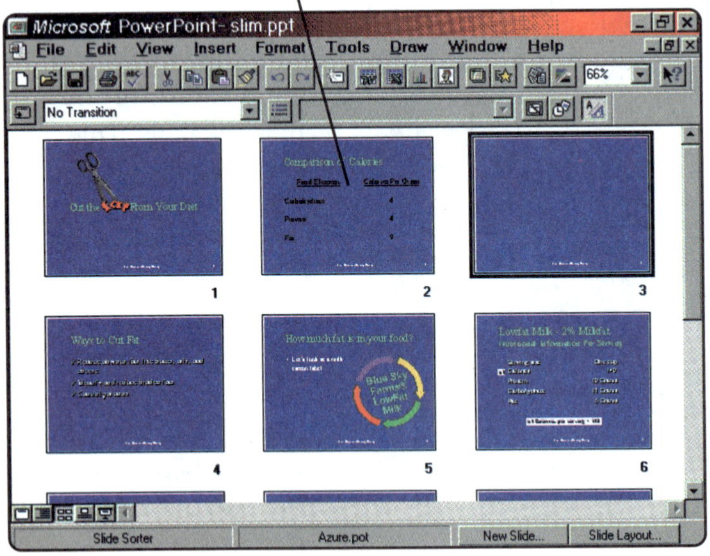

7. **Press** the **Delete key** or backspace key. Slide 2 will disappear, and the remaining slides will be renumbered.

8. **Click** on the **new slide 2** to place a selection border around it.

9. **Press** the **Delete key** or backspace key. The slide will disappear. You will be left with eight slides in your presentation.

CHAPTER 15

Creating an Organization Chart

PowerPoint has a predesigned slide for an organization chart. You can customize it to show the organization chart of an entire company or of a project team. In this chapter you will do the following:

✔ Create an organization chart
✔ Change the format of the chart

USING THE ORG CHART SLIDE

In this section you will create an organization chart in the slim presentation.

1. **Click** on the **Slide View button** if you are not in slide view.

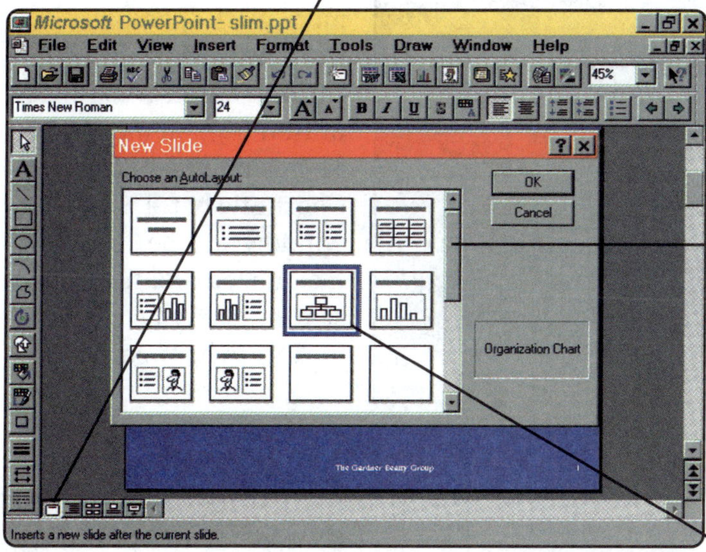

2. **Click** on the **New Slide button** at the bottom of your screen. This will bring up the New Slide dialog box that you see here.

3. If the scroll button isn't already at the top**, move** the **mouse arrow** to the **scroll button** and **press and hold** on the **button** and **drag** it to the top of the scroll bar.

4. **Click twice** on the **Org Chart slide**, which is the third slide in the second row.

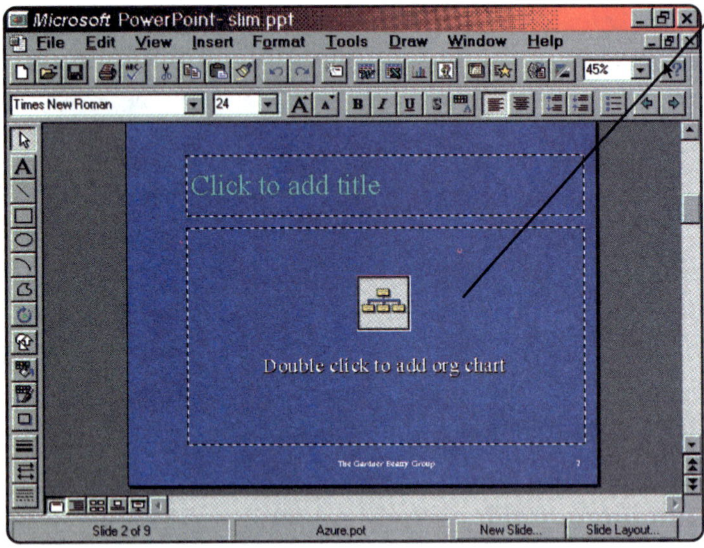

5. **Click twice** on the **org chart text block**. After a lengthy wait, the Microsoft Organization Chart window will appear. The boxes in the chart will be the colors you previously selected for fill and lines. You will change the fill color later in this chapter.

Enlarging the Window

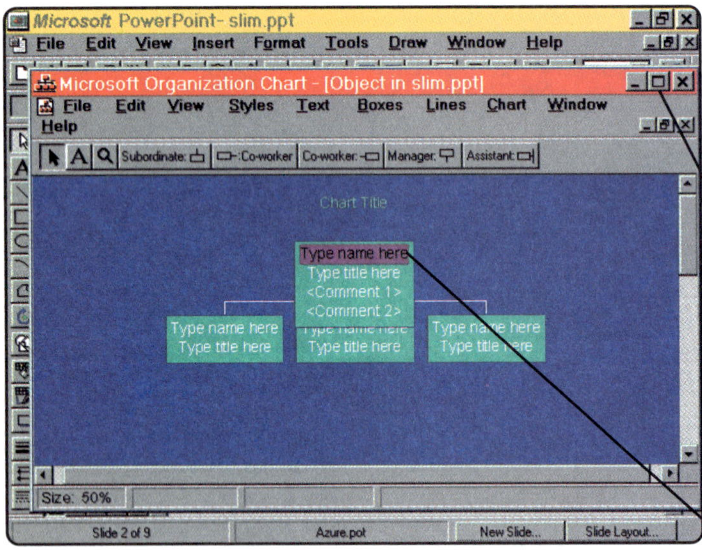

You can enlarge the Organization Chart window to give yourself more work space.

1. **Click** on the **Maximize button** (☐) on the Microsoft Organization Chart title bar. The window will be maximized and fill your screen. It may take a while for this to happen.

Notice that the top box on the chart will be expanded to show four lines and that the top line will be already highlighted. (You may have to click on the top box for this to happen.)

ENTERING NAMES IN THE CHART

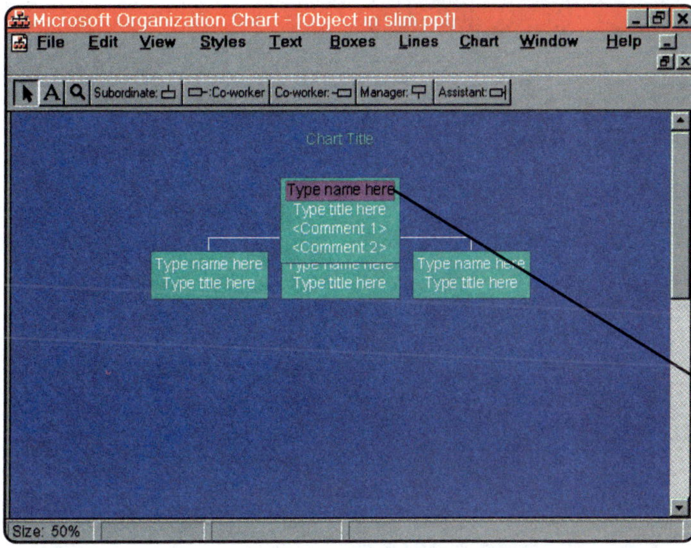

Each box has four lines you can use. The first two lines ("Type name here" and "Type title here") will print as you see them unless you change the text. The "<Comment>" lines will never print unless you enter data in them.

1. **Type Project Leader.**

You will hide the second line of text in this chart box in the next section.

Hiding a Line

The first two lines in a box will print unless you tell PowerPoint to hide one of the lines. In this example you will hide the "title" line in the Project Leader box.

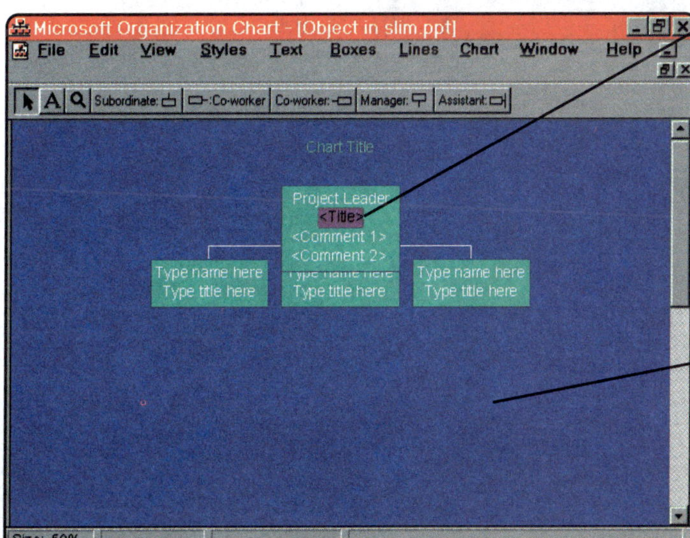

1. **Press Enter** to move to the second line and highlight it.
2. **Press** the **Delete key**. "<Title>" will appear. The angle brackets mean this line will not print.
3. **Click** on the **background** to close the box.

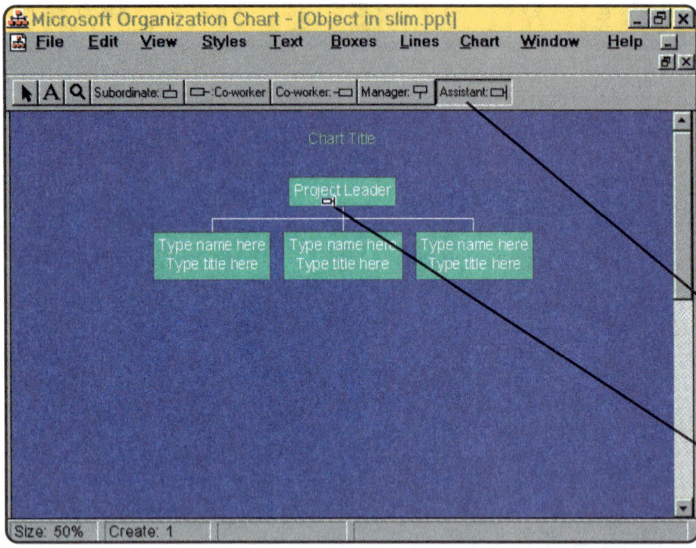

ADDING AN ASSISTANT

In this section you will add an Assistant Project Leader.

1. **Click** on the **Assistant button** in the toolbar. It will appear to be pressed in.

2. **Place** the **cursor** in the Project Leader box. The cursor will change to a box.

3. **Click** the **mouse button**.

A box will be added to the chart. The box will have a black center.

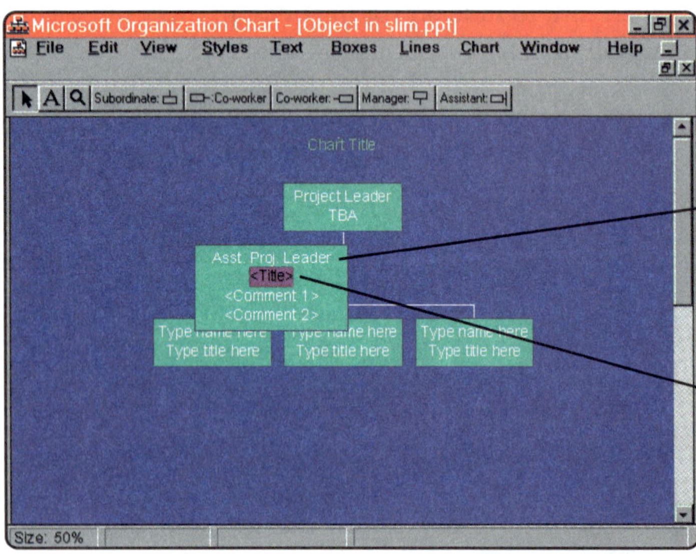

4. **Click inside** the **box**. It will be opened for editing and the first line will be highlighted.

5. **Type Asst. Proj. Leader** and **press Enter**. The second line will be highlighted.

6. **Type TBA**.

7. **Click** on the **background** to close the box.

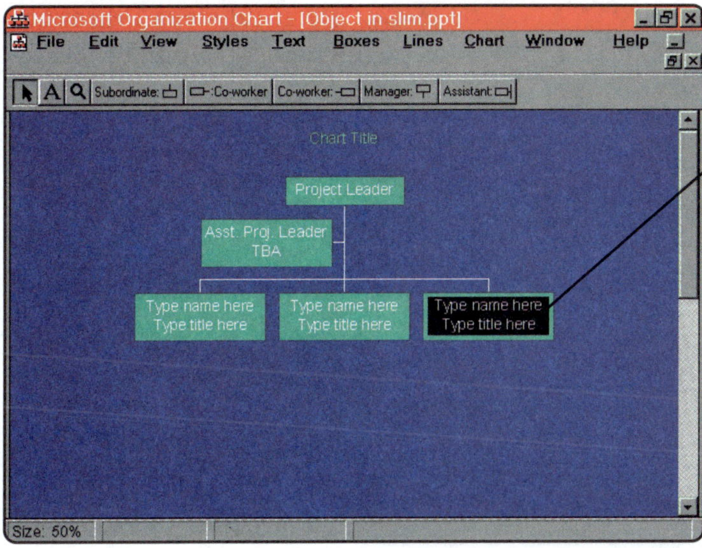

DELETING A BOX

1. **Click** on the **third box** in the third line. It will become black.
2. **Press** the **Delete key** on your keyboard. The box will be removed from the chart.

ADDING MANAGERS

In this example, you will add a Programming Manager and a Training Manager as direct reports to the Project leader.

1. **Click** on this **box** to select it and make it black.

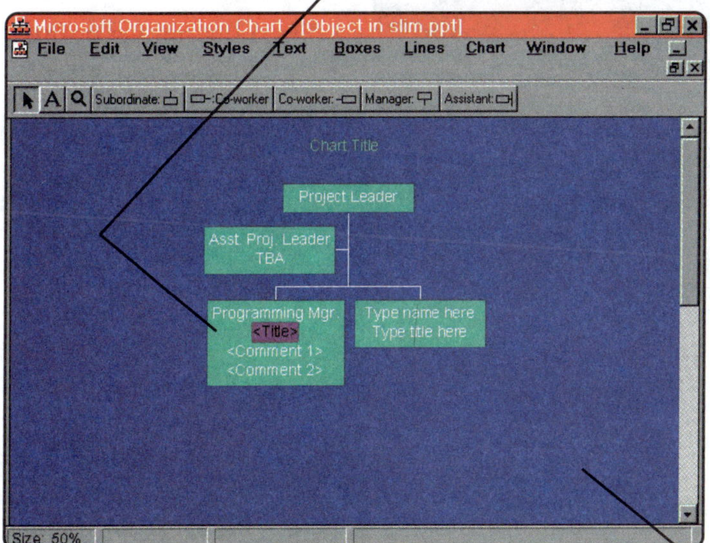

2. **Click** on the **box** a second time to open it for editing.
3. **Highlight** the **first line** and **type Programming Mgr.** Then **press Enter** to go to the second line and highlight it.
4. **Press** the **Delete key**. "<Title>" will appear, indicating that the line will not print.
5. **Click** on the **background** to close the box.

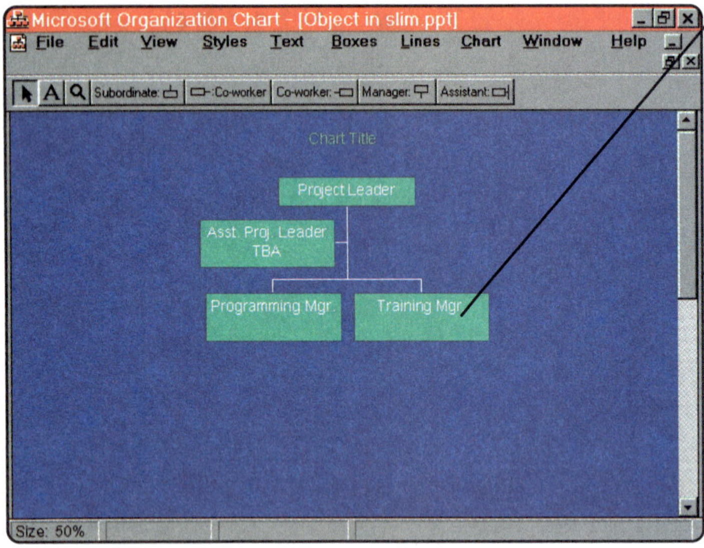

6. **Repeat steps 1 through 5** to insert Training Mgr. in this box.

ADDING SUBORDINATES

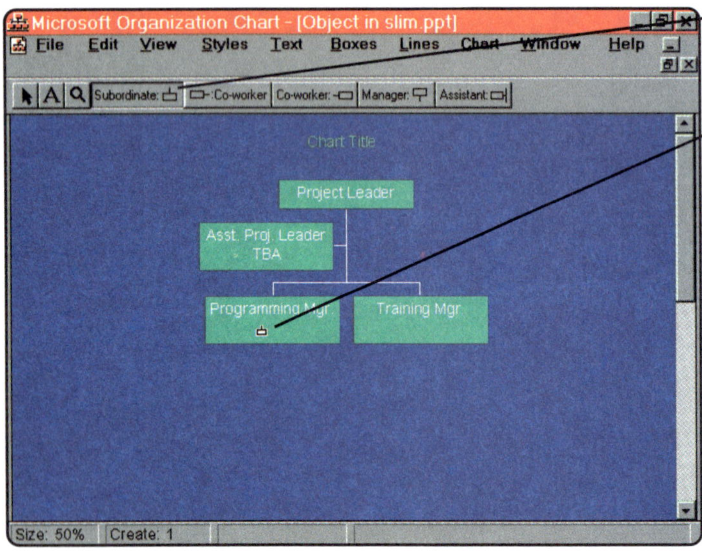

1. **Click** on the **Subordinate button** in the toolbar.

2. **Place** the **mouse pointer** in the Programming Manager's box. The pointer will become a box.

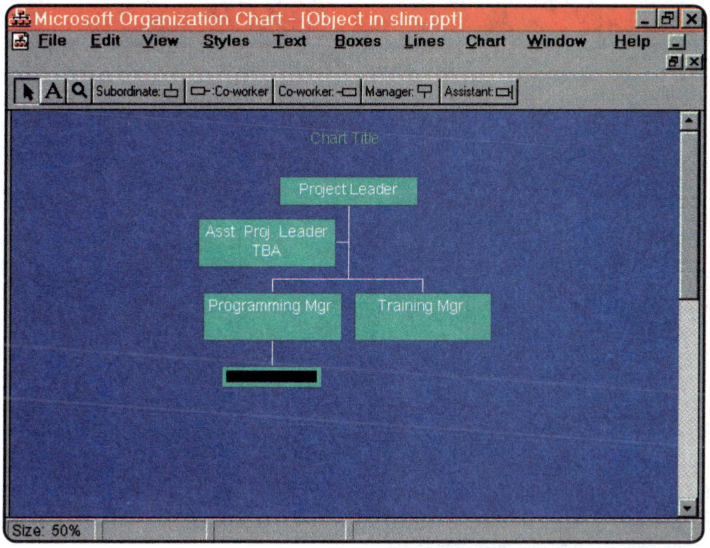

3. **Click** the **mouse button**.

A box will be added below the Programming Manager's box.

Using a Comment Line

1. **Click inside** the **new box**. It will expand to show four lines. The first line will be highlighted.

2. **Type Programmer**.

3. **Press Enter** to move to the title line. Notice that it appears in angle brackets to indicate that it will not print. Each level takes its cue from the previous. Because the previous level has a second line, this level has one also. (You can, of course, add text here if you want.)

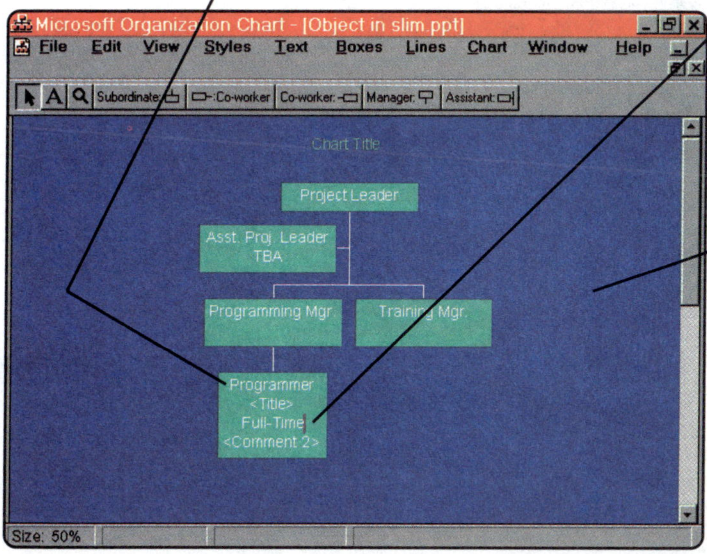

4. **Press Enter** to move to the first comment line and highlight it.

5. **Type Full-Time**.

6. **Click** on the **background** to close the box.

ADDING A CO-WORKER

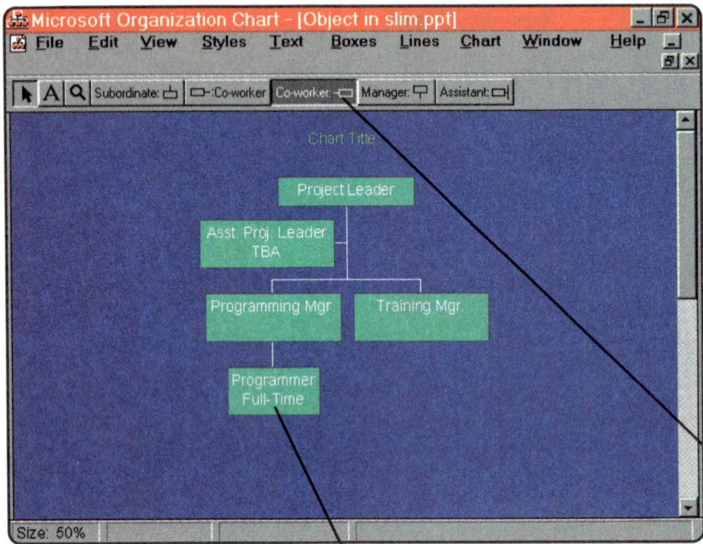

A co-worker can be added to any level of the chart. There are two co-worker buttons. One button adds a box to the left of an existing box. The second adds a co-worker box to the right of the existing box. In this example, you will add a co-worker to the full-time programmer.

1. **Click** on the **right Co-worker button** in the toolbar.

2. **Place** the **mouse pointer** in the **Programmer's box**. The pointer will become a box.

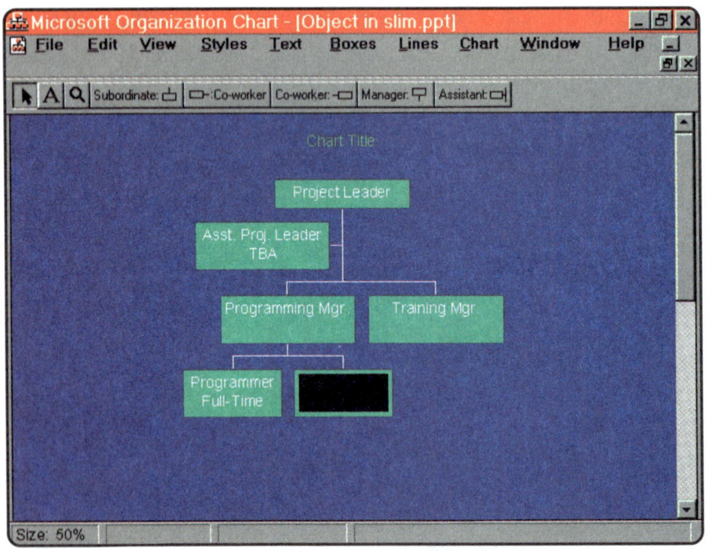

3. **Click** the **mouse button**. A box will be added to the right of the full-time programmer.

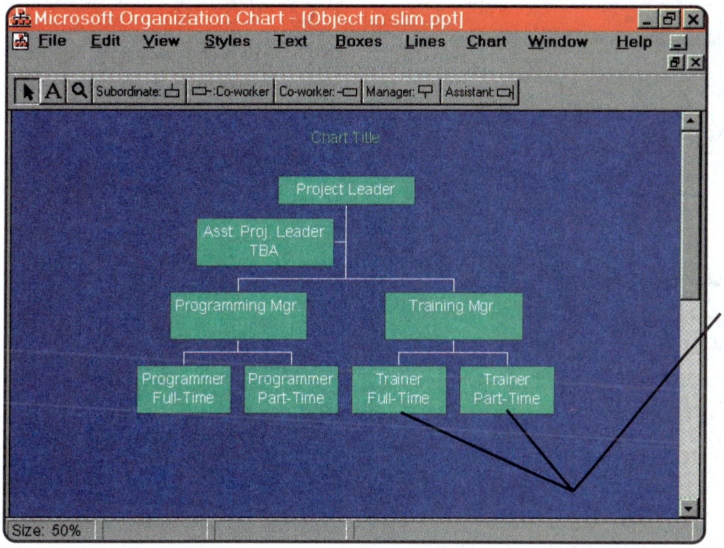

4. **Repeat steps 1 to 5** in "Using a Comment Line" to type the following information in the co-worker's box:
   Programmer
   Part-Time

5. **Repeat** the steps in the previous sections "Adding Subordinates", "Using a Comment Line", and "Adding a Co-Worker" to add the full- and part-time trainers you see here.

INSERTING THE ORGANIZATION CHART INTO YOUR PRESENTATION

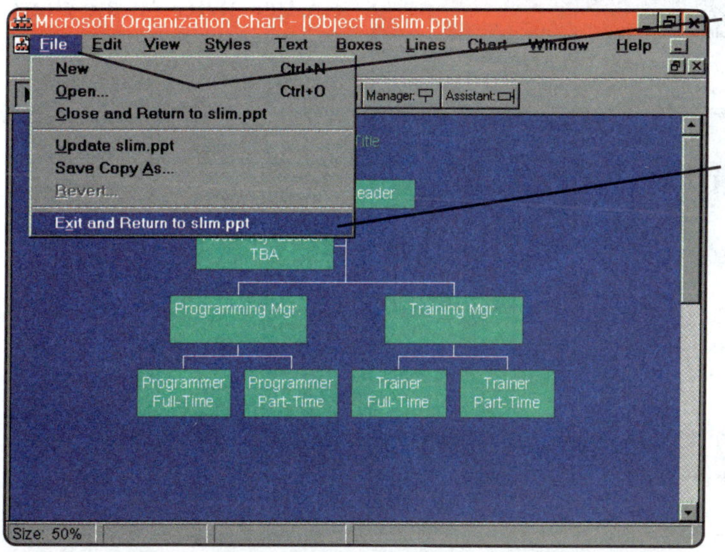

1. **Click** on **File** in the menu bar. The File menu will appear.

2. **Click** on **Exit and Return to slim.ppt**. The Microsoft Organization Chart dialog box will appear.

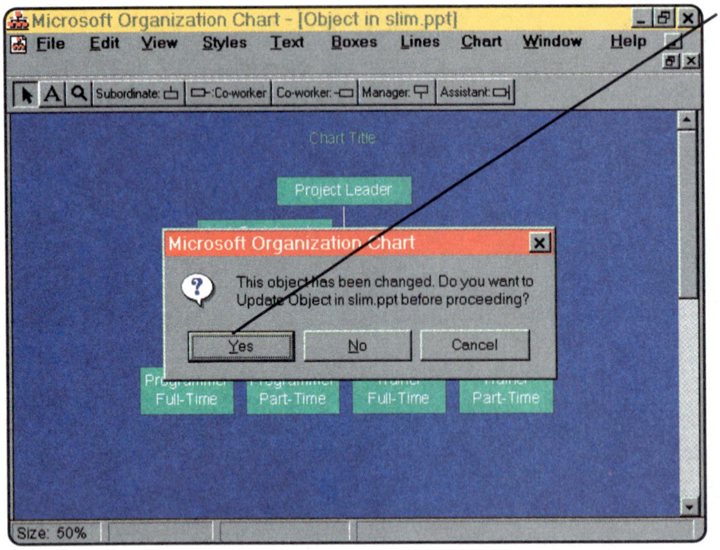

3. **Click** on **Yes**. The window will close, and the organization chart will be inserted in the presentation slide.

EDITING THE ORGANIZATION CHART

You can edit the chart even after it has been inserted into the presentation.

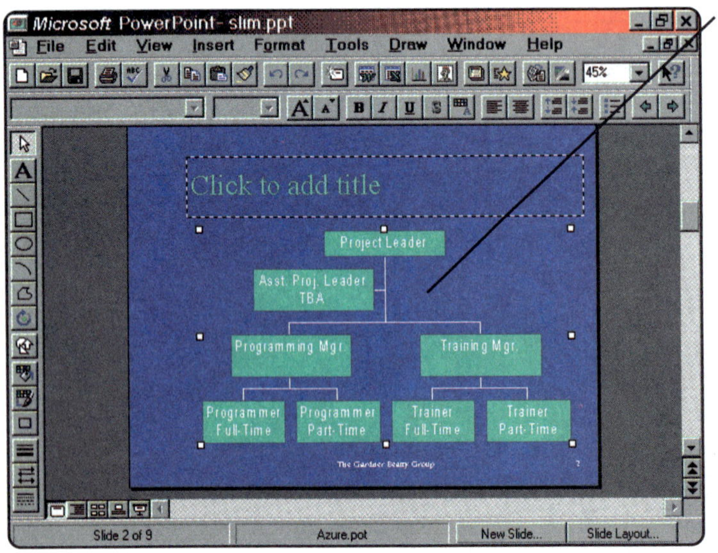

1. **Click twice** on the **chart**. The Microsoft Organization Chart window will appear. Keep in mind that it may take a while.

2. **Click** on the **Maximize button** (□) to increase the size of the window as you did at the beginning of this chapter.

Selecting All Levels

You can select all boxes on the chart and apply a command to all of them at once.

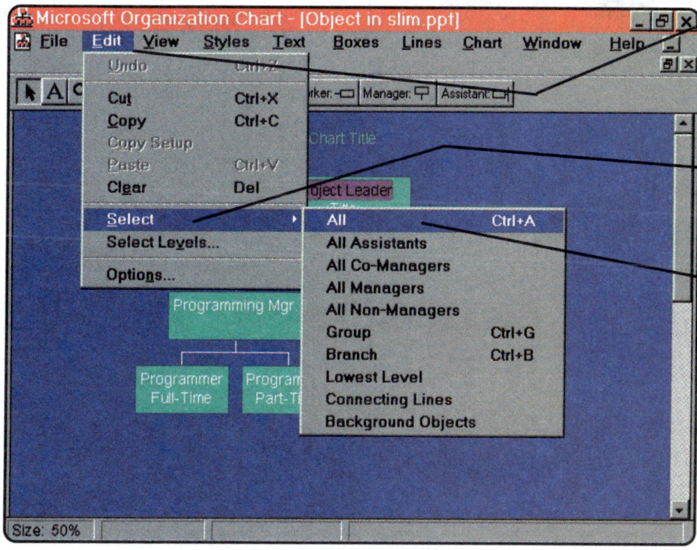

1. **Click** on **Edit** in the menu bar. A pull-down menu will appear.
2. **Click** on **Select**. A second menu will appear.
3. **Click** on **All**. All of the boxes will be selected.

Notice that you can select specific levels and the connecting lines.

CHANGING BOX COLOR

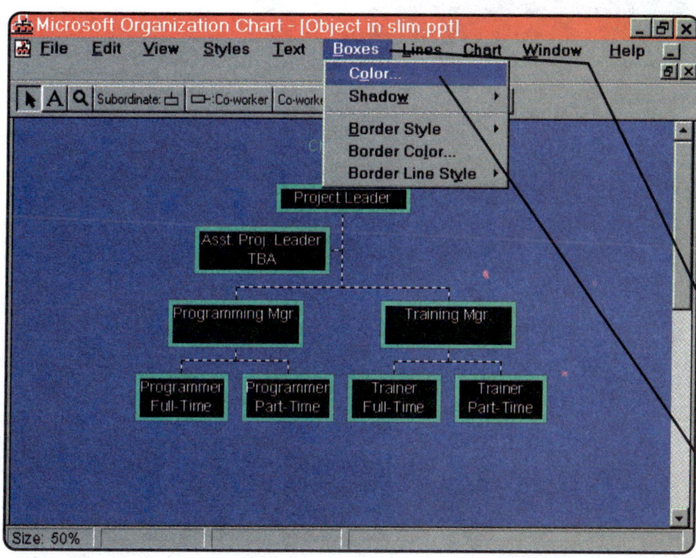

In this section you'll change the color of all of the boxes.

1. **Do** steps **1 to 3** in the section above if you haven't already done so.
2. **Click** on **Boxes** in the menu bar. The Boxes menu will appear.
3. **Click** on **Color**. The Color dialog box will appear.

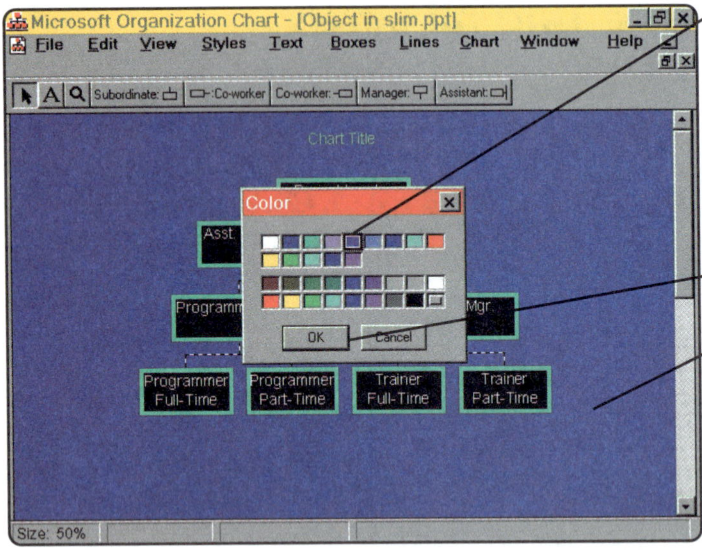

4. **Click** on the **color** you want the boxes to be. In this example, it is purple. You may have different colors on your screen. If so, choose another color.

5. **Click** on **OK.**

6. **Click** on the **background** to remove the selection borders so you can see the boxes clearly.

UNDOING A CHANGE

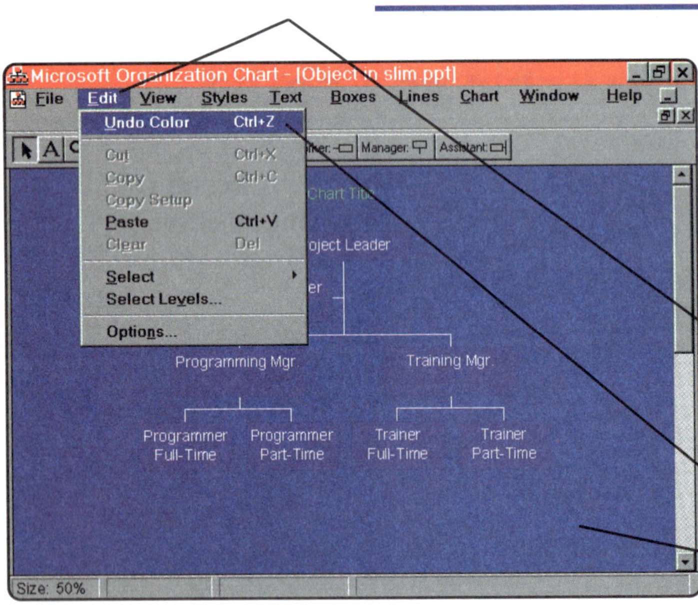

You can use the Undo feature to reverse the change you just made in the color if you use Undo before you do any other function.

1. **Click** on **Edit** in the menu bar. The Edit menu will appear.

2. **Click** on **Undo Color.**

3. **Click** on the **background** to apply the change.

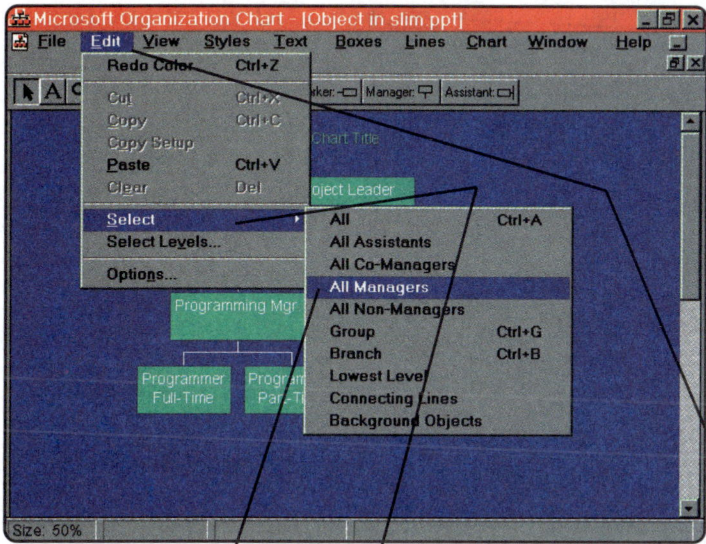

CHANGING THE STYLE OF THE CHART

You can change the style of the chart with a click of your mouse. In this example, you will reorganize around the managers.

1. **Click** on **Edit** in the menu bar. The Edit menu will appear.

2. **Click** on **Select**. A second menu will appear.

3. **Click** on **All Managers**. All levels that have direct reports will be highlighted.

4. **Click** on **Styles** in the menu bar. A pull-down chart of Group styles will appear.

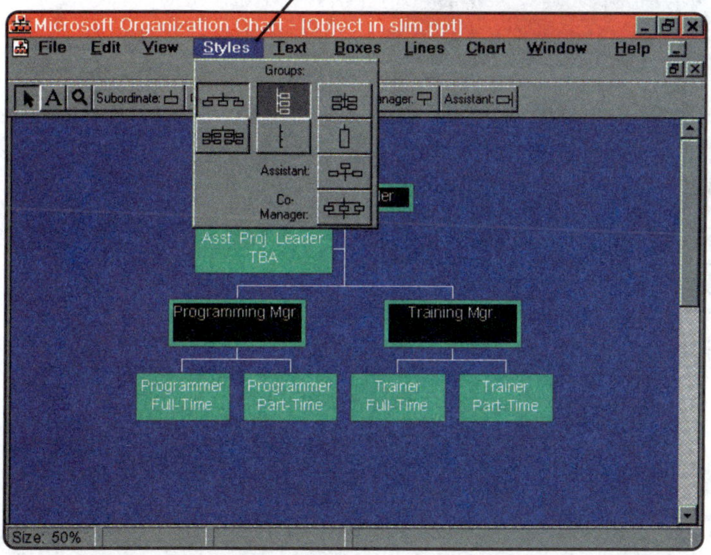

5. **Click** on the **style** of chart you want. In this example, click on the middle button in the top row to change to a vertical arrangement by managers.

If you change your mind, use Undo to go back to the previous chart setup.

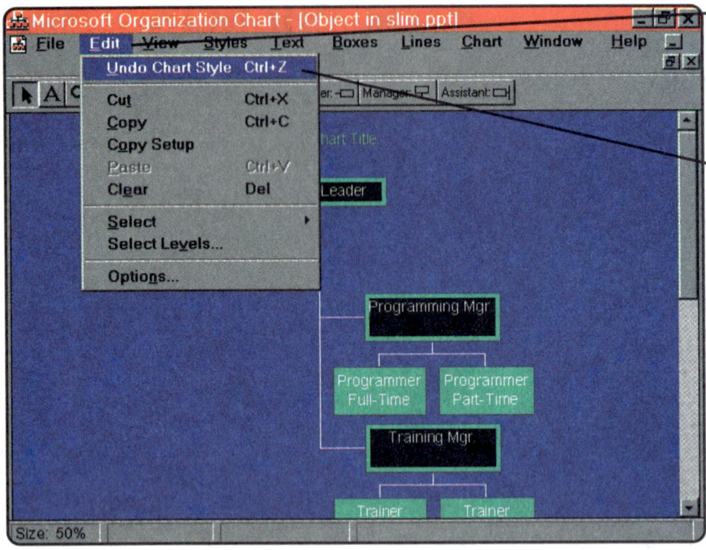

6. **Click** on **Edit** in the menu bar. The Edit menu will appear.

7. **Click** on **Undo Chart Style**. Notice that PowerPoint knows that your last move was to change the chart.

8. **Repeat** the **steps** in the section entitled, "Inserting the Organization Chart into the Presentation," earlier in this chapter.

CLOSING A PRESENTATION WITHOUT SAVING

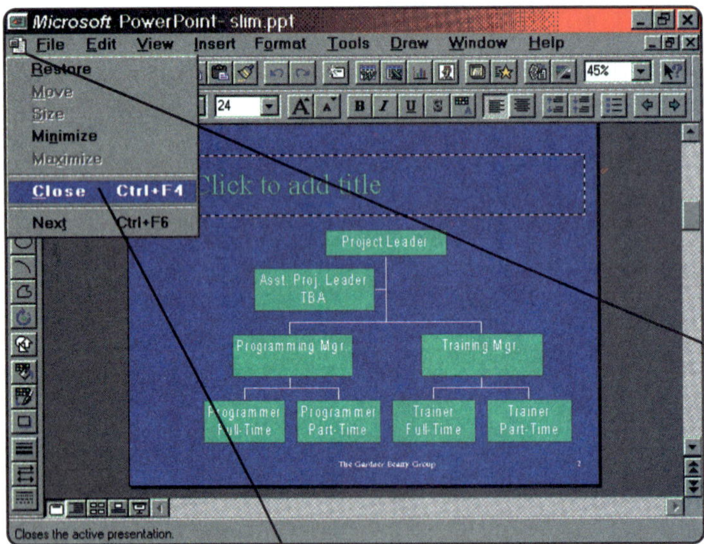

In Chapter 14 you created two practice tables. Because this was only for practice, you don't need to save the work you did. In this section, you will close the slim presentation without saving it.

1. **Click** on the **document icon** on the left of the menu bar. A menu will appear. This Control menu box controls this particular presentation. Be careful not to click on the top Control menu box. It controls the PowerPoint program.

2. **Click** on **Close**. A Microsoft PowerPoint dialog box will appear.

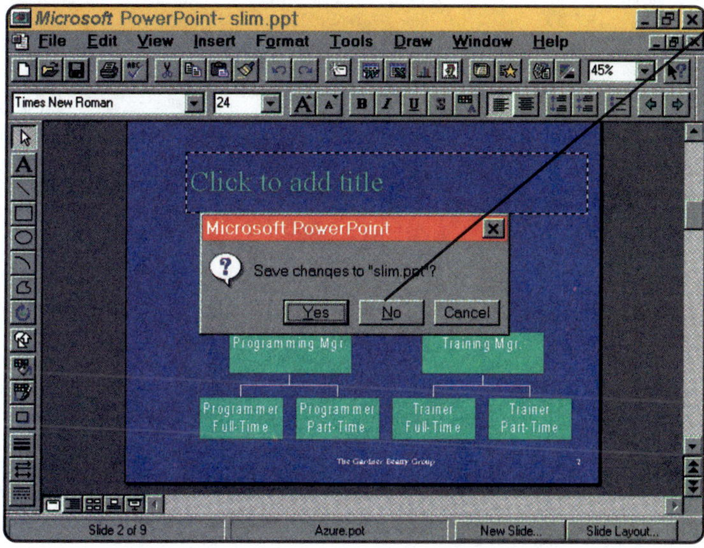

3. **Click** on **No** to close the presentation without saving it.

The slim presentation will close without saving the changes you made since you last saved it.

Part IV: Running a Slide Show

CHAPTER

16

Setting Up and Rehearsing a Slide Show

PowerPoint provides exciting special effects and rehearsal tools to help make your presentation top notch. In this chapter you will do the following:

✔ Add a black slide
✔ Apply and edit slide transitions
✔ Create a build slide
✔ Hide a slide
✔ Rehearse a slide show
✔ Run a slide show

ADDING A BLACK SLIDE

A black slide at the end of a presentation focuses the audience's attention back on the speaker. This is useful for both a 35mm slide presentation and an electronic presentation.

1. **Open** the **slim presentation** if it's not already open.

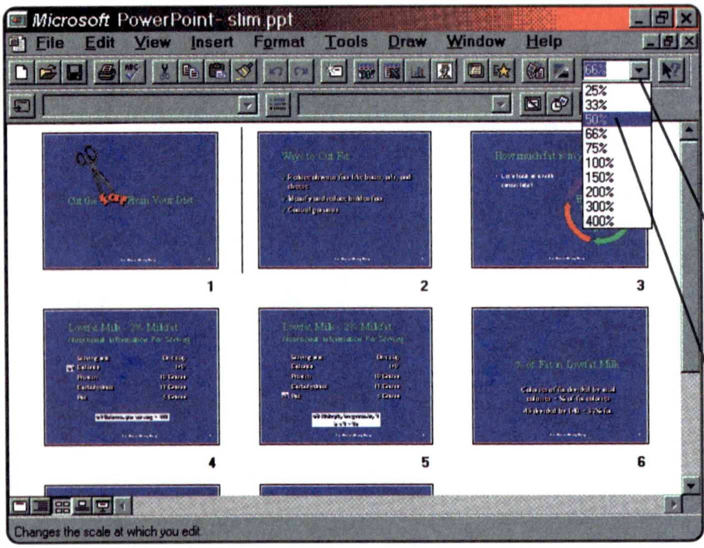

2. **Click** on the **Slide Sorter View button** at the bottom of your screen. It's the third button from the left.

3. **Click** on the ▼ next to the zoom box. A pull-down menu will appear.

4. **Click** on **50%**. The slides will appear in a 50% view, and you will be able to see all the slides at once.

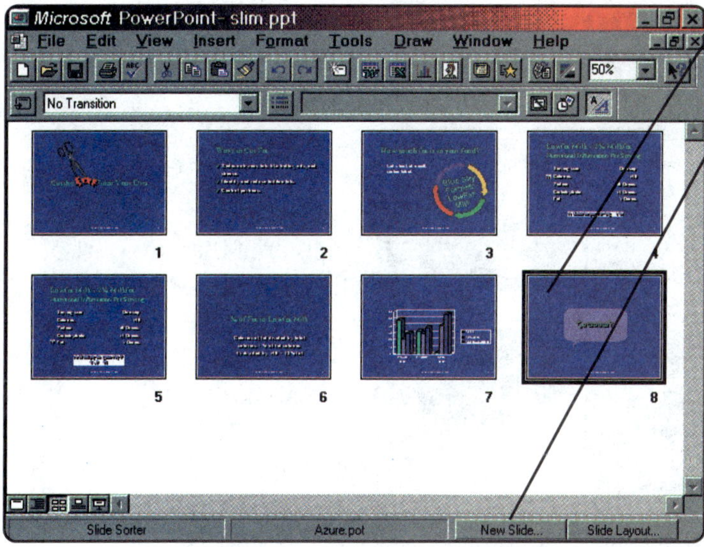

5. **Click** on **slide 8** to select it.

6. **Click** on **New Slide**. The New Slide dialog box will appear.

7. **Click twice** on the **Blank slide**. A blank slide will be added to your presentation.

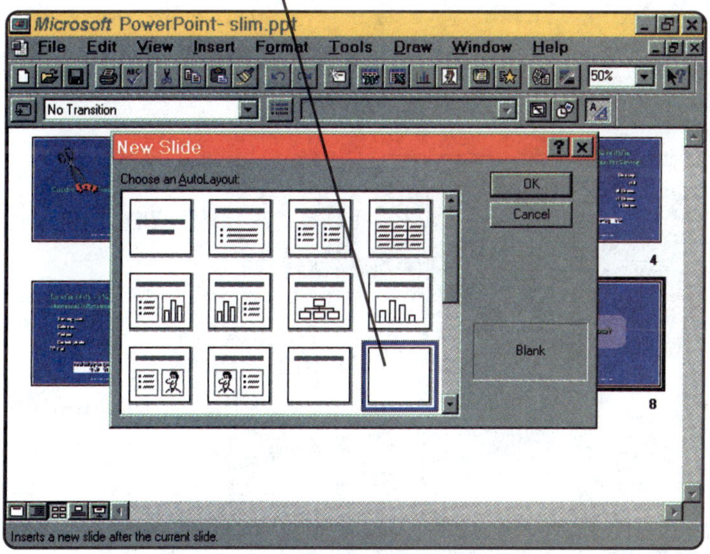

Removing Background Elements from a Slide

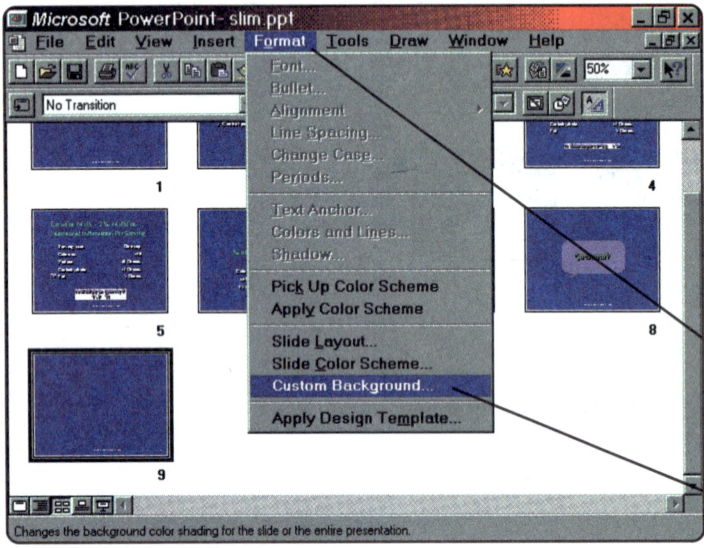

In order to color this slide entirely black you have to remove the background elements that are part of the template.

1. **Click** on **slide 9** if it is not already selected.

2. **Click** on **Format** in the menu bar. The Format menu will appear.

3. **Click** on **Custom Background**. The dialog box will appear.

4. **Click** on **Omit Background Graphics from Master** to place a ✔ in the box. This will remove the design objects from the slide.

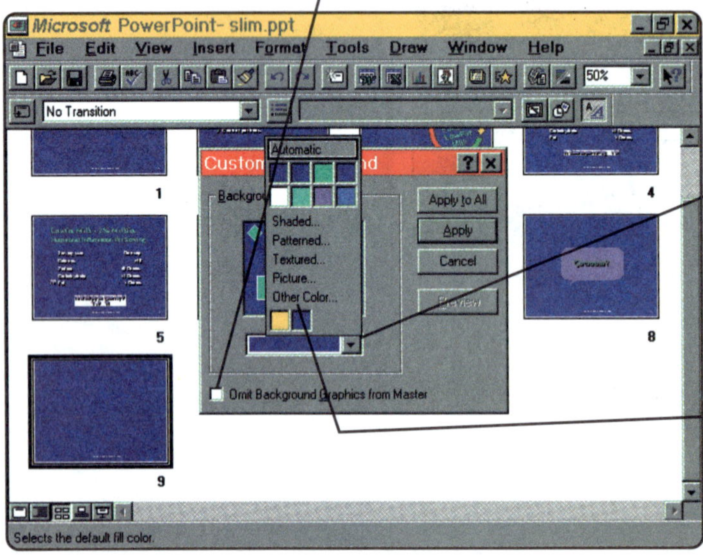

Changing the Background Color

1. **Click** on the **▼ to the** right of the blue rectangle beneath the Background Fill box. The Background Fill dialog box will appear.

2. **Click** on **Other Color.** The Colors dialog box will appear.

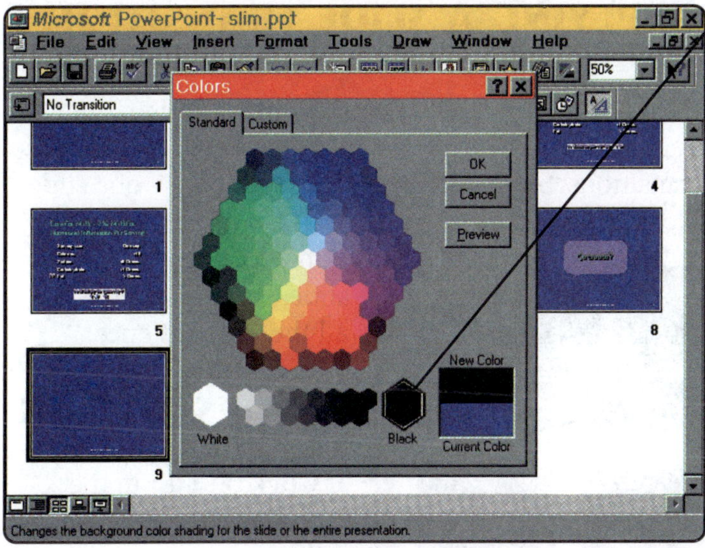

3. **Click** on the large **black hexagon**. The color black will appear in the New Color portion of the Current Color box.

4. **Click** on **OK**. The Colors dialog box will disappear and the Custom Background dialog box will reappear.

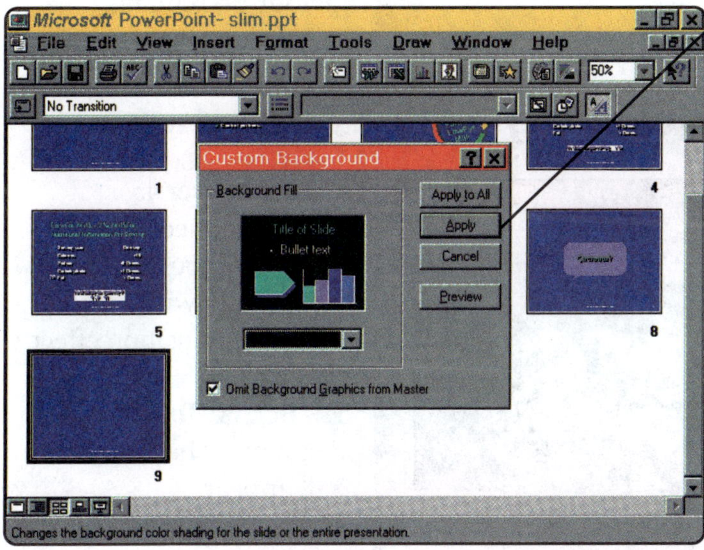

5. **Click** on **Apply**. (Be sure not to click on Apply to All!) The Slide Sorter view will appear with a black slide 9.

APPLYING A SLIDE TRANSITION

If you run your slide show on your computer, one very impressive special effect you can add is slide transitions. Slide transitions determine how one slide fades or dissolves into the next. You can apply transitions to individual slides, multiple slides, or all the slides at once.

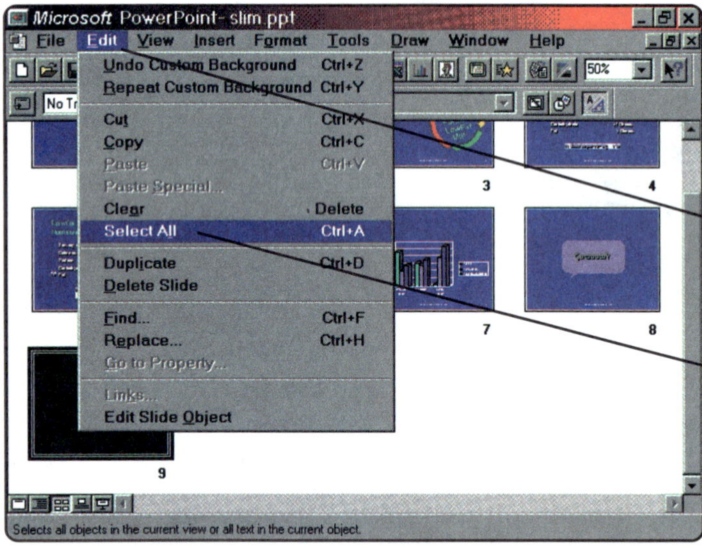

Using Select All

1. **Click** on **Edit** in the menu bar. The Edit menu will appear.

2. **Click** on **Select All**. The Slide Sorter view will appear with all the slides in your presentation selected.

Selecting a Slide Transition

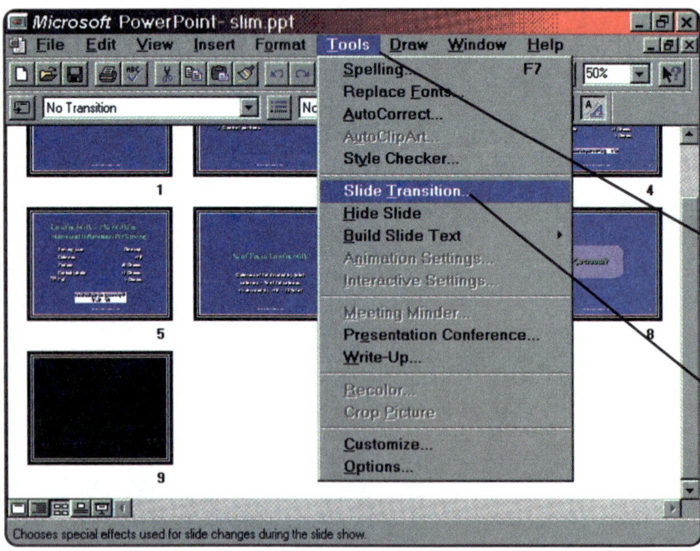

There are over 45 transition effects from which to choose. In this section you will choose a Random Transition effect.

1. **Click** on **Tools** in the menu bar. The Tools menu will appear.

2. **Click** on **Slide Transition**. The Slide Transition dialog box will appear.

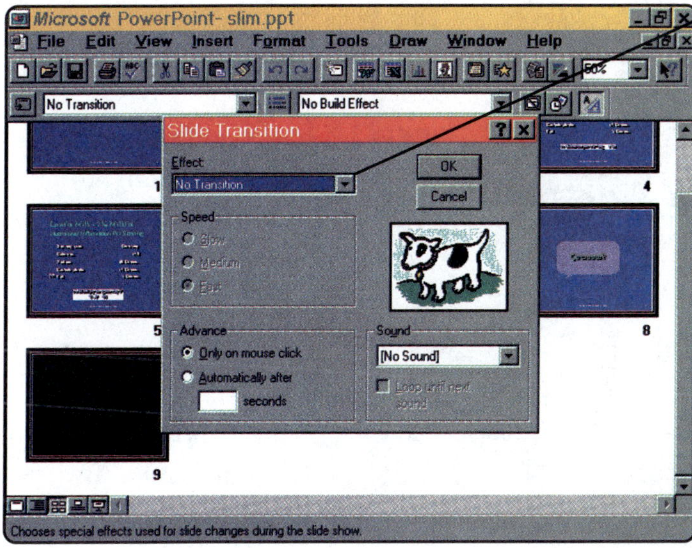

3. **Click** on the ▼ next to the Effect box. A pull-down list will appear.

4. **Press** the ▼ on your keyboard to scroll through the list of transitions. Notice that an example of the effect is shown in the lower right corner of the dialog box. Pause when you reach the end of the list.

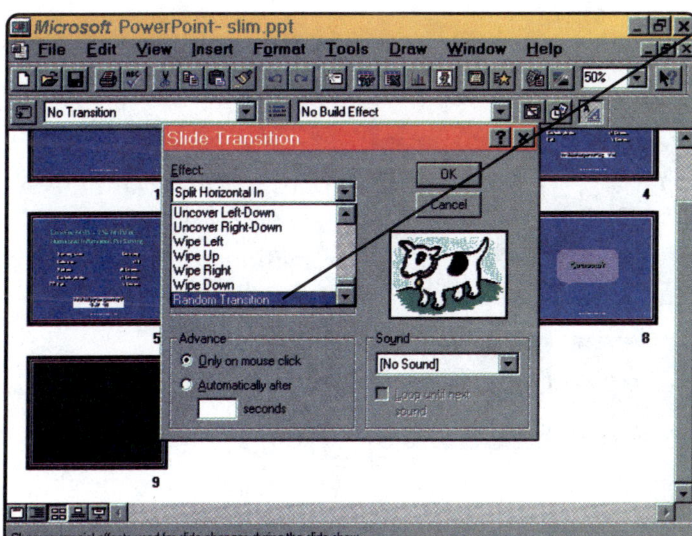

5. **Click** on **Random Transition**. The pull-down list will disappear.

Selecting a Transition Speed and Advance

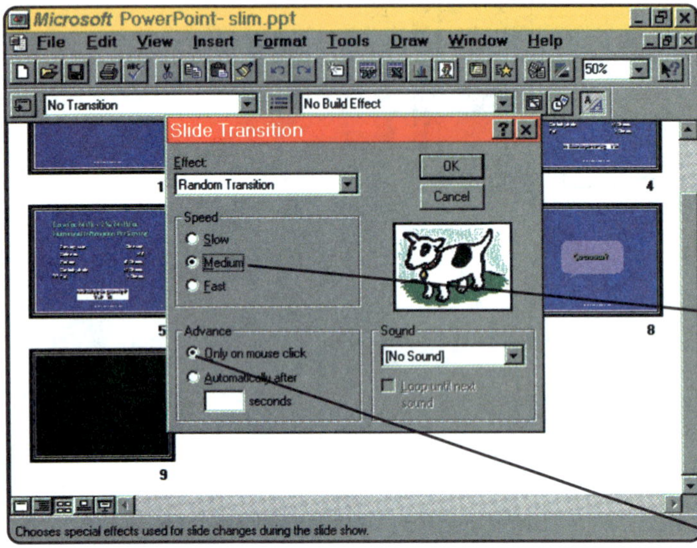

You can control the speed of slide transitions. You can also decide if you want your slides to advance automatically or when you click your mouse.

1. **Click** on **Medium** to put a dot in the circle. An example of this transition speed will appear in the display box.

2. **Click** on **Only on Mouse Click** to put a dot in the circle, if it is not already selected.

3. **Click** on **OK**. The Slide Sorter view will appear.

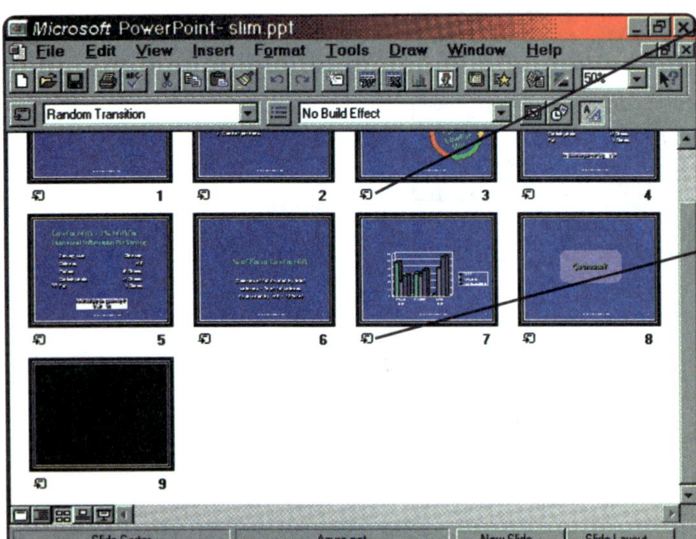

Notice the symbol that appears underneath the slides indicating that a transition has been applied.

4. **Click** on one of the transition symbols. An example of the transition that is applied to the slide will be displayed. Pretty neat!

USING SLIDE SHOW VIEW

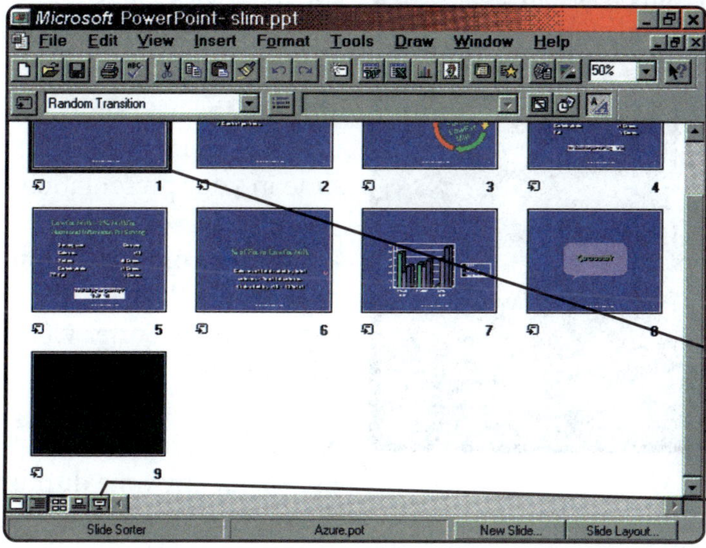

Slide Show view allows you to preview the transitions you have applied.

1. **Click** in the **white space** on the screen to deselect all the slides.
2. **Click** on **slide 1** to select it. The slide show starts with the active slide.
3. **Click** on the **Slide Show button**. After a pause, the first slide in your presentation will appear.

4. **Click** your **mouse button** or press the Page Down key to go to slide 2. Notice the transition effect.

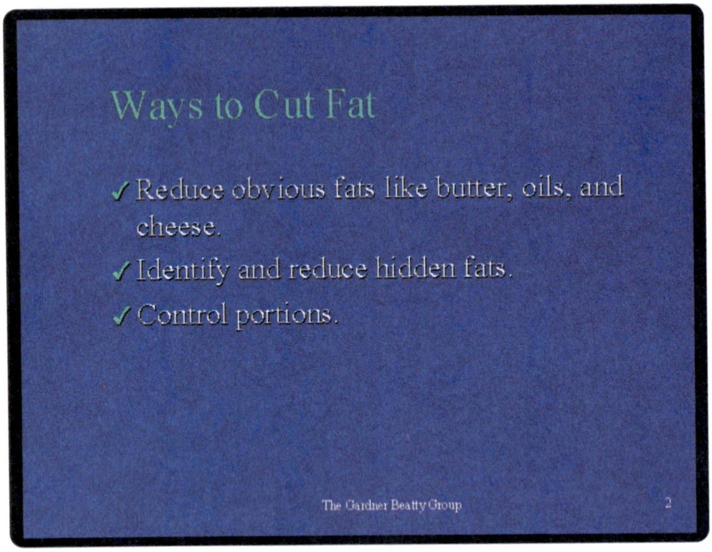

5. **Click** the **mouse button** or press the Page Down key to move slide 3.

6. **Continue** to **click** to move to the next slide until you reach the last slide in your presentation.

7. **Click** the **mouse button** or press the Page Down key. The Slide Sorter view will appear.

Note: You can press the Esc key at any time during the presentation to exit the Slide Show view.

EDITING TRANSITIONS BETWEEN SLIDES

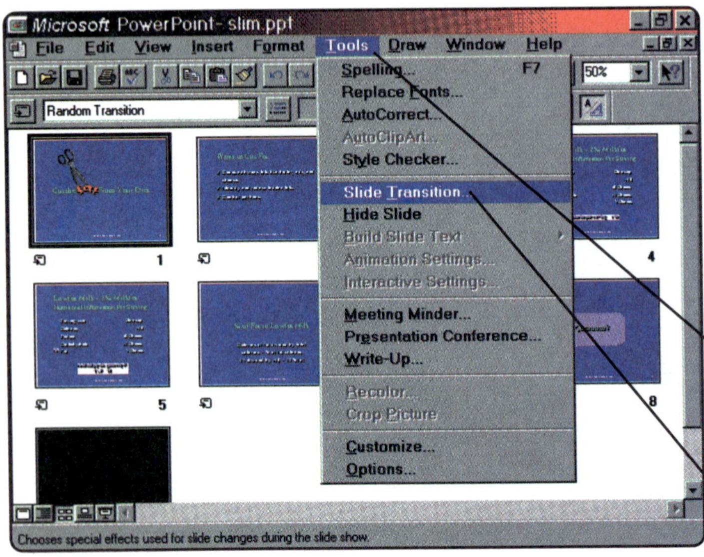

After previewing your slide show, you may wish to change some of the transitions. It's very easy to edit a slide transition.

1. **Click** on **slide 1** or the slide you wish to edit.

2. **Click** on **Tools** in the menu bar. The Tools menu will appear.

3. **Click** on **Slide Transition**. The Slide Transition dialog box will appear.

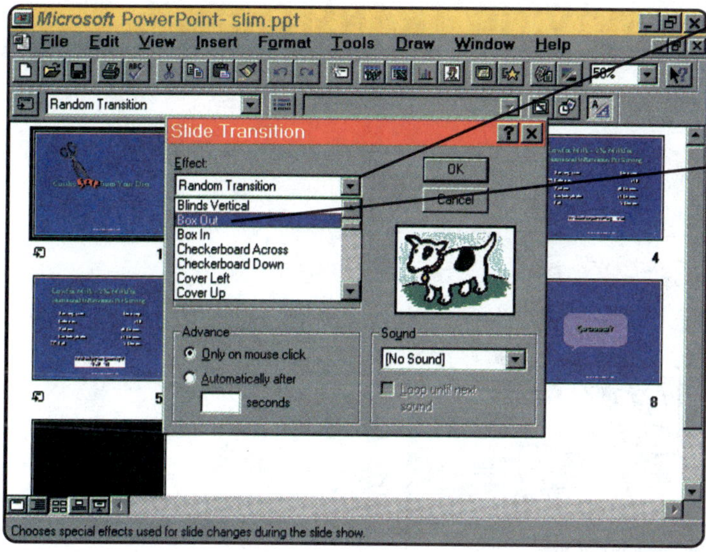

4. **Click** on the ▼ next to the Effect box. A pull-down list will appear.

5. **Click** on **Box Out** or a transition you prefer. The pull-down list will disappear, and a sample of the transition will be displayed.

6. **Click** on **Slow** to put a dot in the circle. An example of this transition speed will appear in the display box.

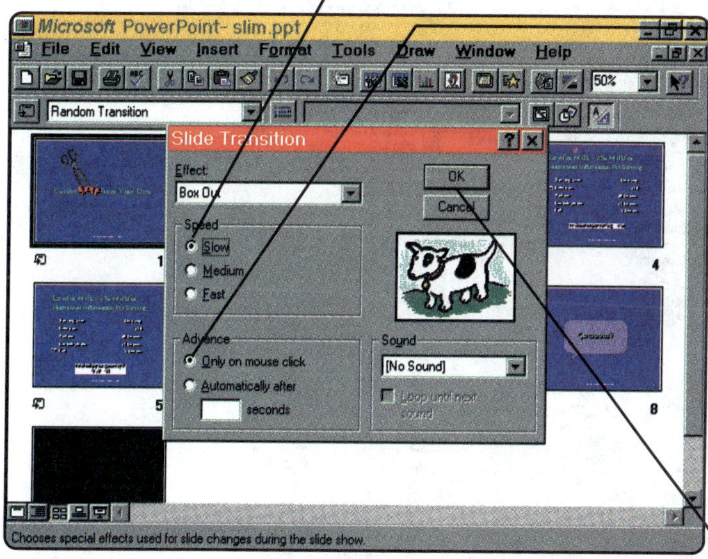

7. **Click** on **Only on mouse click** to put a dot in the circle.

Notice that you can also select Automatically after and specify a time so that the next slide in your presentation will appear automatically. You will learn how to automate your presentation later in this chapter.

8. **Click** on **OK**.

REMOVING TRANSITIONS

You can remove transitions completely if you wish.

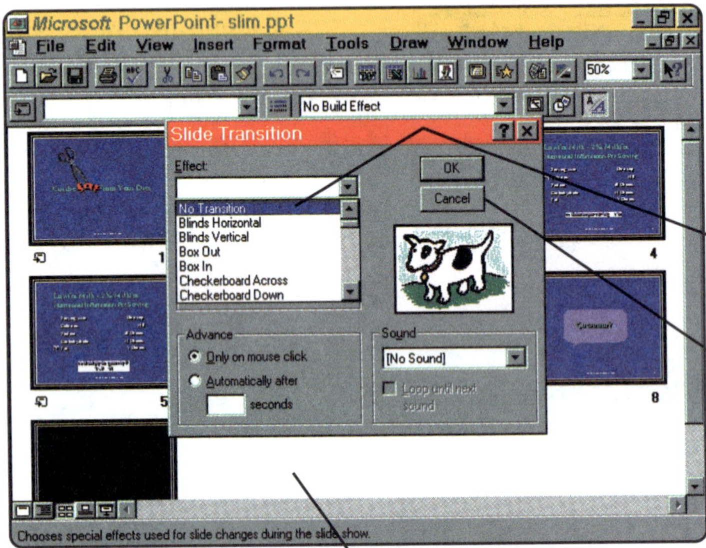

1. **Select all** the slides and open the Slide Transition dialog box. See "Applying a Slide Transition" if you need help on page 192.
2. **Click** on **No Transition** in the Effect box.
3. If you are following the steps in this chapter, **click** on **Cancel.** (Normally, you would **click** on **OK** to remove all transitions.)
4. **Click** on the **white space** to deselect the slides.

CREATING A BUILD SLIDE

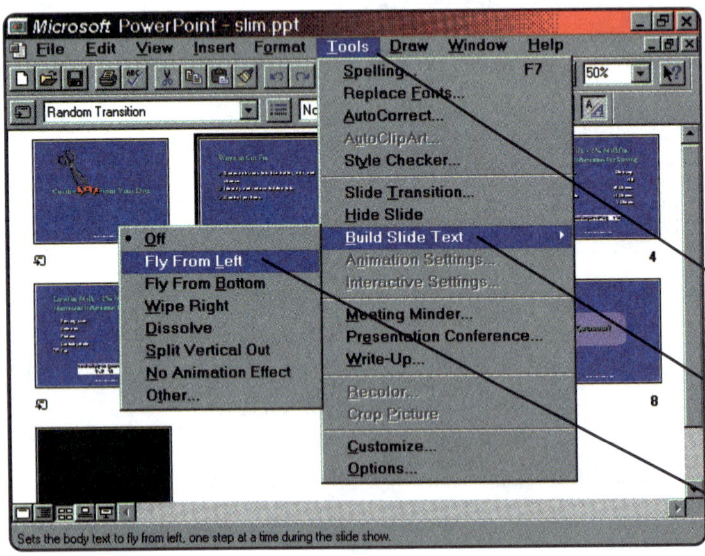

A *build slide* is an exciting effect that allows you to reveal bulleted points on a slide one at a time.

1. **Click** on **slide 2**.
2. **Click** on **Tools** in the menu bar.
3. **Click** on **Build Slide Text**.
4. **Click** on **Fly From Left**. The dialog box will appear.

Choosing a Color For Dimmed Bullets

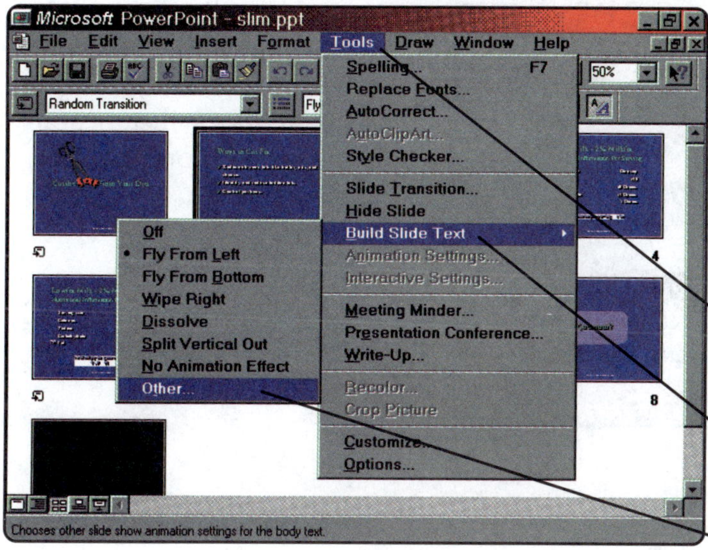

When a second bulleted item appears on the screen, you can make the first item dimmer in color. But first you must get to the Animation Settings dialog box.

1. **Click** on **Tools** in the menu bar.
2. **Click** on **Build Slide Text**.
3. **Click** on **Other**. The Animation Settings dialog box will appear.

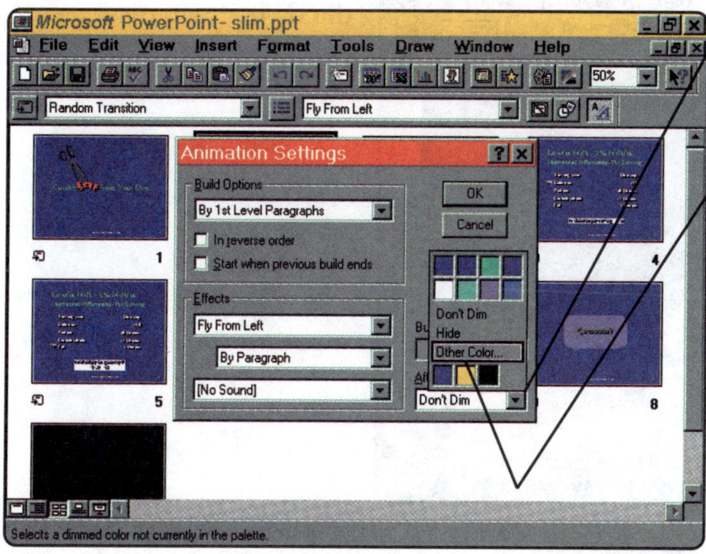

4. **Click** on the ▼ to the right of Don't Dim in the After Build Step box.
5. **Click** on **Other Color**. The Other Color dialog box will appear.

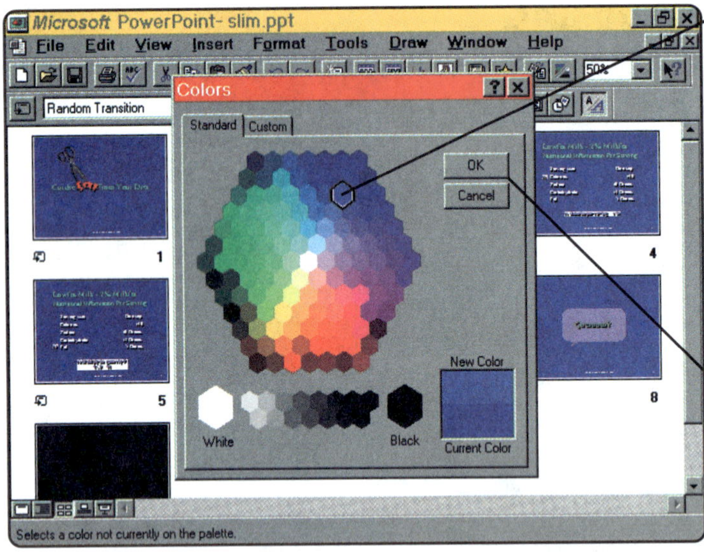

6. **Click** on the **light blue hexagon** in the third row from the top and three over from the right. It may be in a different place on your screen. An example of the color will appear in the New Color half of the preview box.

7. **Click** on **OK**. The Animation Settings dialog box will reappear.

Notice that the new color is now displayed in the After Build Step box.

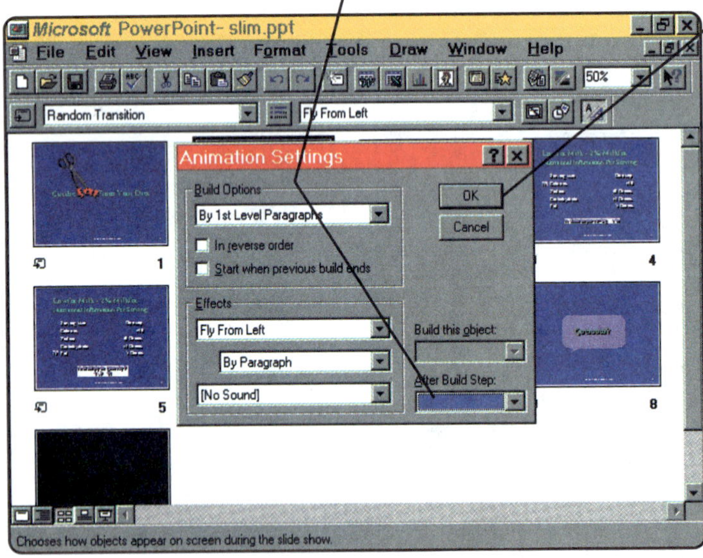

8. **Click** on **OK**. The Build dialog box will disappear.

Notice the symbol resembling a bulleted list that appears below slide 2. This indicates that this is a build slide. You will learn how to display this effect later in this chapter.

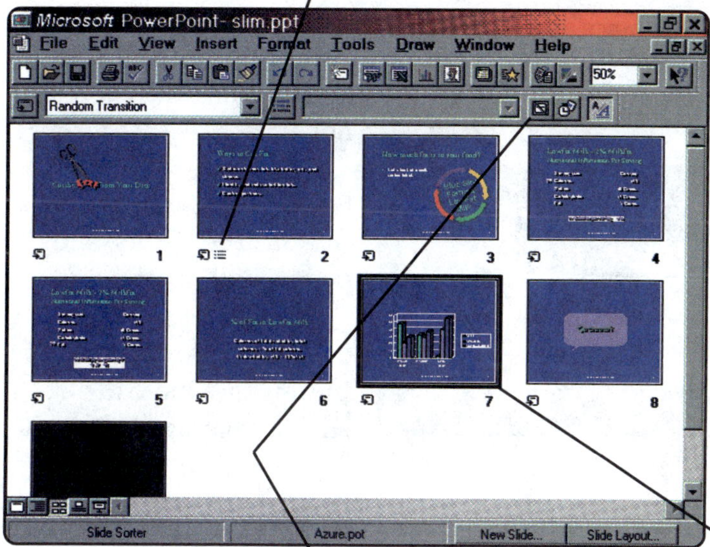

USING THE HIDE SLIDE BUTTON

Hidden slides are set up so you have the choice of including or not including them during a presentation.

Hiding a Slide

In this example we will make slide 7 a hidden slide.

1. **Click** on **Slide 7** to select it.
2. **Click** on the **Hide Slide button** in the toolbar. The button will appear pressed in and lighter in color.

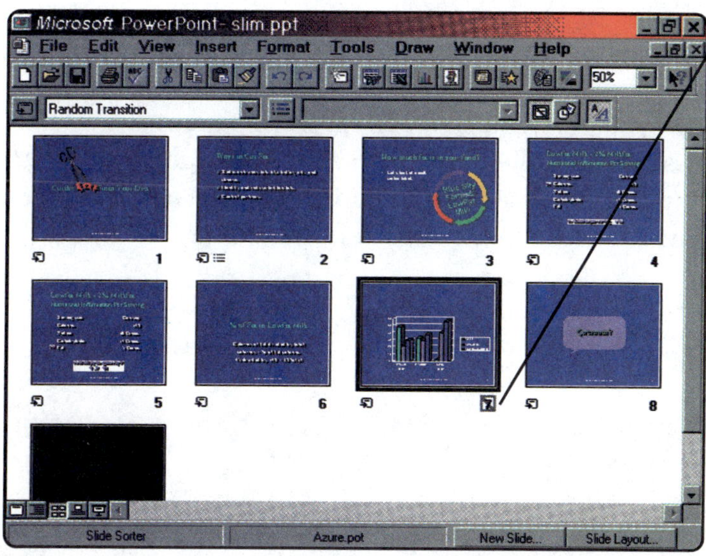

Notice the hidden slide symbol that appears below slide 7. You will learn how to use a hidden slide later in this chapter.

Removing the Hide Slide Option

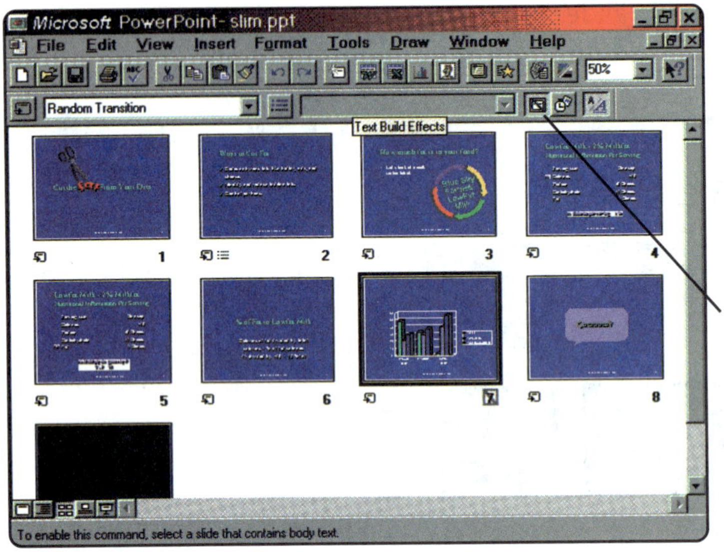

The Hide Slide button works like a toggle switch. Click once to turn it on. Click again to turn it off.

1. **Click** on **slide 7** if it is not already selected.
2. **Click** on the **Hide Slide button.** The hidden slide symbol will disappear.
3. **Click** on the **Hide Slide button** once more to make slide 7 a hidden slide again.

REHEARSING A PRESENTATION

PowerPoint has several nifty tools to help you practice your presentation.

The Rehearse Timings feature lets you time how long you spend on an individual slide and/or the entire presentation. You can then record the times and use them in the "Slide Timings" advance option when you run your slide show. The slides will then advance automatically at the predetermined times.

Using the Rehearse Timings Button

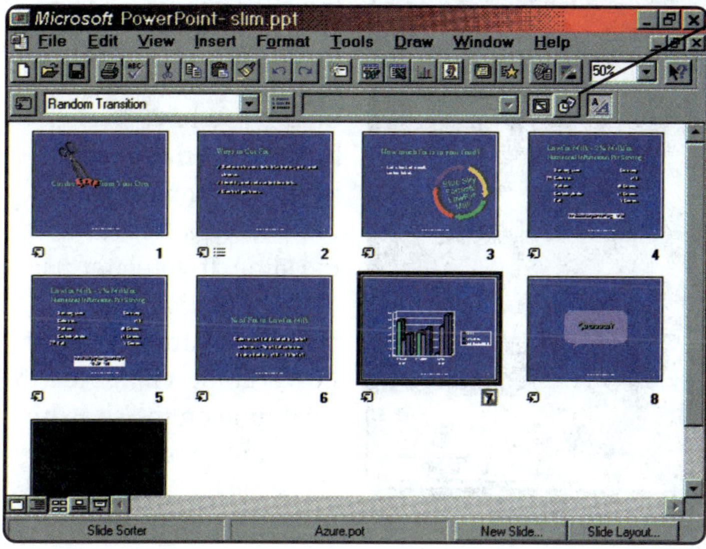

1. **Click** on the **Rehearse Timings button**. Slide 1 will appear in Slide Show view. The Rehearse Timings button always starts at slide 1 regardless of which slide is selected. Your screen will go black and after a pause you'll see the first slide.

Notice the timer that appears in the lower-right corner of your screen. It will be counting off seconds while the slide is showing.

2. **Rehearse** what you plan to say for this slide so that you can time it.

3. **Click** your **mouse** or press the Page Down key when you are done with this slide. The timer will stop for slide 1 and begin at 0:00 for slide 2.

Displaying a Build Slide

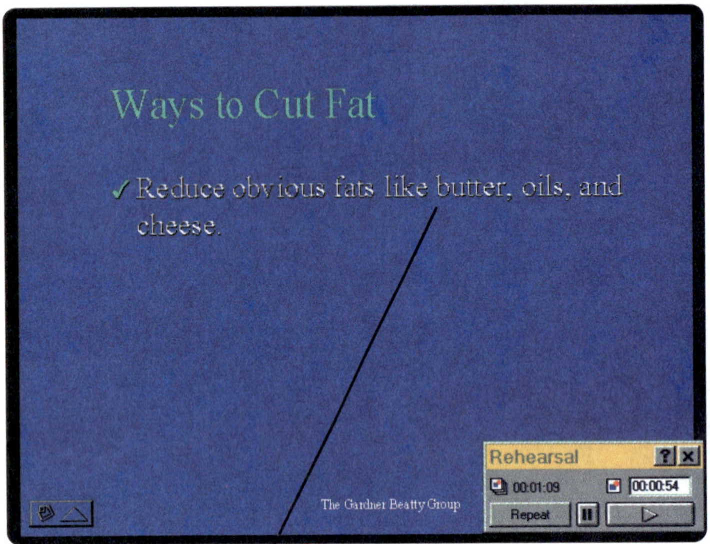

Notice that only the title of the slide shows when a build slide first appears. In the Rehearse Timings mode, you have to click to bring up each bulleted item. The timing device will record a total time for the slide. If you later use the automatic timed advance feature, PowerPoint will divide the total time on the slide by the number of bullets to show each bullet.

1. **Click** your **mouse button once** to bring the first bullet into view.

Notice that the text of the first bullet is bright.

2. **Click again** to bring the second bullet onto the slide.

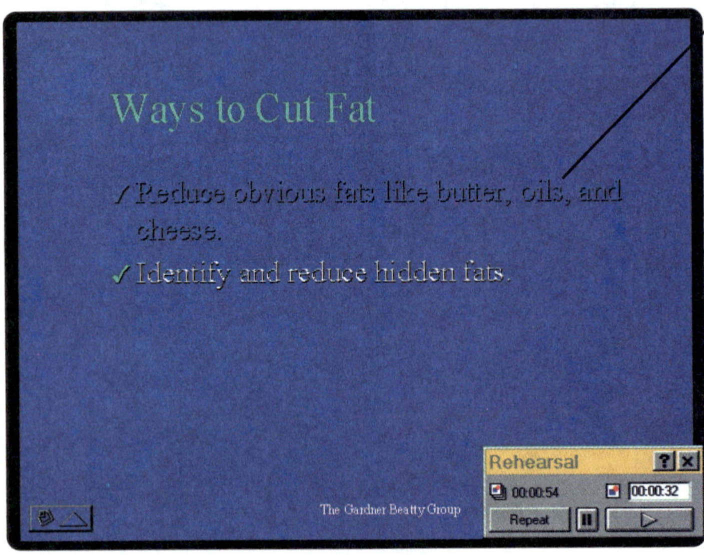

Notice that the first bullet is now dimmed and the second bullet is now bright.

3. **Click once again** to bring the third bullet into view.

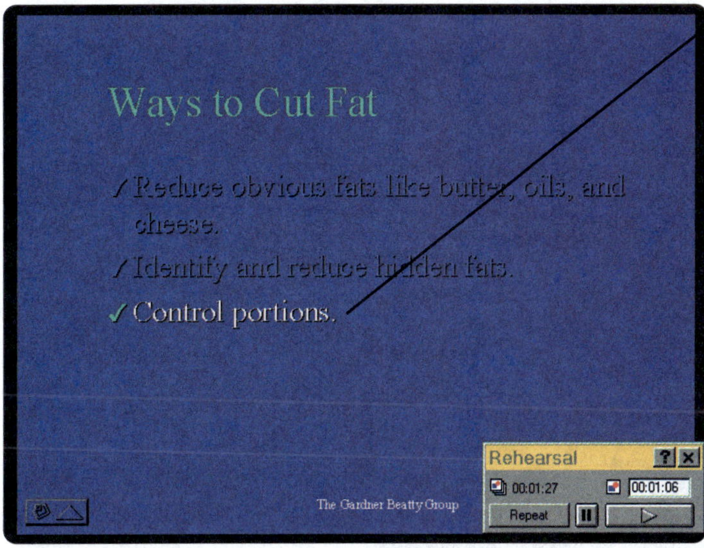

Notice that the first two bullets are now dimmed and the third is now the bright bullet.

4. **Click** your **mouse** or press the Page Down key to go to slide 3. The timer will stop for slide 2 and begin at 0:00 for slide 3.

5. **Click** to show **slides 3, 4, 5, and 6**. Slide 6 will appear on your screen as shown in the example below.

Using the Annotation Pen

PowerPoint provides a handy annotation pen option so you can write on slides as you are presenting the slide show. Once you go to the next slide, the temporary markings you made on the prior slide will disappear.

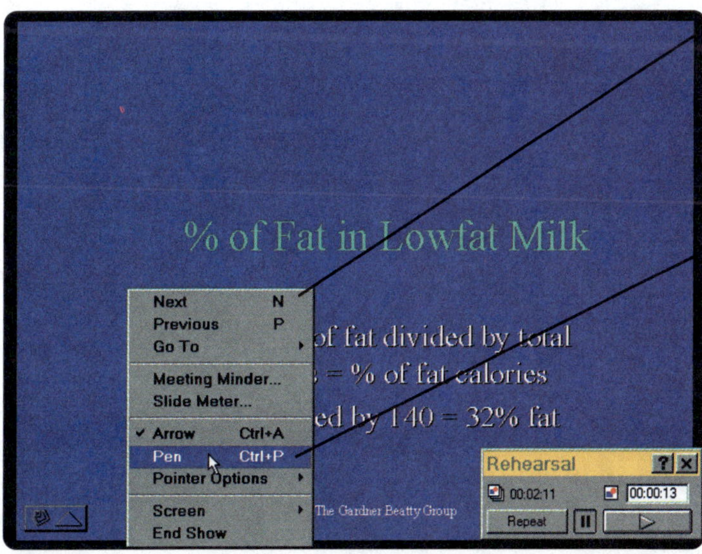

1. **Place** the **mouse arrow anywhere** on the slide and **click** the **right mouse button**. The Slide View menu will appear.

2. **Click** on **Pen** to **place** a ✔ in front of it. The menu will close.

Notice that your pointer now has the shape of a pen.

3. **Place** the **mouse pointer** where you wish to begin drawing or writing on your slide. In this example, place it under 32.

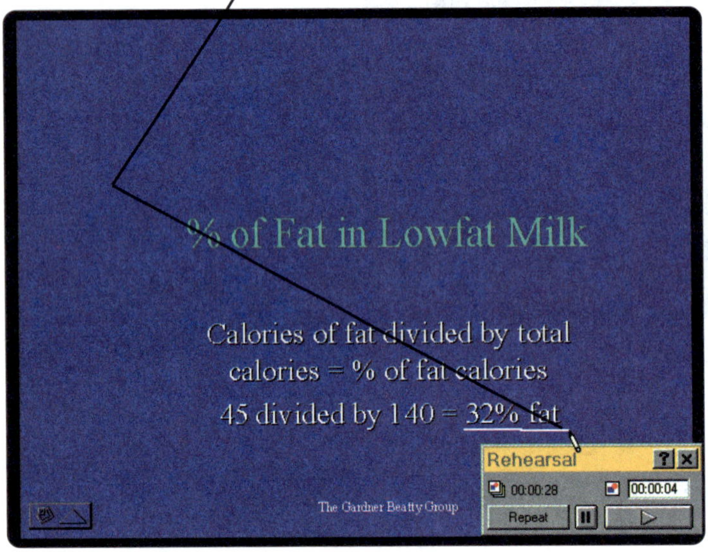

4. **Press and hold** your **mouse button** and **underline "32% fat." Release** the **mouse button**.

If you feel like you're in kindergarten when you first use this tool, practicing will make it go more smoothly. The marks you make on the slide during annotation mode are only temporary. Once you change slides, they will disappear.

5. **Remove** the **pen** by **repeating steps 1 and 2** on the previous page or press the Page Down key on your keyboard to move to the next slide. The pen will not be on the next slide. (Clicking the mouse button will not move you to the next slide when the pen is present. You must press the Page Down key.)

Revealing a Hidden Slide

You have two options with a hidden slide. You can skip slide 7 by clicking your mouse or you can reveal slide 7 as the next slide. In this example you will reveal the hidden slide.

1. **Press** the **H key** on your **keyboard.** This reveals the next slide which is a hidden slide.

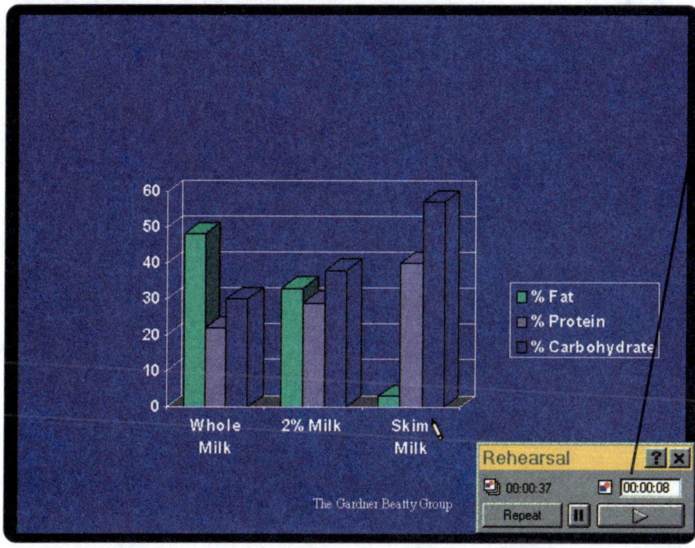

Notice that the hidden slide shows a timer in the corner. If you had chosen not to reveal the hidden slide it would not have had a time applied to it. It would have remained a manual slide. This might be an option to consider during your presentation.

2. **Click** your **mouse** or press the Page Down key to go to the next slide. The timer will start at 0:00 for this slide.

3. **Repeat step 2** for the remaining slides in your presentation. A Microsoft PowerPoint dialog box will appear after you have clicked on the last slide in your presentation.

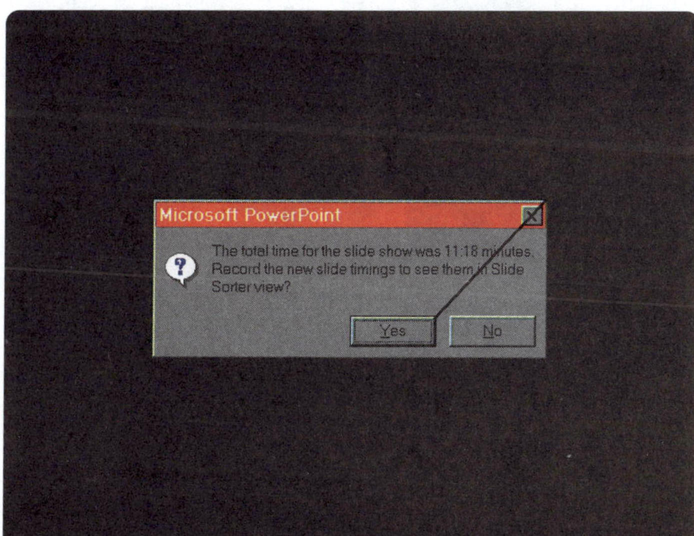

4. **Click** on **Yes** if you are happy with your rehearsal or **click** on **No** and the new times will not be applied. You will return to Slide Sorter view.

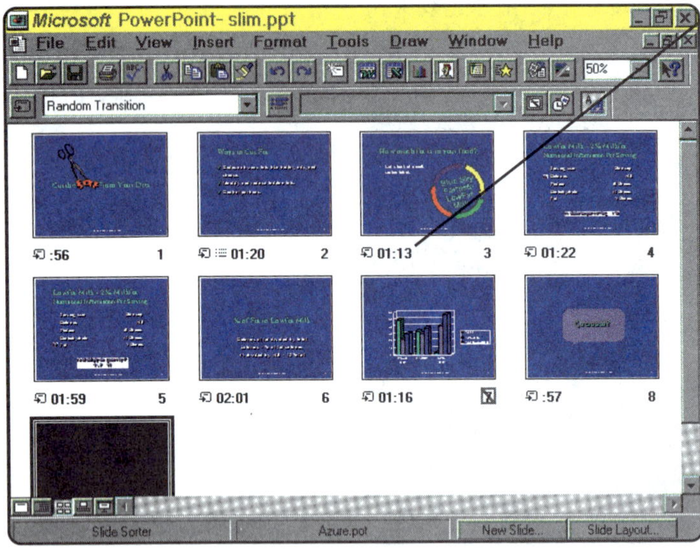

Notice that if you clicked on yes in the previous step, the practice times have been applied to your slides.

RUNNING A SLIDE SHOW

There are two ways to start your slide show.

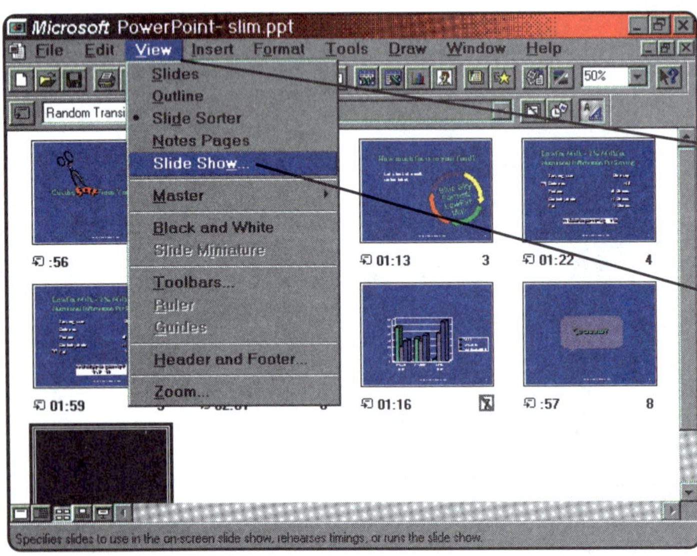

Using the View Menu

1. Click on **View** in the menu bar. The View menu will appear.

2. Click on **Slide Show**. The Slide Show dialog box will appear.

You can either select all of the slides in your presentation or a range of slides.

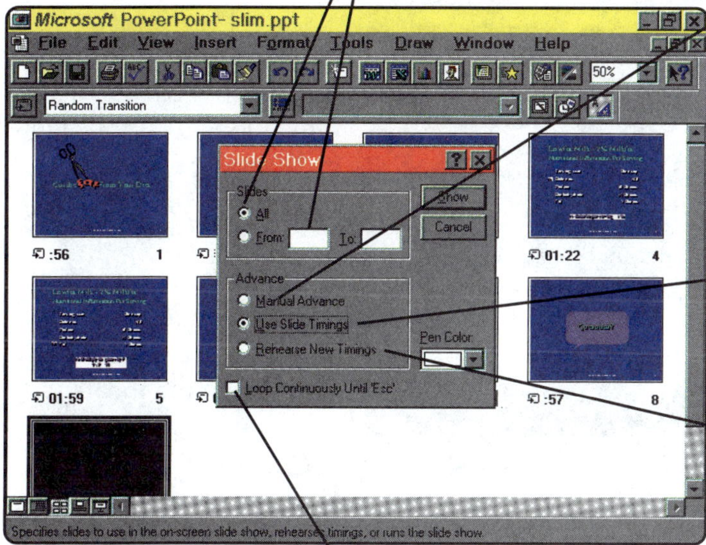

You can select Manual Advance. This allows you to run your slides manually without erasing the times you have set for an automatic slide show.

Select Use Slide Timings to run your slide show with the existing slide times.

If you are unhappy with your slide times you can select Rehearse New Timings.

An exciting PowerPoint feature is the ability to run an automatic slide show continuously. This is a wonderful option to use in a display booth.

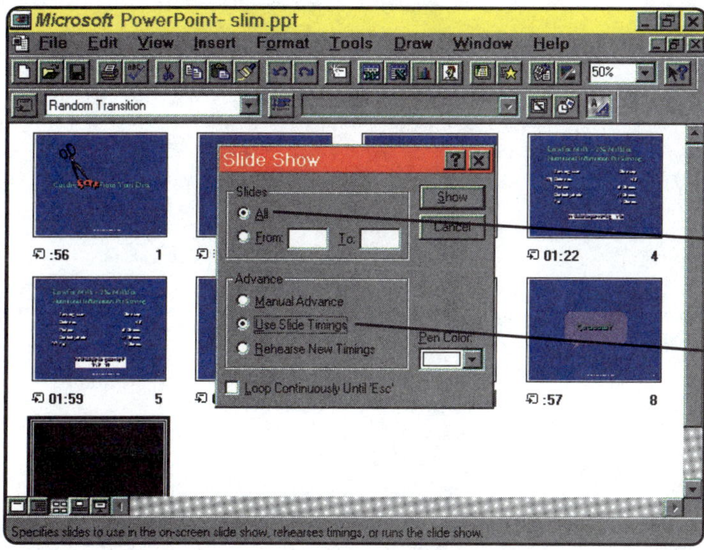

Choose your slides and advance by clicking on the options of your choice. In this example we will select All and Use Slide Timings.

3. **Click** on **All** if it is not already selected.

4. **Click** on **Use Slide Timings**.

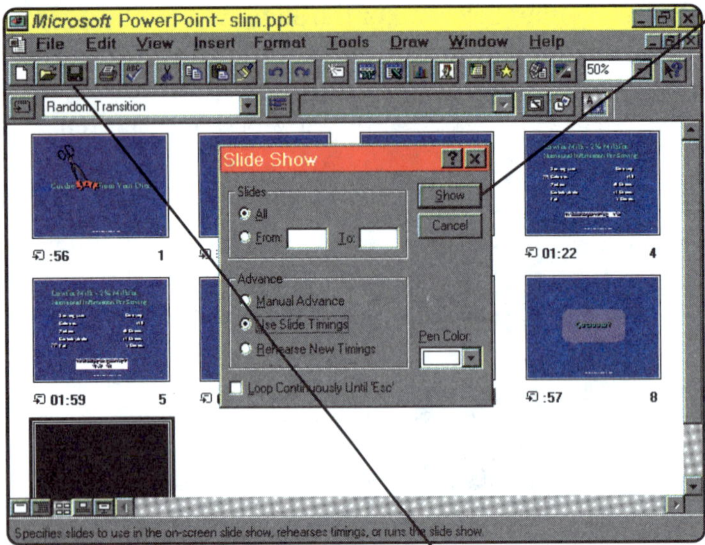

5. **Click** on **Show**. After a pause, your slide show presentation will begin.

Practice your slide show or **press** the **Esc key** to return to Slide Sorter view if you don't wish to view your entire presentation.

Now that you're a pro at presenting your slide show, "break a leg" as they say in the theater.

6. **Click** on the **Save button** to save your presentation.

CHAPTER

17

Taking Your Show on the Road

If you want to take or send a presentation off-site and show it on a computer that does not have PowerPoint, there are a few things you should do first. In this chapter, you will review the following:

- ✔ Use the Pack and Go Wizard to download your presentation to a disk
- ✔ View your presentation immediately
- ✔ Install the presentation and view it at a later time

USING THE PACK AND GO WIZARD

PowerPoint for Windows 95 has a wonderful feature called the Pack and Go Wizard that walks you step-by-step through the process of putting your presentation on a disk so you can take it with you or send it to another site.

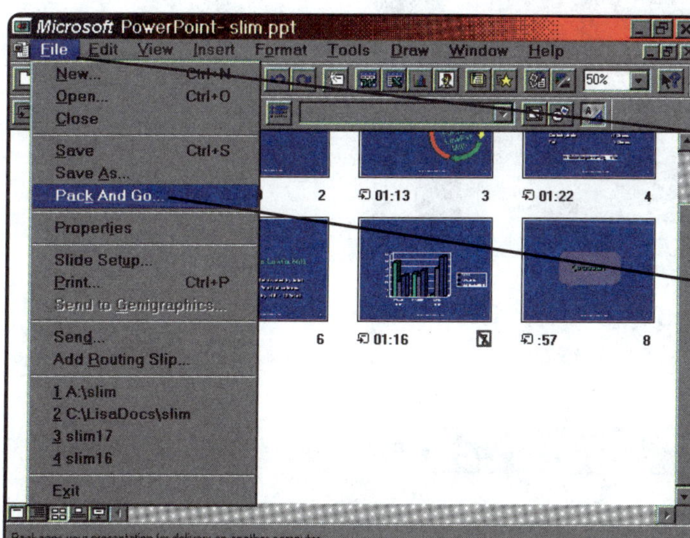

1. **Insert** a **disk** into the appropriate disk drive.
2. **Click** on **File** in the menu bar. The file menu will appear.
3. **Click** on **Pack and Go**. The Pack and Go Wizard dialog box will appear.

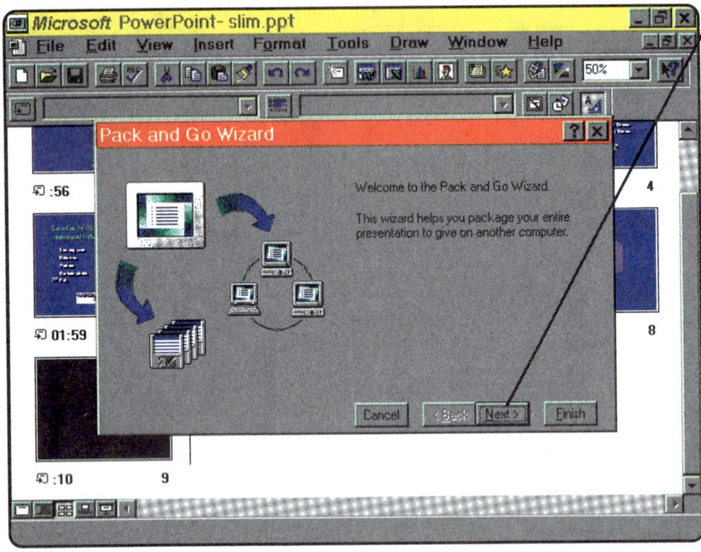

4. **Click** on **Next>**. The next dialog box will appear.

5. **Click** on **slim,** or the name of your presentation, to place a dot in the circle if it's not already there.

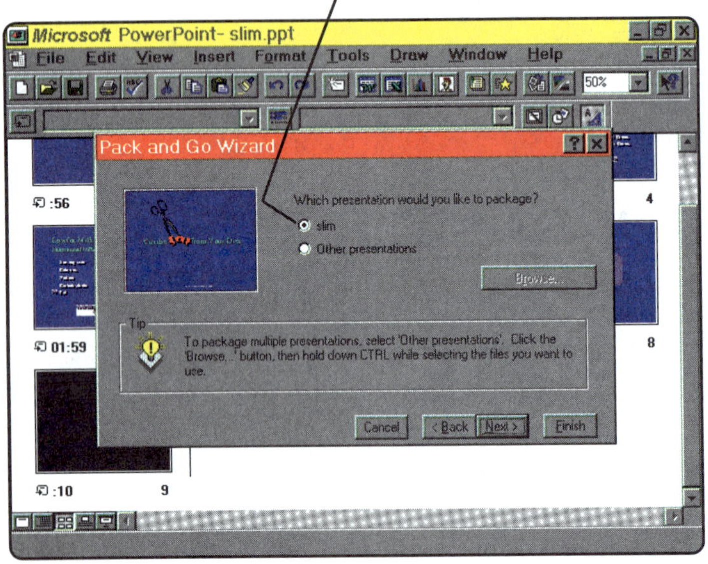

6. **Click** on **Next>**. The next dialog box will appear.

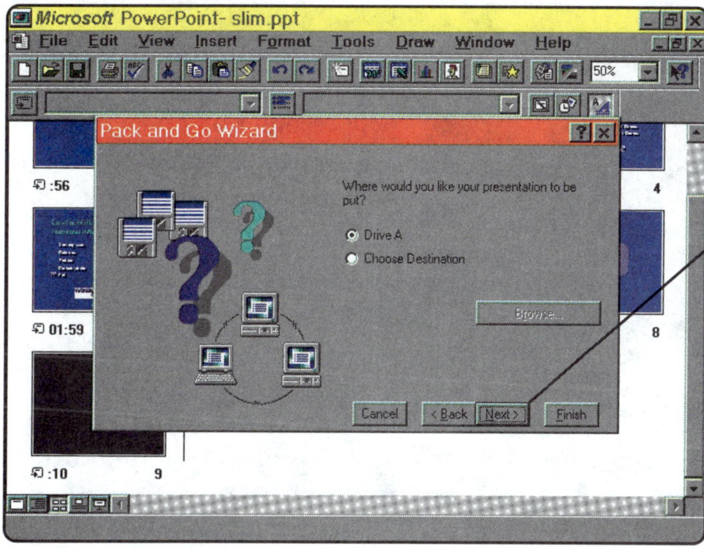

7. **Click** on **Drive A** (this may be a different drive on your computer) to place a dot in the circle if it's not already there.

8. **Click** on **Next>**. The next dialog box will appear.

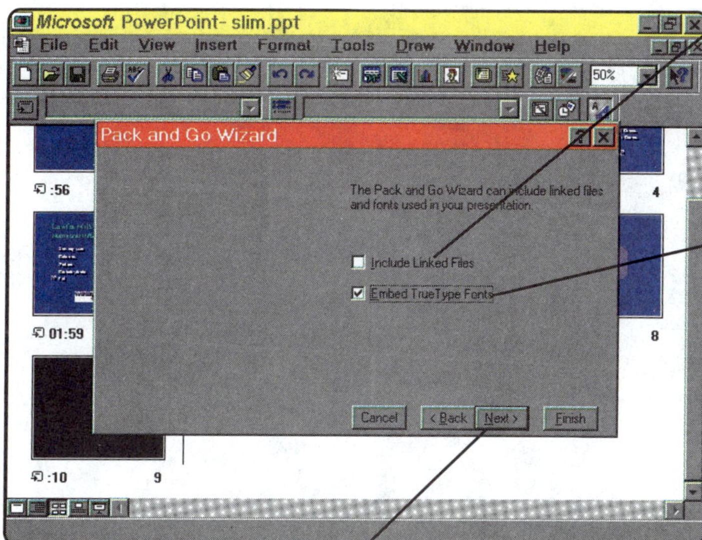

9. **Click** on **Include Linked Files** to place a ✔ in the box only if your presentation has linked files.

10. **Click** on **Embed True-Type Fonts** to place a ✔ in the box, if it's not already there. This will ensure that the type fonts you used in your presentation will show up on other computers that may not have the same fonts.

11. **Click** on **Next>**. The next dialog box will appear.

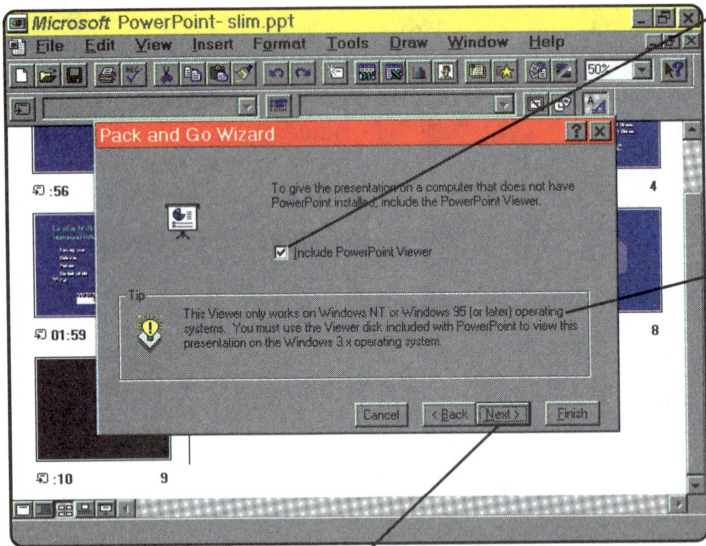

12. **Confirm** that this **box** has a ✔ in it, so that you will be able to show your presentation on a computer that doesn't have PowerPoint.

Notice that this Viewer only works with Windows NT or Windows 95. You will need to use the Viewer disk included with Powerpoint in order to view the presentation on a computer with Windows 3.1.

13. **Click** on **Next>** to go to the next dialog box.

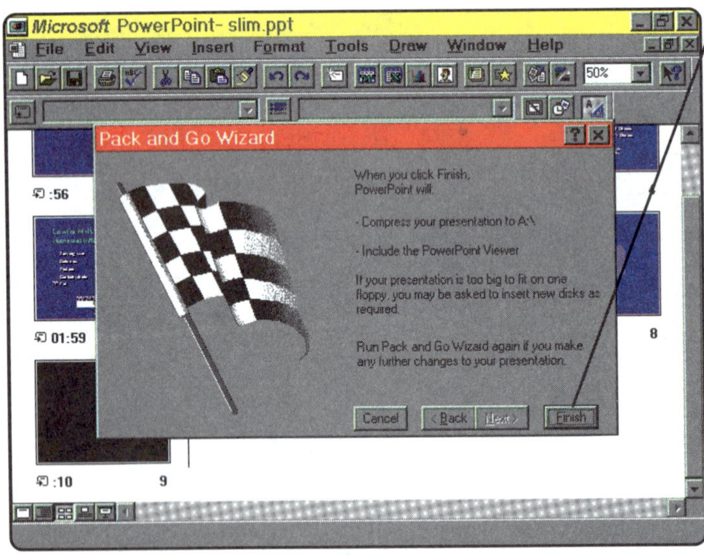

14. **Click** on **Finish.**

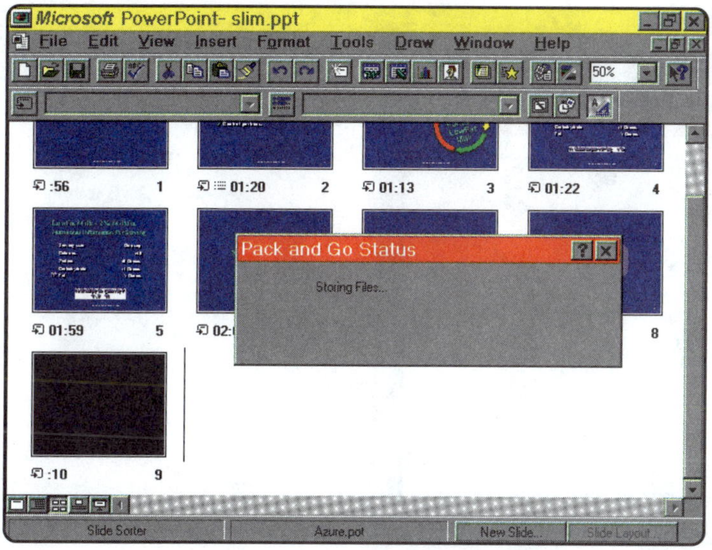

You will see the message "Storing Files," while the presentation is being stored on the disk in the disk drive. When the process is done, remove the disk and save it for later use on another host computer.

VIEWING A PRESENTATION ON A WINDOWS 95 COMPUTER WITHOUT POWERPOINT

This section assumes that you have used the Pack and Go Wizard, described above, to put your presentation on a disk. In this section, you'll use the disk to view your presentation on a host computer. This will work whether or not the computer has PowerPoint installed, if it has Windows 95. This method makes it easy to show your presentation on another computer.

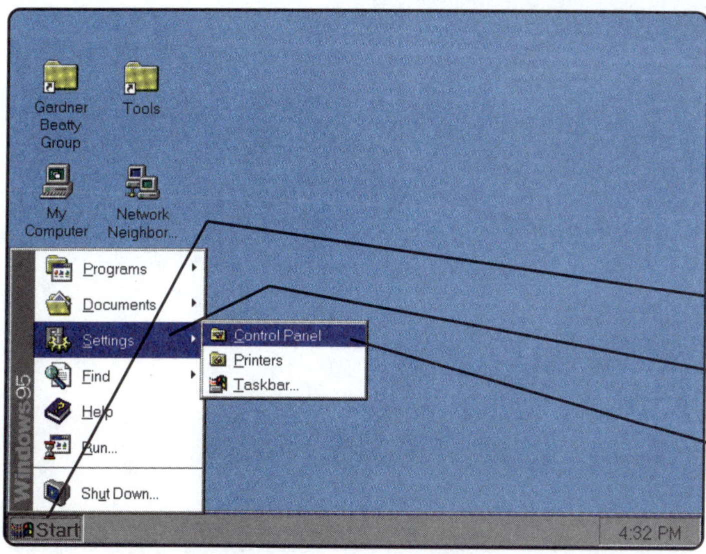

1. **Click** on **Start.**
2. **Click** on **Settings.**
3. **Click** on **Control Panel.** The Control Panel icon box will appear.

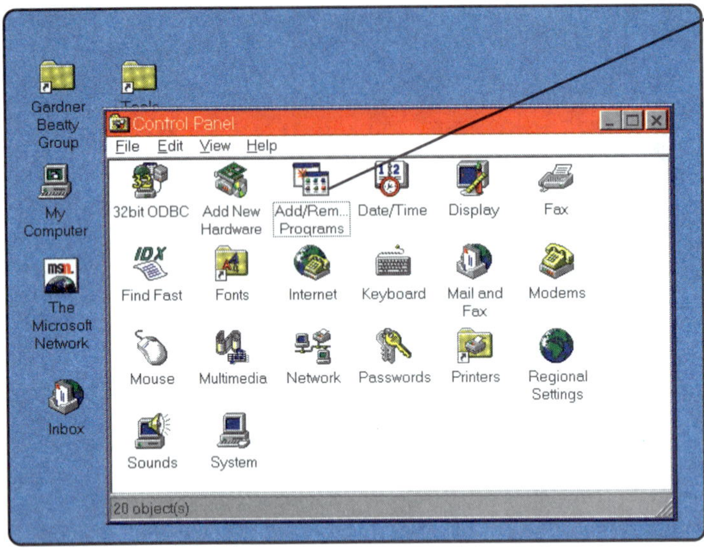

4. Click twice on **Add/Rem... Programs**. The Add Remove Programs Properties dialog box will appear.

5. Click on the **Install/Uninstall tab** if it is not already on top.

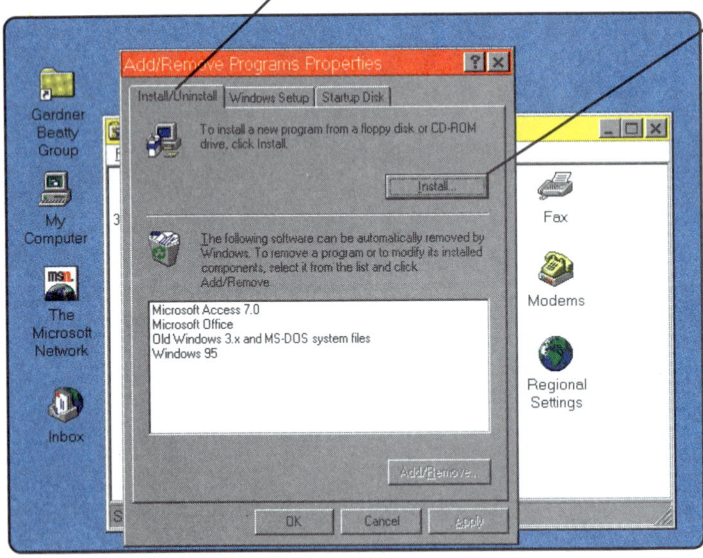

6. Click on the **Install button.**

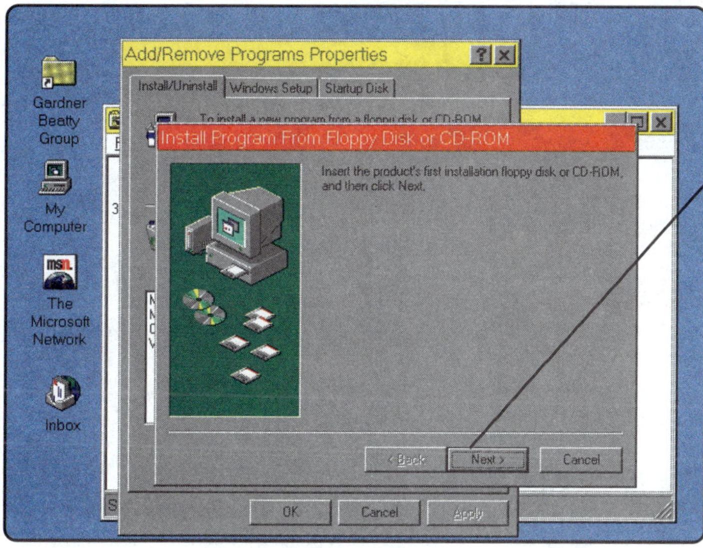

7. **Insert** the **Pack and Go disk** into the appropriate **disk drive.**

8. **Click** on **Next>**. The next dialog box will appear.

Notice that the correct execution file automatically appears in the Command Line box. If need be, you can also use the browse button to locate the execution file.

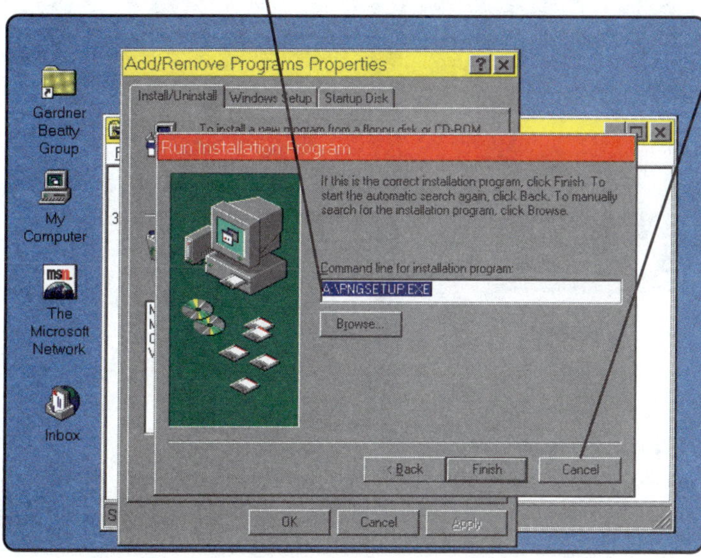

9. **Click** on **Finish.**

Installing the Presentation in a Specific Directory

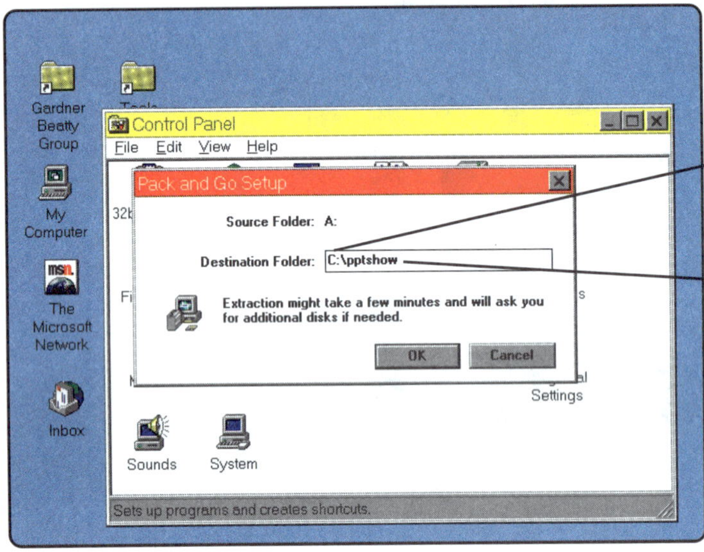

In this example, you'll create a directory on the C: drive.

1. **Click** to the **right** of **C:** to place the cursor.
2. **Type pptshow** or the name of the directory into which you want to install the presentation. If the directory does not exist, you'll see the message box below.

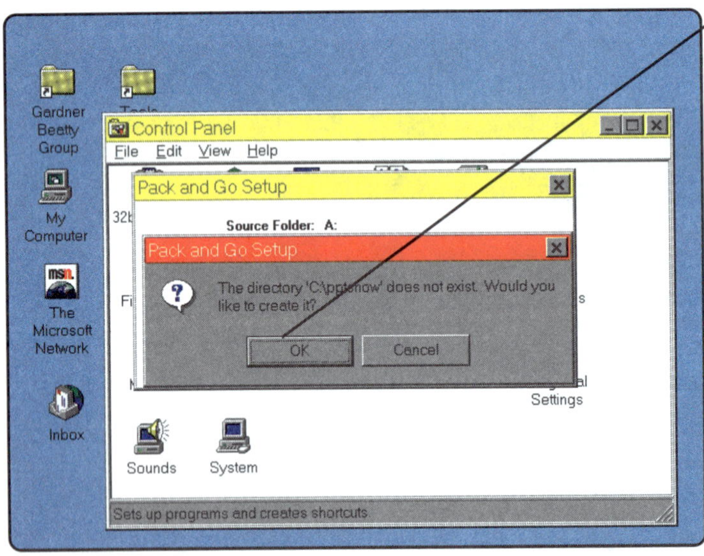

3. **Click** on **OK** to create the new directory.

Viewing the Presentation

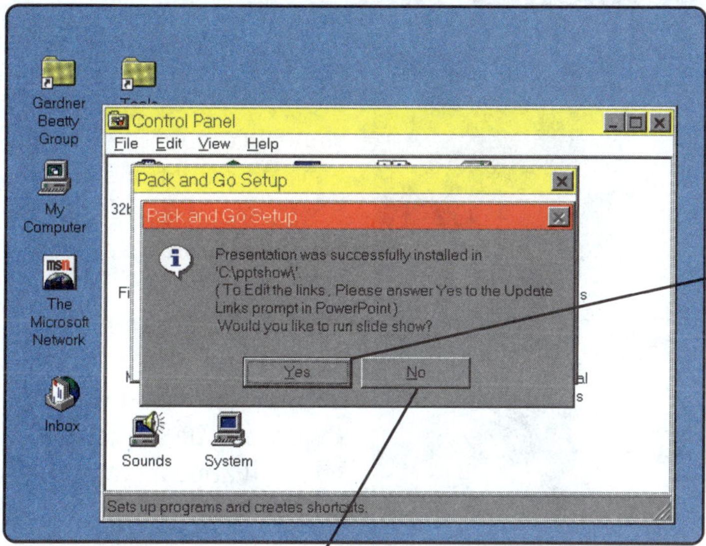

You can choose to view the presentation right away or to save it on the hard drive for later viewing. Just choose one of the following:

1a. If you want to see the presentation now, **click** on **Yes**. The control panel will appear and after a while, the screen will black out for a brief time. Don't panic! It's all part of the process. After a time, the first slide will appear as you see below.

1b. If you don't want to view the presentation now, **click on No**, then go to the section entitled, "Viewing a Presentation at a Later Time" on the next page.

Note: Once the presentation comes on the screen, use the Page Down key on your keyboard or click the mouse to move through the slides. Press the Esc key on your keyboard to shut down the presentation.

Viewing the Presentation at Another Time

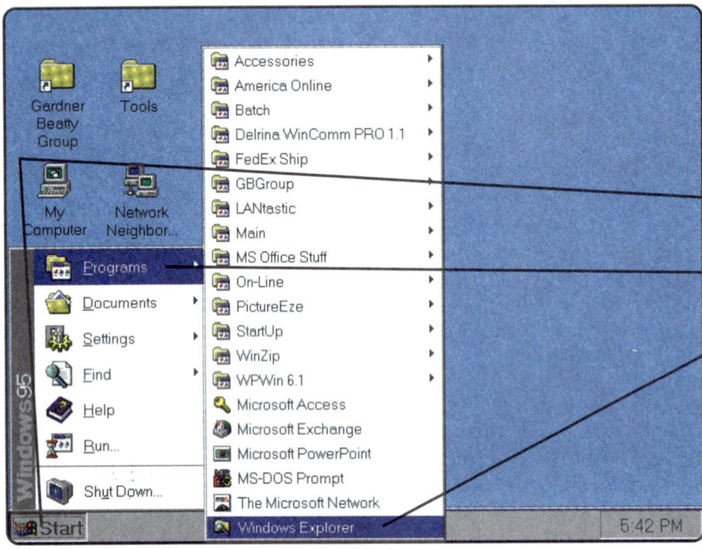

Once the presentation is installed on the Windows 95 host computer, you can view it at any time.

1. Click on **Start.**

2. Click on **Programs.**

3. Click on **Windows Explorer.** The Exploring box will appear.

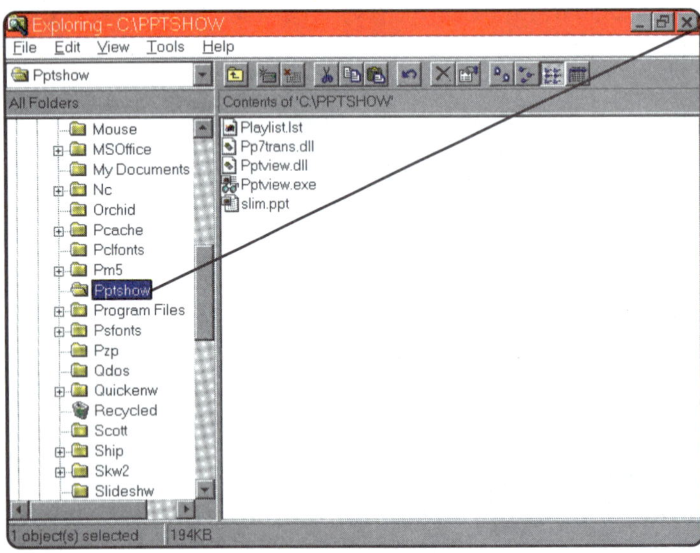

4. **Click twice** on the **directory** where you installed the PowerPoint presentation from disk. In this example, it is in the Pptshow directory. The directory files will appear.

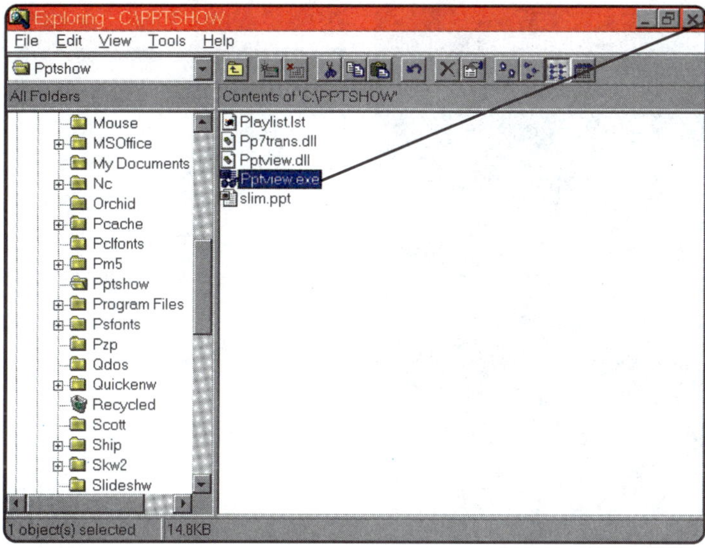

5. **Click twice** on **Pptview.exe.** This is the viewer file that allows you to boot up a PowerPoint presentation on a computer that doesn't have PowerPoint installed. The Microsoft PowerPoint Viewer box will appear.

6. **Click** on **slim.ppt** or the name of your installed presentation.

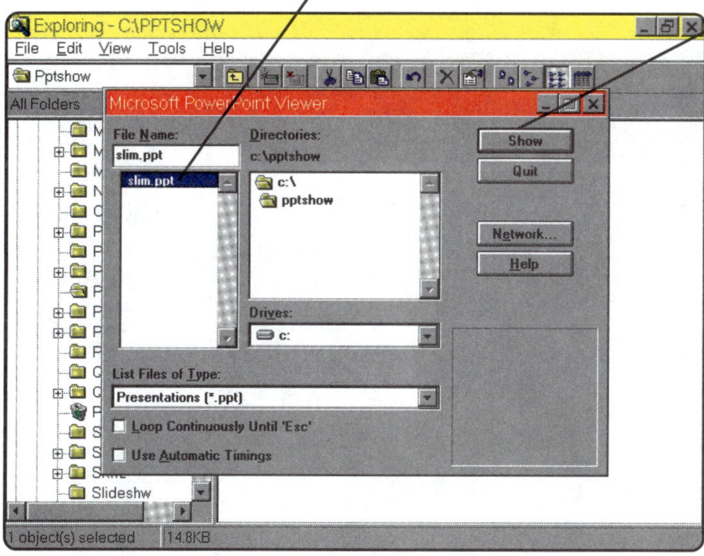

7. **Click** on **Show.** The presentation will boot up.

Note: Once the presentation comes on the screen, use the Page Down key on your keyboard or click the mouse to move through the slides. Press the Esc key on your keyboard to shut down the presentation.

When you finish viewing the presentation, you will return to the Microsoft PowerPoint Viewer screen.

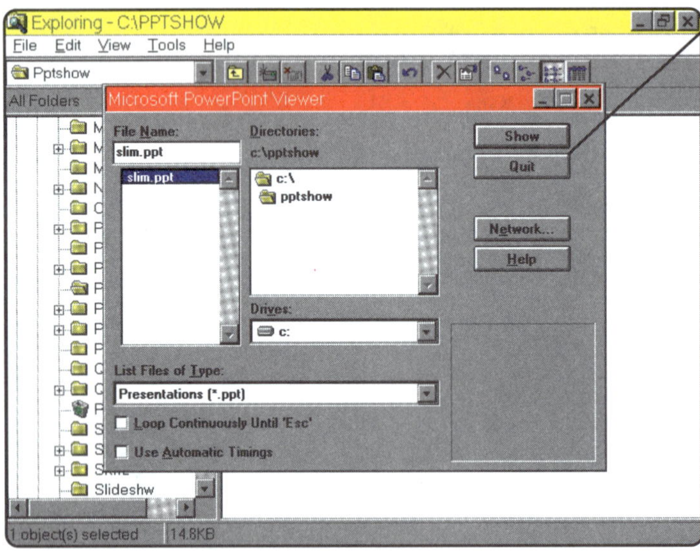

8. **Click** on **Quit** to close down the presentation viewer.

If you want to show your presentation on a host computer with Windows 3.1, consult your Windows 95 manual for details.

Part V: Special Features

CHAPTER 18

Using AutoContent Wizard

If you're unsure about how to begin a new presentation, you can use the AutoContent Wizard. There are six presentation formats that include such topics as presenting a strategy, training, and reporting progress. After you select a topic, AutoContent Wizard gives you a content-related outline that can be edited to fit your specific situation. The outline can then be turned into slides with a mouse click. In this chapter you will do the following:

✔ Use the AutoContent Wizard
✔ Work in Outline view

SELECTING AN AUTOCONTENT PRESENTATION

Begin AutoContent Wizard with a new presentation. To do this, you need to save and close whatever is on your screen. If you are starting PowerPoint, you can select AutoContent Wizard from the dialog box that appears after the Tip of the Day. In this example, you'll start a new presentation and then choose AutoContent Wizard.

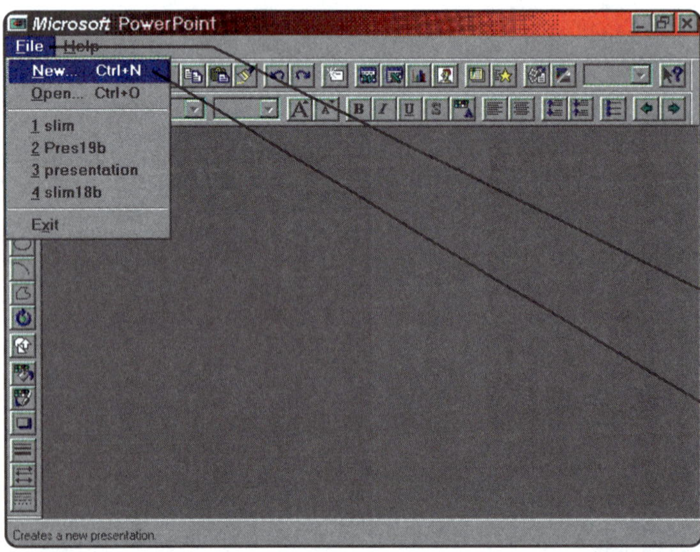

1. **Click** on **File.** The File menu will appear.

2. **Click** on **New.** The New Presentation dialog box will appear.

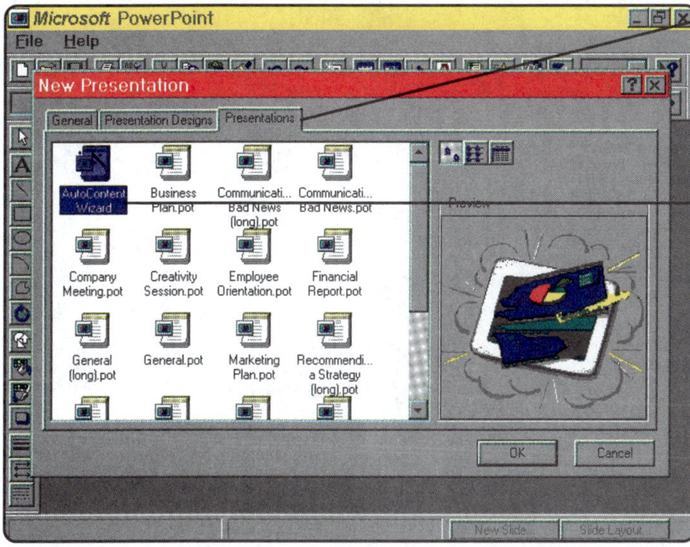

3. Click on the **Presentations tab** to bring it to the front of the dialog box.

4. Click twice on **AutoContent Wizard.** The AutoContent Wizard dialog box will appear.

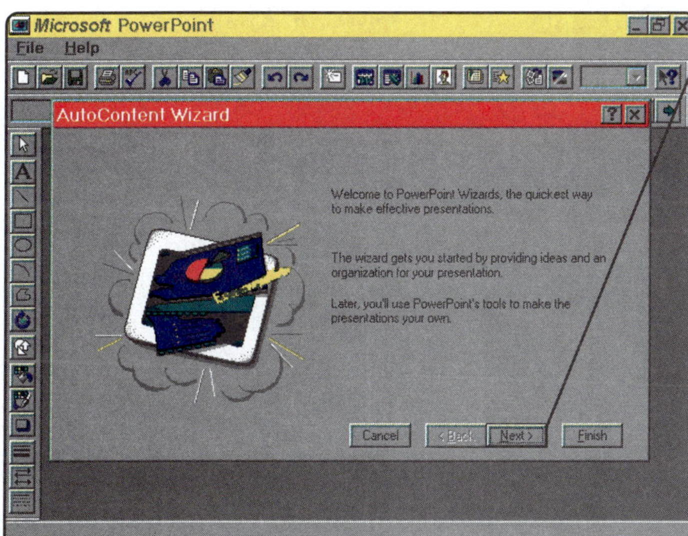

5. Click on **Next>**. The next dialog box will appear.

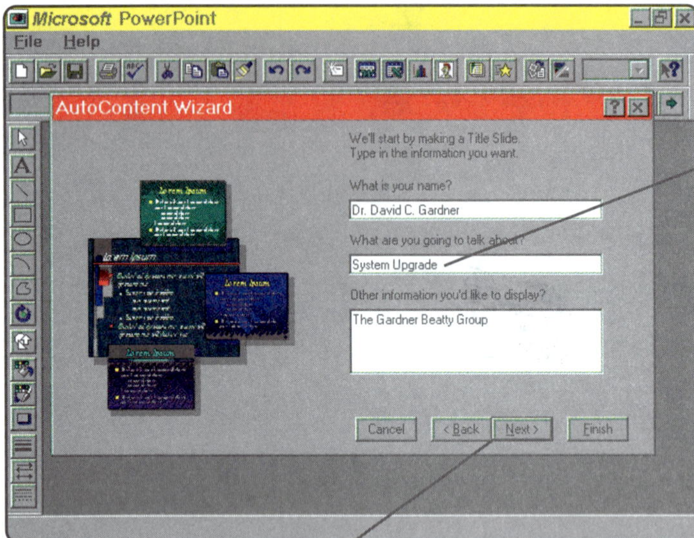

Notice your cursor is already flashing in the subject text box.

6. **Type** the **topic** of your presentation. You can, however, leave this blank and add it later.

The name and company information that was used during the installation process will appear in the name and other information text boxes.

7. **Place** the **mouse arrow** in one of the **other boxes** and **click** the **mouse button** to edit the information if necessary.

8. **Click** on **Next>**. The next AutoContent Wizard dialog box will appear.

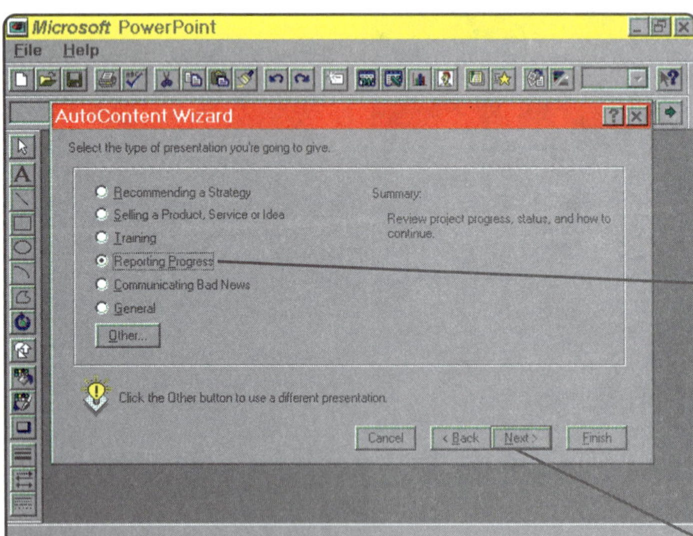

There are six different types of presentations in the AutoContent Wizard. As you click on a choice, a summary will appear to the right.

9. **Click** on the **presentation** that best approximates your slide show objective. In this example, it is Reporting Progress.

10. **Click** on **Next>**. The next AutoContent Wizard dialog box will appear.

Note: You may not see these two dialog boxes when you use AutoContent Wizard. If not, skip to the following page.

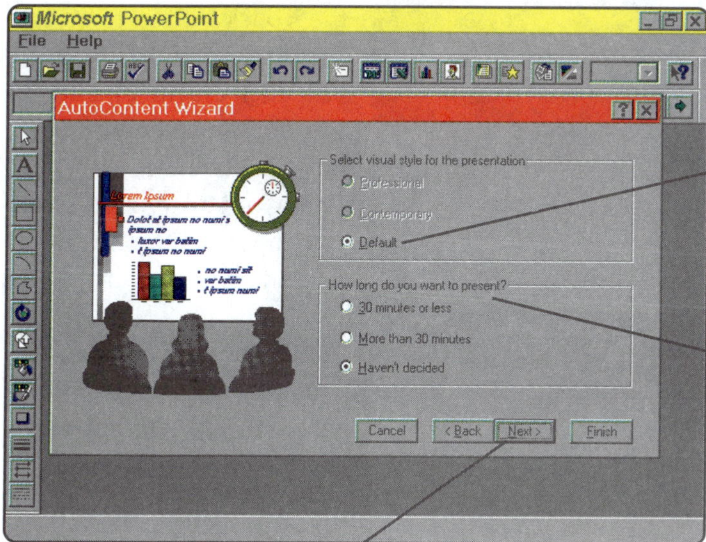

This box gives you options to select a visual style and a presentation length.

Notice that Default is selected for visual style. It is the only available option for this particular template.

11. The How long do you want to present options allow you to choose a specified length for your presentation.

12. Click on **Next>**. The next AutoContent Wizard dialog box will appear.

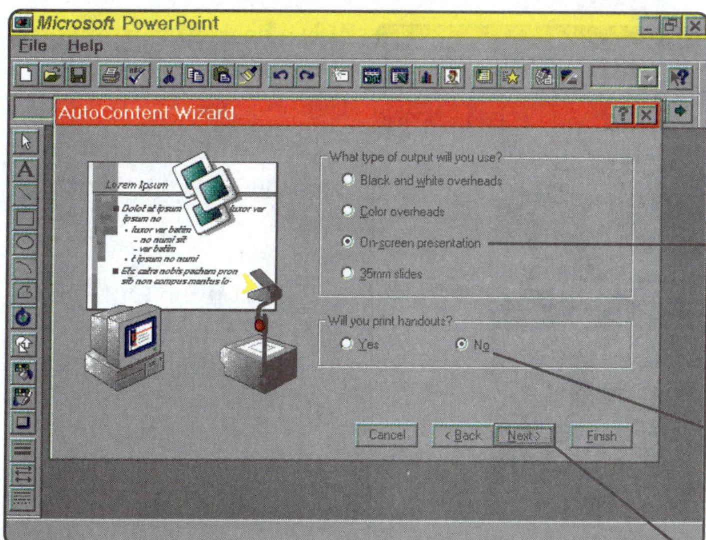

This AutoContent dialog box gives you options to select a specific output and indicate whether or not you want to print handouts.

13. Click on **On-screen presentation** if you are following along with this book.

14. Click on **No** under the handouts option, unless you want handouts.

15. Click on **Next>**. The next AutoContent dialog box will appear.

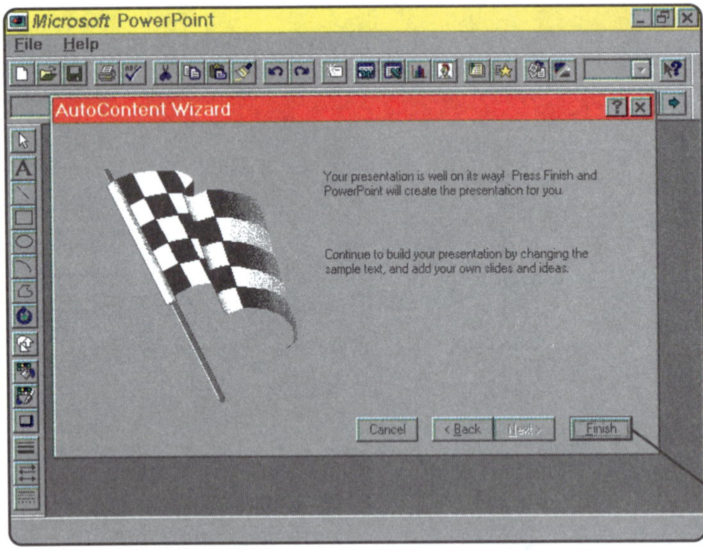

If you change your mind at any point while you are in the AutoContent Wizard, you can click on the <Back button to go to previous screens. Once you click on the Finish button, however, you will have to start the AutoContent Wizard over to choose a different presentation outline.

16. **Click** on **Finish**. After a pause, the presentation you selected will appear on your screen in Slide view.

WORKING IN OUTLINE VIEW

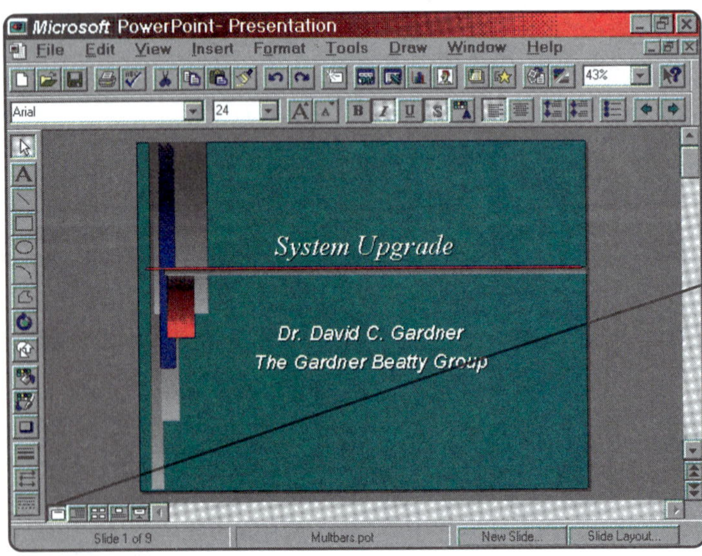

It is a snap to rearrange your presentation in Outline view. In this section, you will change to Outline view and delete a slide.

1. **Click** on the **Outline View** button. It is the second button from the left.

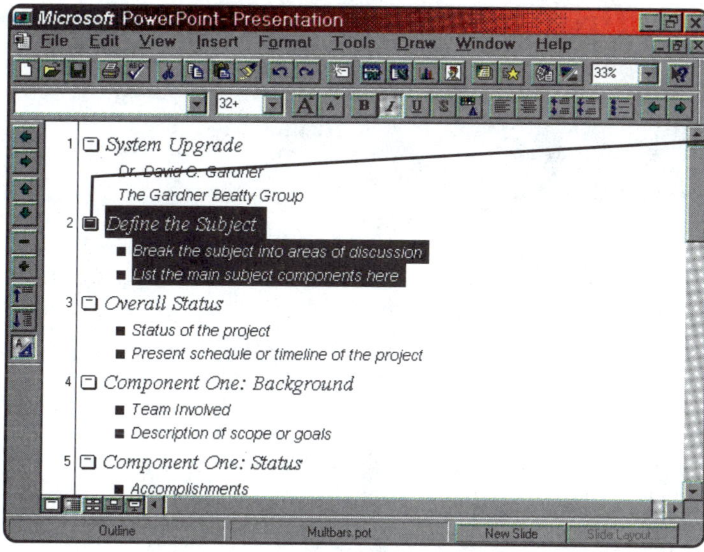

Deleting a Slide in Outline View

1. Click on the **symbol** beside slide 2. All of the text in slide 2 will be highlighted.

2. Press the **Delete** (or Backspace) **key** on your keyboard. The highlighted text will be deleted, and the remaining slides renumbered.

Editing Text in Outline View

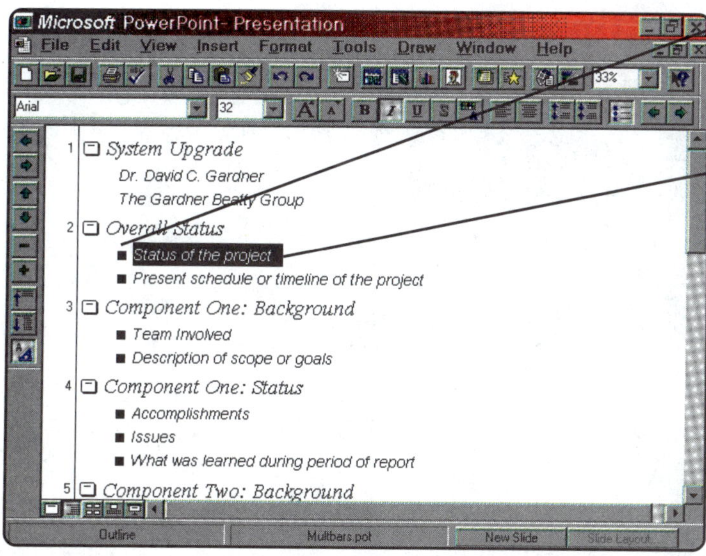

1. Click on the **first bullet** under slide 2. The entire line will be highlighted.

2. Type New Service Contract. It will replace the highlighted text.

Adding a Slide in Outline View

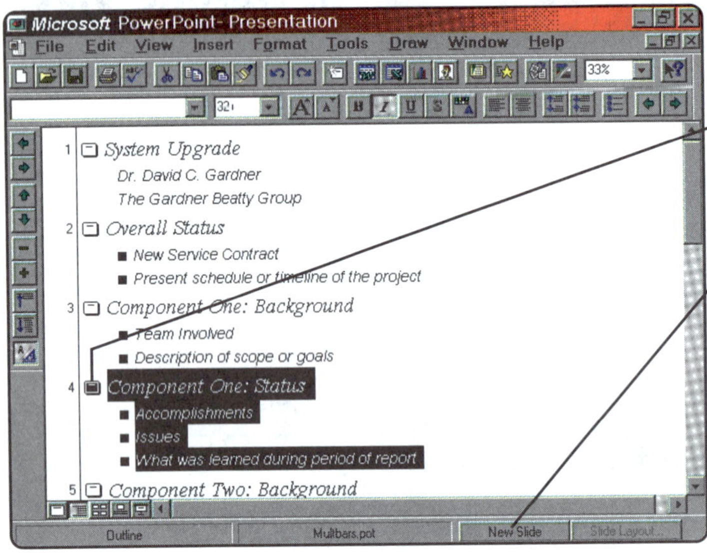

In this example you will add a slide after slide 4.

1. **Click** on the **symbol** beside slide 4. The text on slide 4 will be highlighted.

2. **Click** on the **New Slide button** at the bottom of your screen. A new slide symbol will be added, and the following screens will be renumbered.

3. **Type Component One: Network.** Notice that it appears as a heading.

Adding a Subheading in Outline View

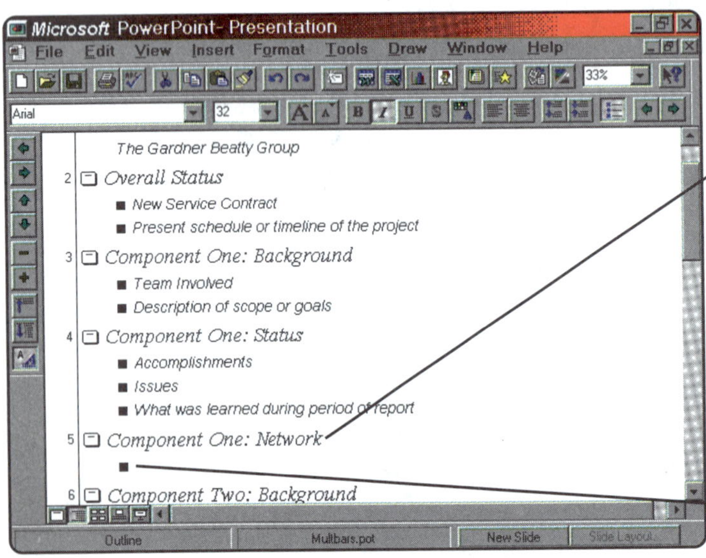

In this example you will add a subheading to a new slide.

1. **Click** after **Network** if your cursor is not already there.

2. **Press Enter**. A new level will be added that is comparable to the previous level.

3. **Press Tab**. The new line will be converted to a subheading line.

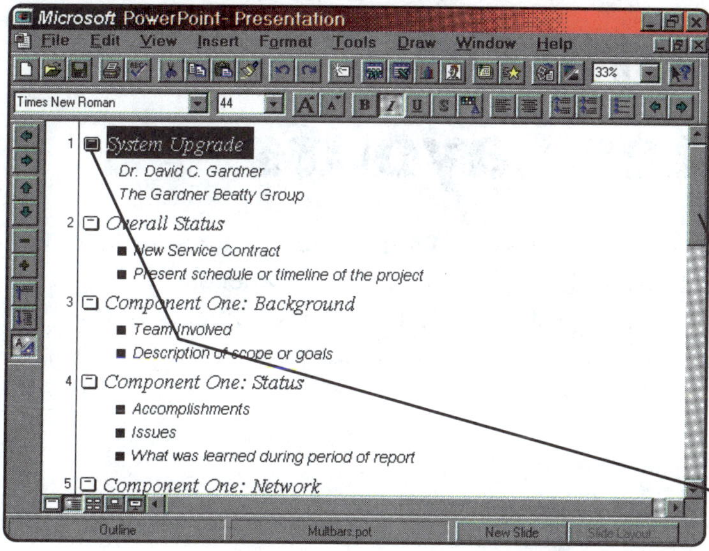

SWITCHING TO SLIDE VIEW

You can switch to Slide view at any time.

1. **Place** the **mouse arrow** on the **scroll bar. Press** the **mouse button** and **drag** the scroll bar to the top. **Release** the **mouse button.**
2. **Click twice** on the **symbol** beside slide 1. Slide 1 will appear in Slide view.

A predesigned template has already been applied to the presentation. You can, of course, change this template if you want.

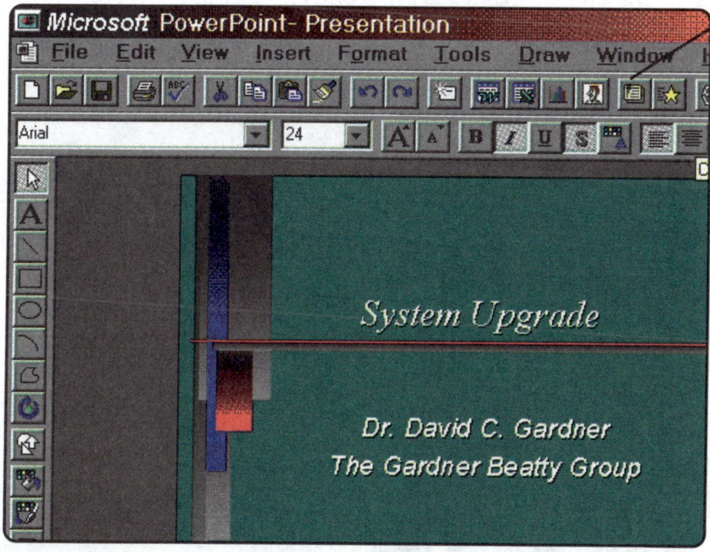

3. **Click** on the **Apply Template Design button** in the toolbar. (It's four buttons to the left of the zoom box.) The Apply Design Template dialog box will appear. Refer to Chapter 3, "Choosing a Predesigned Template," if you need help.

Close this presentation without saving it. We will not be using it in the next chapter. Refer to the end of Chapter 15 on page 184 for details on closing a presentation without saving.

CHAPTER 19

Customizing Master Layouts

PowerPoint for Windows 95 contains two master layouts. There is a master layout for the title slide and a different master layout that controls all other slides. You already learned how to change the color scheme of a layout in Chapter 3. In this chapter you'll learn how to customize the elements that make up the graphic design. In this chapter, you will do the following:

✔ Customize the text on a Slide Master
✔ Customize the graphic design on a Slide Master
✔ Add a logo to a Slide Master

OPENING A NEW TEMPLATE

There are two ways to get to new templates. If you are just opening PowerPoint, do Method #1 below. If PowerPoint is already open, then do Method #2.

Method #1:

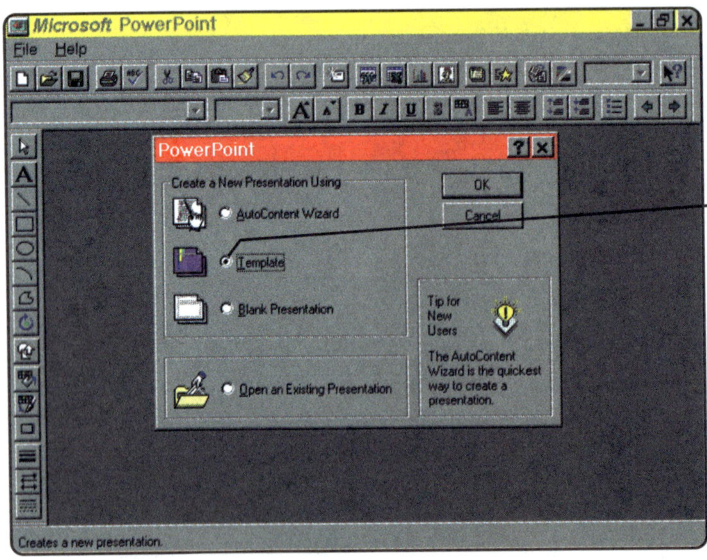

You can choose a template for your presentation as soon as you open the PowerPoint program.

1. **Click** on **Template** to put a dot in the circle.

2. **Click** on **OK**. The New Presentation dialog box will appear.

3. **Go to "Choosing a New Template"** at the bottom of the next page.

Method #2:

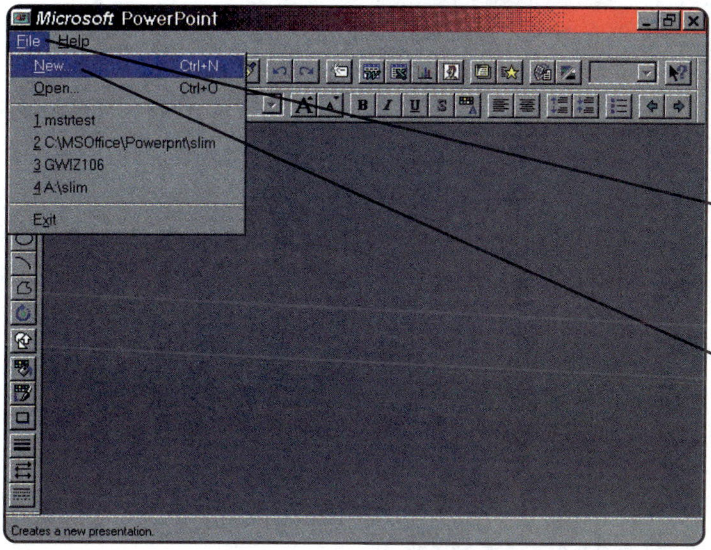

This example shows a blank screen, but you can choose a new template at any time.

1. **Click** on **File** in the menu bar. The File menu will appear.

2. **Click** on **New**. The New Presentation dialog box will appear.

CHOOSING A NEW TEMPLATE

1. **Click** on the **Presentation Designs tab** to bring it to the front.

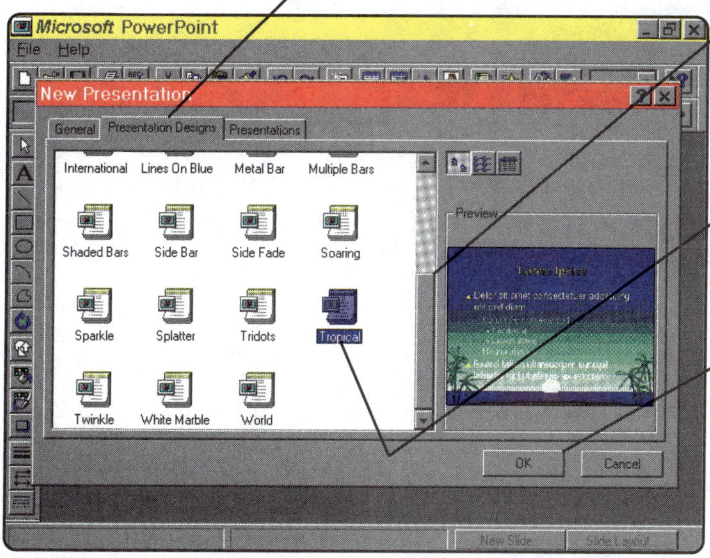

2. **Press and hold** on the scroll button and drag it to the bottom of the scroll bar.

3. **Click** on **Tropical**. A sample of this design will appear in the Preview box.

4. **Click** on **OK**. The New Slide dialog box will appear.

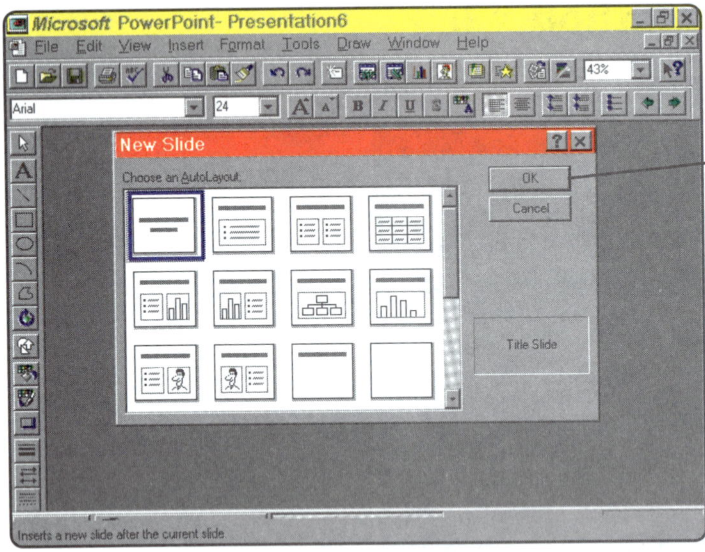

5. **Click** on the **title slide** if it does not already have a border around it.

6. **Click** on **OK** to select the title slide.

The placement of the text, the choice of font, and the graphic design you see in the slide in the next example are all controlled by a master layout.

CUSTOMIZING THE MASTER LAYOUT

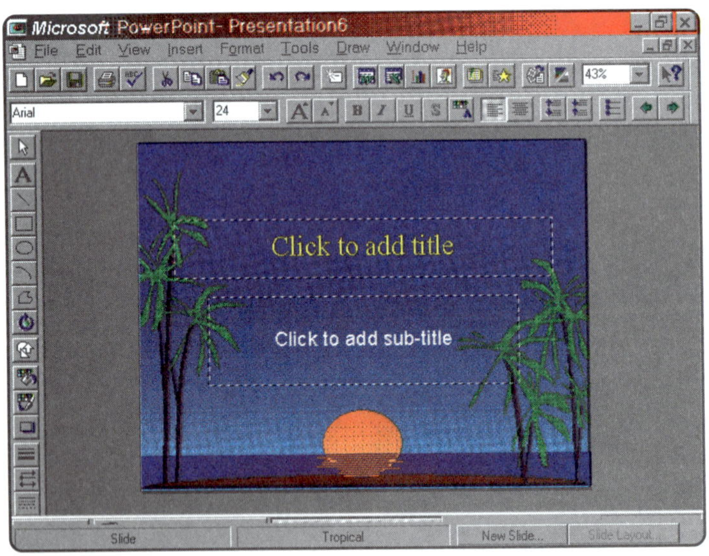

Each template has two master layouts. There is a master layout for the title slide and another master layout for all other slides. Each of these master layouts must be customized individually because changes made in the master layout for the title slide will not carry over to other slides and vice versa.

In the next step you'll go to the master layout view.

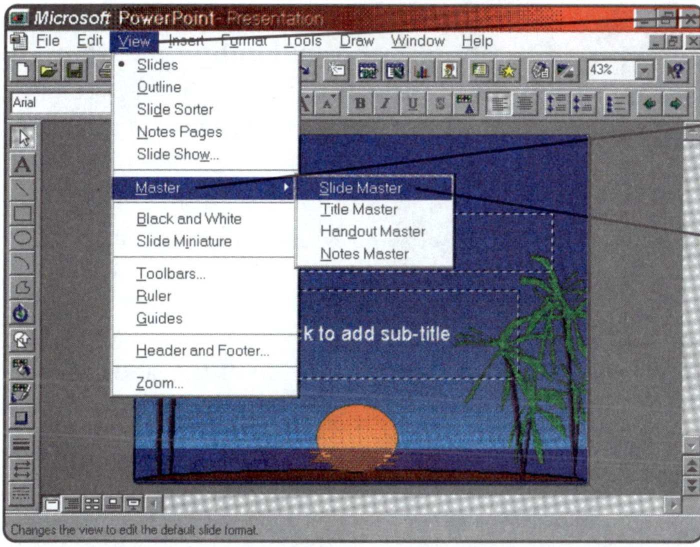

1. **Click** on **View.** The View menu will appear.
2. **Click** on **Master**. Another menu will appear.
3. **Click** on **Slide Master.** The Slide Master dialog box will appear.

Viewing Both Master Layouts

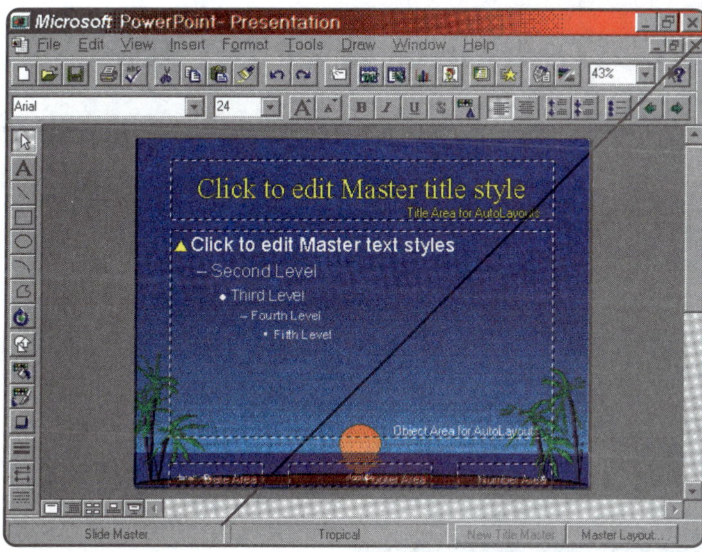

This view shows the "Slide Master." Notice that the graphic design has been modified on this slide to make more room for text. This is why there are two master slides. The title slide can usually handle more graphics than other slides because there isn't much text.

The next step will take you to the master that controls the title slide layout.

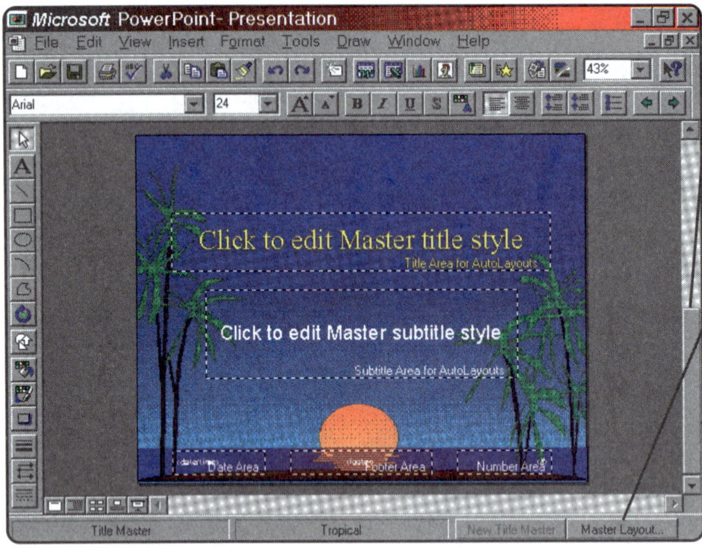

1. **Press and hold** the **scroll button** and **drag** it to the bottom of the scroll bar as you see in this example. When you release the mouse button, the Title Master slide will appear.

Notice that "Title Master" appears in the box at the bottom of the screen.

2. You won't be changing the Title Master in this chapter so **repeat step 1** and **drag** the **scroll button** up to the top of the scroll bar to go back to the Slide Master.

CUSTOMIZING TEXT ON THE SLIDE MASTER

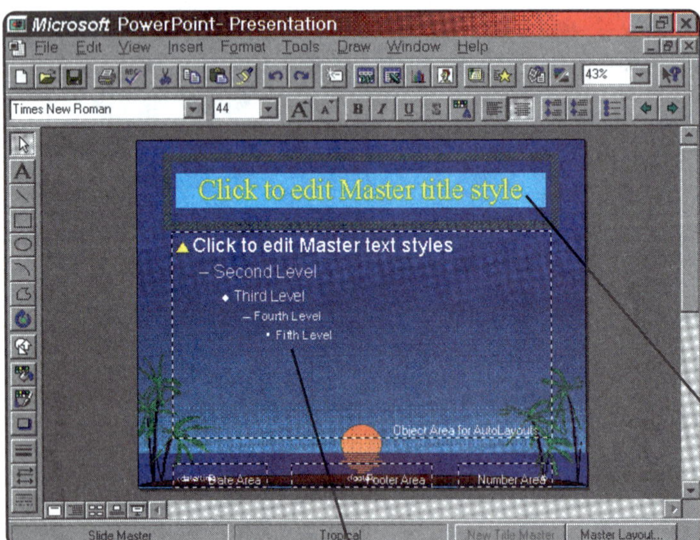

The Slide Master controls the font type, point size, and location of text. You can change any or all of these.

Changing the Font on the Slide Master

1. **Click** in the **text block** in which you want to change the font. The text will be highlighted.

Notice that in this example the text is Times New Roman 44 points.

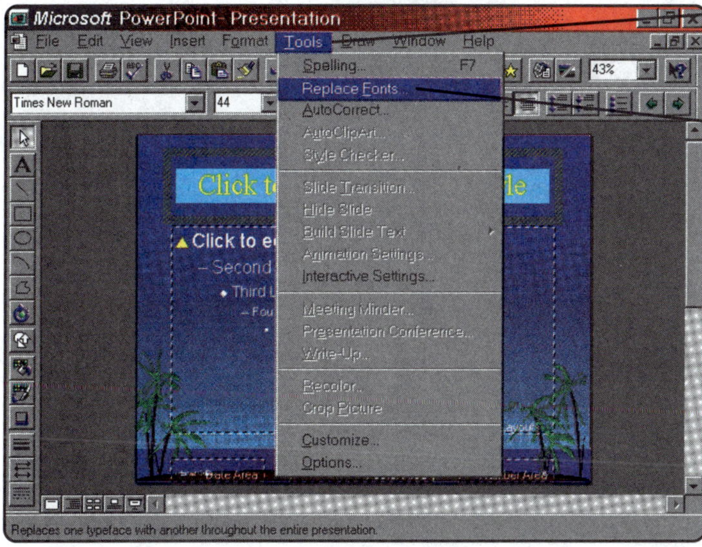

2. **Click** on **Tools.** The Tools menu will appear.

3. **Click** on **Replace Fonts.** The Replace Fonts dialog box will appear.

In this example, we will replace the Times New Roman font with Arial.

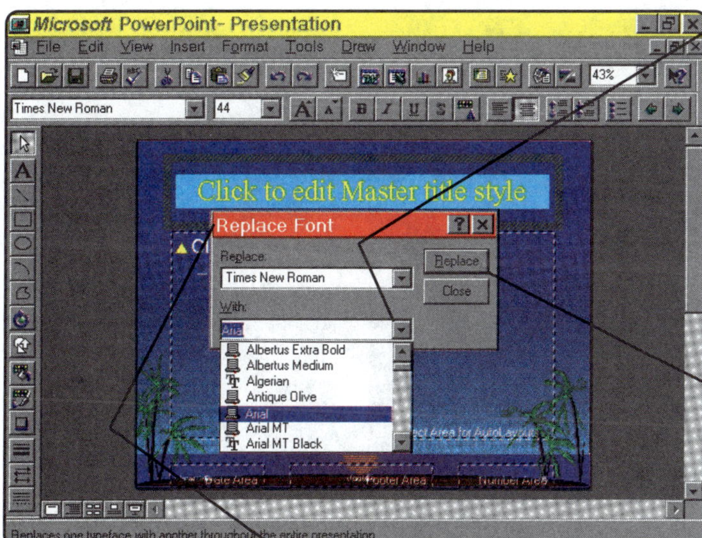

4. **Click** onthe bottom ▼ to get the drop-down list of fonts which are available on your computer. You list will be different from this one.

5. **Click on Arial** or a font that you prefer.

6. **Click** on **Replace.** After a pause, the highlighted text will change to the chosen font.

Note: If the Replace Font box covers the text that you want to change, press and hold on the title bar of the Replace Font dialog box and drag the dialog box to another spot on the screen.

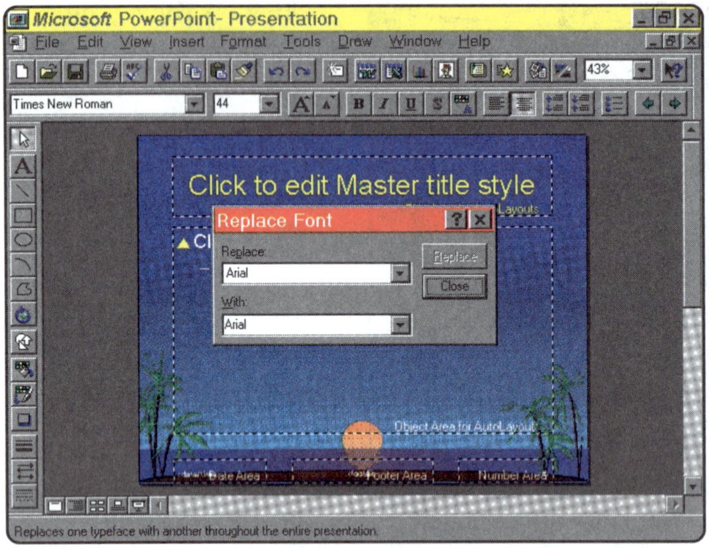

7. If you don't like the change in the font style, **repeat steps 4 through 6** until you find a font you like.

8. If you like this change, **click** on **Close.**

9. **Click** on the **slide background** to remove the highlighting.

Adding Text to a Slide Master

In this example, you will add the name of the conference, "New Horizons Symposium," in the top right corner of the slide above the text block.

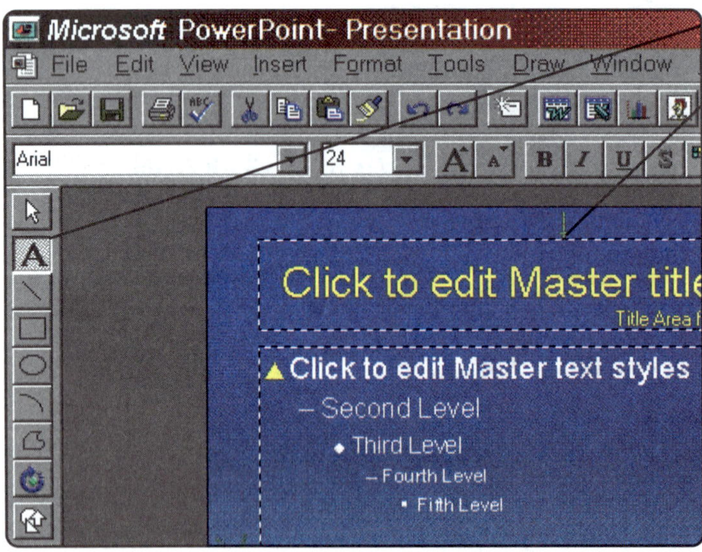

1. **Click** on the **Text tool.**

2. **Place** the **Text tool cursor** above the text block just to the left of "s" in "Master."

3. **Click** the **mouse button**. A new text block will appear.

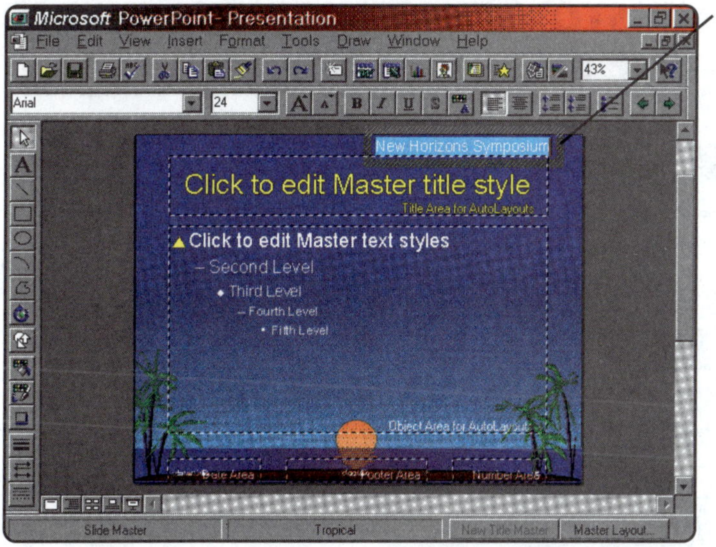

4. Type New Horizons Symposium. Voilà! A permanent text block.

5. Click on the **slide background** to remove the highlighting. This text will appear on any slide that is not in the title slide format.

Note: This new text block can be positioned and moved just like any other text block. See Chapter 6, "Working with Text Blocks."

Deleting a Permanent Text Block

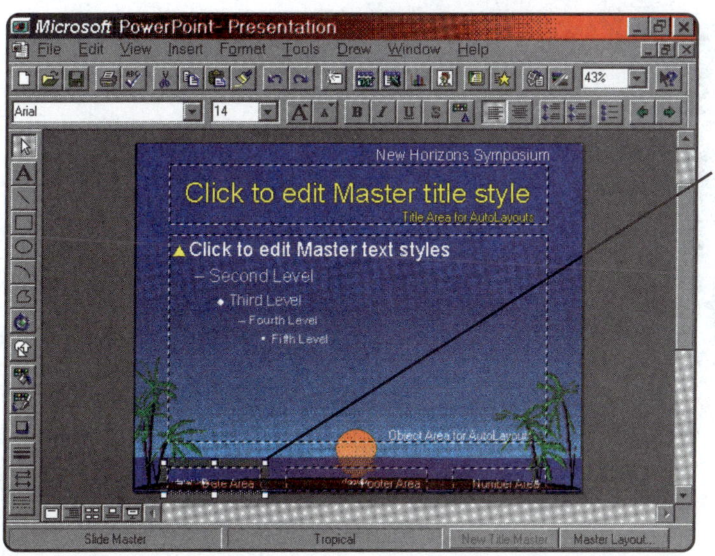

In this example, you'll delete the date text block in the lower left corner.

1. Click on the **border** of the **Date Area text block.** Handles will appear.

2. Press the **Delete key.** The text block will disappear.

CUSTOMIZING GRAPHICS ON THE SLIDE MASTER

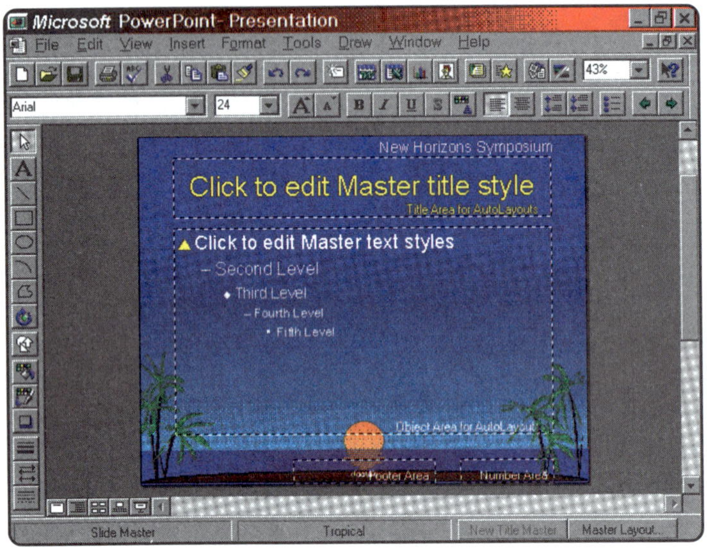

The graphic elements of the template can be customized in the master slide. The graphic design you see on this slide is made up of several different elements. In the steps below, you will select the graphic design, break it into its separate pieces (ungroup it), and then delete the palm tree on the left.

Ungrouping Graphic Elements

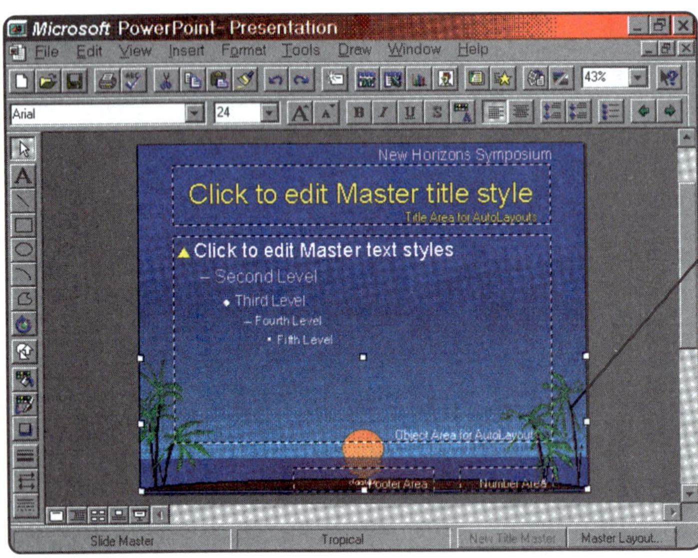

In order to separate a graphic design into its component pieces, you must first select the entire design.

1. **Click** on **one** of the **design elements**. In this example it's the palm tree on the right of the slide.

Note: Be sure that handles appear around the edge of the entire design and not around the text block.

2. **Click** on **Draw.** The Draw menu will appear.

3. **Click** on **Ungroup.**

Notice that all the individual elements of the design have handles. This indicates that they are now separate elements.

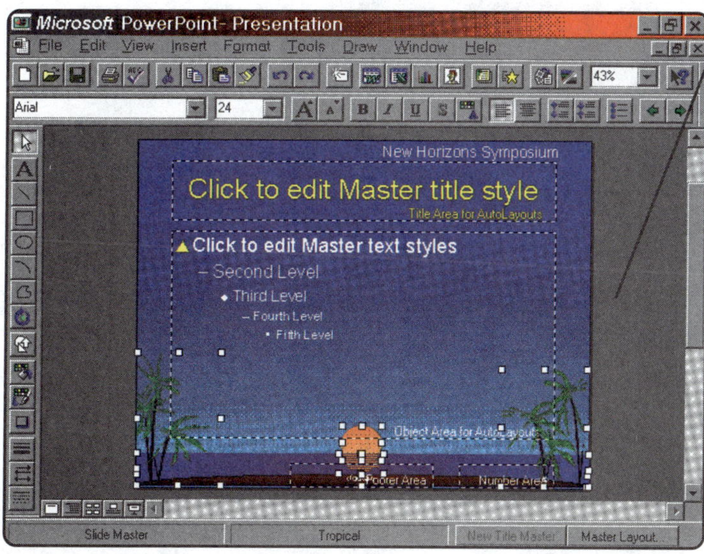

4. **Click** on the **light gray background** to deselect all elements. The handles will disappear.

Removing a Graphic Element

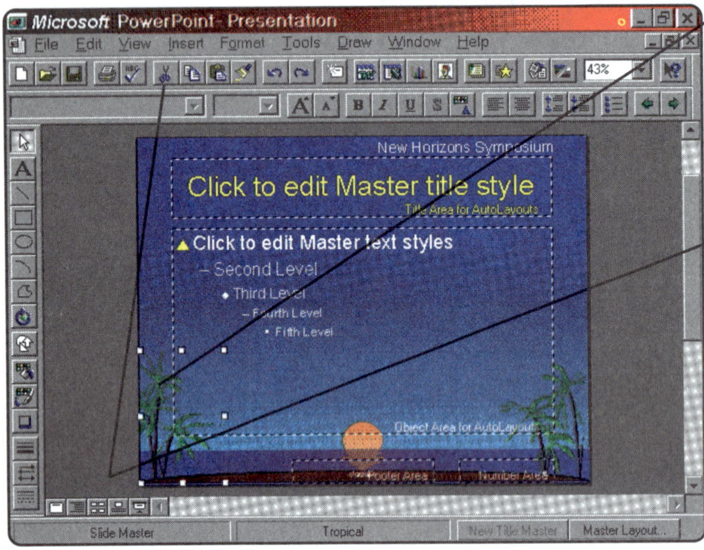

1. **Click** on the **lower left palm tree.** This will select the part of the design that contains only the left palm tree.

2. **Click** on the **Cut button** in the menu bar. The palm tree in the lower left corner will disappear from the Slide Master.

ADDING A LOGO TO THE MASTER SLIDE

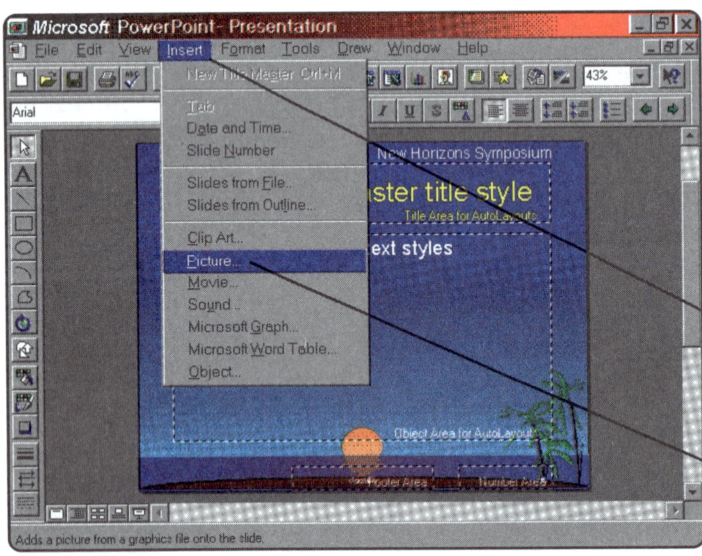

If you have a graphic file that contains your company logo, you can add it to the Slide Master. The logo can be a .tif, .pcx, .bmp, or other format. The steps are the same.

1. **Click on Insert** in the menu bar. The Insert menu will appear.

2. **Click on Picture.** A Choose Picture dialog box will appear.

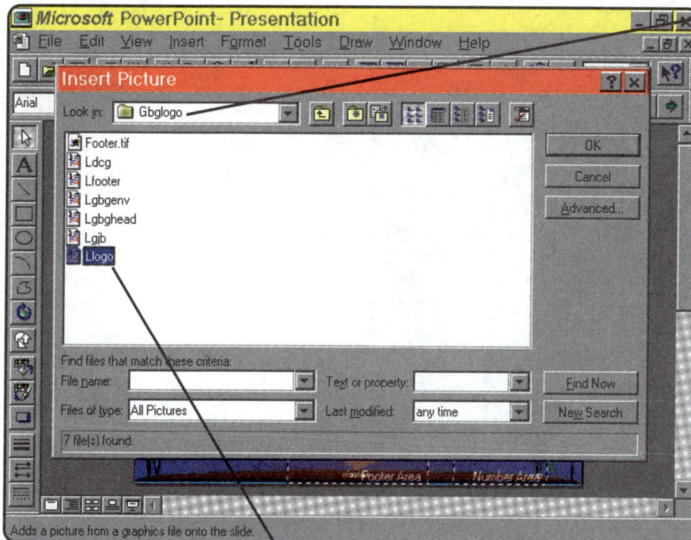

3. Go to the **directory** that has your logo file in it. It should be showing in the Look in box. In this example, it's in the Gbglogo directory. A list of all files in that directory will appear in the box beneath the directory.

For details on how to navigate through the file system and get to the directory you're looking for, see "Naming and Saving a File" in Chapter 2, on page 19.

4. Click twice on the **file** which has your selected logo in it. In this example, it's named Llogo.

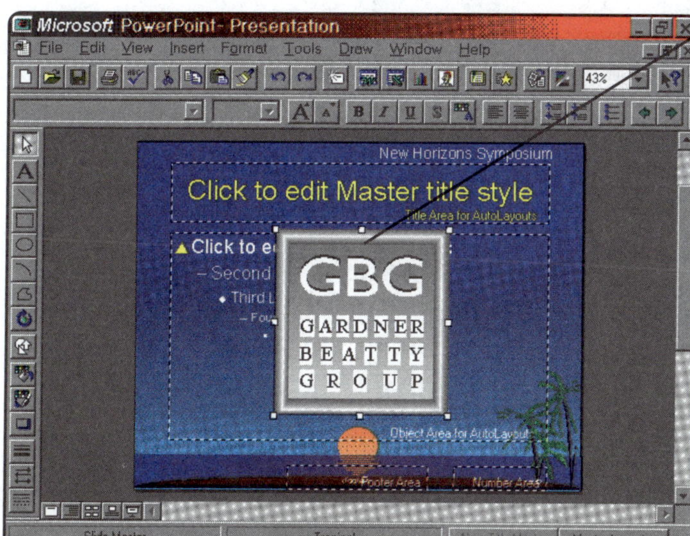

The image you selected will appear in the middle of your Slide Master, ready to be moved, resized, or grouped as described in Chapter 11, "Working with Clip Art."

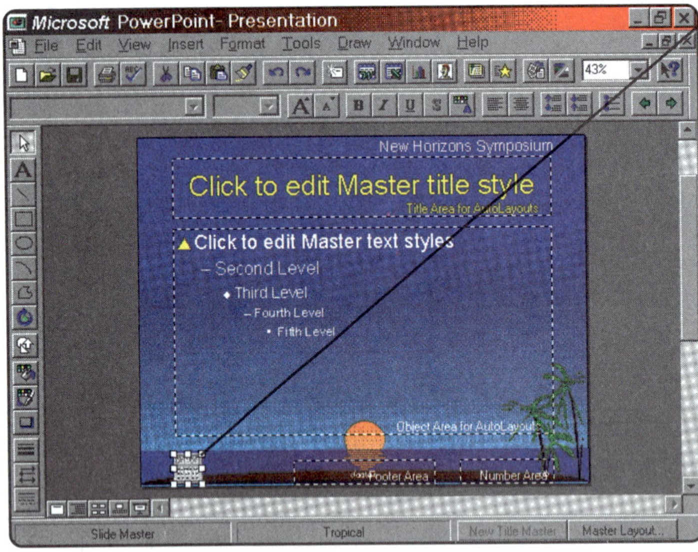

Here is the logo after it was resized and placed in the lower left corner of the slide.

Returning to Slide View

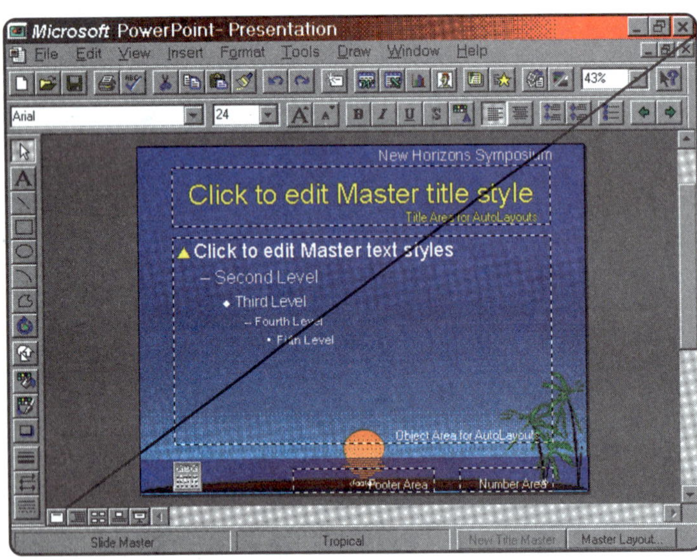

1. **Click** on the **Slide View button** and you will return to the slide that was on your screen when you started this presentation.

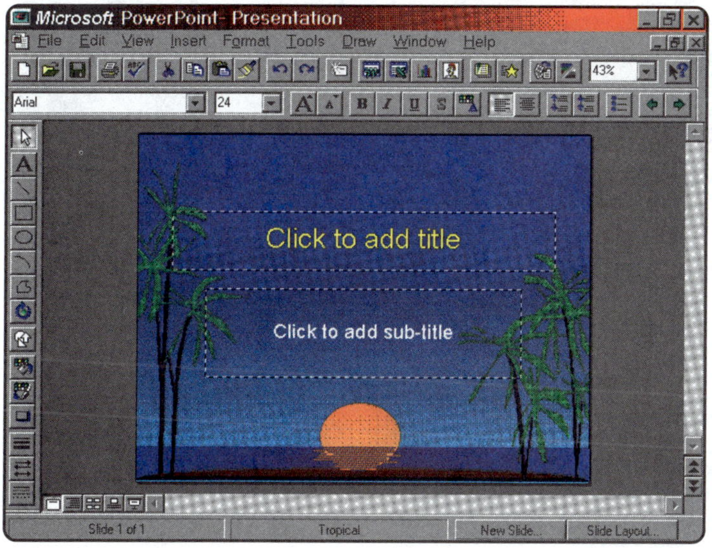

Yikes! Where did all your changes go?

Remember, in the previous part of this chapter you changed the elements on the *Slide Master*. When you went back to Slide view, you went back to the slide that was on your screen when you started the process, which was the Title slide. The changes that you made in the Slide Master are not reflected in the Title slide. If you want to make changes in the Title slide, you must go back to page 236 to select Title Master and edit that master layout.

Viewing the Changes You Made

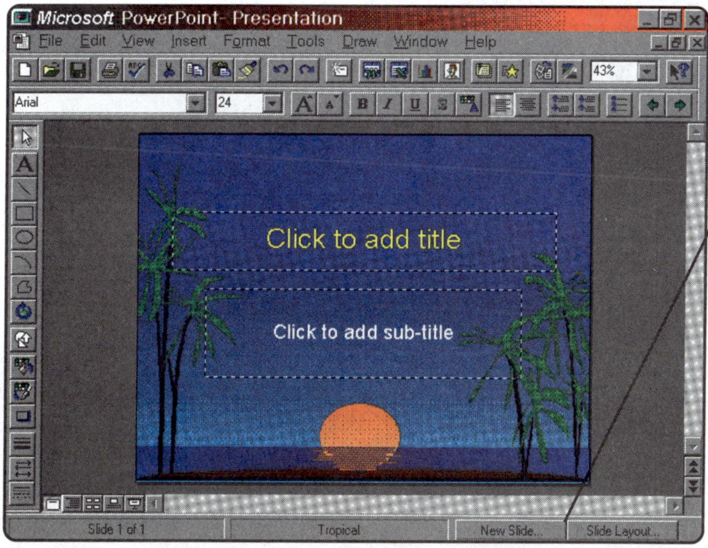

In this example, you will add a new slide. You'll see that the new slide reflects the changes you made.

1. **Click** on **New Slide.** The New Slide dialog box will appear.

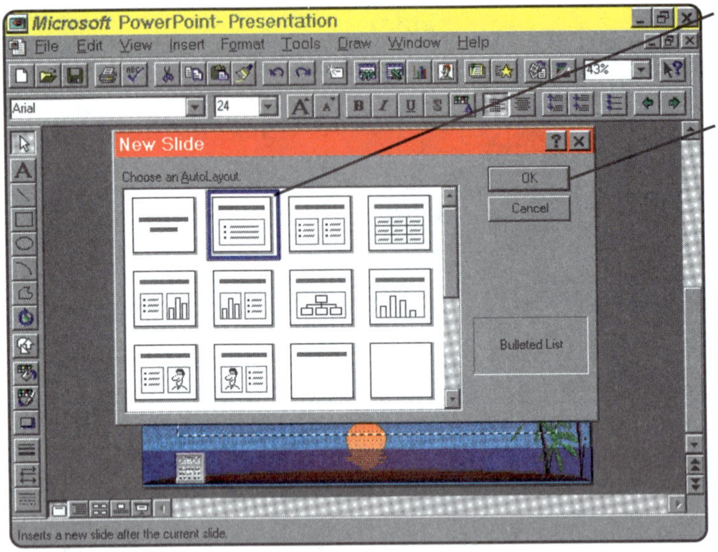

2. **Click** on the **Bulleted List slide.**

3. **Click** on **OK.**

Yeah! The new slide that appears has the text and graphic changes you made on the Slide Master.

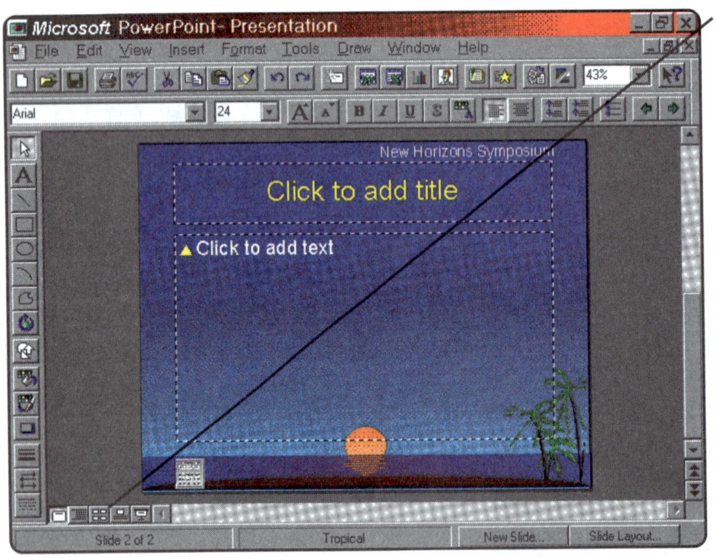

4. **Click** on the **Slide Sorter View.** Your presentation will appear in Slide Sorter view. It will take a while for the color and graphics to be filled in.

The first slide is a Title slide. You didn't change the Title Master, so this slide design remains the same.

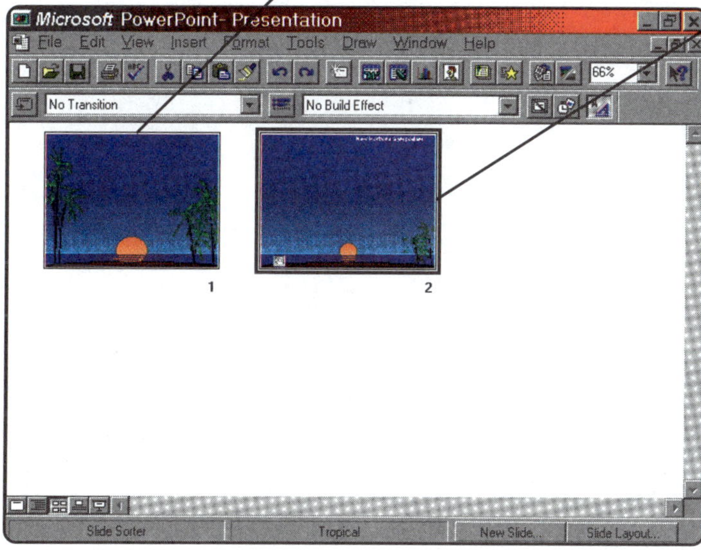

Notice that the Slide Master changes are only reflected in the second slide.

You didn't add any text to these slides, so there is no text showing on these slides.

SAVING THE NEW FILE

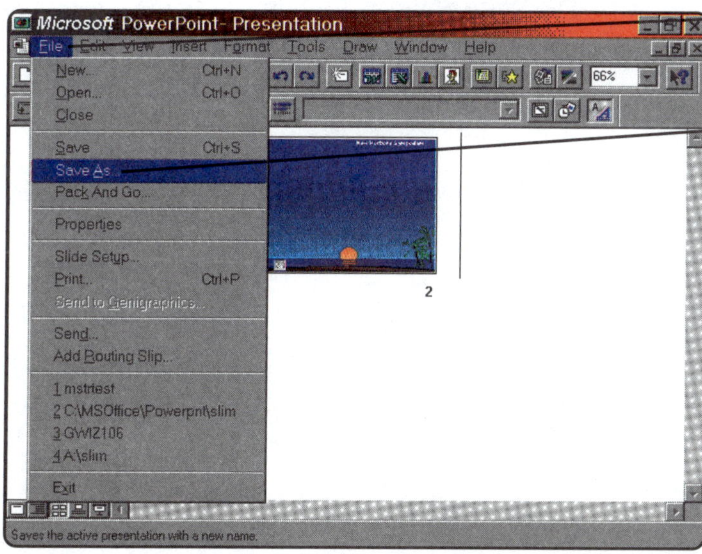

1. **Click** on **File**. The File menu will appear.
2. **Click** on **Save As**. The Save dialog box will appear. Give the file a new name so that you will be able to reopen it at another time.

The changes you made to your presentation design will be saved in this new file. The original design template will remain unchanged.

Part VI: Appendices

APPENDIX

A

Installing PowerPoint for Windows 95

Windows 95 has simplified the way you install programs. In fact, if your computer has a CD-Rom drive, the process is not only simple, it is very FAST. In this chapter, you will do the following:

✔ Install PowerPoint for Windows 95 as a part of the Microsoft Office installation, using the custom option.

OPENING THE CONTROL PANEL

Before you can begin to install the Microsoft Office programs, you must open up the Control Panel.

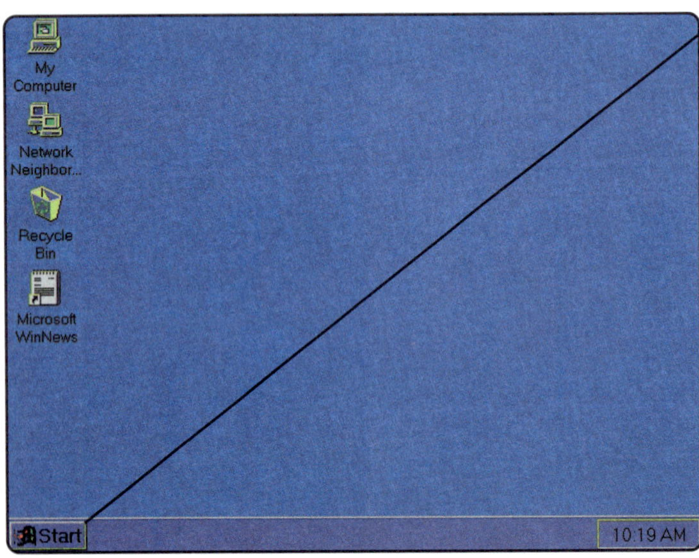

1. **Click** on the **Start button** in the taskbar. A pop-up menu will appear.

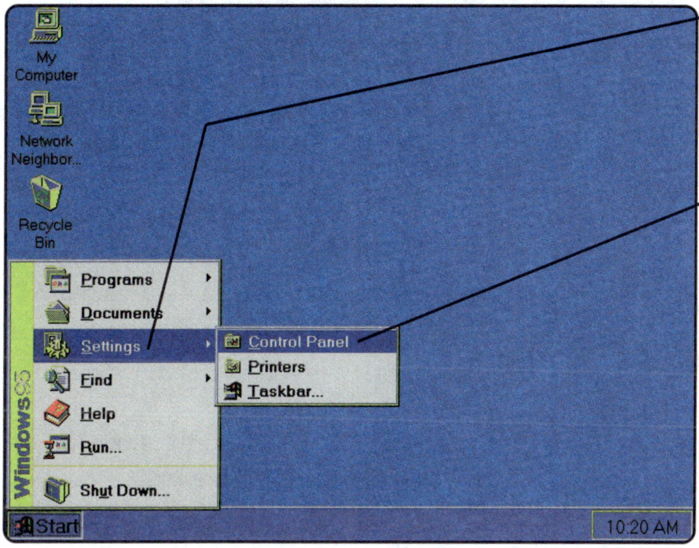

2. **Move** the **mouse arrow up** the menu to Settings. A second pop-up menu will appear.

3. **Move** the **mouse arrow over** to highlight Control Panel.

4. **Click** on **Control Panel**. The Control Panel dialog box will appear.

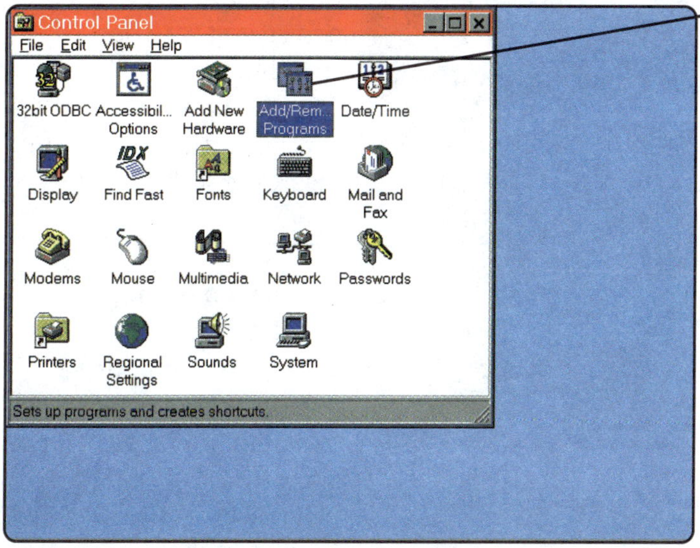

5. **Click twice** on **Add/Rem Programs**. The Add/Remove Program Properties dialog box will appear.

INSTALLING A PROGRAM

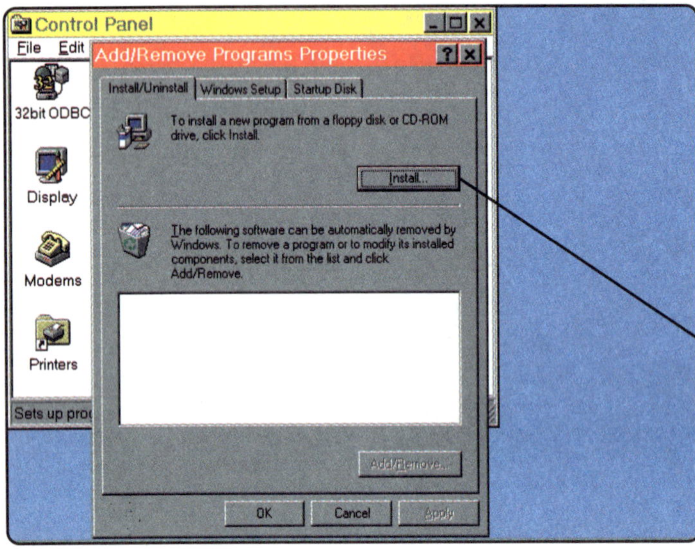

The following sections illustrate an installation using a CD-ROM disk. However, if you are using floppy disks for your installation, your screens will vary from these examples.

1. **Click** on the **Install button**. The Install Program From Floppy Disk or CD-ROM dialog box will appear.

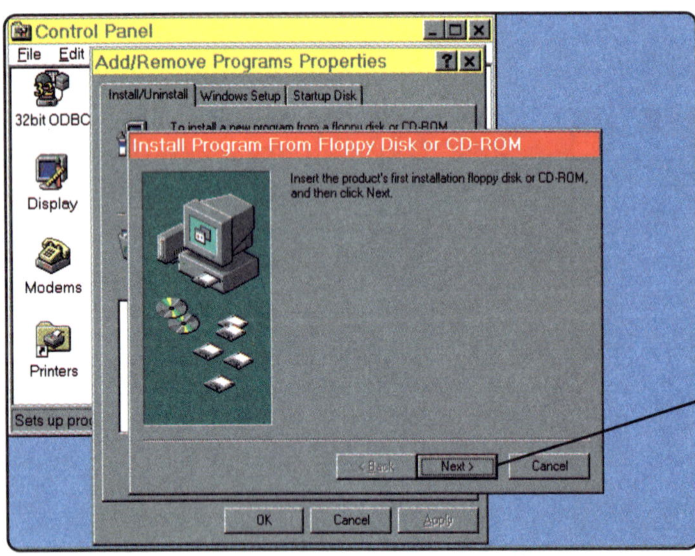

2. **Insert** your **CD-ROM** disk into your CD-ROM drive. Remember, for some drives you may be required to place the CD-ROM disk into a special carrier before you insert the disk into the drive.

3. **Click** on **Next**. Windows 95 will quickly read drive A and drive B as it searches for the installation program. Once Windows 95 finds the installation program disk in the CD-ROM drive, the Run Installation Program message box will appear.

Notice that the command line for the installation automatically appears in the text box.

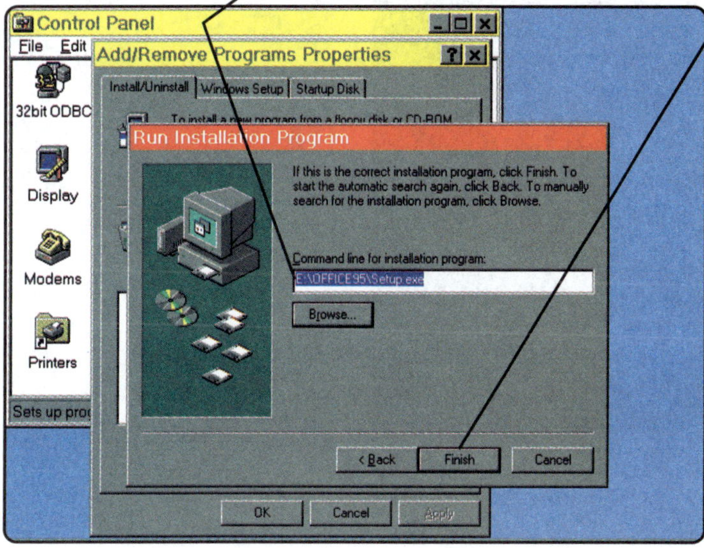

4. **Click** on **Finish**. The Setup Message box will appear.

After a few minutes, the Microsoft Office 95 Setup dialog box will appear.

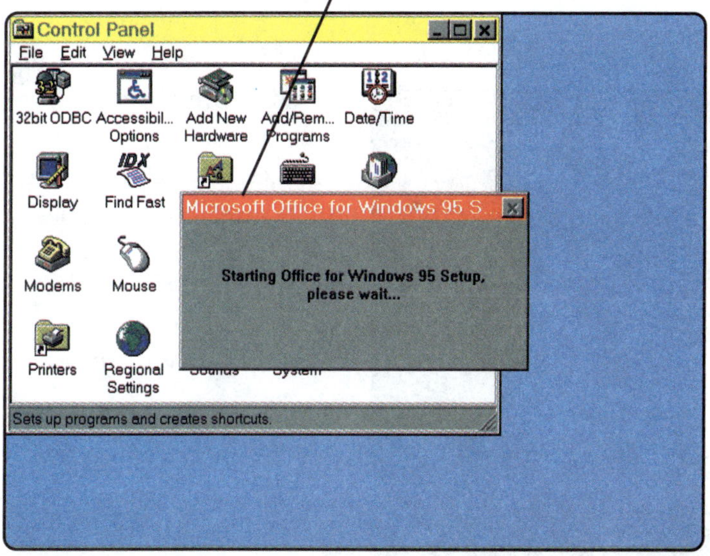

Next, a Microsoft Office '95 welcome message screen will appear.

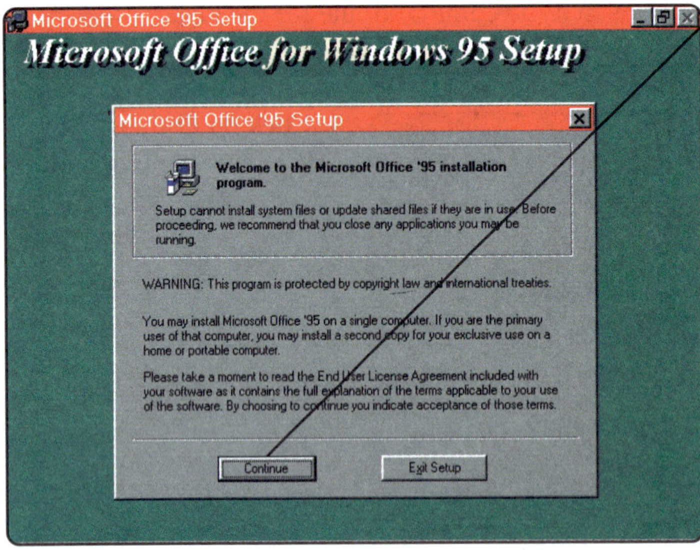

5. **Click** on **Continue**. The Name and Organization Information dialog box will appear.

Notice that the name and organization information used in registering Windows 95 automatically appears in the text box below.

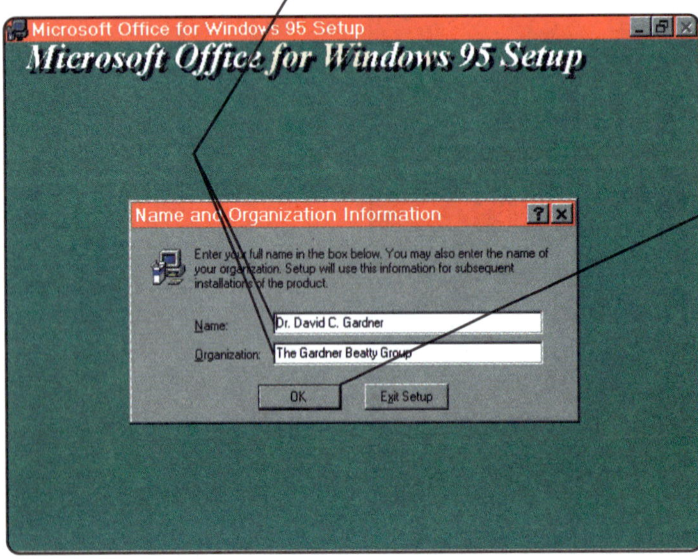

If this information is not correct, you can make the changes now. Or you can fill in new information.

6. **Click** on **OK**. Another Microsoft Office '95 message box will appear.

7. **Click** on **OK** if the information is correct. The Microsoft Office '95 Setup dialog box will appear.

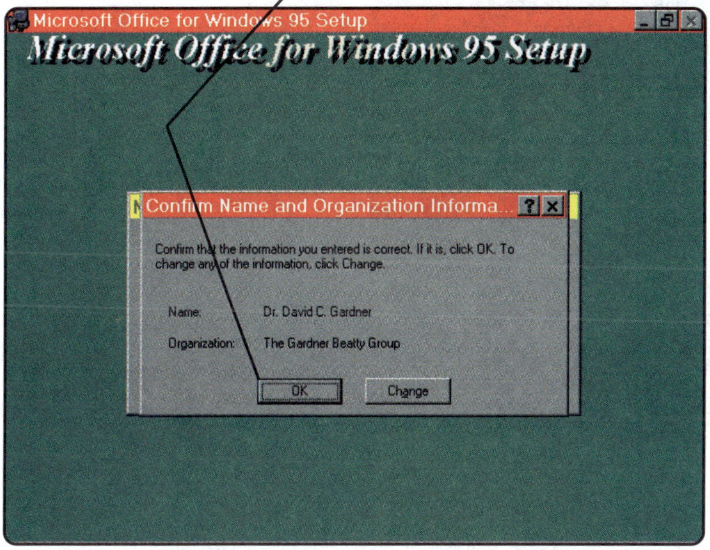

If the information is not correct, **click** on **Change**. The previous dialog box will appear. After making your corrections, **click** on **OK** to return to this dialog box.

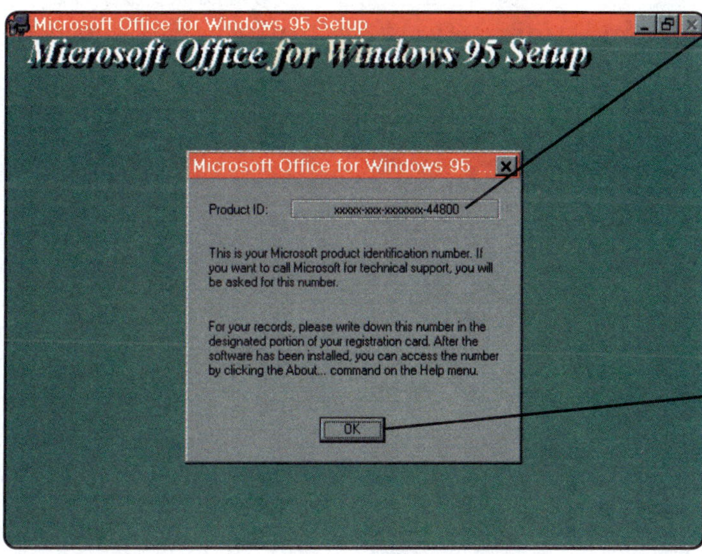

Notice that your registration number appears on this screen. It is important that you make a note of the number and keep it handy. If you call Microsoft for technical support, you will need this number for identification.

8. **Click** on **OK**.

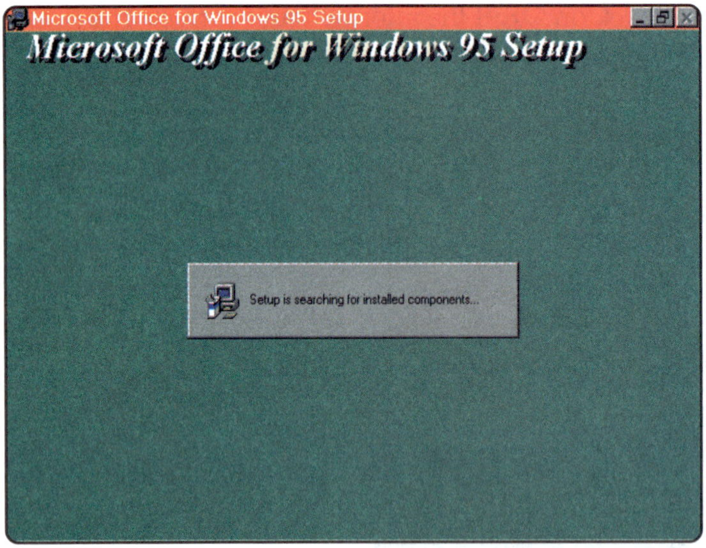

The hourglass will appear briefly along with a Microsoft message box that says "Setup is searching for installed components."

Selecting a Folder for OFFICE95

Microsoft Office will automatically be installed to a new folder (directory) MSOffice which will be created on the C drive (C:\MSOffice).

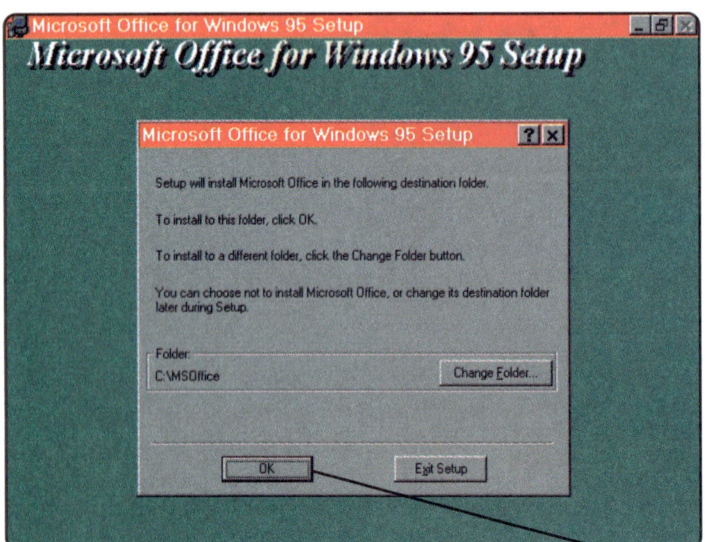

If, however, you wish to install this program in another directory (folder) or on another drive, select the **Change Directory button**. A Change Directory dialog box will appear. **Type** in the new **folder (directory) name and path** and **click** on **OK**.

A confirmation destination message box will appear. **Click** on **Yes** to confirm.

1. **Click** on **OK**. A dialog box will appear.

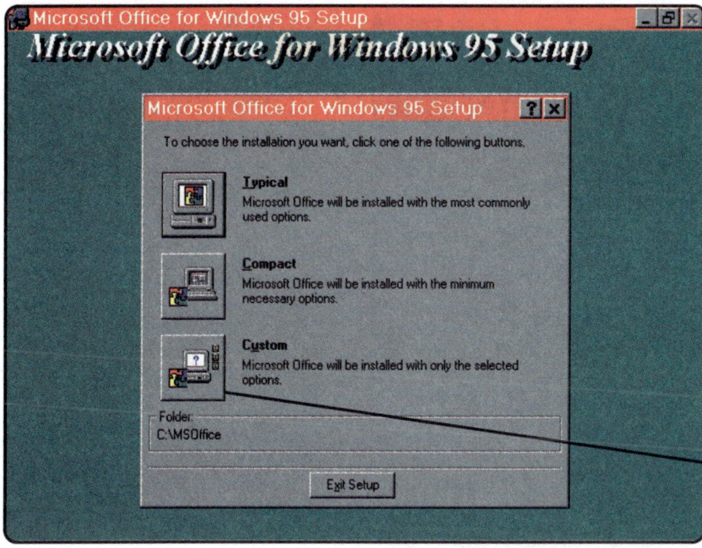

SELECTING THE INSTALLATION TYPE

We recommend the Custom installation so that you can install the different features you will need to fully utilize PowerPoint for Windows 95.

1. **Click** on **Custom.** The Microsoft Office for Windows 95 - Custom dialog box will appear.

2. **Click** in a **box** to *remove* the ✔ from any programs you *don't* want to install at this time. Or, click on the Install All button at the bottom of the dialog box to install everything.

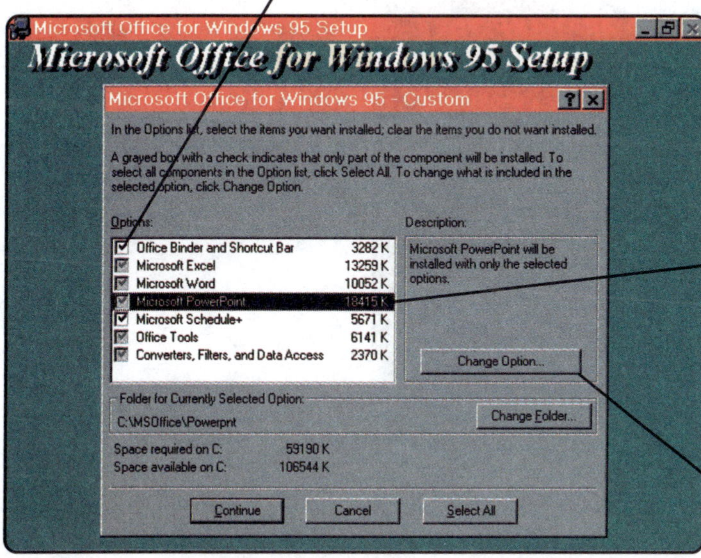

In this example, we will install all of the options.

Adding Custom Features

1. **Click** on the **words "Microsoft PowerPoint"** to highlight the line. Don't click on the box or you'll remove the ✔.

2. **Click** on **Change Option.** The Microsoft Office for Windows 95 - PowerPoint dialog box will appear.

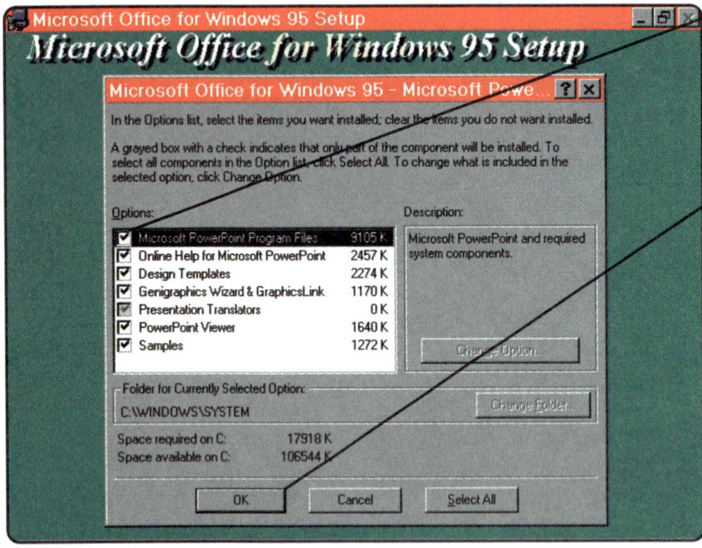

3. **Click** in any of the **boxes** which don't have a ✔ in them already, so that they are all selected.

4. **Click** on **OK.** You will return to the Microsoft Office for Windows 95 - Custom dialog box.

5. **Click** on the words **"Office Tools"** to highlight the line. Don't click on the box or you'll remove the ✔.

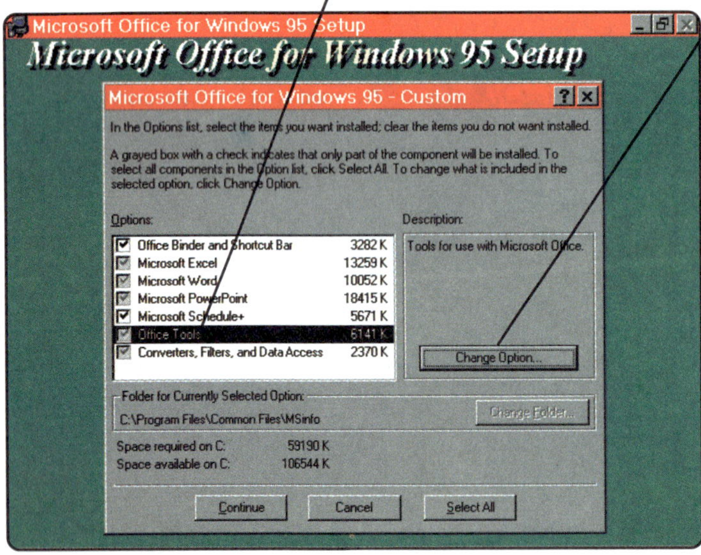

6. **Click** on **Change Option.** The Microsoft Office for Windows 95 - Office Tools dialog box will appear.

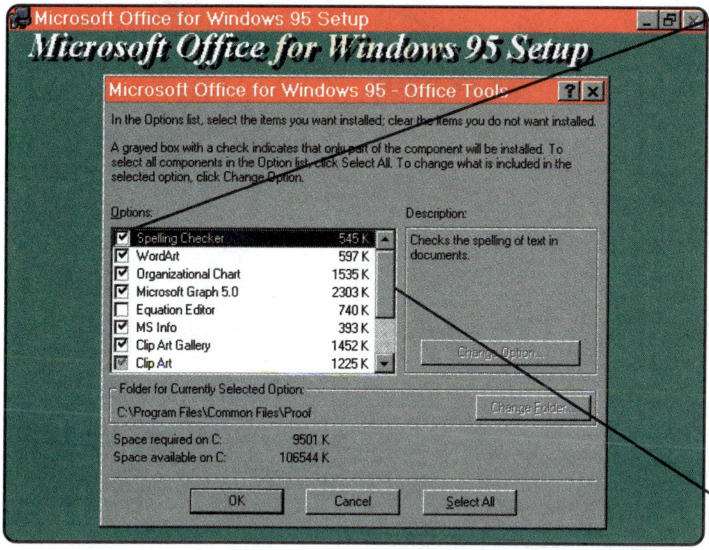

7. Click on the box to the left of the **options** you want to install, to place a ✔ in the boxes. We recommend that you include Spelling Checker, WordArt, Organizational Chart, Microsoft Graph 5.0, MS Info, Clip Art Gallery, and Clip Art, so you can follow along with the chapters in this book.

8. Place the **mouse arrow** on the **scroll bar** and **press and hold** as you **drag** the scroll bar down.

9. Click in the box to the left of the **remaining options** you want to install, to place a ✔ in the boxes. We recommend that you also include Microsoft TrueType fonts.

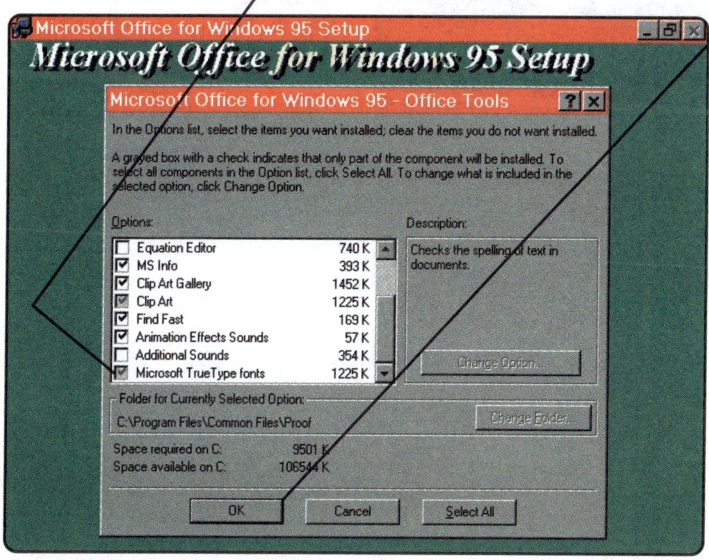

10. Click on **OK.** You will return to the Microsoft Office for Windows 95 - Custom dialog box.

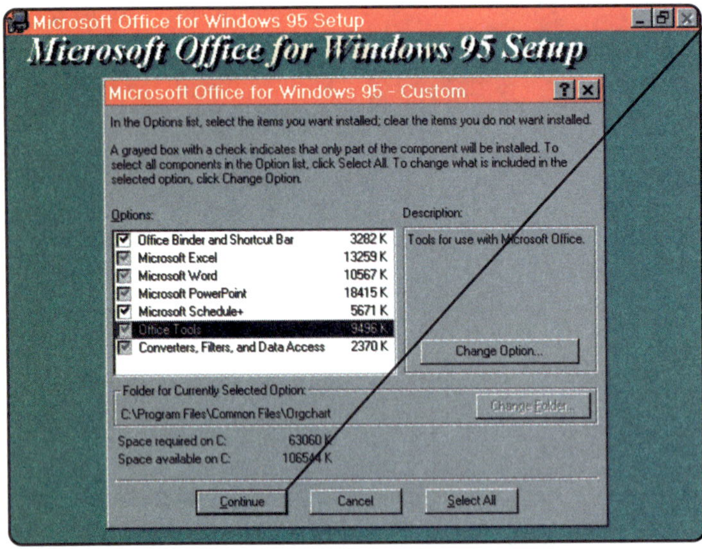

11. **Click** on **Continue.** The dialog box will close, and the Microsoft Office Setup: Disk 1 dialog box will appear.

Watching, Watching

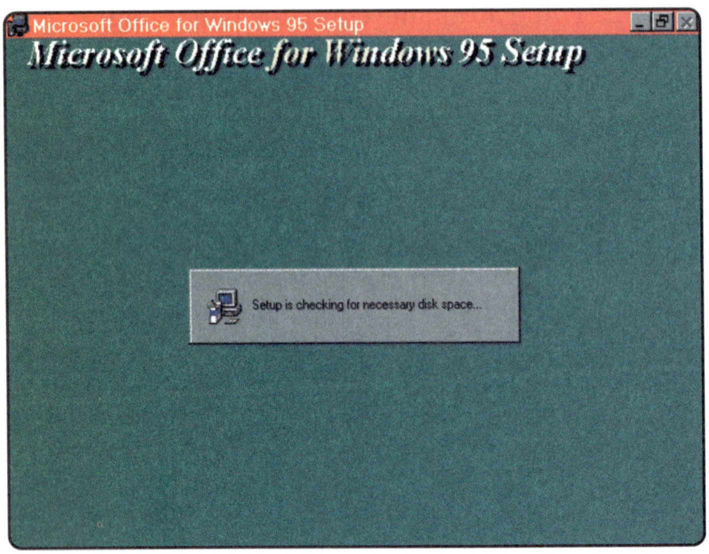

At this point sit back and relax. It's out of your hands. Using a CD-ROM certainly makes life easier. No more of the old "insert disk #x" routine.

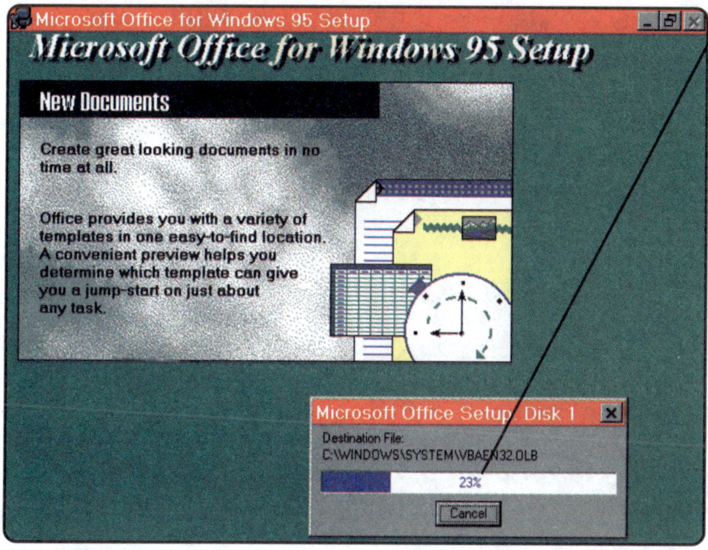

The Microsoft Office Setup Disk 1 dialog box will show you the percentage of completion in copying files from the installation disk.

Closing the Installation

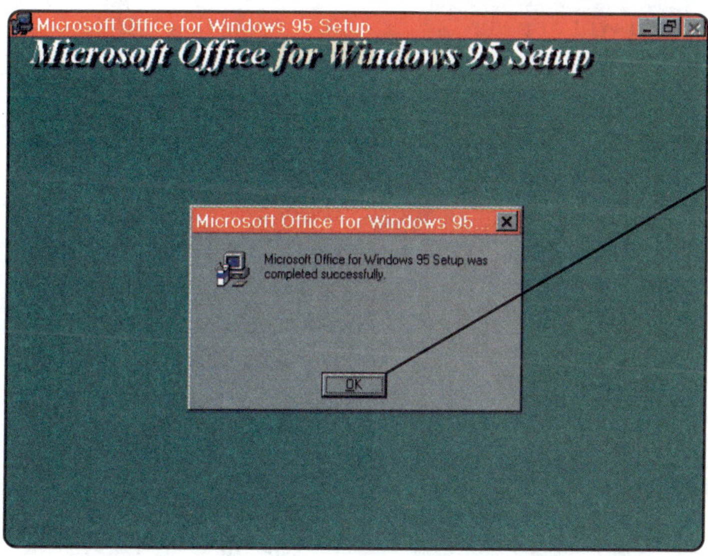

Everything is complete, and you are nearly finished.

1. **Click** on **OK.** You will be returned to the Control Panel.

You may at this point, get a message that says it is rebooting your computer. If so, you won't see the control panel in the next screen.

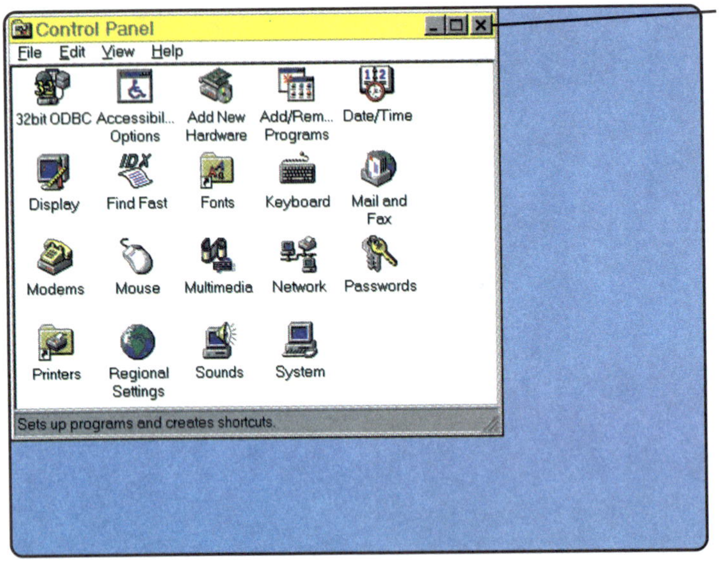

2. **Click** on the **Close button** (☒). Your Microsoft Office programs are only a few clicks away.

VIEWING MICROSOFT OFFICE

Now it's time to have fun and explore your new programs.

1. **Click** on the **Start button** on the taskbar. A pop-up menu will appear.

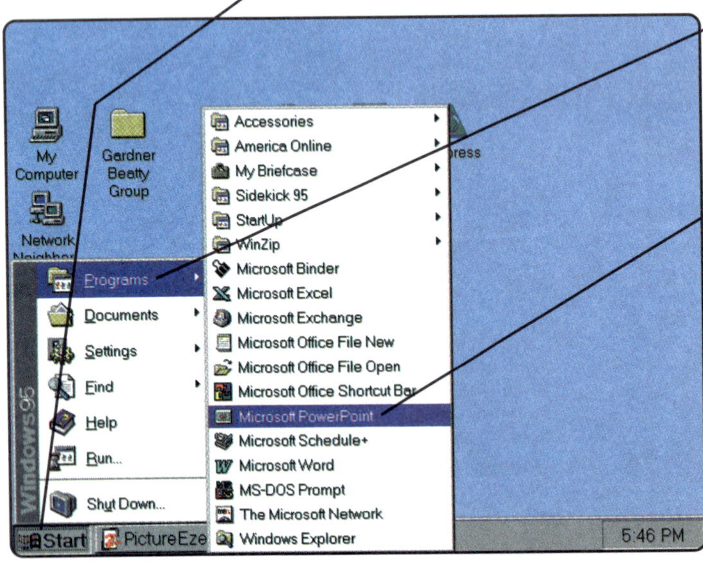

2. **Move** the **mouse arrow** up the menu to Programs. A second menu will appear.

3. **Move** the **mouse arrow** over to Microsoft Office and click. Your next menu will be filled with all of your new Microsoft programs. Click on PowerPoint. . . and you will be on your way!

APPENDIX

B

Hiding the Taskbar

If you do not want the taskbar showing on your screen all the time, you can hide it from view and get it back anytime you need it with a simple mouse movement. In this chapter, you will do the following:

✔ "Hide" the taskbar
✔ Get the hidden taskbar back

REMOVING THE TASKBAR FROM VIEW

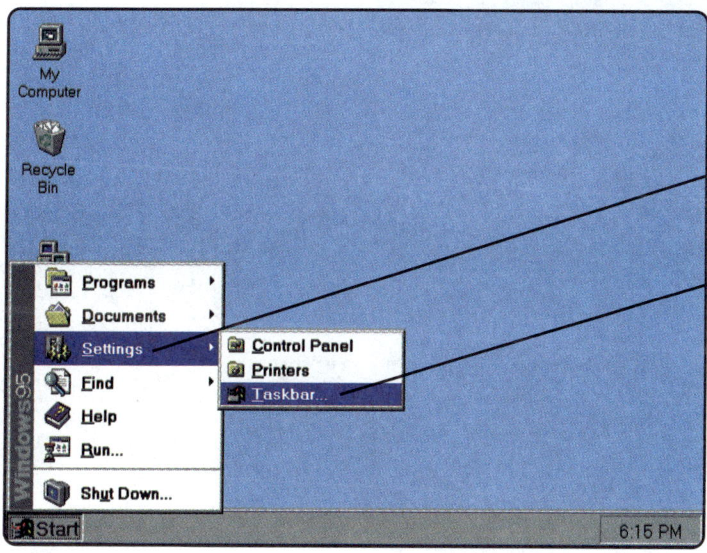

1. **Click** on **Start** in the left corner of the taskbar. A pop-up menu will appear.

2. **Click** on **Settings.** Another menu will appear.

3. **Click** on **Taskbar**. The Taskbar Properties dialog box will appear.

4. **Click** on **Always on top** to put a ✔ in the box if one isn't there already.

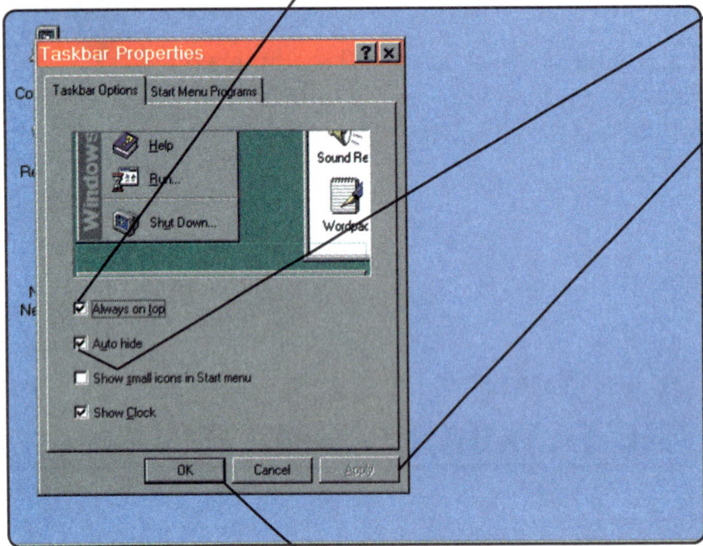

5. **Click** on **Auto hide** to put a ✔ in the box.

6. **Click** on **Apply**.

7. **Click on OK**. The dialog box will close.

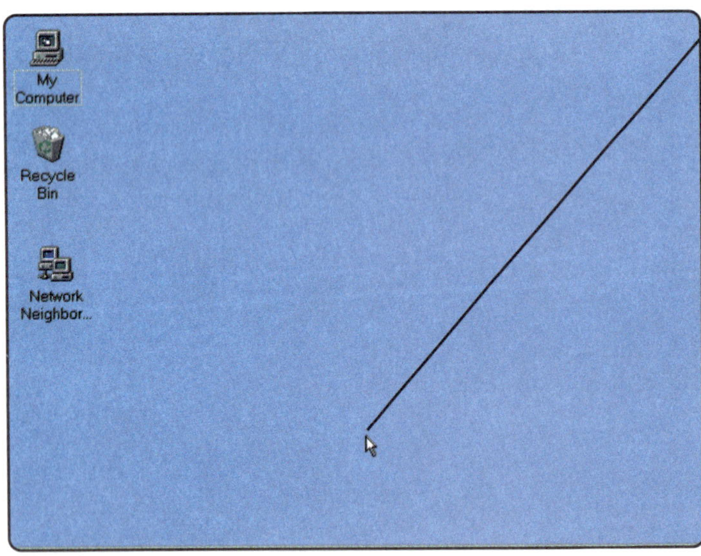

8. **Click anywhere** on the **desktop**. Voilà! The taskbar is gone. Magic, but how do I get it back when I need it? Go on to the next page.

GETTING THE HIDDEN TASKBAR BACK

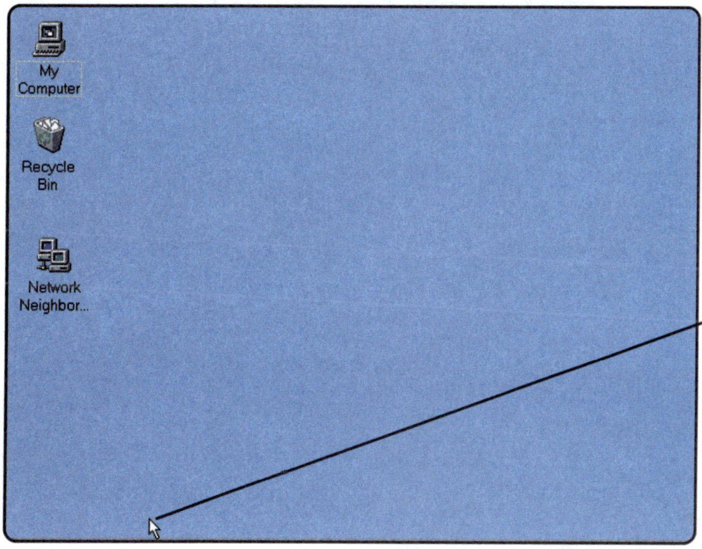

You can get the taskbar back anytime you want to by a simple mouse movement. You can do this at anytime from any program that you have running.

1. **Move** the **mouse arrow** towards the bottom of the desktop.

2. **Continue** to **move** the **mouse arrow** until the taskbar reappears.

Note: To hide the taskbar, simply move the mouse arrow up on the desktop again.

Note: If you want to get the taskbar back permanently, repeat steps 1 to 6 in the first section of this chapter to remove the ✔ from the Auto hide box.

Index

A

B

C

D

E

F

G

H

I

L

M

N

O

P

R

S

T

U

V

W

Z